FOLLOWING IN YOUR FOOTSTEPS

The Lotus-Born Guru in Tibet

VOLUME III

SAMYE TRANSLATIONS
An imprint of Rangjung Yeshe Publications
Boudha, Kathmandu, Nepal
samyetranslations.org

First Edition
Printed in the United States of America
Distributed to the book trade by: Ingram Book Distributors

Title: Following in Your Footsteps: The Lotus-Born Guru in Tibet.
Foreword by Neten Chokling Rinpoche.
Description: First edition. | Kathmandu: 2023
ISBN: 978-1-7328717-5-5 (paperback)
Library of Congress Control Number: 2019913567

BISAC: RELIGION / Buddhism / Sacred Writings. |
RELIGION / Buddhism / History. | RELIGION / Buddhism /
Tibetan.

FOLLOWING IN YOUR FOOTSTEPS
The Lotus-Born Guru in Tibet
VOLUME III

The Spoken Words of
Guru Padmasambhava and Khandro Yeshé Tsogyal

As Revealed by
Nyangral Nyima Özer, Orgyen Lingpa, Taksham Nüden Dorjé,
Tulku Zangpo Drakpa, Chokgyur Dechen Lingpa, Dudjom Lingpa,
and Trinlé Drodül Lerap Dewa Tsal

Supported by the Writings and Teachings of
Jamyang Khyentsé Wangpo, Jamgön Kongtrul Lodrö Thayé,
Jamyang Khyentsé Chökyi Lodrö, Kyapjé Dudjom Rinpoche,
Kyapjé Chatral Rinpoche, Orgyen Tobgyal Rinpoche.

Introduced by
Neten Chokling Rinpoche and Phakchok Rinpoche

Compiled and Narrated by
Samye Translations

CONTENTS

PART THREE: INVOKING THE LOTUS-BORN GURU

FOREWORD

— *Neten Chokling Rinpoche*

I would like to say thank you to Phakchok Rinpoche and Norbu-La for making this book, the third in a three part series dedicated to the sacred sites of the Lotus-Born Guru, and which closely follows Orgyen Lingpa's *Pema Kathang*. My thanks too, for the accompanying guidebook app, "Nekhor: Circling the Sacred." These resources have been of immense help and benefit to people like me, who yearn to visit and learn about these sacred sites and be immersed in their profound blessings. Despite the challenges of accessing many of these holy places, especially those in Tibet which are restricted, nonetheless through these books I see, and I learn, and I receive the blessings. So it has been very beneficial and helpful.

Especially for those who have entered the path and are practitioners, I think it is very important to see these places and learn about their sacredness. Using myself as an example, especially these days, finding genuine inspiration can be difficult, as the surroundings often focus on worldly matters. However, through this book, and through seeing this book, I feel a renewed sense of diligence and dedication to my spiritual path. As I learn about the life stories of these extraordinary mahasiddhas and great masters of the past who followed in the footsteps of the Lotus-Born Guru, and how they traversed the path to enlightenment, I am deeply inspired and motivated to become a better practitioner myself, and to strive towards becoming a mahasiddha like them.

Of course, there are numerous other reasons to appreciate this book. Even the mere act of seeing and hearing about the significance of these sacred places is believed to bring liberation. The benefits are manifold, but for me, the most significant aspect is the deep inspiration to become a dedicated and accomplished practitioner, following the example of the great masters of the past.

Neten Chokling Rinpoche
Chökhor Düchen 2023

When you recount my life-story,
You will be filled with inspiration. ⁂
When you see my qualities and understanding,
Deep faith will be born within you. ⁂
When that faith turns to unshakeable conviction,
My blessing will enter and transform you. ⁂
When your mind is free of all doubts,
Whatever you wish can be achieved. ⁂

————⚬◠◡◠⚬————

Guru Padmasambhava's advice to Khandro Yeshé Tsogyal
upon leaving Tibet, from the Le'u Dünma,
The Prayer in Seven Chapters,

revealed by Tulku Zangpo Drakpa.

THE "LOOKS LIKE ME" IMAGE OF
GURU PADMASAMBHAVA

During Guru Rinpoche's stay at Samyé monastery, skilled artisans sculpted a beautiful statue of his likeness. When the statue was formally presented, he responded, "It looks like me," and then blessed it, saying, "Now it is the same as me!" Thus it was named Guru Ngadrama, the 'Looks-Like-Me Guru.' The statue itself was destroyed in the 20th century. The famous black and white photograph still captures its presence.

ASPIRATION

ཀྱེ༔ ཀུན་བཟང་རྡོ་རྗེ་འཆང་ཆེན་མན་ཆད་ནས༔ །
དྲིན་ཆེན་རྩ་བའི་བླ་མ་ཡན་ཆད་ཀྱི༔ །
འགྲོ་བའི་དོན་དུ་སྨོན་ལམ་གང་བཏབ་པ༔ །
དེ་དག་ཐམས་ཅད་དེང་འདིར་འགྲུབ་པར་ཤོག༔ །

From the great Samantabhadra Vajradhara
Down until our kind root guru,
May the aspirations made for the benefit of beings,
Be fulfilled this very day.

In memory of my father, Pema Lodrö Gyaltsen,

Khenchen Jampal Dewé Nyima,

who first introduced me to Guru Rinpoche.

INTRODUCTION

Over these past years, our journey in the footsteps of the Lotus-Born Guru has taken us through the rolling hills and valleys of Nepal and across the vast plains of India. Now, as we enter Tibet, where Guru Padmasambhava's enlightened activities found their most fertile soil, we are both humbled and inspired by the examples set in these stories that played out across this Snowy Land. Through this journey, as translators and editors, and joined, as we hope, by you our readers, we have grown ever more familiar with the Mahaguru, imagining what it must have felt like to encounter him in one of his myriad forms, to have heard his lion-like speech, to have been in the presence of his penetrating wisdom. Our link with Guru Padmasambhava and his destined disciples is now beyond question, for we have at the very least had the good fortune to learn some of the accounts of his extraordinary deeds. It is with the continuing aspiration to connect our present generation with the life of Guru Padamsambhava that we present *Following in Your Footsteps: The Lotus-Born Guru in Tibet*, the last of three volumes tracing his journey across Greater India, Nepal, and Tibet.

The lotus flower from which Padmasambhava took birth on Lake Dhanakosha still blooms in the heart of the faithful, just as the charnel grounds of Ancient India still blaze with the fierce presence of the dakinis. The mountains of Nepal, too, still harbor sites of practice and pilgrimage, all established in perfect preparation for this, greatest of his feats: the transmission of the Dharma to Tibet, and thence to the world at large. When Guru Padmasambhava was leaving Tibet for the last time and heading for the land of the rakshasa demons in the southwest, his closest disciple, Khandro Yeshe Tsogyal, was grieving at the prospect of losing her beloved master. Guru Rinpoche consoled her with the following pith instruction, a jewel from among the vast treasury of his teachings:

> *When you recount my life-story,* ⁓
> *You will be filled with inspiration.* ⁓
> *When you see my qualities and understanding,* ⁓
> *Deep faith will be born within you.* ⁓
> *When that faith turns to unshakeable conviction,* ⁓
> *Then my blessing will transform you.* ⁓
> *When your mind is free of all doubts,* ⁓
> *Whatever you wish can be achieved.*[1] ⁓
>
> — *Revealed by Tulku Zangpo Drakpa*

The editors, as they have throughout the series, continue to take Kyapjé Domang Yangthang Rinpoche's (1930–2016) words of advice to heart: "Primarily follow the *Pema Kathang, The Chronicles of Padma*, and use it as your guiding reference." Guided thus, we have followed the amazing accounts of Guru Padmasambhava's life and liberation[2] in Tibet, penetrating deep into the principal places where his activity unfolded, and learning that his influence was vaster than we could ever have imagined. Our heartfelt wish is that through this journey we may all share in the good fortune of experiencing Guru Rinpoche's blessings. May they saturate our body, speech, and mind, and so may we never be apart from the Mahaguru!

Samye Translations
Chötrül Düchen 2023

OUR MISSION

We started our research with a simple purpose in mind: to connect today's practitioners with the extraordinary life and accomplishments of Guru Padmasambhava. From this, there grew an interest in the actual places where the Mahaguru practiced and a wish to make them more widely known to long-term practitioners of Tibetan Buddhism and to newcomers alike. With this series of books, we begin to fulfill this goal. In recognizing and bringing to life the great holy places of Guru Padmasambhava, we offer all practitioners the opportunity to follow in the footsteps of past masters and bring their blessings onto their path.

In this, the third book of the series, we present Guru Rinpoche's life and deeds as they occurred in Greater Tibet, turning an entire land into a sanctuary for the Dharma—a safe haven where practitioners could pursue the Dharma wholeheartedly. This was by no means an easy task. In many ways, the Mahaguru's rigorous study in India and his practice in Nepal had been but preparation for his work in Tibet. Once in Tibet, the Mahaguru was faced with the challenges posed by the hordes of wild, untamed beings inhabiting the land. In a quite spectacular way, the Mahaguru rose to the challenge, establishing spirits as guardians of the Dharma, laying the foundations for Tibet's first monastery at Samye, translating the Dharma into Tibetan, establishing a Sangha, and hiding countless treasure teachings. It is through these immeasurable acts of kindness that many of Guru Padmasambhava's priceless teachings are still practiced and readily available to us today. It is our aspiration that this guide will connect you with Guru Padmasambhava and serve as a catalyst for your own spiritual journey.

As a companion to this book series, you are welcome to visit our website, **www.nekhor.org**. At **Nekhor** ("pilgrimage" in Tibetan, literally "circling the sacred") there is an expanding selection of resources to aid your exploration of the Mahaguru's sacred sites. As part of the larger effort of Samye Translations to present authentic, practice-related literature from the Tibetan tradition, we have also translated and made available a variety of traditional prayers and compositions that honor Guru Padmasambhava and his activities. All these are freely available online. Furthermore, the **Nekhor** mobile app, available in major app stores, now offers quick, convenient access to our online resources, providing practical travel information and much more. If you are interested in on-the-ground guidance to these sites, our team welcomes the opportunity to connect with you as you consider embarking on your own pilgrimage.

HOW TO USE THIS BOOK

Our Nepal and India volumes provided an extensive introduction to Guru Padmasambhava's life, and to traditional Buddhist pilgrimage in general, and with this third volume we aim to extend the reader's appreciation of the Mahaguru's influence. Thus, the introductory material in this volume begins with *The Wish-Fulfilling Tree*, a concise account of the Mahaguru's life, revealed by one of the greatest treasure revealers of the 19th century, Chokgyur Dechen Lingpa. There follows a teaching, offered by Phakchok Rinpoche, on the origin of the Mahayoga *Kagyé* and its transmission to Greater Tibet. Finally, there is a general introduction to Tibet from the editors. Whether you are at home or on pilgrimage, we hope that these will inspire you as you embark on this journey. If you would like to explore Guru Rinpoche's life more deeply, we encourage you to read the translations mentioned in our cited sources.

In the main part of the book, you will find the stories behind a selection of the many sacred sites connected with the Mahaguru in Tibet. Their descriptions are arranged according to the main overarching themes in the *Pema Kathang*, Padmasambhava's most extensive life story, and the sequence follows its chapters chronologically, with just a few changes for clarity. Indeed, in the *Pema Kathang* we find an astonishing number of sacred sites touched by Guru Padmasambhava's awakened activities during his stay in Tibet, and many more that were discovered and opened by his followers. As the famous Tibetan saying goes, "there is not so much as a clod of earth the size of a horse-hoof print that the Mahaguru did not cover."[3] We are talking here about a vast area that could be termed "Greater Tibet," unbound by the vicissitudes of political boundaries, its regions linked by common linguistic and cultural characteristics during Guru Rinpoche's time. This would include not only Central Tibet (Ü Tsang), but also Eastern Tibet (Kham and Amdo) and the kingdoms of Bhutan and Sikkim, as well as Ladakh, Zanskar, Lahual and Spiti.[4] The treasure trove of sacred sites found in these blessed lands is so extensive that it would be challenging to cover, even in many volumes. In this volume, we have focused our attention on some of the main events and sacred sites associated with Guru Padmasambhava's bringing of the Dharma to the heart of Tibet—an accomplishment which quickly filtered into the wider cultural landscape of Greater Tibet, transforming it into a vast realm still blessed to this day.

In order to provide some insight into how the upholders of Guru Padmasambha's legacy engaged with the Mahaguru's sacred sites, we have concluded several chapters in this volume with stories from contemporary Tibetan masters. As you will discover, the sacred sites discussed in this book served vital roles in the transmission of the Mahaguru's *nyingtik* (heart essence) teachings—those of the Great Perfection. Therefore, we will share stories of key upholders of the Nyingtik tradition, such as Gyalwang Longchenpa (1308–1364) Rikdzin Jikmé Lingpa (1730–1798), and as other Nyingtik masters active at these sites. We also include stories of some of the more important *tertöns* (treasure revealers) have who retrieved the Mahaguru's legacy in the form of *termas* (treasures) from these very sites. In particular, we focus on the accounts of the great master and pilgrim Jamyang Khyentsé Wangpo (1820–1892), who traversed the Mahaguru's sacred landscape in the 19th century. On his pilgrimage, not only did he teach and practice, but he also revealed treasures and composed prayers at many of the places that he visited. His pilgrimage was captured in his extraordinary *Guide to Central Tibet*—which has since become a major resource on the Mahaguru's sacred sites, and on pilgrimage sites in general.[5]

As in our previous volumes, each sacred site is depicted in a painting that evokes a sacred landscape of the past. These are visions of how the sites may have looked when Guru Padmasabhava was present there, and they feature the major sacred landmarks described both in the Mahaguru's biography and as witnessed by later pilgrims.

In the third part of this book, *Invoking the Lotus-Born Guru*, we have again included advice from Phakchok Rinpoche on how to go on pilgrimage authentically, and have again included a collection of some of the most famous prayers to Guru Rinpoche. Thus, wherever you are, you may find inspiration, strength, and blessings by using the sacred words intoned by masters past and present. For this book to be a lightweight travel companion, we have included only a droplet from the ocean of prayers to the Mahaguru. For those who wish for more, the many supplementary prayers that we have translated are readily accessible through our website.

Finally, there are endnotes providing further information, a list of our sources, and a bibliography. The endnotes provide suggestions for further reading, enabling an in-depth exploration of the topics mentioned. To make the guide more accessible and readable, we have removed all diacritics from the Sanskrit words. For Tibetan words, we are following the Samye Translations phonetic system.

The vision of the *Following in Your Footsteps* series is to allow readers to follow Guru Rinpoche's journey through the geographical landscape of our world. While we strive to tell the stories in full, we have decided not to include practical travel information, since such details are liable to change. Instead, we have made them available on the **Nekhor** website and app. Please also note that we have focused our research on the sacred sites mentioned in the few select biographies listed in our sources. Thus, this series does not present Tibet's *beyuls* (hidden lands), as are recognized in several pilgrimage guides, and in the rich oral traditions of Tibet, Bhutan, Sikkim, Ladakh, Zanskar, Lahual and Spiti, and even in Mongolia. Rather than discussing these in our book, we will feature these sacred *beyul* sites on our **Nekhor** website and app.

OUR APPROACH AND SOURCES

This series follows the kind advice of our teachers in its portrayal of Guru Padmasambhava as a fully enlightened being whose life transcends the confines of space and time while still appearing within them. While we follow a traditional approach to the Mahaguru's life, we also acknowledge the diversity of views that our traditional and academic research has brought forth. We have refrained from lengthy discussion of these issues in the main text of the book in the interests of simplicity and ease of access. However, for the interested reader, there are endnotes where we keep careful track of our sources. This is where further clarification is provided where possible, and suggestions for further reading.

The spirit in which this pilgrimage guide is offered is perhaps captured in

Guru Rinpoche's own reply to Tibet's Dharma King Trisong Detsen, who had requested him to tell his life story:

> I myself have not really come into the world, ⁞
> For I am the unelaborate dharmakaya, ⁞
> Like the mandala of the sun. ⁞
> Yet from the perspectives of my disciples ⁞
> My life story appears in myriad ways ⁞
> According to every limited viewpoint, ⁞
> Like wavering moons in bodies of water. ⁞[6]

This statement reveals how, in terms of the Buddhist view, inconsistencies and contradictions naturally occur because of the dualistic world we inhabit. While it is indeed important to acknowledge these often-alluring differences, they may not actually be relevant for penetrating the heart of the spiritual path. Alternatively, perhaps it is the way we deal with them that helps the spiritual path to unfold.

Kyapjé Yangthang Rinpoche's direction to us, to follow the *Pema Kathang* in presenting these sacred sites, has been a guiding light throughout our project. The *Pema Kathang* was discovered in the 14th century by the great treasure revealer Orgyen Lingpa (b. 1323) and it represents the very speech of Guru Padmasambhava, as flawlessly remembered and set in writing by his chief consort and devoted disciple Khandro Yeshé Tsogyal. In the wake of its discovery, the *Pema Kathang* quickly rose to become one of the Mahaguru's most celebrated biographies. Its language is highly poetic, written in verse, with a hundred and eight chapters, and running to approximately five hundred pages in length. Orgyen Lingpa also revealed a companion treasure volume, the *Kathang Dé Nga* (*The Five Part Chronicles*), which elaborates on various episodes and key figures in Guru Padmasambhava's life.

Soon after the *Pema Kathang* was revealed, Sangyé Lingpa (1340–1396), a contemporary of Orgyen Lingpa, discovered the *Sertrengwa* (*The Golden Garland Chronicles*). Closely following the *Pema Kathang*, written in prose, with a hundred and seventeen chapters, and somewhat longer than the *Pema Kathang*, this is considered by many as a kind of auto-commentary on the *Pema Kathang*. We have found that these two works are integral supports for each other, forming a master narrative of the Mahaguru's life.

Of these three major biographies, the *Pema Kathang* was translated into French as *Le Dict de Padma* by Gustave-Charles Toussaint in 1912.[7] In 1978, it was translated from French into English by Kenneth Douglas and Gwendolyn

Bays.[8] It is our heartfelt aspiration in the coming years to bring out a modern translation of the *Pema Kathang*, along with translations of the *Kathang Dé Nga* and the *Sertrengwa*, neither of which are currently available in the English language.

Drawing also from the *Sertrengwa* and *Kathang Dé Nga*, we have covered every chapter of the *Pema Kathang* in brief, presenting summaries of its chapters over the course of this three-part series. From the *Pema Kathang* itself, we have provided fresh translations of key passages that relate to the sacred places, so that the reader can more closely follow the original spirit of Guru Padmasambhava's incredible journey.

While the *Pema Kathang* plays a central role in revealing the life of the Mahaguru, it does not always provide a detailed account of each and every sacred site. Nor do all the sites it mentions have a clear place in the modern landscape. Furthermore, at times we found other authoritative sources providing more information or even telling different accounts of certain places. Thus, we have carefully selected some of the most trusted compositions, prayers, and stories from great masters past and present—those that provide insight into these sacred sites.

Such sources include the *Zanglingma* (*The Copper Palace*) by Nyang Ral Nyima Özer (1124–1192);[9] the summary prayer *A Beautiful and Wondrous Udumbara Garland* by Jamyang Khyentsé Wangpo (1820–1892) ;[10] The *Le'u Dün Ma* (*Prayer in Seven Chapters*) by Tulku Zangpo Drakpa (14th century); *The Wish-Fulfilling Tree* by Chokgyur Dechen Lingpa (1829–1870); and two biographies written in verse and entitled *The Tenth Day Prayer*, one by Jamgön Kongtrul and the other by Kyapjé Dudjom Rinpoche (1904–1987).[11]

For the sacred sites of the five wisdom dakinis, the spiritual consorts of Guru Rinpoche, we have relied on the biographies of Khandro Yeshé Tsogyal and Lhacham Mandarava, as revealed by Samten Lingpa (1655–1708) and Trinlé Drodül Lerap Dewa Tsal (19th century). These biographies have been translated into English as, respectively, *Lady of the Lotus-Born: The Life and Enlightenment of Yeshe Tsogyal* and *The Lives and Liberation of Princess Mandarava*[12]. We have also provided footnotes referencing the relevant passages in the respective English translations. Yeshé Tsogyal's biography includes accounts of the other three spiritual consorts, Belmo Shakyadevi, Belbang Kalasiddhi, and Mönmo Tashi Kyidren.[13] Finally, for the life stories of the masters and students as presented in this book, we are mainly following the accounts given in the *Pema Kathang*, in Jamgön Kongtrül Lodrö Thayé's *A Garland of Beryl: Brief Accounts of Profound Terma and the Siddhas Who Have Revealed Them*,[14] and in Kyapjé Dudjom Rinpoche's *History of the Nyingma School*.[15]

Finally, we have relied on two extraordinary pilgrimage guides—*The Guide to Central Tibet* by Jamyang Khyentse Wangpo and, for more recent descriptions, *The Pilgrimage Guide to Central Tibe*t by Katok Situ Chökyi Gyatso (1880–1925).[16]

ACKNOWLEDGEMENTS

The writing of these books began several years ago at the request of Norbu-la. Her wish was for those who feel connected to Guru Padmasambhava to form an even deeper connection. Her aspiration and inspiration have continuously breathed life into the series as it has unfolded. Our work began auspiciously on Dakini Day, September 18, 2014, and an initial edit was completed in 2020, the Tibetan Mouse Year, which marks the 200th anniversary of Jamyang Khyentse Wangpo's birth, the 150th anniversary of Chokgyur Dechen Lingpa's *parinirvana*, and the 100th anniversary of Kyapjé Tulku Urgyen Rinpoche's birth. Most of the initial research for the series took place in 2016, the Tibetan Monkey Year, the astrological year of Guru Padmasambhava's birth. Since then, our work on the series has continued, and now, the final volume auspiciously concludes on Treldha Tsechu, celebrating the births of Guru Rinpoche, Khandro Yeshé Tsogyal and Terchen Chokgyur Dechen Lingpa in the Monkey month of the Water Rabbit Year.

We would first and foremost like to offer our deep gratitude to all the lineage masters of the past who have made this book possible. We are also deeply grateful to all our precious teachers, who constantly guide and connect us with Guru Rinpoche. We thank especially Kyapjé Domang Yangthang Rinpoche, Kyapjé Chatral Rinpoche, Neten Chokling Rinpoche, Phakchok Rinpoche and Orgyen Topgyal Rinpoche—all of whom have initiated, inspired, supported, and guided this project with great care and wisdom.

This pilgrimage guidebook is the result of generous contributions from many Dharma brothers and sisters. Foremost among them is Samye Translations' Stefan Mang, who because of his karma and being introduced to the Dharma early in life by his precious teacher Sogyal Rinpoche, has been unwavering in his commitment to this project since its inception. Likewise, Peter Woods has been hugely instrumental in terms of translation, research, and writing. We would like to thank our researchers, translators, scouts, and editors: Theresa

Bachhuber, Hilary Herdman, Nata Kryvolapchuk, Oriane Lavolé, Marcela Lopez, Robert Offner, Nick Schmidt, Monica Thunder and Kaleb Yaniger. Also, were it not for the tireless work of our copy editors, Libby Hogg and Liz Miller, this book would surely lack the eloquence and polish that all such epic undertakings deserve.

We would like to thank our wonderful artists. The cover image is a photo of the murals at Mindrolling Monastery in Dehradun, India. The "Looks Like Me" image of Guru Padmasambhava on page 8 is from a photograph taken by the late Queen Mother of Sikkim and is courtesy of the *Tertön* Sogyal Trust. The pictures depicting the sacred sites were painted by Tenzin Gyurmé Dorjé. Our wonderful graphic designer Julian Pang and our amazing typesetters Linda Joyce Baer and Lana O'Flaherty designed this book. With their creative and visual input, this guide more fully conveys the color and vibrancy of these places of pilgrimage.

We offer our thanks to Adam Pearcey and the translators, editors, and programmers of Lotsawa House. Without their efforts and dedication, we could not have included all the wonderful Tibetan translations found within this guide.

We are grateful to all the many academics, scholars, and professors on whose work we have relied. Without their dedicated research, this would not be such a rich and detailed guide.

We offer many thanks to our production advisor and publisher Marcia Schmidt, and our deep gratitude to our production patron Owsley Brown III. Our gratitude also goes out to all those not mentioned here who have in myriad ways created the causes and conditions, knowingly or not, that have allowed this guide to manifest, as well as to all those pilgrims who will take this book and visit the sites of the precious Lotus-Born Guru. It is you who will truly bring this work to life.

May this book be a guide for all who wish to follow in
The Mahaguru's footsteps as they tread the path of awakening!
May this book be dedicated to the Lotus-Born's teachings,
To their continuance and proliferation,
And to the fulfilled aspirations of all who uphold them!

PART ONE

Entering the
Sacred Landscape

THE LIFE AND LIBERATION
OF GURU PADMASAMBHAVA

In our previous volumes, *The Lotus-Born Guru in Nepal* and *India*, we shared acounts of the Mahaguru's life by Jamgön Kongtrül Lodrö Thayé and Jamyang Khyentsé Wangpo. In this, the third volume, we are honored to present one of the most treasured life stories of Guru Padmasambhava: *The Wish-Fulfilling Tree*, revealed by the Great Tertön Chokgyur Dechen Zhikpo Lingpa. Chokgyur Lingpa was born in Sangyal, at the base of the sacred mountain Namkha Dzö (Sky Treasury) in the province of Nangchen, on the tenth day of the sixth month of the Earth Ox Year (August 10, 1829). Prophesied by Guru Padmasambhava as the last of the hundred major *tertöns*, Chokgyur Lingpa was also one of the most prolific treasure revealers of the 19th century. His revelations—together with their ancillary materials—span more than forty volumes of Tibetan pecha. Chokgyur Lingpa's revelations are replete with profound teachings meant for our times—practices that are concise, easy to apply and full of blessings. They include all three practice categories required to qualify a treasure revealer as a great treasure revealer (*terchen*)—practices related to Guru Rinpoche, to the Great Perfection, and to Avalokiteshvara. Like Jamyang Khyentsé Wangpo, Chokgyur Lingpa was particularly renowned as an entrusted holder of the full range of Dharma lineages, the Seven Transmissions (*khapap dün*)— the oral lineage, the earth treasures, the rediscovered treasures, the mind treasures, the oral instructions, the visionary revelations, and recollections from past lives.[17]

At the age of twenty-eight, on the fifteenth day of the fourth month in the Fire Dragon Year (May 19, 1856), at the sacred site of Akanishta Karma in Tibet, Chokgyur Lingpa revealed as an earth treasure (*sater*) the Mahaguru's life story, *The Wish-Fulfilling Tree* (*Paksam Jönshing*)—part of *The Sevenfold Cycle of Profundity* (*Zapa Kordün*). The verses of *The Wish-Fulfilling Tree* were uttered by the Mahaguru himself, and thus reflect his personal perspective on an extraordinary life—unlike biographies written by another, who can only ever have partial knowledge of the subject.[18] Although it consists of only ten short chapters, *The Wish-Fulfilling Tree* covers the full span of his life story, from his birth to his departure for the Glorious Copper-Colored Mountain. Each chapter focuses on one important aspect of his enlightened activity, making it easy to get a sense of the unfolding of his journey in our world. *The Wish-Fulfilling Tree* is thus an autobiography that is truly rare and precious, and is sure to bring blessings to the devoted heart.[19]

ཨོཾ༔ རབ་པ་སྤྱོར་བདུན་ལསཿ ཨོ་རྒྱན་རྣམ་ཐར་དཔག་བསམ་ལྗོན་ཤིང་བཞུགས་སོ༔

The Wish-Fulfilling Tree
The Life-Story of the Master of Uddiyana
as found in Padmasambhava's Sevenfold Cycle of Profundity

revealed by Chokgyur Dechen Lingpa

ཐོན། སྙ།རྗ།༔

Emaho. How marvelous! ༔
I, Padma, shall here present the story of my life— ༔
How I mastered the sacred Dharma, all three vehicles, ༔
How my deeds for beings became a constant flow, ༔
And how I have unceasingly spun the Wheel of Dharma. ༔

Each and every sentient being of the sixfold classes ༔
Strays incessantly through samsara, confused, unknowing. ༔
Especially in the Age of Strife,[20] the dregs of time, ༔
beings are steeped in the five poisons and act in errant ways. ༔
To inspire them, hard as they are to change, ༔
The dharmakaya buddhas directed their attention; ༔
The sambhogakaya buddhas asserted their command; ༔
And the nirmanakaya buddhas in conference all agreed ༔
That I, the Lotus Master, should appear in this world, Jambudvipa. ༔

Perceived by some, I magically appeared in Uddiyana, ༔
Upon a lotus flower on the waters of Dhanakosha. ༔
Perceived by others, I was the son of Uddiyana's King. ༔
Perceived by still others, I descended as a thunderbolt ༔
Onto the peak of Mount Meteoric Iron. ༔

In any case, it was twenty-four years after Shakyamuni's passing ༔
That Amitabha took the form of a bodhisattva, ༔
The Great Compassionate One,[21] and from his heart ༔
Magically conjured me, Padma, as the letter *hrih*.༔

What's more, I arrived in all the worlds like the rain, ༔
Descending upon countless millions of billions of places. ༔
Indeed, the deeds of the Conquerors surpass the reach of thought: ༔
Who could ever measure them or limit their scope? ༔

Nevertheless, conjured I was to Jambudvipa, ༔

As the destined son of Uddiyana's King. ⁑
Over that kingdom I reigned, turning the Wheel of the Mahayana Dharma, ⁑
So that everyone together would realize true awakening. ⁑
Then, I journeyed through the lands of India ⁑
And learned to perfection the fivefold fields of knowledge.[22] ⁑

This was the first chapter in Padma's Wish-Fulfilling Tree, *my story of liberation, on how I came into this world and trained in the fields of knowledge.* ⁑

ཟ་ཚ༑ཟཧྲུ༔

In India, I raised questions on the sutras with Ananda, ⁑
Buddha Shakyamuni's close disciple. ⁑
In Prabhahasti's presence I became a renunciant monk, ⁑
And studied all the teachings of the triple yogas.[23] ⁑

Then I went before the master Prahevajra[24] ⁑
And requested every doctrine on the heart essence of the Great Perfection. ⁑
And, at the feet of the master Buddhaguhya, ⁑
I received the *Secret Essence, Net of Illusion*[25] hundreds of times. ⁑

At Shri Singha's feet I then bowed down,[26] ⁑
Receiving all the tantras of Mahottara Heruka.[27] ⁑
I went before the master Mañjushrimitra ⁑
And received, without exception, every Mañjushri Yamantaka tantra.[28] ⁑

Then I went to the great master Nagarjuna ⁑
To request the tantras and sadhanas of Lotus Speech.[29] ⁑
I visited the great master Humkara and from him received ⁑
All the tantras and sadhanas for Yangdak, Mind of Perfect Purity.[30] ⁑

In the presence of the master Vimalamitra ⁑
I received the tantras and sadhanas of Amrita Qualities.[31] ⁑
I went before the master Dhanasamskrita ⁑
and requested the tantras and sadhanas of Kila Activity.[32] ⁑

Once again, I journeyed back to Prabhahasti ⁑
And received from him the *Sublime Knowledge of Kila* collection.[33] ⁑
At the feet of the great master Shantigarbha ⁑
I received the tantras and sadhanas for Jikten Chötö[34] and Möpa Drakngak.[35] ⁑

Furthermore, from accomplished masters in great numbers ⁑

I received a plethora of empowerments, explanations, and instructions ⚬
On a plethora of tantras, statements, and sadhanas ⚬
From the Tripitaka[36] and the outer and inner Secret Mantra. ⚬

This was the second chapter in Padma's Wish-Fulfilling Tree, *my story of liberation, on how I requested key instructions from all the masters and resolved all uncertainty.* ⚬

ཟ་ཚ༷།ཟ་རྗེ༵༔

Then I reached perfection in my practice ⚬
In India's eight major charnel grounds and sacred places, ⚬
And with diverse siddhi signs I overcame the hordes of maras. ⚬
Above all, when trouble arose at the Vajra Throne of India, ⚬
Caused by evil-minded teachers preaching extreme beliefs, ⚬
I settled it with logic and used my power to defeat them. ⚬
Five hundred panditas then placed me on a throne, ⚬
And as the Buddha's regent I preserved the doctrine for a hundred years. ⚬
Later, Vimalamitra, the great pandita, became my successor. ⚬

I, Guru from Uddiyana, went to the land of Zahor, ⚬
Where the ruler, in his ignorance, had me burned alive. ⚬
I displayed a miracle, transforming the pyre into a lake, ⚬
Which set everyone in the kingdom onto the Dharma path. ⚬
I upheld the Buddha's teachings there for two hundred years. ⚬

Then I went to attain immortality in Maratika, ⚬
And Lord Amitayus appeared before my eyes, ⚬
Bestowing one hundred and eight sadhanas on longevity. ⚬
I proceeded to the Akanishta Realm of Dense Array, ⚬
And to the pure realms of the five buddha families. ⚬
There I requested tantras from all the sugatas ⚬
And conversed with the nirmanakaya buddhas, all of whom declared: ⚬
"There is no buddha apart from your own mind!" ⚬

In the upper practice cave of Yangleshö,[37] ⚬
In order to attain the siddhi of the Great Seal,[38] ⚬
I performed the practice of glorious Yangdak Heruka. ⚬
Hindrances arose, inflicting pain on India and Nepal, ⚬
So I asked my masters to send Dharma methods to repel them. ⚬

The messengers carried back the *Sublime Knowledge of Kila*, ༔
And by its mere arrival in Nepal, all hindrances were quelled. ༔
Thus, I achieved the supreme siddhi, the Great Seal. ༔

While I was practicing at Yari Gong, Upper Slate Mountain, ༔
Argumentative extremists again challenged the Vajra Throne. ༔
Dakinis appeared before a group of five hundred Buddhist scholars ༔
And told them to send a message to Surya Singha, the Indian king, ༔
And his priests, to call me back to the Vajra Throne. ༔
There, I once again defeated all the extremist teachers. ༔

Next, with the eight great masters[39] I traveled to Cool Grove cemetery,[40] ༔
Where we remained in meditation for seven days. ༔
On the final night, at the Great Enchanting Mound Stupa,[41] ༔
We all beheld, as we meditated there, ༔
That the stupa was glowing, sparks of light flashing. ༔
A dakini[42] appeared and gave us each a casket of treasure teachings. ༔
While I personally received the instructions for the *Assembly of Sugatas*,[43] ༔
Each of the masters also received a mandate of their own. ༔
For a long time we remained at the Vajra Throne, preserving the Dharma. ༔

This was the third chapter in Padma's Wish-Fulfilling Tree, *my story of liberation, on how I upheld the teachings in the land of India and established every
country in the Dharma.* ༔

ཐ་ཅ།བཞི༔
Then, through the force of past aspirations, ༔
Trisong Detsen, who was a Dharma-upholding king, ༔
Gave rise to deep-felt wishes that a temple be built ༔
and invited the great pandita Shantarakshita to come and pacify the site. ༔
While the land was actually tamed without a problem, ༔
The pandita pretended otherwise and spoke of the prophecy of my arrival. ༔
Three emissaries[44] were thus sent with an invitation and gold. ༔

They requested permission from the Indian king and his priests, ༔
Who discussed whether I should be allowed to go. ༔
Even though the Indian lands were under threat from extremist teachers, ༔
the predicted time had come for spreading the Dharma in Tibet. ༔
Therefore they decided that I should undertake the journey ༔

And signed the letter; the messengers were sent ahead, ⁣⁣
And I set out from India.

As I approached central Nepal, Tibet's gods and demons
Grew concerned—soon all were wracked with worry.
Once again, five messengers were dispatched
And we met in Mangyul. These were the first Tibetans
To have faith in my miraculous abilities.

In Tibet, on the shore of Nyima Khü (Sun Rim Lake),
I bound the yakshas and rakshasas under oath.
I bound the Tenma Sisters on the heights of the Khala Pass,[45]
I bound Gangkar Shamé,[46] Tingmen of Jang,
Tinglomen,[47] and the local guardians of Jang.[48]
In Tsang at Oyuk, on the dreadful pass of Shang,
I subdued Dorjé Lekpa,[49] and, in Yeru and Yönru,
The malicious mountain spirits Osham and Tanglha.[50]

On sacred Mount Kailash I subdued the *gyukar* constellation gods,[51]
And on Targo's Snowy Range the *zadü* planetary demons.[52]
At Namtso Chükmo I bound the *mentsün* medicine ladies,[53]
And at Ma Tsongön the *lumen* naga goddess.[54]
At Dentig Cliff I bound the Magyel mountain god,[55]
And at Rotam Nakpo, likewise, the *mayam* plague mothers.[56]
In Atarong Gorge I bound the *gongpo* demons,[57]
And at Melung Cliff I subdued the *genyen* deities.[58]
At Red Wang Shumar I bound the *lhatsen* warrior deities,[59]
And on Kham's snowy range, the *lutsen* warrior nagas.[60]

At Divine Zhakra Peak I bound the *kulha* body guardians,[61]
And at Black Thökar Nakpo I subdued the *lhatsen* warrior deities.
At Black Trigo Nakpo I bound the *gya* deities under oath,[62]
And at Dark Changra Mukpo all the *gyalpo* sovereign spirits.[63]

In Tsawarong Gorge I bound the *sadak* earth lords,[64]
And at La Kangchik, all the *te'u-rang* hammer-wielders.[65]
At the Bo Gorge I bound the *lutsen* warrior nagas,
And across the Six Ranges of Nédruk Gang all the *ludü* demon nagas.[66]

At Anchung Dzong Fortress the *genyen* spirits came to greet me,
And at Sengé Dzong I bound the *yapang* spirits of meadows and crags.[67]

At Namkha Dzong I bound the *lhanyen* spirits,[68] ﹖
And at Mara's Rock of Dükyi Drak all the *barlön* deputy spirits.[69] ﹖

At Mayo Glacier I bound the great *nyenchen* spirits,[70] ﹖
And on Poyi Drak Cliff I subdued a *dümen* demoness.[71] ﹖
At Khyungto Nakpo I bound a *dütsen* warrior demon,[72] ﹖
And on Düri Nakpo Mountain, a *dügyal* demon king.[73] ﹖

At the holy site of Buchu[74] I bound the minor *lutren* nagas, ﹖
And at Lharu Tse the menial *lhatren* gods. ﹖
At the holy site of Dakpo I bound the *gurlha* hunting gods,[75] ﹖
And likewise, at Maldro, all the nagas. ﹖

In the southern land of Mön I bound the *mudü* demons,[76] ﹖
And in Sikkim, Land of Crops, the *rongdü* valley demons.[77] ﹖
On Lapchi's snowy range I bound the four *semo* sisters,[78] ﹖
And at the Jamtrin Temple in Kyirong all the *mamo* mother goddesses.[79] ﹖

In the valley of Tsang, gods and humans welcomed me, ﹖
And everyone in Tölung turned out in greeting. ﹖
All along the way emerged springs of siddhi nectar. ﹖

At Drakmar's Tamarisk Grove, the king came forth to greet me. ﹖
Although he was emperor, an emanation of Mañjushri, ﹖
The veil of his human birth was extremely dense, ﹖
And so he failed to see my qualities in full. ﹖

High and mighty, full of pride, the king's attitude was offensive. ﹖
So I sang a song of my greatness and displayed my magic. ﹖
The emperor's faith was kindled; he bowed down low ﹖
And presented a throne of gold, and gifts in great abundance. ﹖
All Tibet's gods and humans came to pay their respects. ﹖

This was the fourth chapter in Padma's Wish-Fulfilling Tree, *my story of liberation, on how the Tibetan monarch invited me to his land and how the gods
and demons were subdued.* ﹖

ཐ་ཅ།ཐཇཱ﹖
Then I summoned every god and demon in the kingdom of Tibet, ﹖
Gave them orders, bound them to oaths, and consecrated the land. ﹖

With vajra dance and song of *hung*, they were brought under my command. 𐩒
During the day, the people laid down Samye's foundations, 𐩒
But it was the gods and demons who took up the work at night. 𐩒
The Four Great Kings[80] assisted, supervising their endeavor, 𐩒
And so the walls went up with joyful, clamorous song, 𐩒
Gods and demons raising them higher at night than humans could by day!𐩒

Meanwhile, between the King and nagas a covenant was made, 𐩒
And the nagas were assigned to fill the land with gold dust. 𐩒
Samye was constructed in differing designs— 𐩒
The central temple with three stories was built like Mount Meru, 𐩒
The two yaksha temples like the sun and moon, 𐩒
And the whole was adorned with the four continents and eight minor isles. 𐩒
One hundred and eight stupas were placed on the Iron Mountain wall,[81] 𐩒
And four female dogs of copper were set on four stone pillars. 𐩒

The three stories were made in the styles of India, China and Tibet. 𐩒
Samantabhadra was the central figure in the upper storey, 𐩒
With the mandala of *Vairocana's Awakening*.[82] 𐩒
In the middle storey, the chief figure was Vairocana, 𐩒
Surrounded by the deities of the Vajradhatu mandala.[83] 𐩒
Central on the ground floor was the Great Awakened One,[84] 𐩒
With all the buddhas of the ten directions and their closest heirs. 𐩒

All the temples were consecrated, flower petals strewn, 𐩒
And wisdom deities descended into the statues, for all to see. 𐩒
Rays of light blazed forth and the sound of music was heard. 𐩒
The gods all showered down a rain of flowers 𐩒
And the nagas came to offer gifts of precious gems; 𐩒
Thus the world was filled with auspiciousness of every kind. 𐩒

Male and female protectors arrived to flank the temple's sides. 𐩒
The stone pillars shot forth flames, and the dogs growled and barked. 𐩒
Three times *arura* fruits[85] showered down like rain. 𐩒
Over all Tibet, auspicious signs and goodness reigned. 𐩒
Both gods and men were filled with joy, again and yet again— 𐩒
And so the banner of fame was unfurled across the land. 𐩒

This was the fifth chapter in Padma's Wish-Fulfilling Tree, *my story of liberation, on how I built the monastery of Samye and performed its consecration.* 𐩒

ཐ་ཅེ།ཐཞྲེཿ

Then, we, Abbot and Master,[86] conferred together: ༂
"This kingdom of Tibet is a land of savages. ༂
They don't know good from evil, so how can Dharma's truth be taught? ༂
Tibetan ministers are all puffed up with pride. ༂
So, once the King's wishes are fulfilled, let's go back to our own lands." ༂

The emperor caught wind of our discussion ༂
And grew deeply saddened, shedding many tears. ༂
Yet again, he presented us with a priceless gold mandala. ༂

"Masters, pay heed, out of your deepest kindness! ༂
I, King Trisong Detsen, indeed have lofty wishes, ༂
For this land of Tibet is savage, shrouded in darkness, ༂
And not a single word of the Dharma here resounds. ༂
Masters, perhaps you're disappointed, but take pity upon us: ༂
I beg you, please, care for us with your awakened compassion! ༂

"As enlightened emanations you entered this wretched land, ༂
And as bodhisattvas, your work is to care for others. ༂
You have no other task than to fulfill the needs of beings. ༂
I, Trisong Detsen, beseech you—please fulfill my prayers! ༂

"Although I have built shrines for the awakened body, speech, and mind, ༂
and have brought the Dharma of Sutra and Tantra to Tibet, ༂
Still it needs to spread through study, practice and meditation. ༂
So, masters, please ensure that this takes place! ༂
Abbot, Master, I beseech you both—don't leave, but stay here, in Tibet!" ༂

We, Master and Abbot, again conferred, and decided to remain. ༂
I could foresee all those young Tibetans of noble birth ༂
Who should be assembled, and we taught them to translate. ༂
From among this multitude, one hundred lotsawas emerged,[87] ༂
Including Ka, Chok and Zhang[88] and, foremost of all, Vairocana. ༂
I myself led the translation of the outer and inner tantras, ༂
While the Abbot was in charge of all aspects of Sutra and Vinaya. ༂

Since the basis for the Dharma is the precious Sangha, ༂
Eleven hundred Tibetan youngsters then took the vows of monks. ༂
We taught them the names of each and every Indian master, ༂
And sent a hundred lotsawas off to the land of India. ༂

One hundred great panditas they invited to Tibet— §
Vimalamitra, Buddhaguhya, and others of their kind. §
And so, in the temple—panditas, lotsawas, Abbot and Master— §
We all took our seats §
Upon beautiful and lofty thrones, all wrapped in rich brocade, §
And were served the finest treats and offered mandalas of gold. §

The teachings of Sutra and Tantra we translated in their entirety. §
The Three Collections of Vinaya, Sutra and Abhidharma we translated, §
And the *Paramita* [89] in its longer, medium and shorter forms— §
Thus all the Sutra teachings, without exception, we translated. §
The definitive teachings, such as the *Mahaparinirvana Sutra*—[90] §
All of them, without exception, likewise we translated. §

Kriya and Yoga tantras such as the Vajra Summit—[91] §
all the outer tantras, without exception, we translated. §
The eight tantras of the *Net of Illusion*, including the *Secret Essence*, §
The transmissions of the *Scripture of Assembly*, the Mind Section cycles, §
The *Eight Sadhana Teachings*, the five root tantras §
And ten specific tantras, fifteen in all— §
Untold numbers of Secret Mantra's inner tantras we translated. §

Moreover, countless teachings of Sutra and Tantra §
were, day and night, translated, studied, and explained. §
Throughout the Tibetan kingdom we established Dharma schools §
And compiled myriad volumes of sutras and tantras. §

With parasols and banners, pennants and streamers, §
With articles of offering, countless in number, §
All so very beautiful and resplendently arranged, §
The volumes were carried upon the monks' shoulders, §
And in between were carried all kinds of offerings. §

The panditas and lotsawas were seated in horse-drawn chariots, §
With parasols above and banners at their flanks. §
Untold numbers of instruments filled the air with music §
As they circled the temples, led always by fragrant incense. §
This was the day when Namkhé Nyingpo displayed miracles §
And all the scriptures were ceremoniously installed in the middle storey. [92] §

Then thrones were erected upon Yobok Meadow §

And all were offered a golden mandala and a brick of gold, ៖
A set of garments each, and a roll of silk and wool, ៖
A horse, a mule, and a male and female dzo,[93] ៖
A lamb's wool coat, a woolen jacket, leather case, and block of tea, ៖
A hundred coins of gold apiece, and a thousand pieces of silver. ៖

Once these were offered, the King rose from his seat. ៖
He spoke about his royal lineage, Tibetan customs, and his vision, ៖
And he extolled the virtues and kindness of the panditas and lotsawas. ៖
Then Vimalamitra spoke, and other great panditas, ៖
On the origins of the Dharma and the reasons for its greatness. ៖

Next, Vairocana spoke, and the other lotsawas, ៖
About the great panditas' virtues and the translation of the Dharma. ៖
Gö and other ministers distributed gifts, ៖
And spoke of the ways in which their wishes had been fulfilled. ៖
All the citizens, in turn, created merit, each according to their means. ៖

Then the great panditas, each escorted by their lotsawa, ៖
Embarked upon their journeys back to their own lands. ៖
Like the rising sun, the Dharma now shone upon Tibet. ៖

This was the sixth chapter in Padma's Wish-Fulfilling Tree, *my story of liberation, on how panditas and lotsawas were invited to translate the Sutra and
Tantra teachings.* ៖

ཟ་ཅ། ཟརྒུ ៖
Then, as I, the Lotus Master, was engaged in sadhana practice ៖
At the secluded hermitage of Samye Chimpu, ៖
King Trisong Detsen, the monarch of Tibet— ៖
Accompanied by Namkhé Nyingpo and Sangyé Yeshé, ៖
Gyalwang Chöyang and Lady Yeshé Tsogyal, ៖
Palkyi Wangchuk and Dorjé Düdjom, ៖
And Vairocana and the other royal subjects— ៖
Came with mandalas of gold, and requested repeatedly ៖
That I reveal the mandala of *The Assembly of Sugatas.* ៖

I revealed the mandala to the King and subjects ៖
And conferred the *Assembly*'s grand empowerment on them. ៖
This was when the monarch's flower fell on Mahottara,[94] ៖

Namkhé Nyingpo's flower fell on Yangdak Heruka, ༔
Sangyé Yeshé's flower fell on Yamantaka. ༔
Gyalwang Choyang's flower fell on Hayagriva, ༔
Yeshé Tsogyal's flower fell on Kila, ༔
Palkyi Wangchuk's flower fell on Mamo, ༔
Dorjé Düdjom's flower fell on Jikten Chötö, ༔
and Vairocana's flower fell on Möpa Drakngak. ༔
And so they practiced, each within their destined mandala.[95] ༔

King and disciples all brought forth signs of accomplishment: ༔
Trisong Detsen overpowered the others' experience with his splendor; ༔
Namkhé Nyingpo rode on the sun's rays, as though astride a horse; ༔
Sangyé Yeshé plunged his dagger into solid rock; ༔
Gyalwang Chöyang sent forth horse neighs from his crown; ༔
Yeshé Tsogyal was able to revive human corpses; ༔
Palkyi Wangchuk caused paralysis by pointing his dagger; ༔
Dorjé Düdjom moved about freely, swift as the wind; ༔
And Vairocana employed the spirits as his servants. ༔
Indeed, many were the siddhi signs in King and disciples. ༔

I gave the ripening empowerments and liberating instructions ༔
For the myriad mandalas of *The Embodiment of the Gurus' Realization*, ༔
The Embodiment of the Yidams' Realization, ༔
The Embodiment of the Dakinis' Realization, ༔
And *The Embodiment of the Protectors' Realization*. ༔
Thus, I disseminated the teachings for the retreat centers of Tibet. ༔

This was the seventh chapter in Padma's Wish-Fulfilling Tree, *my story of liberation, on how I gave the ripening empowerments, and how the King and disciples showed the signs of accomplishment.* ༔

ཐ་ཅ།ཐཀྲུ༔
It was then that I, the Lotus Master, had a realization: ༔
"Here in Tibet, all the teachings of Sutra and Tantra, ༔
And of the outer, inner, and innermost Vajrayana, ༔
Have been studied, contemplated, and practiced, and siddhi signs achieved. ༔
Yet the essence of them all, an indispensable teaching— ༔
The Ocean of Dharma, the Gathering of Transmitted Precepts— [96] ༔
I must now with care bestow upon the King and disciples." ༔

At that very same moment, the King and the three princes ⁂
Requested me to give it, in Chimpu Cave, in the expanded way. ⁂

Later, while I was concealing many treasures of awakened mind, ⁂
The Tibetan emperor, King Trisong Detsen, ⁂
With Muné Tsenpo, the senior prince, ⁂
And Murup Tsenpo, the second prince, ⁂
And Mutik Tsenpo, the youngest prince, ⁂
Along with Gyalwang Chöyang, the Lotsawa of Langdro, ⁂
The great Jñanakumara of Nyak, and others, ⁂
With Vairocana and Palkyi Sengé of Shübu, ⁂
With Tingdzin Zangpo and Dorjé Düdjom, ⁂
Palkyi Wangchuk and Wangchuk of Odren, ⁂
With Acharya Salé and Dorjé Tsomo of Shelkar, ⁂
With Drokpen Lotsawa, and Tsogyal with her three servants, ⁂
And the three brides of the three princes, among so many others— ⁂
All came, each with their following, to Namkha Dzong in Kham. ⁂

After unveiling *The Ocean of Dharma, the Gathering of Transmitted Precepts*, ⁂
I gave the King and disciples the ripening empowerments ⁂
And thoroughly explained the essential liberating instructions. ⁂
After practicing this one-pointedly for seven years, with his retinue, ⁂
The King could freely move through rocks and mountain. ⁂
Muné Tsenpo beheld the deity in person, ⁂
Murup Tsenpo gained the wakefulness of greatest bliss, ⁂
Mutri Tsenpo saw the very essence of his mind, ⁂
Vairocana soared like a bird into the sky, ⁂
Gyalwang Chöyang transformed his body into a bonfire, ⁂
Könchok of Langdro's form became a fiery mass of light, ⁂
Sangyé Yeshé arrived at the stage of Universal Light, ⁂
The great Jñana of Nyak realized the exhaustion of phenomena, ⁂
Kharchen Tsogyal drew immortal nectar out of solid rock, ⁂
Salé the Acarya shattered boulders with bare hand, ⁂
Drokmi Palkyi Yeshé's gaze burned down forests, ⁂
Dorjé Düdjom's gaze evaporated an entire lake, ⁂
Tingdzin Zangpo pierced straight into a mountain wall, ⁂
And Lady Shelkar used the mamo spirits as her servants. ⁂
Many were the siddhi signs displayed by the disciples. ⁂

All the scriptures were then written down in magical letters ༔
And concealed as treasures at seven supreme sites. ༔
Moreover, I predicted those who would reveal them, ༔
Sealed them with commands, aspirations, and conferred empowerments. ༔
In the Age of Strife, when the lifespan is but thirty years, ༔
These treasures will appear; such is my prediction, my samaya! ༔

This was the eighth chapter in Padma's Wish-Fulfilling Tree, *my story of libera-tion, on how I revealed The Ocean of Dharma, the Gathering of Transmitted Precepts and concealed it as a treasure.* ༔

ཐ་ཅ༑ པ་རྒྱ༔
After this, I wrote down all the profound Dharma teachings ༔
In five kinds of writing upon scrolls of five kinds of material, ༔
And inserted it in caskets, extraordinary and wondrous. ༔
In Lhasa, and in Samye, Yoru, and Tramdruk, ༔
At the Border Taming and Further Taming Temples,[97] ༔
At the Sheldrak Cave of Yarlung and the Lhodrak Cliff of Kharchu, ༔
At the Yangdzong Fortress of Drak, and in Dawaphuk Cave at Yerpa, ༔
In Yamalung Valley, and Zabu Valley in Tsang, ༔
At Mount Trapzang and at Riwoché in Tsang, ༔
On Lapchi's snowy range and Yolmo's snowy ridge, ༔
At Namkechen and the eight sites of Bhutan, ༔
At Tsari Gyala and the holy site of Sengdam Buwo, ༔
At the extraordinary Drakar Cliff of Tidro, ༔
And at the twenty-five sacred places of Upper and Lower Kham— ༔
Five for awakened form, five for speech, and five for awakened mind, ༔
Five for qualities and five for the awakened activities— ༔
At all these places I practiced, consecrating the sites, ༔
And concealing countless treasures there, both major and minor. ༔

Even though the teachings now shine like the light of the sun, ༔
Within three generations of the present King's descendants ༔
There will appear a King with ox-shaped head and malicious plans. ༔
That is when, due to an obstructing minister with raven-like head, ༔
The Buddha's teachings will be torn to the ground. ༔

Following this, the royals and disciples now present ༔
Will reappear in the future, due to their noble aspirations, ༔

As two supreme treasure-revealers,[98] twenty lingpas,[99] ⚬
Another hundred *tertöns*, lords of the teachings, ⚬
And a further retinue of a thousand and two minor *tertöns*. ⚬
Moreover, re-concealed termas will be countless in number. ⚬

The propagators of these teachings, doctrine-holding masters, ⚬
Will appear by the hundreds, accompanying each great *tertön*. ⚬
Each area will have its own treasure revealer, ⚬
And each place of my sadhana practice will have a treasure site. ⚬

In each district there will appear a siddha of renown, ⚬
And every town will have a venerable master. ⚬
For each householder there will be a monk, worthy of offerings, ⚬
And a yogin to subdue their hindrances and threats. ⚬
Thus, in the future, the teachings will fill every corner of the land. ⚬
All of this shall be the work of my awakened emanations. ⚬
So bring forth pure perception, future people of Tibet and Kham! ⚬

This was the ninth chapter in Padma's Wish-Fulfilling Tree, *my story of liberation, on how I concealed the treasures and predicted their revealers.*⚬

ཟ་ཙ་ཟརྒྱ⚬
Then I declared, "Our teacher Buddha Shakyamuni, ⚬
In the *Sutra of Predictions in Magadha*, spoke these words: ⚬
'The rakshasa hordes will pour out from the lands of the southwest; ⚬
They will invade and extinguish this Jambu continent." ⚬
My work for the Tibetans, in my direct form, is now complete, ⚬
So I must head southwest now, to tame the rakshasa ogres. ⚬

When the prince[100] heard these words, ⚬
He cried out, deeply saddened, ⚬
And tried to dissuade me from departing. ⚬
Out of kindness then, and to benefit the Tibetan people, ⚬
I predicted representations of my body, hid treasures to represent my speech, ⚬
And entrusted my heart-realization to predestined heirs. ⚬
As I explained this point, the prince's sadness disappeared, ⚬
And so again I made ready to set off for the land of the rakshasas. ⚬

Everyone escorted me to the mountain pass of Mangyul, ⚬
Where I gave my final testament to the prince and Tibetan people, ⚬

Along with thirteen pith instructions for clearing away obstacles ༔
And protecting descendants, in the form of a prayer,[101] ༔
And the inner sadhana with its many applications.[102] ༔
These were concealed at Khala Rongo in Mangyul. ༔

All those not present then, those unable to meet me in person, ༔
all beings of times to come, ༔
Should study and recite this, my story of liberation. ༔
Memorize it to perfection and understand it to its depths! ༔
When you read this biography during your six sessions, ༔
Bring me to mind, then call upon me in this way: ༔

ༀ ཨེ་མ་ཧོཿ ཆོས་སྐུ་ཀུན་བཟང་དྲུག་པ་རྡོ་རྗེ་འཆང་༔
emaho, chöku künzang drukpa dorjé chang ༔
Emaho. Dharmakaya Samantabhadra, Vajradhara, The Sixth, ༔

སྤྲུལ་པ་རྡོར་སེམས་བཅོམ་ལྡན་ཤཀྱེ་གྱི་རྒྱལ༔
tönpa dorsem chomden shakyé gyal ༔
Vajrasattva, our teacher, the blessed King of the Shakyas, ༔

མགོན་པོ་ཚེ་དཔག་མེད་དང་སྤྱན་རས་གཟིགས༔
gönpo tsepakmé dang chenrezik ༔
Lord of Boundless Life, Amitayus, and All-Seeing Avalokiteshvara— ༔

དབྱེར་མེད་པདྨ་དེ་ལ་གསོལ་བ་འདེབས༔
yermé pema dé la sölwa dep ༔
To you, Padma, inseparable from them all, we pray! ༔

སྐུ་ཡི་བདག་ཉིད་འཇམ་དཔལ་གཤིན་རྗེའི་གཤེད༔
ku yi daknyi jampal shinjé shé ༔
In essence, your awakened body is Manjushri Yamantaka; ༔

གསུང་གི་བདག་ཉིད་དབང་ཆེན་རྟ་སྐྱད་འཚོར༔
sung gi daknyi wangchen také tser ༔
In essence, your awakened speech is mighty Hayagriva; ༔

ཐུགས་ཀྱི་བདག་ཉིད་ཡང་དག་ཧེ་རུ་ཀ༔
tuk kyi daknyi yangdak héruka ༔
And, in essence, your awakened mind is Yangdak Heruka— ༔

གུ་རུ་ཡིད་བཞིན་ནོར་བུ་ལ་གསོལ་བ་འདེབས༔

guru yizhin norbu la sölwa dep ༔

To you, our Wish-Fulfilling Guru, we pray! ༔

ཡོན་ཏན་ཟིལ་གནོན་ཆེ་མཆོག་ཧེ་རུ་ཀ༔

yönten zilnön chemchok héruka ༔

Your overwhelming qualities are Mahottara Heruka; ༔

ཕྲིན་ལས་བདག་ཉིད་རྡོ་རྗེ་གཞོན་ནུའི་སྐུ༔

trinlé daknyi dorjé zhönnü ku ༔

Your awakened activity is Vajrakumara, in essence; ༔

མ་མོ་མཁའ་འགྲོའི་གཙོ་བོ་མངོན་རྫོགས་རྒྱལ༔

mamo khandrö tsowo ngön dzok gyal ༔

And you rule over the mamos and dakinis as Ngöndzok Gyalpo— ༔

དཔལ་ཆེན་ཐོད་ཕྲེང་རྩལ་ལ་གསོལ་བ་འདེབས༔

palchen tötreng tsal la sölwa dep ༔

To you, Supremely Glorious Tötreng Tsal, we pray! ༔

སྐུ་ཡི་དབྱིངས་སུ་སྒྱུ་འཕྲུལ་ཞི་ཁྲོའི་ངང་༔

ku yi ying su gyutrül zhitrö ngang ༔

Your form encompasses the illusory net of peaceful and wrathful deities, ༔

གསུང་གི་གདངས་སྐད་ཡན་ལག་བཅུ་གཉིས་ལྡན༔

sung gi dang ké yenlak chunyi den ༔

The melody of your speech holds the twelve special qualities, ༔

ཐུགས་ཀྱི་དགོངས་པ་ཟང་ཐལ་ཡོངས་ལ་ཁྱབ༔

tuk kyi gongpa zangtal yong la khyap ༔

And your unimpeded wisdom pervades everywhere— ༔

མཁའ་འགྲོའི་གཙོ་བོ་རྗེ་ལ་གསོལ་བ་འདེབས༔

khandrö tsowo jé la sölwa dep ༔

To you, sovereign lord of dakinis, we pray! ༔

སྐུ་ཚབ་ལུང་བསྟན་གསུང་ཚབ་གཏེར་དུ་སྦས༔

kutsap lungten sung tsap ter du pé ༔

You prophesied representatives of your body, hid treasures of your speech, ༔

ཐུགས་ཀྱི་དགོངས་པ་ལས་ཅན་བུ་ལ་གཏད༔

tuk kyi gongpa léchen bu la té ༔

Entrusted your heart-realization to destined heirs, ༔

བརྩེ་བའི་ཞལ་ཆེམས་བོད་འབངས་ཡོངས་ལ་བཞག༔

tséwé zhal chem bö bang yong la zhak ༔

And left your loving testament for all the Tibetan people— ༔

དྲིན་ཆེན་སྤྲུལ་པའི་སྐུ་ལ་གསོལ་བ་འདེབས༔

drinchen trülpé ku la sölwa dep ༔

To you, kindest of awakened emanations, we pray! ༔

བཀའ་དྲིན་དྲན་ནོ་གུ་རུ་རིན་པོ་ཆེ༔

kadrin drenno guru rinpoché ༔

We recall your overwhelming kindness, Guru Rinpoche. ༔

ཐུགས་དམ་ཞལ་བཞེས་དགོངས་པས་གཟུང་དུ་གསོལ༔

tukdam zhal zhé gongpé zung du sol ༔

Please remember your promise to hold us in your embrace, ༔

དུས་ངན་འདི་ལ་རེ་ལྟོས་གཞན་མ་མཆིས༔

dü ngen di la ré tö zhen ma chi ༔

For in these troubled times we have no hope but you. ༔

ཐུགས་རྗེས་གཟིགས་ཤིག་ཨོ་རྒྱན་སྤྲུལ་པའི་སྐུ༔

tukjé zik shik orgyen trülpé ku ༔

Look upon us with compassion, awakened emanation of Uddiyana! ༔

མཐུ་རྩལ་ནུས་པས་དུས་ངན་གཡོ་འཁྲུག་བཟློག༔

tutsal nüpé dü ngen yo truk dok ༔

With your power and strength, dispel the turbulence of this dark age, ༔

བྱིན་རླབས་ཡེ་ཤེས་དབང་ཆེན་བསྐུར་དུ་གསོལ༔

jinlap yeshé wangchen kur du sol ༔

Bestow your blessings and the great empowerment of wisdom, ༔

ཉམས་དང་རྟོགས་པའི་རྩལ་ཤུགས་རྒྱས་པ་དང་༔

nyam dang tokpé tsal shuk gyepa dang ༔

Increase the strength of our experience and realization, ༔

བསྟན་འགྲོར་ཕན་པའི་མཐུ་རྩལ་རབ་བརྟན་ཅིང་༔

ten dror penpé tu tsal rapten ching ༔

Grant us powerful skills to benefit beings and the teachings, ༔

ཚེ་གཅིག་སངས་རྒྱས་འགྲུབ་པར་མཛད་དུ་གསོལ༔

tsé chik sangyé drupar dzé du sol ༔

And bring us, we pray, to buddhahood, in this very life! ༔

After instructing them to call upon me in this way, I mounted a fine horse held aloft by four dakinis, and declared: ༔

"Once every month I shall return for the sake of Tibetans. In particular, on the tenth day of the Monkey month, I will come to clear away the troubles of all Tibetans. Call upon me, don't forget!"

Then I turned my gaze directly to the southwest and took my leave. The prince and the other Tibetan disciples returned to their homes, where they each continued with their own practice. ༔

This was the tenth chapter in Padma's Wish-Fulfilling Tree, *my story of liberation, on how I gave my testament and then departed to subjugate the rakshasas in the southwest.* ༔

ཐ་ཙ་ཐཀྲུ༔

I, Tsogyal, later wrote down this biography and concealed it as a treasure. ༔
May it meet with the worthy one endowed with the right karma. ༔

Having met with him, may its benefit for beings be boundless. ༔

Samaya, seal, seal, seal. ༔ ཨིཐྱཻཐི༔

— I, Orgyen Chokgyur Lingpa, one of the great incarnated revealers of treasure, brought this forth from Akanishta Karma's Damchen Drak Cliff.

THE MAHAGURU IN GREATER TIBET

In the earlier volumes in our Following in Your Footsteps series—The Lotus-Born Guru in Nepal and The Lotus-Born Guru in India—we introduced you to Buddhist pilgrimage, to the Mahaguru and his teachers, to his consorts and disciples, to his grand enlightened feats in Nepal and India. Taking these introductions as a starting point, we now invite you to read about his activities in Greater Tibet, his transmission of Buddhism there, and some of the key elements required for Buddhism to flourish and spread in any country. Greater Tibet, as the treasury that has kept the Mahaguru's spiritual legacy vibrant and alive for over a millennium, is, was, and ever will be one of the world's most sacred destinations for any follower of Guru Padmasambhava. Greater Tibet is also where the influence of Guru Padmasambhava is all-pervasive, as seen in its vast wealth of Dharma treasures in every form—whether written, spoken, or as the sacred sites themselves. This the Mahaguru entrusted to the Tibetan people, a profound legacy they are now sharing with the world

The Land of Snow

Stretching across the northern side of the Himalayas, Greater Tibet is a land guarded by towering peaks and vast expanses of natural beauty. This, the world's largest plateau, has for centuries been called the Land of Snow for its position high above the plains of India, at an altitude that in modern times has earned it another name: Roof of the World. A curtain of high mountains blocks the summer monsoon downpours of neighboring countries to the south, a feature which has transformed Tibet into a dry, wind-swept land. And yet, rising from the parched earth of western Tibet, we equally find the source of four great rivers—the Brahmaputra, Sutlej, Indus, and Karnali—all flowing, according to ancient Indian lore, from Sumeru, home of the gods, the very center of the world. These life-giving waters flow down to India, Pakistan, and Bangladesh, nourishing their vast plains with fertile soil. When we look to eastern Tibet, too, we find the sources of the Yangtse, Mekong, and Yellow Rivers, the waters that have sustained Chinese civilization.

In this land of great richness, and great extremes, the Tibetans made their home, often living a simple life, deeply in touch with the natural world, as farmers, shepherds, and traders. It was heart-felt aspirations that eventually manifested and brought the Buddhadharma to such an isolated region of the world. And, while huge challenges lay in the way, the Tibetans succeeded in the truly marvelous endeavor of establishing the Dharma in their homeland. In the lines of their descendants we have great meditators such as Gyalwa Longchenpa, Jamyang Khyentsé Wangpo, Chokgyur Dechen Lingpa and Jamgön Kontrul Lodrö Thayé—whom we continue to revere to this day. Through their efforts, the realm of Tibet has proved time and again to be a unique spiritual haven in which the Dharma can safely blossom for over a millennium. This, the final book in our three-part series on the Lotus-Born Guru, brings us to the fascinating turning point that was the establishment of Buddhism in Tibet, and the role that the Mahaguru played in this grand endeavor.

The Dharma Takes Birth in Tibet

Traditional Tibetan histories recount how the Buddhadharma gradually came to the snowy lands of Greater Tibet.[103] Well before the arrival of Guru Padmasambhava, back in the mists of time, the fields of awakening were already being sown through the kindness of Avalokiteshvara, Buddha of Compassion. It began when Avalokiteshvara instructed a single monkey to go and meditate in the Yarlung Valley of central Tibet. There the monkey practiced diligently, guided by compassion, until eventually he encountered a local rock-ogress. They came together and had six children who would go on to become the Tibetan people.[104]

In a later age, a young prince was forced to leave his homeland in India, and after great hardship eventually arrived in the same Yarlung Valley.[105] When the local farmers asked him where he was from, the prince pointed into the sky.[106] Presuming that he must be a divine being, the Tibetan people made him their King. The prince came to be known as Nyatri Tsenpo (c. 127 BCE), the first King of Tibet, who built the Yumbu Lhakhang Palace.[107] Twenty-seven generations later, the King Lha Totori Nyentsen (c. 374–493), an emanation of the bodhisattva Samantabhadra, became the twenty-eighth ruler of Tibet. During his rule, representations of awakened body, speech and mind miraculously fell from the sky and landed upon the palace—including a golden stupa and a jewel, a scripture dedicated to Avalokiteshvara called *The Basket's Display* (*Karandavyuha Sutra*),[108] and several other relics.[109] Thus scriptural and material Dharma first came to the land.

Five generations later, an emanation of Avalokiteshvara, Dharma King Songtsen Gampo (c. 605–650), became the thirty-third ruler of Tibet. During this period, the Tang Dynasty of China and the Licchavi kingdom of Nepal were not only powerful neighbors, but cultures that strongly supported the Buddhadharma. King Songtsen Gampo thus wed Bhrikuti, the Newar princess of the Licchavi kingdom, and Wencheng, the Chinese princess of the Tang royal dynasty, establishing them both as royal queens in Tibet. These two queens, respectively emanations of Green Tara and White Tara, brought with them the precious statues of Jowo Mikyö Dorjé and Jowo Shakyamuni, to be enshrined in newly built temples at Trülnang and Ramoché in Lhasa.[110] King Songtsen Gampo also brought a self-arisen statue of Avalokiteshvara to bless the land,[111] and commissioned one hundred and eight stupas holding relics of awakened masters to tame the borderlands.[112] Still further, Songsten Gampo sent his trusted minister Thönmi Sambhota to India to learn the art of writing, and, having undergone many hardships, Thönmi returned to Tibet, where he devised the first Tibetan script, basing it on a northern form of the Indian Gupta alphabet. Thönmi proceeded to translate the *Karandavyuha* Sutra and several other Buddhist scriptures into Tibetan, thus initiating the first translations of Buddhist scriptures from Indian languages into Tibetan.[113]

All of this compassionate activity set the stage for the coming of Dharma King Trisong Detsen (c. 742–800), thirty-eighth in the line of Yarlung Kings and an emanation of Manjushri. Although King Songtsen Gampo had laid a strong foundation for the Dharma in Tibet, still, by the 8th century, the teachings of the Buddha, and in particular the Vajrayana, had yet to take deep root in the Land of Snow. King Trisong Detsen would thus take up the mission of transforming Tibet into a nation unshakeable in its commitment to the Dharma, so that generation after generation would benefit from the teachings. In the King's mind, the key to achieving this was to build Tibet's first monastery: Samye (The Inconceivable).

Indeed, it was the destiny of three former brothers to carry the Buddha's teachings far to the north and establish them in the uncharted Snowy Land of Tibet—the fully ripened result of aspirations made lifetimes ago in front of the Jarung Kashor Stupa in Boudha, Nepal.[114] They took rebirth, this time, as Abbot Shantarakshita, Dharma King Trisong Detsen, and Guru Padmasambhava, specifically to reunite and fulfill this virtuous purpose. As we will discover in this book, however, they did not achieve this alone; a host of similarly destined individuals—such as the vidyadhara Vimalamitra, the wisdom dakini Yeshé Tsogyal, the lotsawa Vairocana—also played a part in this grand awakened vision. It was their combined efforts that finally ensured the establishment of Buddhism in Tibet, on the roof of our world.

Overcoming Great Challenges

While there was a growing interest in the Dharma among 8th century Tibetans, many still showed more similarity to their rock-ogress ancestor, rather than to the kind monkey sent by the Buddha of Compassion. Their adherence to old ways of sacrifice and revenge, and the power these brought, proved to be stubborn habits that threatened the full flourishing of the Dharma.

Furthermore, Tibet's wild landscape had long attracted savage spirits who considered the mountains and valleys their private realms, wreaking havoc upon anyone who questioned their dominion. Thus, when Dharma King Trisong Detsen invited his destined teachers Abbot Shantarakshita and Guru Padmasambhava to the land, and started constructing edifices to the Triple Gem, these spirits perceived his actions as threats to their sovereignty. The Mahaguru, needless to say, recognized that these haughty spirits and their supernatural abilities could be useful allies; if they would only direct their powers in the right direction, they could become friends instead of foes. Through his extraordinary methods and mastery of the Vajrayana path, the Mahaguru thus overpowered the spirits, getting them to swear allegiance to the Dharma and serve as protectors of the profound teachings.

Nevertheless, malignant forces both human and spiritual still secretly remained, lurking around Guru Rinpoche, trying everything in their power to stop Buddhism from taking root in Tibet. They took the form of wicked ministers, sowing seeds of mistrust and suspicion among those in power. These demons of ill-intent nearly succeeded in their endeavor, even managing to get the Mahaguru banished into temporary exile. However, it was but one of many such turns of events, and Guru Padmasambhava transformed what was a dire situation into a means to further his practice and spread the Dharma to the outlying regions.

Earlier, while still on his way to Tibet, the Mahaguru had begun his great taming of these spirits, instilling faith as a result in all the Tibetans he encountered. As he traveled to meet King Trisong Detsen, the Mahaguru would overpower the ravening spirits and bind them to oath, using every opportunity he could to inspire faith and devotion in whomever he encountered. While the story of this grand endeavor is one of glory, triumph, and the overcoming of all obstacles, the hardships and challenges that each devotee had to undergo were many, as we will see in the pages to come.

Establishing the Support for Enlightened Body

In the heart of Tibet, the Mahaguru and the Dharma King finally met, and their joint aspiration became clear: this land desperately needed a temple for the Three Jewels, a place for their veneration and devotion, and a permanent residence for the Sangha. An outer residence for the Sangha meant creating a sacred space for enlightened activity, where teachers and students would meet in a most intimate way, transmitting and receiving the Dharma on a grand scale. The grander this outer foundation could be, the better also would it serve to inspire spiritual seekers and create a sacred environment in which the Dharma could fully blossom.

As we learn from the *Pema Kathang*, no expense or effort were spared in the building of Samye Monastery. The most skilled artisans from Nepal worked alongside Tibet's best builders—together crafting the temples, stupas, and statues. Even the spirits joined in this endeavor, while the Dharma King Trisong Detsen emptied his entire treasury to fund the great work. Thus, Samye Monastery was built in the grandest way possible, replete with precious statues all filled to the brim with sacred relics. This outer foundation would provide the ideal home, in turn, for the inner foundation of enlightened speech, the scripture of the Dharma.

Establishing the Support for Enlightened Speech

While, through their teachings and blessings, Guru Padmasambhava and Abbot Shantarakshita were able to bring the authentic Dharma to Tibet, both were non-native speakers, and the vast majority of written teachings were only accessible to those who read Sanskrit. This meant that most Tibetans still had no way to read the precious Dharma, no matter how great their faith. A massive undertaking of translating the sutras and tantras into Tibetan was required, if the Dharma was to truly enter into the heart-blood of Tibetan culture. The Guru and Abbot therefore proposed the great task of translating the Buddha's words into the native Tibetan tongue, a request to which the Dharma King Trisong Detsen assented. So began a great wave of Dharma transmission into the Tibetan language, an activity that would unfold for centuries to come, thereby establishing the Tibetan language as one of the world's most precious vessels for the enlightened speech of the Buddha.

They would need translators to accomplish this task. One hundred and eight of the most intelligent youths in the land were gathered and trained in the ancient languages of India. Despite the severe hardships involved, these young savants traveled across the Himalaya and down to the Gangetic plains, in search of teachers from India's most prestigious institutions of learning—such as the universities of Nalanda and Vikramashila. Upon returning to Tibet, these *lotsawas*, skilled now both in their own tongue and in those of ancient India, brought back physical Dharma scriptures, along with some of the greatest scholars of the time. These priceless resources were gathered at Samye Monastery, where the work of translating the full scope of the Dharma began. Included were texts related to Sutra and Mantra, as well as treatises on medicine and science, all of which would serve as the backbone to Tibet's fledgling monastic education system. To this day, the fruition of this massive endeavor continues to benefit beings throughout the world, in the form of canons that preserve the scriptures of the buddhas, but also their indispensable explanations by some of the greatest Buddhist scholars who have ever lived and taught the Dharma.

Establishing the Support for Enlightened Mind

Guru Padmasambhava embodied so fully the magnificence of the Buddha's teaching that his sheer presence inspired faith and devotion in the fortunate ones who met him. Even before arriving in King Trisong Detsen's court, the Mahaguru gained the support of the envoys sent to invite him; they became his first Tibetan students.[115] By the time Guru Rinpoche's stay in Tibet concluded, thousands had been brought to the Dharma, many of them becoming his close heart disciples. More was needed, however, if these new devotees were to properly engage in the Buddhist path; they also had to live and practice these teachings and, most importantly accomplish them. For it is only when realized individuals are present that transmission of the "Dharma of realization" can be accomplished, as opposed to the Dharma of scriptural presence alone.

To ensure that this happened, Dharma King Trisong Detsen installed Shantarakshita, the great Mahayana scholar-practitioner-monk, as abbot of Samye Monastery. Shantarakshita identified seven of the most promising Tibetans and transmitted his Sarvastivadin lineage of the Vinaya to them, within the halls of this great new monastery. These first monks would prove that the Tibetan people were truly capable of monastic discipline, setting the stage for many more to join the monastic sangha. The community beyond the monastery walls would need a strong practitioner presence as well, and so Guru Rinpoche took to initiating householders into the path of the *ngakpa*, thus establishing the tradition of lay practitioners of Secret Mantra in Tibet. Through the efforts of these two great masters, the core pillars of ordained and lay sangha were established, just as they had been in India.

Indeed, Guru Padmasambhava's heart students were drawn from these lay and monastic communities—the most outstanding of them being King Trisong Detsen himself, along with twenty-five other supremely devoted disciples. To these heart disciples Guru Rinpoche transmitted the entire Buddhadharma by means of extensive teaching and transformative empowerment. This meeting of a perfect teacher with the perfect students, supported by perfect teachings and in the perfect location, allowed Tibet to become a realm conducive to the very highest level of spiritual realization. Therefore, when Guru Rinpoche finally departed from Tibet, his profound instructions could be perfectly upheld despite his physical absence. As the Buddhadharma was beginning to fade in India, the torch was thus passed to the Tibetans to uphold the priceless Vajrayana teachings. This vast lineage of realization continues to be transmitted, unbroken from generation to generation, continually granting the support of the Buddha's enlightened mind, right down to this present day.

A Trove of Treasures

The later incarnations of Guru Rinpoche's twenty-five disciples would prove instrumental in preserving these precious Dharma teachings. Skillful master that he was, Guru Padmasambhava hid many teachings as treasures for the sake of future generations, to be revealed only when the time was ripe. The knowledge of these treasures was entrusted to his heart disciples, whose later incarnations held the keys to their discovery. They were soon to be known as *tertöns*, revealers of treasure. These treasures, known as *termas* in Tibetan, were hidden as physical objects to be revealed from natural elements of the Tibetan landscape—such as rocks, cliff faces, caves, rivers, and lakes. Aside from these tangible *termas*, Guru Rinpoche concealed many teachings in his disciples' own mind-streams, to be spontaneously recalled by later revealers. Further still, the Mahaguru enlisted spirits to act as guardians, tasked with protecting the treasures until an authentic incarnation was ready to reveal it.

The wisdom dakinis also played a vital role in preserving the hidden teachings of the Mahaguru—foremost among them his Tibetan consort, Khandro Yeshe Tsogyal. The *terma* teachings, for example, were transcribed in "dakini script," a form of writing only decipherable by a master of great realization. Even if an ordinary person were to somehow come into contact with one of these treasures, the secret nature of the encryption would prevent anyone from unpacking its true depth or meaning. Indeed, only a genuine reincarnation of Guru Rinpoche's heart disciples can read such a script, due to their unique connection to the dakinis—a level of realization well beyond our ordinary modes of experience. From just a few short lines of dakini script, entire cycles of teachings have been unraveled.

Other forms of *terma* include statues or other sacred objects used by Guru Rinpoche or his disciples. As mentioned, these treasures are only revealed at the proper time, depending on the inclinations of beings in a certain age. A *tertön*'s mind will be triggered to reveal these objects or teachings, based on the occurrence of certain signs or significant dreams that outline their location. It is by means of these *terma* treasures that the Mahaguru's teachings never grow stagnant or corrupted, staying ever fresh and pristine as new treasures are revealed.

Establishing Sacred Sites

They are described as beyond count, the places that Guru Rinpoche visited, practiced in, and blessed with his presence. It is said that there was not a single place in the whole of Tibet, not even as small as a hoofprint, that lacked the Mahaguru's impression.[116] The features of the Snowy Land were absolutely filled with his blessings. Among all the many sites in the vast Himalayan landscape, though, he chose specific places—often caves—for extended retreat on particular elements of Vajrayana practice. These sites, due to their unique qualities, serve as powerful catalysts, enhancing the practice and thereby swiftly propelling progress along the path. Unfolding realization unlocks the sacred blessings held in such places, revealing the sacred profundity of their features.

A whole host of factors had to come together for any given location to be recognized by the Mahaguru as such a site. These factors were geographical, historical, and spiritual—elements that might make a site truly unique. Examples of this would be a valley's peculiar shape, maybe resembling an auspicious symbol, or the geological features of a particular cave or spring, or the fact that the site had already been visited by an awakened being, or that it served as the abode of a deity or protector. The site thus becomes something extraordinary, especially when several of these factors come together, rendering it capable of bringing vast benefit to all who encounter it.

Once Guru Padmasambhava had consecrated the various mountains, caves, and valleys of Tibet's vast landscape, he instructed his own students to practice at these designated sites. With these powerful settings as locations for their strict retreat, his close students, following his extensive instructions, likewise reached great accomplishment, further imbuing the sites with blessings. And just as with the termas described above, these practice sites themselves would later be revealed as treasures, unlocked by highly realized *tertöns* over the many years that have elapsed since the Mahaguru was in Tibet. With their rediscovery, these sacred places could once again serve as havens for Dharma practice for present and future generations. A constant stream of practitioners and pilgrims have thus sought to maintain an unbroken connection with Guru Rinpoche through receiving his blessings at these sites of profound realization, entering into retreat there so that their own profound realization and extraordinary revelations might occur. Through this activity, treasures and teachings have continued to emerge, and the lineage and traditions of Guru Padmasambhava have been maintained to this day. Our journey through the sacred sites of the Mahaguru in Tibet, and beyond, allows us to walk in those same footsteps and join in this extraordinary journey of awakening.

THE KAGYÉ

Their Origin and Significance and Their Transmission to Greater Tibet
— *Phakchok Rinpoche*

Central to the establishment of the Vajrayana in Greater Tibet was the Mahaguru's transmission of the yidam deities that he had practiced and accomplished in Greater India—a topic we will explore in depth in the chapters on The Eight Caves of Accomplishment. This transmission allowed the Mahaguru's students to develop a profound connection of their own with a particular tutelary deity and thereby swiftly attain accomplishment. Within the Nyingma tradition, there are eight principal yidam deities that collectively form the mandala of the Kagyé (The Eight Instructions). Guru Rinpoche initially practiced and accomplished each of these in the charnel grounds of Greater India. To establish the Kagyé teachings in Greater Tibet, he sought out specific sites and practiced all eight of the yidam deities in specifically chosen sacred caves. He then initiated his closest students into the mandala of the Kagyé and, based on their individual karmic connections, instructed them to practice in one or other of the caves. Following the Mahaguru's guidance, his students found these sacred locations, practiced, and swiftly attained great siddhis. Subsequently, the Mahaguru and his students together concealed the Kagyé teachings, to be revealed as terma-treasures in future times—ensuring that disciples, even now, can likewise make rapid progress on the path. To gain a deeper understanding of this profound dissemination, we requested Phakchok Rinpoche to give a teaching on the Kagyé.

Guru Rinpoche organized the Buddhadharma into nine yanas (vehicles): the three of the Shravakas, Pratyekabuddhas, and Bodhisattvas; the three of Kriya, Upa, and Yogatantra; and the three of Maha, Anu, and Atiyoga. Each of these vehicles has its respective point of origin in the human realm.

The Buddha's teachings can be classified as belonging to the dharmakaya, the sambhogakaya, or the nirmanakaya. The Atiyoga teachings belong to the dharmakaya, while the Mahayoga and Anuyoga belong to the sambhogakaya. Mahayoga tantras such as the *Guhyagarbha*, for example, were taught by the sambhogakaya deities Vajrasattva and Vajradhara. Here, of these nine yanas, we will focus on the Mahayoga, looking first at its origins, with reference to *The Pond of White Lotuses: A History of the Nyingma Tradition*, a text by Shechen Gyaltsab Gyurmé Pema Namgyal:

The Mahayoga teachings are divided into two sections—the Tantra section and the Sadhana section. First, let us consider the Tantra section. Perpetually, since time without beginning, Buddha Samantabhadra abides in enlightenment, never experiencing delusion. Steadfastly adhering to unchanging time, he manifests as the Universal Lord Vajradhara. As Vajradhara, he imparts the profound teachings of the Mahayoga to the Five Family Buddhas, embodiments of primordial wisdom, and the Three Family Lords, Avalokiteshvara, Manjushri, and Vajrapani. He does this in non-conceptual language, encompassing the entirety of the generation and completion stages (*kyerim* and *dzogrim*), and spanning the whole of the past, present and future.

The Three Family Lords, in particular, were then entrusted to disseminate the Dharma of Secret Mantra in different realms: Manjushri in the god realm, Avalokiteshvara in the naga realm, and Vajrapani in the yaksha realm. Historically, in the human realm, the teachings emerged twenty-eight years after the passing of Buddha Shakyamuni. Five disciples, called The Five Noble Ones, representing different spiritual lineages, gathered on Mount Malaya in Lanka. Together, they expressed their sorrow at the Buddha's departure. Seeing this, Buddha Samantabhadra manifested as Vajrapani, one of the Three Family Lords, and condensed all the Secret Mantra tantras from the god realms into a single quintessence. These quintessential tantras were then transcribed by one of the disciples, a rakshasa named Matyaupayika, onto golden leaf paper using molten blue star sapphire as ink. Knowing that these tantras would be disseminated in the future by the Dharma custodian King Ja, The Five Noble Ones then hid these sacred scriptures as wisdom treasures in space, guarded by wisdom dakinis. As foreseen, when the auspicious conditions had gathered, the Mahayoga tantras descended from the sky upon King Ja's palace in Zahor, marking the beginning of the human lineage. In a succession of teacher-disciple transmissions, these teachings were then passed down all the way to the Mahaguru.

The Sadhana section, to which the *Kagyé* (*The Eight Instructions*) belongs, can be further divided into the direct transmission (*kabab*) and the treasure transmission (*terma*). In terms of the direct transmission, the Sadhana section was directly transmitted to five sublime beings who had entered the ranks of the vidyadharas. As a result of their spiritual accomplishment, they each received the mandate for one particular yidam deity. In this way: Humkara received Yangdak Heruka, representing awakened wisdom; Manjushrimitra received Yamantaka, symbolizing awakened body; Arya Nagarjuna received Hayagriva, embodying awakened speech; Vimalamitra received Chemchok Heruka, representing awakened qualities; and Prabhahasti received Vajrakilaya, representing awakened activity. These five principal transmissions symbolize the

Five Buddha Families: Manjushri Yamantaka belongs to Vairocana's Buddha Family; Hayagriva belongs to Amitabha's Padma Family; Yangdak Heruka belongs to Akshobhya's Vajra Family; Chemchok Heruka belongs to Ratnasambhava's Ratna Family; Vajrakilaya belongs to Amoghasiddhi's Karma Family. That is how the direct transmission of the Sadhana section was established in the human realm.

Regarding the treasure transmission, the Sadhana section—like the Tantra section—was initially taught by Buddha Samantabhadra, who in his wrathful heruka form compiled the fifteen root tantras and transmitted these teachings to Vajrapani, Lord of Secrets. Vajrapani arranged these tantras into nine separate sadhana sections and entrusted them to the dakini Karmendrani, establishing her as the treasure guardian. The dakini Karmendrani, in turn, placed the sadhanas within nine caskets and concealed them as treasures inside the naturally-arisen stupa of Shankarakuta, located in the great Sitavana charnel ground.

Then, when the auspicious conditions had assembled, Guru Rinpoche, along with eight great vidyadharas, gathered in front of the Shankarakuta stupa and entered into samadhi. As a result of their profound practice, each received a casket containing their karmically destined teachings:

Vimalamitra was given the practice of Chemchok Heruka in a golden casket, while Humkara received Yangdak Heruka in a silver casket. Manjushrimitra was given Yamantaka in an iron casket, and Nagarjuna was granted Hayagriva in a copper casket. Prabhahasti was given Vajrakilaya in a turquoise casket; Dhanasamskrita received Mamo Bötong in a casket of rhinoceros horn; Rambuguhya was given Jikten Chötö in an agate casket, and Shantigarbha received Möpa Drakngak in a dzi stone casket. Each of the eight vidyadharas received their allocated set of instructions and accomplished their key points. Subsequently, they transmitted to Guru Rinpoche the tantras, transmissions, and pith instructions they had received. Finally, from the stupa, Guru Rinpoche revealed a casket made of all eight substances, containing the tantras, transmissions, and pith instructions for the whole of the *Kagyé*—collectively called the *Kagyé Deshek Düpa* (*The Gathering of All Sugatas*) which was later revealed by the great tertön Nyangral Nyima Özer. To receive all the empowerments for this, Guru Rinpoche turned directly to Vajrapani in his pure land. From this, it is accurate to say that Guru Rinpoche accomplished Vajrakilaya as part of the *Kagyé*, even though Prabhahasti received the individual practice of Vajrakilaya. Both statements are valid without contradiction. Having received the empowerments and teachings directly from Vajrapani and the treasure transmissions directly from all the eight vidyadharas, the Mahaguru thereby became the principal custodian of the *Kagyé* teachings.

It is important to highlight that the great Indian siddhas—Arya Nagarjuna, Guru Padmasambhava, Humkara, Dhanasamskrita, Rambuguhya, Shantigarbha, Vimalamitra, Manjushrimitra, and Prabhahasti—all attained immortality. Some achieved this through manifesting the rainbow body, while others attained the stage of "vidyadhara with mastery over longevity." By transcending death, these great masters co-existed in the same era, as well as originating from different time periods. There are many such examples of immortal great masters in history. Some of them would occasionally withdraw from human society to live in remote, sacred places, but would return when needed, as Marpa Lotsawa saw Naropa do. Thus it was that these nine great masters assembled at the Sitavana charnel ground during the same time period. In modern times, some people doubt the story of the *Kagyé* transmission, arguing that the chronology is incorrect. They claim that Guru Rinpche and the eight vidyadharas lived in different centuries—suggesting that all nine vidyadharas could not have physically met each other. However, this perspective does not take into consideration that these vidyadharas had transcended death through their tantric practices and were therefore perfectly capable of gathering at the Sitavana charnel ground at the same time. Guided by their realization, they sensed that the time had come for the transmission of the Secret Mantra teachings. Meeting the dakini Karmendrani, they individually received the tantras, empowerments, and sadhanas related to their yidam deity, accomplished their practices, and attained siddhis. Thus, the treasure transmission of the Mahayoga Sadhana section was initially transmitted in this manner.

According to the Dharma of Secret Mantra, all aspects of our existence—our body, speech, mind, qualities, and activities—are inherently awakened. At their essence, they are Buddha. This is why they can manifest as different deities. Within the *Kagyé* these aspects manifest in the form of the five wisdom deities: Yamantaka personifies the body; Hayagriva represents speech; Yangdak Heruka embodies the mind; Chemchok Heruka symbolizes qualities, and Vajrakilaya signifies activities. Additionally, there are three deities for accomplishing worldly objectives: Mamo Bötong, Jikten Chötö, and Möpa Drakngak, bringing the total to eight.

Why are all these deities wrathful? The Secret Mantra teachings encountered significant challenges to their propagation in this world. Humans, gods, and demons resisted the spread of the teachings, sometimes resorting to violence. Even Guru Rinpoche faced great difficulties, in both India and Tibet.

He emanated Sengé Dradrok in Greater India and Dorjé Drolö in Greater Tibet because the Buddhadharma was under threat from various groups of people. Non-Buddhists were widely opposed to its spread, and kings were suppressing Buddhist teachers and communities. Non-Buddhist *tantrikas* were using mantras and black magic to attack Buddhists, while Buddhist teachers themselves lacked the power of mantra. To counteract these circumstances, Guru Rinpoche accomplished such wrathful deities as Mamo Bötong, Jikten Chötö, Möpa Drakgnak, and others, including Simhamukha. For example, through his accomplishment of Simhamukha, the Mahaguru manifested as Sengé Dradok, hurled his kila dagger, and pulverized the yaksha spirits. Many of these stories are recounted in the Mahaguru's autobiographies and in prayers such as the *Barché Lamsel (Prayer to Dispel Obstacles on the Path)*. Newcomers to Buddhism may be reluctant to approach these wrathful deities because they do not comprehend their origins or purpose. Understanding these stories becomes crucial if one is to grasp the significance and relevance of wrathful practices like those found in the *Kagyé*.

As for the *Kagyé* teachings found within the *Chokling Tersar (The Profound Treasures of Chokgyur Lingpa)*, Guru Rinpoche structured his *Kagyé* teachings around four essential instructions: view, meditation, conduct, and pith instruction. Meanwhile, the pandita Vimalamitra had taught the *Kagyé* in terms of ground, path, and fruition. Guru Rinpoche combined these two approaches through study, contemplation, and meditation—into a profound teaching that became known as the *Kagyé Deshek Kündü (The Assembly of All Sugatas)*. Later, in Tibet, Guru Rinpoche transmitted and entrusted the *Kagyé Deshek Kündü* in its entirety to the King's second son, Murup Tsenpo Yeshé Rölpa Tsel. Having established the prince as its main custodian, the Mahaguru then hid the *Kagyé Deshek Kündü* as a treasure and prophesied that the prince would reveal it at an auspicious time in a future age.

Following the Mahaguru's prophecy, when the auspicious circumstances had gathered, the Great Tertön Chokgyur Dechen Lingpa—the thirteenth reincarnation of Murup Tsenpo—revealed the *Kagyé Deshek Kündü*, from Yubel Rock, situated on the southern slope of Yegyal Mountain in Namkha Dzö, on the tenth day in the waning half of the fourth month of the Male Wood Rat Year (May 30, 1864). This became the Chokling Tersar cycle of the *Kagyé Deshek Kündü (The Assembly of All Sugatas)*.

The colophon of the *Kagyé Deshek Kündü* further explains that each of the vidyadharas and acharyas, having received their personal yidam, diligently practiced and accomplished the key points of their individual practices.

Subsequently, they expounded the tantras for their respective yidams, based on the key points they had mastered. According to the colophon then, Vimalamitra accomplished Chemchok Heruka, the embodiment of awakened qualities, and transmitted this lineage through the eight categories of the *Kagyé*—body, speech, wisdom, qualities, activities, Mamo Bötong, Jikten Chötö, and Möpa Drakngak. Following Vimalamitra's explanation, one can understand that the essence of Secret Mantra revolves around these eight aspects. Acharya Humkara accomplished Yangdak Heruka, the wisdom aspect, and then elaborated on the practice in terms of view, meditation, and conduct. Manjushrimitra accomplished Manjushri-Yamantaka and expounded on the practice through the stages of generation, completion, and great perfection (*dzokchen*). Arya Nagarjuna accomplished Hayagriva, awakened speech, and transmitted this practice through tantra, transmission, and pith instruction, which he considered most essential. Dhanasanskrita accomplished Mamo Bötong and transmitted it by way of ground, path, and fruition. Rambuguhya, the holder of Jikten Chötö (Tamer of Haughty Spirits), an emanation of Vajrakilaya, expounded the Secret Mantra in terms of fortress (view), mountain path (meditation), and life-force (conduct). These are wrathful practices, focused on Vajrakilaya, and include the three clarities, the three winds, etc. They were Rambuguhya's unique way of presenting the wrathful practice of Jikten Chötö. Shantigarbha held the practice of Möpa Drakngak and presented it as a method to control and neutralize the life-force of samsara and nirvana, and the life-force of enemies. Guru Rinpoche accomplished Vajrakilaya and, based upon this accomplishment, he explained the essence of all tantras by means of six categories: view, empowerment, samaya, samadhi, conduct, and pith instruction.

Understanding the organizational structures of these texts provides valuable insight into how these great masters comprehended tantra. Knowing this framework allows practitioners to hold onto and utilize the teachings effectively for each practice; it is fascinating to delve into the texts themselves, for the profound understanding of tantra that they reveal, beyond just the stories of the enlightened masters associated with them.

In conclusion, I share with you this beautiful passage from *The Wish-Fulfilling Tree*—the autobiography of the Mahaguru that was revealed by Terchen Chokgyur Lingpa—which captures the precious moment of the Mahaguru's initial transmission of the *Kagyé* to his heart-disciples at Samye Chimpu:

> Then, as I, the Lotus Master, was engaged in sadhana practice ᠄
> At the secluded hermitage of Samyé Chimpu, ᠄

King Trisong Detsen, the monarch of Tibet— ༔
Accompanied by Namkhé Nyingpo and Sangyé Yeshé, ༔
Gyalwang Chöyang and Lady Yeshé Tsogyal, ༔
Palkyi Wangchuk and Dorjé Düdjom, ༔
And Vairocana and the other royal subjects— ༔
Came with mandalas of gold, and requested repeatedly ༔
That I reveal the manadala of *The Assembly of Sugatas.* ༔

I revealed the mandala to the King and subjects ༔
And conferred the *Assembly's* grand empowerment on them. ༔
This was when the monarch's flower fell on Mahottara, ༔
Namkhé Nyingpo's flower fell on Yangdak Heruka, ༔
Sangyé Yeshé's flower fell on Yamantaka. ༔
Gyalwang Choyang's flower fell on Hayagriva, ༔
Yeshé Tsogyal's flower fell on Kila, ༔
Palkyi Wangchuk's flower fell on Mamo, ༔
Dorjé Düdjom's flower fell on Jikten Chötö, ༔
and Vairocana's flower fell on Möpa Drakngak. ༔
And so they practiced, each within their destined mandala. ༔

King and disciples all brought forth signs of accomplishment: ༔
Trisong Detsen overpowered the others' experience with his splendor; ༔
Namkhé Nyingpo rode on the sun's rays, as though astride a horse; ༔
Sangyé Yeshé plunged his dagger into solid rock; ༔
Gyalwang Chöyang sent forth horse neighs from his crown; ༔
Yeshé Tsogyal was able to revive human corpses; ༔
Palkyi Wangchuk caused paralysis by pointing his dagger; ༔
Dorjé Düdjom moved about freely, swift as the wind; ༔
And Vairocana employed the spirits as his servants. ༔
Indeed, many were the siddhi signs in King and disciples. ༔

I gave the ripening empowerments and liberating instructions ༔
For the myriad mandalas of ༔
The Embodiment of the Gurus' Realization, ༔
The Embodiment of the Yidams' Realization, ༔
The Embodiment of the Dakinis' Realization, and ༔
The Embodiment of the Protectors' Realization. ༔
Thus did I disseminate the teachings for the retreat centers of Tibet. ༔

This was the seventh chapter in Padma's Wish-Fulfilling Tree, *my story of liberation, on how I gave the ripening empowerments, and how the King and disciples showed the signs of accomplishment.* ༔

Finally, I invite you to join me in offering these aspiration prayers, seeking the swift accomplishment of the Dharma for us all:

༁ྃ རྩ་བརྒྱུད་བླ་མའི་བྱིན་རླབས་སྙིང་ལ་ཞུགས༔
ཡི་དམ་མཁའ་འགྲོ་ལུས་དང་གྲིབ་བཞིན་འགྲོགས༔
ཆོས་སྐྱོང་སྲུང་མས་བར་ཆད་ཀུན་བསལ་ནས༔
མཆོག་ཐུན་དངོས་གྲུབ་འགྲུབ་པའི་བཀྲ་ཤིས་ཤོག༔

༁ྃ ལྷ་རྣམས་མཁའ་ལས་མེ་ཏོག་ཆར་ཆེན་འབེབས༔
ཀླུ་རྣམས་ཀུན་གྱིས་ས་གཞི་འབྱོར་པས་བཀང༔
བར་དུ་སྐྱེ་རྒུ་ཐམས་ཅད་བདེ་དང་ལྡན༔
མཐར་ཕྱུག་མཛོན་སངས་རྒྱས་པའི་བཀྲ་ཤིས་ཤོག༔

༁ྃ རྒྱལ་བ་ཀུན་གྱི་ཉེ་ལམ་གཅིག་པུ་རུ། །
རྒྱལ་བས་ཡོངས་བསྔགས་ཐེག་མཆོག་རྟོགས་པ་ཆེ། །
རྒྱལ་དབང་པདྨའི་རིང་ལུགས་སུ་འགྱུར་བའི། །
རྒྱལ་བསྟན་ཕྱོགས་མཐར་ཁྱབ་པའི་བཀྲ་ཤིས་ཤོག །

May the blessings of the root and lineage gurus enter our hearts! ༔
May the yidams and dakinis accompany us ༔
Like a shadow follows the body! ༔
May the Dharma protectors and guardians dispel all obstacles! ༔
May there be auspiciousness, ༔
That we attain the supreme and common siddhis! ༔

May there be auspiciousness, that the gods stream flowers from the sky ༔
And the nagas fill the whole earth with riches! ༔
And, in the meantime, may all beings enjoy happiness, ༔
And ultimately may they reach full awakening! ༔

Lauded by all buddhas as the sole swift path of all victors
Is this supreme vehicle of the Great Perfection,
This victorious teaching of the Early Translations,
This long-standing tradition of the victorious Lotus-Born.
May there be auspiciousness,
That this teaching of the victors spreads in all directions!

PART TWO

The Lotus-Born Guru in Tibet

Jikten Tsek

Drak Yerpa

Drakmar Yamalung

Drak Yangdzong

Samyé Chimpu

Tibet

Samyé Monastery

Yarlha Shampo

Yarlung Sheldra

Lhodrak Kharchu

Sikkim

Sengé Dzong

Nepal

Lhundrup Tsek

Bhutan

Paro Taktsang

Nalanda

Kusumapura

Sitavana

Varanasi

Tamradvipa

Kukkutapada

Vajra Seat
& Haha Göpa

Pema Tsek

Zahor

PROLOGUE

Three noble brothers stood before the Great Jarung Kashor Stupa in Nepal, and each in turn made an aspiration. One brother aspired to be a king who would uphold the Dharma in the land beyond the Himalaya; another aspired to lead the Sangha there; the third aspired to be born as a great tantric master able to quell the uprisings of spirits and other obstacles. Each vowed to play their part in spreading the Dharma far to the north of India's plains, and farther still, even beyond the endless mountains of Nepal.

These powerful seeds of aspiration would sprout, then fully ripen, in a later age, at the time of Buddha Shakyamuni.[117] Not long after the passing of this sage of the Shakya clan into mahaparinirvana, Guru Padmasambhava took birth in the sacred land of Uddiyana, within the heart of a lotus flower, far to the northwest of the Magadhan plains where the Buddha's activities had chiefly unfolded. Adopted by a king, he would eventually reject the throne and instead take up the life of a wandering yogi, learning from the great masters of India, receiving empowerments directly from the buddhas, and practicing in the charnel grounds of that Noble Land.

Guru Padmasambhava would then travel to the mountains and valleys of Nepal to gain still greater heights of accomplishment, taming troublesome demons and hiding spiritual treasures all the while. Once this work was complete, he resettled at the Diamond Throne of Bodh Gaya, site of the Buddha's awakening, to preserve and protect the precious Dharma at the behest of the Buddhist rulers of that time.

His former brothers' aspirations were coming to fruition as well. A great abbot known as Shantarakshita had already been born in the land of Zahor, in India. The son of kings, Shantarakshita would master of all aspects of the Buddhadharma from his seat at glorious Nalanda, the greatest monastic institution of the day. Meanwhile, far to the north, in the heart of Tibet, a new ruler was soon to be born—Dharma King Trisong Detsen. His exceptional position, combined with a proclivity for the Dharma, would inspire him to send his senior councillors to India to invite the Great Abbot of Nalanda and the Mahaguru of Uddiyana to the Snowy Land of Tibet, thus establishing the Dharma in this vast landscape of gods and demons for the generations to come.

A DHARMA KING IS BORN

Drakmar Drinzang

The Buddha's teachings had first taken root in Tibet under the rule of King Songtsen Gampo, Tibet's first Dharma King and an embodiment of the Buddha's compassion. His two divine consorts, Queen Bhrikuti of Nepal and Queen Wencheng of China, brought with them the sacred relics and statues that were enshrined in the land's very first Buddhist temples. While these initial connections with the Dharma were vital, the land of Tibet had yet to fully incorporate the Buddha's teachings of Sutra and Mantra, and many Tibetans still held fast to the shamanic traditions of their ancestors. Even if one was eager to enter this virtuous path, the land still lacked an authentic lineage of ordination into the monastic Sangha, so there could be no native monks and nuns to teach and uphold the Dharma. The potent aspirations of previous lives were now ripening, however, and a royal heir was soon to be born who would change the course of Tibet's history, firmly establishing the liberating teachings of Buddha Shakyamuni in the Land of Snows.

The Dharma King Trisong Detsen was Manjushri's gift to the land of Tibet. The Bodhisattva of Wisdom emanated into the form of this awakened ruler, with the skill and wisdom to complete the path set out by his forefather, King Songtsen Gampo. This extraordinary life begins in the Drakmar Valley (Valley of Red Rocks), where the royal family had made their residence, at the Drinzang Palace. The unfolding of the King's story, as we will find, is inextricably bound to the foundation of the Buddhadharma in Tibet—for Dharma King Trisong Detsen, fueled by pure motivation and despite all obstacles, made it his mission to build Tibet's first monastery, Samye (The Inconceivable).

The exceptional life of Dharma King Trisong Detsen—devotee, practitioner, and ruler—still resonates to this present day. Had it not been for his unwavering dedication and generosity, the Buddha's teachings of Sutra and Tantra would not have taken root and spread over that vast plateau, transforming an entire culture in the process. Not only was he personally one of the Dharma's greatest patrons ever, but his reign itself was guided by a spiritual quest—not only his own realization, but the establishment of resources for his people to attain realization too. To this day, the blessings of King Trisong Detsen are still invoked, for he embodies all the qualities of a perfect ruler, a true Dharma King.

DRAKMAR DRINZANG

Bodhisattva appearing as a Dharma King—
In this remote Land of Snow you tamed every being in need
Through myriad skillful means.
Trisong Detsen: to you I pray!

— *Chokgyur Dechen Zhikpo Lingpa*

Introduction

When Tibet's great Dharma King Trisong Detsen finally took birth in the royal palace of Drakmar Drinzang, a wondrous display of light filled the red rock valley, a sign of great joy to come. Within these walls, the young King's wish to establish the Dharma in Tibet gradually took root. His wish soon became an unshakeable quest to build Tibet's first monastery, and for this he would seek guidance from the Indian scholar Abbot Shantarakshita. Their initial decisive steps, however, would be met with fierce opposition from forces resistant to change. From his palace at Drakmar Drinzang, King Trisong Detsen negotiated this upwelling of evil spirits, some of whom appeared as ministers who would do anything in their power to block the spread of the Three Jewels—Buddha, Dharma, and Sangha—in the land of Tibet.

Faced with such obstacles, the great Abbot Shantarakshita, this closest spiritual friend of the Dharma King, invoked the aspirations made in their past lives, knowing they must invite the powerful tantric master Guru Padmsambhava from India. Only the Mahaguru could quell the dark forces of the land and let the bright light of the Buddha's wisdom stream in to bless the Tibetan people and the world at large. From the palace, the invitation was carried by hand to India by skilled Tibetan envoys, and into the Mahaguru's presence, fulfilling aspirations made when the three were brothers, lifetimes ago.

Approaching the Sacred Site

The journey by road to Drakmar Drinzang, birthplace of King Trisong Detsen, takes the pilgrim up the Drakmar Valley and past his greatest physical accomplishment, Samye Monastery, a reminder of the importance of this humble site. There now remain only the ruins of the ancient royal palace—yet there it is, a shrine to the greatest of Tibet's Dharma Kings, high up on a rocky escarpment, to the west of the present-day path. Here once stood Drakmar Podrang (Palace of the Red Rocks) built as a residence for Trisong Detsen's father, King Tridé Tsuktsen (704–755), also known as Mé Agtsom. Adjoining the palace was the Buddhist temple of Drinzang, modeled after a temple on Mount Wutai Shan[118], and now treasured as the place where Tibet's greatest Dharma King entered this world.

Twelve centuries have passed since that momentous occasion. Over time, the temple became a place of pilgrimage, a place to recall the collective accomplishments of the King. Today only ruins are left, but Jamyang Khyentsé Wangpo, when he visited in the 19th century, wrote of its recent renovation; and Katok Situ Chökyi Gyatso, visiting some decades later, in the early 20th century, wrote that Drakmar Drinzang featured life-sized statues of Buddha Shakyamuni, Guru Padmsamabhava, and the three great Tibetan Dharma Kings—Songtsen Gampo, Trisong Detsen, and his grandson Tri Ralpachen. Both Khyentsé Wangpo and Katok Situ found King Trisong Detsen's sandalwood *lha shing* (life-force tree) below the temple and encircled within a shrine. Due to the ravages of time, only the foundations of the original site remain, and yet it is through these very ruins that the deeds of the masters can still be remembered, for we have not yet forgotten their impact on our world.[119]

The Dharma King's Journey

The Birth of a Dharma King

> *Trisong Detsen, emanation of Manjushri,*
> *Took birth in Tibet, based on previous aspirations.*
> *Reaching full maturity, he joined the supreme noble family*
> *And developed the heartfelt wish*
> *To establish the Dharma in Tibet. Homage to you!* [120]
>
> — *Jamyang Khyentsé Wangpo*

The story of the Dharma King's birth begins with the Gentle-Voiced Lord, Manjushri. One day, from his perch high atop Riwo Tsénga, the Five-Peaked Mountain of Wutai Shan, Manjushri looked out to the West, toward the snow-capped lands of Tibet. He immediately perceived that the Dharma had begun to spread there many years before, yet the roots of the Buddha's teachings had not penetrated deep enough to transform that land into the realm it was destined to become. So Noble Manjushri, embodiment of the wisdom and intelligence of all the buddhas, contemplated the situation thus:

Long ago, Avalokiteshvara, the Great Compassionate One, sent an enlightened emanation to the land. He thus manifested as King Songtsen Gampo, and he erected one hundred and eight shrines, including the Trülnang and Ramoché temples in Lhasa, among many others both large and small. He thereby brought the tradition of the sacred Dharma to Tibet. But now I, the noble Manjushri, must spread that Dharma, allowing it to flourish throughout the Snowy Land. Thus, I shall incarnate as a powerful king and establish my domain over this land of Tibet![121] ८

— Revealed by Nyangral Nyima Özer

With his intention clear, Noble Manjushri directed his gaze at King Tridé Tsuktsen as he lay beside his queen, the Chinese consort Jinchen Gonzhu,[122] on their royal bed at Drakmar Drinzang. From the Bodhisattva's heart, rainbow lights radiated forth, and on their tip was a golden boy, a finger's breadth in size. This golden child entered the womb of Lady Jinchen, and the Dharma King was conceived—a miracle of awakened compassion. When Lady Jinchen fell asleep that night, she had dreams of light rays streaming forth like the dawn of day. Upon these brilliant rays was the baby boy, shining toward her and entering her belly. When she awoke the next morning, Lady Jinchen recounted the details of these auspicious signs to the King. At the news, he joyfully proclaimed, "A divine messenger from the heavens has come to be our child! What an incredibly auspicious dream!"

As the days of her pregnancy progressed, Lady Jinchen felt an increasing sense of ease. Even when the child moved about, she felt no discomfort. Her mind was clear, her body light, and she was without any disturbance, either in body or mind. Her child, an incarnation of Manjushri's compassion, was born nine months later, during the Year of the Horse (742),[123] under the auspicious Pushya constellation in the first month of spring, Thus, like Buddha Shakyamuni before him, Trisong Detsen came into this world just as the sun was rising, spreading its warmth upon the Snowy Land—a miracle from within the palace walls of Drakmar Drinzang.

The king's Chinese astrologer, an expert in divination by the name of Birje, was quickly summoned to observe the wondrous child, kept safe in these royal grounds. Birjé studied the infant closely, aided by his charts and methods of calculation, and pronounced his findings to the king and queen:

Through the Chinese science of divination with its multi-colored grid, ८
There have arisen the signs of birth of a Glorious Man. ८

From the nine magic numbers and the eight trigrams, ⁑
It is clear that the King's wishes will be attained. ⁑
He will have teeth like spiraled conch shells. ⁑
The pleated hair on his crown will be jet black, clockwise curled. ⁑
Extremely handsome, like a child of the gods, ⁑
He will gather all the most excellent panditas and lotsawas, ⁑
Founding institutions for study and practice, and establishing the Dharma. ⁑
Thus he will build a bridge of Dharma connecting India and Tibet.[124] ⁑

— Revealed by Orgyen Lingpa

His divination pronounced, the court astrologer then gave this child his name, by which he would later become famous—Trisong Detsen, the future Dharma King of Tibet.

Turning to The Inconceivable

The infant child soon grew into a young prince. As was the ancient custom, Trisong Detsen spent his youth training thoroughly in all the arts and crafts of rulership. When he was just thirteen, his father passed away, and it became his duty to ascend the imperial throne and take three brides—Lady Margyen of Tsepang, Lady Jangchup Men of Tro, and Lady Gyalmo Tsin of Phogyong.[125] The young King Trisong Detsen was now charged with guarding the borders of Tibet and expanding them further, all the while ensuring civic harmony among his people. And by all accounts, these early years of rulership were successful.

As he turned sixteen, in the Female Fire Ox Year of 758, his royal attention began to turn toward the Dharma. The young King began reflecting on how his forebears, in particular Dharma King Songtsen Gampo, had not only successfully maintained the kingdom, but also brought the Buddhist teachings to the people. Only this could provide true benefit. As he contemplated just how to further this vision, he soon found the following aspiration growing deep within his heart: To build Tibet's first monastery—a temple for the Three Jewels, a place for their veneration and devotion, and a permanent residence for the Sangha, which would ensure the establishment, spread and transmission of the Dharma throughout the land.[126]

Foundations of The Inconceivable

The King's intention was now clear as day. He would have to marshal the resources of his kingdom and convince his councillors, many from powerful clans, to do his bidding. The King's vision, after all, was far beyond the mundane affairs of foreign conquest and domestic legislation to which his court was accustomed. Predictably, when he announced that they were to build a grand foundation for the Buddha's teachings, the ministers were aghast. "Anything but that!" they lamented. But King Trisong Detsen responded with skill:

> Now listen, all you ministers and subjects! ၜ
> I must act in accordance with our traditions, ၜ
> And so the choice is yours. Pick one of these three: ၜ
> Make the Tsangpo River flow through copper tubes; ၜ
> Build a crystal stupa on Mount Hepori at Samye, ၜ
> Such as can be seen from Shangpo; ၜ
> Or fill the whole of the Valley of Foxes with dust of gold. ၜ
> Otherwise, let us build a monastery with foundations that rise up ၜ
> as fast as an arrow. The choice is yours![127] ၜ
>
> — *Revealed by Orgyen Lingpa*

Faced with these difficult choices, the councillors conferred among themselves. There was not sufficient copper to put the Brahamputra in copper tubes, they reckoned; that was impossible. A crystal stupa of that size would be impossible too; there was not enough crystal even to make a hundred crystal necklaces. As for filling the Valley of Foxes with gold dust, there simply was not enough gold in the vaults; also impossible. So, with only one choice left, they returned to their King: "We beg you," they pleaded, "Please abandon your notions of those three impossible things. We'd prefer to build a monastery!"

The King's plan had worked. His councillors had agreed, albeit reluctantly, to begin the great work of building Tibet's first monastery, akin to those great monastic institutes of India—Nalanda, Vikramashila, and Uddandapuri. It was now only a matter of deciding where to lay the foundations for this new establishment.

Inviting the Sangharaja

> *Requesting his subjects to decide on a site,*
> *The King sent the sage known as Birjé to survey the land.*
> *His purpose and intent were the construction of a temple.*
> *He invited Shantarakshita to come from Zahor* ၜ
> *And joyfully welcomed the great scholar. Homage to you![128]* ၜ
>
> — *Jamyang Khyentsé Wangpo*

King Trisong Detsen dispatched Birjé, his Chinese astrologer, to find a suitable piece of land for the monastery. After surveying the whole domain, Birjé found that all the auspicious geomantic signs were assembled at the Tamarisk Grove, only a short distance from the royal palace of Drakmar. The site was thus decided, and workers began to lay down the monastery's foundations. However, along with this supremely virtuous activity came forces of obstruction with similar power. These demonic forces quickly laid to waste whatever efforts were made for the good. And as the story goes, no matter what was built during the day, spirits would swoop in to demolish it at night.[129]

It soon dawned upon the King that merely employing more workers to build the monastery would not suffice. Trusted envoys were dispatched to India, their mission to search for a learned master who could provide the spiritual guidance necessary for a monastery to be properly established on the untamed ground of Tibet. The emissaries traveled south, over the Himalayan ranges, down to the plains of the Ganges, continuing along their difficult road until they reached the land of Zahor.[130] They quickly learned that the land was famed for a scholar-prince named Shantarakshita (725-788), the son of King Gomati.[131] Shantarakshita was widely celebrated as not only the very best exponent of the Buddhadharma in the whole of Zahor, but also one of the top scholars at Nalanda University, India's most esteemed Buddhist institution. To Nalanda they went, where they finally met the great Buddhist teacher just as he was turning the Dharma Wheel. While they could not understand the foreign speech, his mere presence filled them with a natural sense of wonder.[132] The envoys raced back to the King, who rejoiced at the news: Tibet's first bodhisattva abbot had been found.

The King ordered two of his most trusted councillors, Banang Jñaneshvara and Nyak Jñanakumara, to travel back to Nalanda with gifts of gold and a formal letter of invitation. The letter, addressed to the Great Abbot Shantarakshita, read:

> The jeweled teachings of the Dharma, a supreme parasol held aloft, ⸸
> Do not appear even as a faint star within the darkness of this far realm. ⸸
> Please come and clear away the mist that enshrouds our land, ⸸
> For deities and demons now rise up to block my efforts![133] ⸸
>
> — *Revealed by Orgyen Lingpa*

The Great Abbot accepted the King's invitation, and joined his emissaries on the long journey back to Tibet. When the party finally reached the royal palace at Drakmar Drinzang, King Trisong Detsen received Shantarakshita with great respect, requesting him with the utmost sincerity to help fulfill his aspiration to build the monastery of Samyé (The Inconceivable).

Shantarakshita began this monumental project by laying out the Vajradhatu mandala[134] upon the building site and embarking on the rituals for blessing the land. The Great Abbot then examined the earth and confirmed that everything did indeed appear favorable for the construction of the monastery.[135] And so the work proceeded under the guidance of Shantarakshita, who advised that the institute should be modeled after the prestigious Indian monastery of Uddandapura.[136] In this fashion the foundations of Samye were laid in the year 762, the Water Tiger Year, when the King was only twenty-one years of age.[137]

As the construction progressed, Shantarakshita took up residence in a silken tent on the roof of the nearby palace. There he began teaching the sacred Dharma to the King and any Tibetan disciples gathered around him. The Great Abbot began at the very beginning. He taught these students the ten virtuous deeds, the twelve links of dependent origination, and the eighteen constituents of mind and body.[138] Thus the Dharma Wheel began turning in earnest in the Snowy Land, with this partnership of its ruler and this great Indian teacher.

Inviting the Mahaguru

> *Again and again, Shantarakshita reminded the King*
> *Of the aspirations they had made together, lifetimes ago,*
> *And messengers were sent to invite you, the master Padmasambhava.*
> *Compassionately, you accepted and made your way to Tibet,*
> *Taming countless gods and demons on the way. Homage to you!*[139]

> — *Jamyang Khyentsé Wangpo*

Everything appeared to be off to an auspicious start, yet soon the tides began to turn. A naga who lived in the thicket around Samye began mustering local spirits, all of them keen to oppose this profound shift in the physical and spiritual landscape of their native ground. These demons descended upon the site in great force, in the form of floods, plague, and terrible storms; they even began tearing down the foundations of the monastery, carrying the earth and rocks back to their sources, leaving the place in ruins. At such an impasse, King Trisong Detsen turned to his kind teacher Shantarakshita for guidance:

> Although I have aspired to do well in constructing this monastery, ⸙
> A source of refuge for beings both now and in the future, ⸙

My obscurations seem too great,
Or else you have not given your blessings. ⁜
Rather, it seems as if my aspirations will be left unfulfilled![140] ⁜

— *Revealed by Orgyen Lingpa*

Compassionately, the Great Abbot responded to his royal disciple's plea. His own training was in the peaceful path of a bodhisattva, and these methods were simply not powerful enough to pacify the spirits now wreaking havoc upon the land. Someone more powerful was needed—a siddha who had mastered the arts and crafts taught in the tantras. And he knew of one such siddha—Guru Padmasambhava, who at that moment resided in the lands of India and was precisely the master they needed.[141] The Great Abbot approached the court with a bold proposition:

Right now, in the presence of India's Vajra Throne, ⁜
Dwells the Master from Uddiyana, Padmasambhava. ⁜
A great master in the five fields of learning, ⁜
he has perfected his training ⁜
And attained the siddhis both ordinary and supreme. ⁜
He conquers demons, the eight classes of spirits are in his service, ⁜
Gods and demons tremble before him, and all the spirits bow. ⁜
If this one you invite, supreme among buddhas past and future, ⁜
neither gods nor demons will be able to resist, ⁜
and your aims will succeed.[142] ⁜

— *Revealed by Orgyen Lingpa*

Although the Mahaguru's boundless work on the Indian subcontinent had been essential over the centuries, it had mostly been accomplished in disguise, by means of his many emanations. The Tibetan court had thus never heard of this tantric adept and his miraculous powers, and the Great Abbot's proposal was met with immediate suspicion by King and ministers alike. Might such wrathful activity not only threaten the spirits that opposed them, but also risk their own entrenched position as the Tibetan ruling class?

In his clairvoyance, the Great Abbot Shantarakshita knew better: the three of them— Dharma King, Great Abbot, and Tantric Master—were already bound by a potent karmic connection from many lifetimes ago. He began to introduce their shared history, tracing it back to the tears of Avalokiteshvara, and from the divine realms to Nepal, where an impoverished poultry-keeper formed the pure resolve to build a stupa for the benefit of all beings. The three had been born as her sons in that lifetime and had fulfilled her sacred vow, completing the building of the Great Jarung Kashor Stupa, a source of blessing for the world.[143] The time had now come, Shantarakshita insisted, for the three to be reunited, to fulfill their aspirations of spreading the Dharma far beyond the noble lands of India, into the northern realm of Tibet. "You must invite him," he pleaded, referring to Guru Padmsambhava, "for it is your own former prayer of aspiration!"[144] These powerful karmic links were now ripening; there was no choice but for the King to take them seriously.

Upon hearing this incredible history, King Trisong Detsen took courage, and all hesitations were overcome. His immediately dispatched an invitation to the Vajra Throne of Bodh Gaya, residence of the Mahaguru.[145] Four envoys skilled in the Indian language—Bami Trisher, Dorjé Dudjom, Shakyaprabha, and Shubu Palkyi Senge—made the long journey over the Himalaya and across the Gangetic plains to Bodh Gaya. There they offered a golden vessel filled with gold dust to the local sovereign, another to his court priest, and finally, another to Guru Padmsambhava, along with their urgent request:

> The King of Tibet, Trisong Detsen, has made a vow ⸸
> To build a foundation for the teachings, a monastery, ⸸
> But gods and demons are preventing its construction. ⸸
> We come to invite you to bless and consecrate the ground, ⸸
> And to secure, preserve, and defend the Buddhadharma. ⸸
> Please come—embrace us with your compassion![146] ⸸
>
> — *Revealed by Orgyen Lingpa*

Guru Padmasambhava already knew, even before this request was made, that the time had come for the Tibetan King to become his patron, and so he accepted without question. The Mahaguru thus began the long journey north, and as he reached the vast Himalayan range that lay between India and the Tibetan plateau, he blessed its mountains and valleys with his practice and by hiding countless treasures for times to come. As the Mahaguru approached the borders of Tibet, King Trisong Detsen remained at Drakmar Drinzang, anticipating the moment of their meeting, an event that would change the course of his kingdom's history and the spiritual fortune of the Tibetan people, for all time.

The Mahaguru's Legacy

The Treasures of Drakmar Drinzang

In front of a mountain known as Tségang, ⁝
On a boulder resembling the coiled Nageshvara, ⁝
One known as "King Mañjushri" will appear, ⁝
An exponent of thirteen profound treasures.[147]⁝

— *Revealed by Orgyen Lingpa*

Later, as foretold by Guru Padmasambhava, the reincarnation of King Trisong Detsen appeared as the renowned treasure revealer Jamyang Khyentse Wangpo. This fresh emanation of Manjushri thus shared a natural connection with Drakmar Drinzang, his birthplace and residence in former times. It should not be surprising, then, that Khyentse Wangpo would sometimes dream of Drakmar Drinzang. On a Guru Rinpoche Day in the year 1834, when he was just fifteen, he had this particularly powerful experience:

Before dawn on the 10th day of the eighth month of the Wood Horse Year (1834), when I was fifteen, I dreamt of arriving at a temple I knew to be Drakmar Drinzang. A red woman beautifully dressed in the apparel of a goddess, in silks and jewels, was holding a red flowerbud in her right hand. As soon as she gave it to me, the flower opened and a small red volume appeared inside. I tried to read it, but it was all written in symbolic script, so I could not. Then she passed me the kapala in her left hand, filled with amrita. I drank, and the appearances of ordinary deluded awareness became shrouded in mist, while the symbolic script became easily legible, and there with mounting joy I found the voluminous outer, inner, secret, and innermost secret cycles of the *Deshek Düpa* guru sadhana. There were other prophetic things, too, but apart from the words "In the future, near this very temple a precious wish-fulfilling treasure will materialize", and a few other phrases, I did not remember them.

Then that volume melted into red light and dissolved into me, and as the entirety of the literal meaning shone clearly in my mind, I awoke. Thereupon I wrote down an extensive practice manual for the outer cycle, identical in form to the *Barché Künsel* sadhana, but with eight complete sections. The brief daily practice of the inner cycle, which I also wrote down, was mostly identical to the present

Sampa Lhundrup, also with a mandala arrangement of thirteen Gurus, but, as the time had not yet come for disseminating these teachings, I just practiced them a little myself and reconcealed the texts. The peaceful and wrathful Mahakarunika of the secret cycle and the Varahi and so forth of the innermost secret cycle appeared clearly in my mind, but I did not write them down.'[148]

It was nine years later, on a Guru Rinpoche Day in the year 1848, that Jamyang Khyentse Wangpo finally visited the sacred residence of Drakmar Drinzang. Just as he arrived, an unknown woman approached carrying the clay finger of a Buddha statue. This mysterious lady placed the finger in his hands and, without speaking a single word, then left. The Great Khyensté tucked the finger into his robe and soon forgot about it, unaware of the blessing it held.

When, later, Khyentse Wangpo was loosening his belt, the clay finger rolled out from his robes and promptly fell to the floor, shattering. To his amazement, amidst the broken pieces lay a variety of scripture and unknown sacred substances.[149] Meanwhile, on this very same day, his future companion in treasure revelation, Chokgyur Dechen Lingpa, discovered the *Tukdrup Barché Künsel* cycle at Kala Rongo in Nangchen, at the youthful age of twenty.[150] The prophecies of Khyentse Wangpo's dream had come true. Through his connection with Drakmar Drinzang, a profound treasure was indeed revealed, one that would allow the profound teachings of Mahaguru Padmasambhava to bless the Snowy Land of Tibet all over again.

A WISDOM DAKINI IS BORN

Tsogyal Lhatso

As the Buddhadharma's foundations were being laid by the new Dharma King, another embodiment of enlightened wisdom was about to take birth in the Snowy Land, Khandro Yeshé Tsogyal, Queen of Lake-Born Wisdom. She was a supreme wisdom dakini, destined to become the chief disciple and spiritual consort of Mahaguru Padmasambhava, and her spiritual journey is absolutely vital to the unfolding of the Dharma in the land of Tibet. Indeed, Khandro Yeshé Tsogyal's profound spiritual relationship with the Mahaguru, and her service to his liberating teachings, has allowed the Dharma to reach the hearts and minds of all future generations. Guru Rinpoche shared the entirety of the Dharma with her, so that she became the foremost holder of his life and legacy and was appointed guardian of his most treasured teachings, the *Nyingtik*, the innermost heart essence of the Great Perfection. Her unparalleled devotion to the path, and to her personal guru Padmasambhava, shines as an example of the ideal disciple, and led her to become the first Tibetan to attain enlightenment in a single lifetime.[151]

Along with the Mahaguru, Yeshé Tsogyal traveled the entire length and breadth of the Himalayan plateau. Wherever her guru went, she followed in his footsteps, practicing his pith instructions and attaining marvelous siddhis. This is not only reflected in her life story, but can be witnessed by pilgrims today: the majority of the Mahaguru's sacred sites also feature "secret" caves where she, too, practiced.[152] And wherever Guru Padmasambhava spread the Dharma, any moment that he deemed his treasure teachings ripe for concealment, the wisdom dakini Yeshé Tsogyal was there, constantly enabling this activity to unfold. Her presence, her creative command, was a constant feature that enlivened every step of this grand process of awakening—both for the Tibetan landscape and its people. Thus they are hailed together as *guru yab yum*: Guru Padmasambhava, the father, inseparable from his spiritual consort, the mother, Khandro Yeshé Tsogyal—together the union (and unity) of skillful means and wisdom.

At her birthplace, Tsogyal Lhatso, vast and profound treasures have been revealed, just as they have from the countless other sacred sites where Khandro Yeshé Tsogyal lived, taught, and realized the profound Dharma imparted by her teacher. As followers of the Mahaguru, we can receive her blessings too, through receiving any of the many teachings she wrote down and concealed for our current age. We can also do this through engaging in any of the many Vajrayana practices that invoke Yeshé Tsogyal herself. In fact, invoking this wisdom dakini is considered to be of vital importance for unlocking the higher stages of realization of the path—for her blessings are vast, profound and swift.[153] So, even before we meet Guru Padmasambhava in Tibet and begin following his journey spreading the Dharma throughout the land, we pay homage to the birth of this wisdom dakini who would go on to make this wondrous activity possible. Her birth at Tsogyal Lhatso marks the beginning of this extraordinary path, ushering in the dawn of Dharma in the Land of Snows.

TSOGYAL LHATSO

Mother of Space, foremost of dakinis, Lady Kharchen Za,
Gatherer of Padmakara's secret treasury,
Knower of all—past, present and future,
Mother Tsogyal, Great Bliss Queen, to you we pray:
Grant us siddhis, ordinary and supreme![154]

— *Jamyang Khyentse Chökyi Lodrö*

Introduction

An emanation of the goddess of sublime eloquence, Khandro Yeshé Tsogyal was born to Palkyi Wangchuk, chief of the Kharchen clan, and his fair wife Khandro Getso of Nup. This wisdom dakini's miraculous birth caused a lake to appear, giving it the name Tsogyal Lhatso, "life-force lake." These blessed waters, surrounded by the green growth of birch and willow, still well up from the sandy plains of the lower Drak Valley, a life-giving miracle that connects us with her extraordinary presence to this day.

An extraordinary child, even as an infant Yeshé Tsogyal bore all the signs of a wisdom dakini, awakened from the beginning. Then, as she grew of age, her unsurpassed beauty was such that suitors even took up arms to vie for her hand in marriage. Only Dharma King Trisong Detsen was deemed fit for the betrothal, a match that opened the door to meeting her destined teacher, Guru Padmasambhava. This spiritual partnership unfolded as one of the greatest in the history of great saints, for it led to the Dharma's firm establishment in the hearts of the Tibetan people, and in the landscape of Tibet itself. Tsogyal Lhatso, then, marks the beginning of this incredible journey, for it was from these blessed waters that a dakini was born who would fulfill the Mahaguru's activity, allowing it to shine forth and bless countless generations to come.

Approaching the Sacred Site

To the west of Drakmar Drinzang, along the northern banks of the great Tsangpo River, lies the Drak Valley. This was the ancestral home of the Kharchen clan, and here Khandro Yeshé Tsogyal was born. The life-force lake that gushed forth at her birth is now a tranquil tree-lined pond around which a community of nuns has emerged, nurtured by the flow of Yeshé Tsogyal's blessings. Tsogyal Lhatso rests among the settlements of the lower Drak Valley, known locally as "Zhangda" or "Asha," on the eastern banks of the river bed.

It is reached by following the main road north of Drongmoché. Drak Valley is also the birthplace of the Mahaguru's disciple Nupchen Sangyé Yeshé, and the Drak Yangdzong caves further up the valley became one of the vital retreat places of the Mahaguru.[155]

The sacred pond of Tsogyal Lhatso is now held within a rectangular stone tank roughly thirty feet by twelve, beneath the protection of willow, poplar, and birch trees. To the northern end of the sanctuary is Jangchup Ling, also known as Kashima (Temple of the Four Pillars). This branch of Samye Monastery traces its history back to the 8th century, and it contains a pair of stones bearing the footprints of Khandro Yeshé Tsogyal, impressed upon the living rock when she was only eight years old. There is also a later handprint of Yeshé Tsogyal taken from the meditation caves of Samye Chimpu,[156] and in recent years murals have been commissioned that relate her life story. Perhaps the most celebrated object of devotion within the temple is the sandalwood life-force tree—*lha shing*—given to Khandro Yeshé Tsogyal by none other than Nanda, king of the Nagas. Like the lake, this tree is considered to be Khandro Yeshé Tsogyal's own *lha*, or life-force, and it can still be seen today.

Just outside Jangchup Ling and to the east, one can pay homage to the newly restored stupa that marks the precise location of Yeshé Tsogyal's birth, while west of Tsogyal Lhatso lies the Dakini's Breast Milk stream, where fresh waters pour forth, warm in winter and cool in summer. Tasting these waters is said to cure illness and purify evils and obscurations, so by their blessing one is totally liberated from the lower realms.[157] These and many other wonders await the pilgrim visiting the sacred site of Yeshé Tsogyal's birth.

The Wisdom Dakini's Journey

The Birth of Khandro Yeshé Tsogyal

When the time had come to tame the wild beings of Tibet,
You descended from the sky, means and wisdom united.
In Drak, you entered the womb of a Kharchen maid
And manifested countless auspicious signs. To you, we pray!

In the Bird Year, at sunrise on the tenth of the Monkey month.
The earth quaked, as you were born, and thunder filled the sky;
Flowers fell like rain, the lake overflowed;
Huge canopies of light streamed in rainbows across the sky.
To you, we pray!

Newly born, you uttered the alphabet and recited lines of poetry.
The sky rang with goddesses singing verses of auspiciousness.
After just one month you looked like an eight-year-old child,
And your fame spread through the kingdom. To you, we pray![158]

— *Jamgön Kongtrul Lodrö Thayé*

Far away in the celestial realm of Uddiyana, Guru Padmasambhava had been reflecting. The time for propagating the Secret Mantra of the Vajrayana had come, and to aid him in this work an emanation of Sarasvati should appear in the world. So the Mahaguru and the goddess of enlightened speech embraced, taking delight in the play of bliss. From their union a great light burst forth, and a red *E* within a circle of white vowels and a white *Vam* within a circle of red consonants shot like meteors through the sky toward the land of Tibet, falling into the private chambers of Kharchen Palkyi Wangchuk and Khandro Getso, as they lay together in their marital bed.[159] A vision suddenly arose to Khandro Getso of a sweet humming bee melting into her husband's crown, while he saw a third eye appear upon his wife's brow, and a girl of eight approaching, strumming a viol and intoning sacred sounds, only to vanish into thin air the next moment.

The earth shook then, and lights shone forth and thunder pealed. As the ground quaked, the spring that flowed beside their residence transformed miraculously into a lake. The couple woke from this night of auspicious dreaming to a strange and fair maiden who said, "In the household of this princely father, the Buddha has arisen, and the Dharma and the Sangha. *Alala*, this is a marvelous wonder!"[160] And so began Getso's pregnancy. For nine months the sound of sacred syllables hung in the air, while all sorts of flowers blossomed around the village.

On the tenth day of the Monkey month of the Bird Year, as rainbows filled the skies above Drak Valley, Getso finally gave birth to an exquisitely lovely girl, bearing all the signs of a wisdom dakini.[161] This was clearly no ordinary child, for just as she left her mother's womb, the infant exclaimed, "Great Lord of Uddiyana, please think of me!" The lake that had emerged beside the Kharchen castle had now swelled to double its size, overflowing its banks. Once again, the earth shook, and flowers fell from the sky, and now red and white flowers blossomed around the lake. Her father, chieftain of Kharchen, thus gave her the name by which she would become famous: Yeshé Tsogyal, *Queen of the Lake of Wisdom*.[162]

The child's appearance was amazing. Her body was radiant and rosy, she had a full set of pearly white teeth, and locks of blue-black hair already hung down to her waist. When her mother first brought her nourishment, the infant-child broke into song:

> I, your child, a yogini nirmanakaya, ፨
> Am nourished by the food of pure essences; ፨
> Unclean foods I now have long forgotten! ፨
> But, mother, I will eat—that you may gain in merit. ፨
> Essential teachings will be what I truly eat, ፨
> And all samsara will be what I swallow. ፨
> Awareness, pristine wisdom, will be now my fill. ፨
> *Ah Ye!*[163] ፨

> — *Revealed by Samten Lingpa*

This astonishing child of the Kharchen clan grew swiftly, swifter than any other in the land. After a single month she had the appearance of an eight-year-old girl, and at ten she had become a beautiful maiden. So beautiful was she that suitors began calling from every corner of Tibet, and from all the surrounding kingdoms. All of this attention left her parents helpless. It seemed that Khandro Yeshé Tsogyal would soon have to be given to one of these suitors, but who could be worthy of this amazing child's hand?

Dharma King Trisong Detsen meets Khandro Yeshé Tsogyal

> *Developing renunciation for samsara's prison,*
> *You fled far from the suitors of surrounding kingdoms*
> *And aligned yourself with King Trisong Detsen*
> *And entered his noble court. To you, we pray!*[164]

> — *Jamgön Kongtrul Lodrö Thayé*

The local clansmen and their insatiable interest posed a problem for the Kharchen family; the suitors began to demand her hand in marriage—by force, if need be. For her part, Khandro Yeshé Tsogyal was not at all interested in the ties of marriage; she wished only to follow a spiritual path. Feeling the heat of this brewing conflict, the young Yeshé Tsogyal made her attempt at escape and temporarily hid in the mountains at Önphu Taktsang,[165] only to be found and brought back against her will. The whole land was now on the brink of all-out war, and Kharchen Palkyi Wangchuk was left with no choice but to call upon his emperor, King Trisong Detsen, to intervene.

King Trisong Detsen thus arrived in the Drak Valley in a grand royal procession. To avert war and quell the tempers of his chieftains, he decided to marry Khandro Yeshé Tsogyal himself, and the royal assembly feasted for three months in celebration. It soon became clear, however, that Yeshé Tsogyal herself had little interest in the life of an empress. She begged the King for permission to devote herself to the practice of the Dharma, which in his wisdom he graciously granted, thus clearing the way for her spiritual path to begin.[166] Indeed, Yeshé Tsogyal was soon to meet her karmically destined teacher, with the coming of Guru Padmasambhava, tamer of Tibet's demons and bringer of the teachings of Sutra and Mantra to their wild highland realm.

The Wisdom Dakini's Legacy

The revelation of the Yumka Dechen Gyalmo

> Great Bliss is the reality body, Samantabhadra;
> Bliss-Emptiness is the enjoyment body, the Vajra Queen in actuality;
> Supreme Bliss is the mother of all buddhas, Yeshe Tsogyal.
> To you I pray: grant me the wisdom of Great Bliss![167]

> — Jamyang Khyentse Wangpo

Over the many centuries since Khandro Yeshé Tsogyal's birth, pilgrims have journeyed in devotion to this sacred lake to pay homage to her life and legacy. Among all the pilgrims who have found their way here, the great treasure revealer Rikdzin Jikmé Lingpa (1730–1798) stands out, for his visit left signs still visible to this day. Before his arrival here in 1773, Jikmé Lingpa had practiced in retreat for many years, inspired by the life and legacy of Gyalwa Longchenpa, peerless master of the Great Perfection. With one-pointed devotion, he invoked Longchenpa, again and again, until finally there arose in Jikmé Lingpa's vision the master himself, as if he were present in the flesh. Over the course of the following seven years (c.1757–1764), Jikmé Lingpa received the very essence of Longchenpa's sublime realization, in the form of a practice cycle known as the *Longchen Nyingtik* (*Heart Essence of the Vast Expanse*).

So it was that, some nine years after this period of revelation, Jikmé Lingpa set out on a pilgrimage to the Drak Valley, the sacred birthplace of Khandro Yeshé Tsogyal, the supreme wisdom dakini. On arriving at the lake, he began fervently to pray and make offerings to her. Afterwards, he sat down to rest under a tree, and promptly fell asleep. On waking the next morning, he noticed something odd. Where he had leaned against the base of the tree in his slumber, an imprint had formed in the shape of his back. This tree, and its miraculous imprint, is now a site of reverence for all who visit Tsogyal Lhatso.

But Jikmé Lingpa had another experience too, at this site, that still carries great blessings to this day. At Tsogyal Lhatso he revealed one of the main dakini sadhanas from his renowned *Longchen Nyingtik* cycle: the practice of *Yumka Dechen Gyalmo* (*The Yogini Practice of the Queen of Great Bliss*). The main figure is a wisdom dakini, the radiantly red Yeshé Tsogyal, whom the practitioner invokes, while channeling great devotion for her. We are fortunate to have Jikmé Lingpa's personal account of this revelation, in his *History of the Yogini Practice of the Queen of Great Bliss*:

> On one occasion, when I arrived at Tsogyal Lhatso near the large village of Yoru Drak, I offered to the lake a bowl of ambrosia (*amrita*) which liberates upon taste, together with a silken scarf. The bowl sank slowly, like a living being entering the water, while the end of the scarf remained fluttering above the surface, which amazed me. Then a pure state of consciousness arose spontaneously and my ordinary perception vanished. I drank some of the water and, in the very instant that I touched its surface, a perfectly black bee, like an utpala flower, arose and hovered around. Three times it made a buzzing sound, like the sound of a sitar. This made my ordinary perception dissolve into a state free from objective reference. From within the expanse where appearance, mind, and reality merge, a wisdom dakini appeared. She was bright red and adorned with jewels and the six bone ornaments. She wore a garland of flowers, swaying to and fro. She then fully revealed to me a ritual of her own visualization, which included all the essentials.
>
>> I, a dakini, come from the dharmakaya expanse.
>> I have no thoughts of coming and going.
>> I, a girl, am mistress of the twenty-four sacred places.
>> I come from the emanated realm of Chamara,
>> the glorious mountain.
>> In the arrangement of my body the qualities of
>> mantra are perfected.
>> I, a girl, am the mother of the victorious ones of the three times.
>> There are no Three Jewels but for those that arise from me.
>> If you accomplish me, the dakini,
>> you will accomplish the three kayas.

For the benefit of beings to be tamed,
I am in the south-western direction.
If auspicious interdependent circumstances are not disturbed,
With 🛕 I will nurture fortunate ones in the expanse of the
     six spheres.

As soon as she had said this, the inexhaustible miraculous array of the dakini's secret syllables merged inseparably with me and dissolved into the center of my heart.

The Lord of Dharma Drakpukpa, who was beside me at the time, earnestly paid his respects and asked: 'What did you see in your vision?' I had simply left the vision for what it was, but with his question the auspicious interdependent circumstances were awakened. First, I protected the secret samaya for five days. Then, during the waning phase of the moon, the time when dakinis gather, we performed a feast-gathering with plentiful offerings. In the palace of power of Yangdzong Düdra, through the auspicious interdependent circumstances and profound connections, the seal was released.[168]

Many years later, Jamyang Khyentse Wangpo, Jikmé Lingpa's reincarnation, also visited this sacred site on pilgrimage. He offered one thousand feasts to the wisdom dakini, and, as a result of his prayers, the blessings of Khandro Yeshé Tsogyal flowed forth in a vajra song of aspiration:

All forms are the mandala of the three seats of the illusory net.
All sounds are perfect as the indestructible nada.
All thoughts are liberated into the dharmakaya.
May all beings realize this primordial ground![169]

THE MAHAGURU ARRIVES IN THE LAND OF SNOWS

Mangyul, Tolung Spring, Zurkhar Do & Mount Hepori

Thus far, Dharma King Trisong Detsen's efforts to establish the Buddhadharma in Tibet, despite the compassionate guidance of Abbot Shantarakshita, had met with terrible obstacles. Gods and demons had risen up to block any transformation of their native landscape, and in their aggression were laying waste not only to the foundations of Samye Monastery, but to other already established supports for Dharma too. The success of the Dharma King's grand aspiration now rested upon the shoulders of the supreme tantric master Padmasambhava, who alone might have the skillful means and wisdom to tame the forces of evil that were preventing the Dharma from taking firm root. Through the strength of their karmic connection, the Mahaguru had accepted the King's call to travel to Greater Tibet and establish the Dharma there, once and for all.

And so it was that Guru Padmasambhava made his way from the Vajra Throne in India, through the hills of Nepal, to Mangyul, a border region that was itself ripe for training and conversion. There he remained for three months, practicing and blessing Mangyul's most sacred object, a self-arisen statue of Avalokiteshvara, the Arya Vati Zangpo. When the Tibetan delegation arrived to usher their new teacher into Central Tibet at the King's behest, the Mahaguru granted them initiation. Thus, Guru Rinpoche and this party of royal envoys made their entrance into Tibet as guru and disciples—his first among all Tibetans.

As they traversed the mountains and valleys of the Snowy Land, the Mahaguru subdued the local gods and demons, one by one, just as he had in Greater India and Nepal. However much these spirits tried to defeat the Guru with their magical powers, or even if they simply fled in terror, none in the end managed to escape—all were bound to swear allegiance to the sacred Dharma. When King Trisong Detsen did finally receive the Mahaguru, it was in the company of a vast retinue near his palace at Zurkhar Do, on the shores of the Brahmaputra River. Now reunited, the Dharma King and Tantric Master proceeded to the top of Mount Hepori, where Guru Rinpoche took on his extremely wrathful form, known as Dorjé Drolö (Wild Vajra Wrath), in order to subjugate fully Tibet's terrible gods and demons and set the stage for laying the foundations of Samye, the Dharma's inconceivable support for in the Land of Snows.

MANGYUL

In Mangyul, at the Cloud of Love Temple, ⁝
You granted siddhis to the four bhikshus. ⁝
O supreme Kyepar Phakpé Rikdzin, ⁝
With your compassion, inspire us with your blessing! ⁝
With your love, guide us and others along the path! ⁝
With your realization, grant us siddhis! ⁝
With your power, dispel the obstacles facing us all! ⁝
Outer obstacles, dispel them externally; ⁝
Inner obstacles, dispel them internally; ⁝
Secret obstacles, dispel them into space! ⁝
In devotion, I pay homage and take refuge in you! ⁝
om ah hung benza guru pema siddhi hung[170]⁝

— *Revealed by Chokgyur Dechen Lingpa*

Introduction

Mangyul was Guru Padmasambhava's gateway to the vastness of Tibet. Even before the Mahaguru's arrival, however, the area had been blessed by the Bodhisattva Avalokiteshvara, in the form of a self-arisen statue of sandalwood, the Arya Vati Zangpo. This miraculous image was one of five "brothers" discovered generations earlier by the Dharma King Songtsen Gampo. After his journey through the land of Nepal, Guru Padmasambhava's arrival here, and his three-month stay, would only further imbue its temples and shrines with the influence of the Great Compassionate One.

Mangyul itself lay on the principal route connecting Tibet with the Himalayan valley-kingdom of Nepal, and further south with Greater India. The royal envoys of Dharma King Trisong Detsen, tasked with the mission of inviting Abbot Shantarakshita and Guru Padmasambhava, set out along this route, and it was via this route that they returned with these great masters in their company. Many others too—the wisdom dakinis Khandro Yeshé Tsogyal and Belbang Kalasiddhi, the great Lotsawa Vairocana, and later generations of Indian and Tibetan masters and teachers, scholars, translators, and pilgrims—all took this same path, and countless Indian and Tibetan sages have followed in their wake.[171]

When Guru Padamsambahva did eventually meet the royal delegation at Mangyul's Serthang (Golden Plain), the earth turned to gold and the

Mahaguru's power was immediately apparent to his stunned Tibetan audience. They were initiated as disciples shortly thereafter, at Ngödrup Phuk (Cave of Siddhis). The Mahaguru continued on his way, binding the twelve Tenma goddesses, powerful protector spirits native to Tibet, at nearby Palkü Tso. Mangyul, then, is where the Mahaguru began his activity in the Land of Snows, and where his mastery over the gods, demons, and people of Tibet was displayed for all to see.

Approaching the Sacred Site

Out of unending space, its extent beyond fathom,
The magic of the buddhas' compassion appears
As a conjurer, evoking every kind of display.
Sublime and noble Vati Zangpo, to you I pray![172]

— *5ᵗʰ Dalai Lama, Ngawang Lobzang Gyatso*

With its lush hills of evergreen and its towering snow peaks, Mangyul has served as a place of refuge for countless generations of traders and pilgrims—an ideal transition point between the plains of India and the heights of Tibet.[173] Typically, traders from India would wait until winter to cross the thick jungles of lowland Nepal, known as the Terai; at any other time they would be at risk of catching malaria. These traders would then pause in Kathmandu, where they could comfortably wait for the snow-covered mountain passes to clear with the coming of spring and summer; only then would they continue north along the Trisuli River valley and up to Mangyul, before crossing onto the high plateau of Greater Tibet.

Mangyul became not only an important center of commerce, but also a vital refuge for the many pilgrims crossing the Himalayas from south to north or vice versa in search of the Dharma. The prosperity brought by its trade-route connections meant that the people of Mangyul were well-equipped to provide food and lodging for pilgrims, as well as to support the building of temples, stupas and other sacred monuments.[174] Its material and spiritual resources made it a haven, too, for Tibetan translators seeking to avoid the intense summer heat of India and Nepal, while allowing them to stay in close proximity to the Sanskrit scholars of the Kathmandu Valley.[175] Furthermore, Mangyul's considerable distance from Central Tibet made it an ideal refuge for sacred objects, not to mention practitioners, during times when the Tibetan capital of Lhasa was in danger of attack by either foreign invaders or local demons. [176]

The most famous of Mangyul's sacred sites is the Jamtrin Lhakang (Cloud of Love Temple). This temple was one in a geomantic network of thirteen, built by Dharma King Songtsen Gampo (c. 605–650) at the request of his Chinese consort Queen Wencheng, in order to safeguard the country and suppress a demoness that lay supine across the land.[177] Jamtrin Lhakang was positioned on the left foot of the demoness.[178] While the temple presents an invaluable sacred and historic relic in itself, the main draw for pilgrims has primarily been its central object of devotion: the Arya Vati Zangpo. A wooden statue depicting the Bodhisattva Avalokiteshvara in his standing, two-armed guise, the Arya Vati Zangpo is one of five naturally-arisen Avalokiteshvara statues hidden by this Buddha of Compassion to bless the beings of this degenerate age.[179]

Since the time of their revelation during the reign of Dharma King Songtsen Gampo, these statues have served as some of the most revered and sacred relics of Avalokiteshvara, right up to the present day. Four of the five statues still remain in their original locations. Fearing that the statue of Arya Vati Zangpo might be damaged in the cultural revolution, in an extraordinary collective effort Tibetan refugees took the statue to Nepal.[180] In the process, a text was revealed that had been hidden within the statue itself, a history entitled *Tajang* (*The Emerald Horse*), composed by the master Drakkar Chökyi Wangchuk (1775–1837), and one of the three most important sources on the history of these statues now available to us today.[181] In secrecy, the statue was eventually ushered to the private quarters of His Holiness the 14th Dalai Lama, Tenzin Gyatso, at his residence in Dharamsala, India. There, Arya Vati Zangpo now remains and is publicly displayed once a year, so that pilgrims have a chance to see and receive its blessings once again.

The Mahaguru's Journey

Approaching Tibet

> The gods and demons of Tibet have risen up in fury, §
> But I shall come to tame them, before long... §
> Gods and demons with bodies born of womb §
> Should hold their peace. §
> Lotsawas, go on ahead![182] §
>
> — *Revealed by Orgyen Lingpa*

Upon accepting the invitation of King Trisong Detsen, Guru Padmasambhava sent his emissaries ahead, for he knew there was some work to do first. Along the road to Tibet, the Himalayan land of Nepal was under threat too. As we may remember, the Mahaguru had provided vast benefit to this country during a previous visit, culminating in his awakening at the Asura and Yangleshö caves.[183] Unable to resist the calls for help, the Mahaguru now took up residence at E Vihara in Patan, where he assisted the Newar prince Vasudhara, taught the Dharma, bound evil spirits, and hid *terma* treasures throughout the land, thus ensuring that the Buddhadharma in Nepal would last long into the future.[184]

Meanwhile, King Trisong Detsen was becoming increasingly worried, as the situation in Tibet had not improved. He decided to dispatch a second party of seven, led by Namkhé Nyingpo, with a royal letter and much gold. They met the Mahaguru on the shores of Lake Nyima Kü, more commonly known as Lake Taudaha, not far below the caves of Asura and Yangleshö.[185] The Mahaguru again promised the envoys that he would come to Tibet soon, and sent the party back to Tibet. After another two months had passed, the King sent three more envoys with an invitation and more gold—to ask the Mahaguru yet again to come. The first day of the first month of the summer season had arrived, and auspicious signs began pointing to the journey ahead. The flowers of Nepal all began to bloom, turning their fresh blossoms northwards, towards the land of Tibet. Guru Padmasambhava decided the time had come to continue north, and so he flew through the sky and landed in the area of Mangyul, where he took up residence at Yari Gong, Upper Slate Mountain, awaiting the Tibetan delegation.[186]

The Story of the "Five Brothers" and the Blessings of Arya Vati Zangpo

Long before, when Dharma King Songtsen Gampo was laying the foundations for the Dharma in Tibet, he had developed the strong wish to bring a sacred image of his tutelary deity Avalokiteshvara, to bless the land. As the result of his aspiration, King Songtsen Gampo had received a vision of Avalokiteshvara, who told him that there were five statues buried as treasures within a *hari* sandalwood tree in a forest in Nepal.[187] The King immediately sent an emanation, the noble monk Akaramati, to Nepal, who found, within a great forest, an amazing sandalwood tree, radiating light in all ten directions. Akaramati split the trunk into five pieces, from which five noble brothers burst forth: Arya Vati Zangpo, Arya Akham, Arya Bhukham, Arya Jamali, and Arya Lokeshvara.[188] Thus Avalokiteshvara, the Great Compassionate One, became five distinct objects of veneration, each of which then declared where it wished to reside. Thus, like a garland of jewels, the Self-Arisen Avalokiteshvara Brothers positioned themselves along an ancient trade route that begins in Patan, once a small kingdom in the Kathmandu Valley and now a part of the city of Kathmandu, and continues north through the Kathmandu Valley, tracing the Trisuli River all the way through Mangyul and continuing to Lhasa in Central Tibet.[189]

A century or so later, the Mahaguru was following this same path from the Kathmandu Valley to Lhasa in Central Tibet. Pausing before each of the Self-Arisen Avalokiteshvara Brothers, he recited verses of auspiciousness and performed the consecration ritual, and at the Arya Vati Zangpo of Mangyul he did this not just once, but three times. Thus, these statues are at once actual emanations of Avalokiteshvara and sacred sources of Guru Rinpoche's immense blessings and activity. His enlightened wisdom mingled with these sacred representations, enhancing their potency even further. To this day, it is said that the blessings of Arya Vati Zangpo have been so strongly ingrained in the landscape of Mangyul that anyone who focuses on reciting the six-syllable mantra of Avalokiteshvara in Mangyul will reach the state of Avalokiteshvara in a single lifetime.[190]

When Earth Turns to Gold

When the third Tibetan delegation arrived in Mangyul, Guru Padmamsambhava had already been there for three months, teaching the Dharma, erecting stupas, taming evil spirits, and hiding *terma* treasures throughout the land.[191] They met on a plain, right on the modern-day border of Nepal and Tibet, a region that is still referred to as Serthang (Plain of Gold), for the miracles that took place on that fateful day:

> Upon meeting with the emissaries, the Mahaguru asked, "Who are you and where are you going," although he already well knew who they were.
>
> Mangjé Salnang of Bé replied, "We were sent by the King of Tibet to request the presence of Master Padmasambhava. Are you indeed that Master?"
>
> "Ah! Well, yes indeed, and I was summoned here three months ago by the protectors. While you emissaries have been delayed by doubt and fatigue, here I've been, left waiting. You really did take your time! Now, give me whatever offering you've prepared!"

The party prostrated to the Mahaguru, and each offered him a full measure of gold.

"Now, another offering!"

So the emissaries gave him whatever they had in their pockets.

"Now give me whatever else you have!"

The emissaries were distressed, saying, "But the King gave us nothing else to offer! And we ourselves haven't anything else but that!" All they could do was to offer their body, speech, and mind to the Mahaguru, to prostrate and circumambulate him, and touch the crown of their head to his feet.

This pleased the Master, who said, "I was just checking to see whether or not Tibet has faithful people who could really be transformed and changed. To me, everything that appears is gold!" Then, as the Mahaguru stretched out his arm toward Mangyul Gungthang, all the mountains to the right moved to the left. As he stretched out his left arm to the west, all the earth and stones turned to zi, agate, coral, and gold. Of these, he gave to each of the emissaries a measure.

He then let loose a destructive stare, and the sun and moon both fell to the earth.

"Now you believe!" he said. "Personally, I have no need of gold. Nevertheless, I will accept some so that your ruler may accomplish his aspiration and gain merit in the process."

The Mahaguru took up their gold and tossed it in the air, toward Mangyul and Nepal, declaring, "In the future, Tibet's gold will come from these areas of Mangyul and Nepal, and there'll be plenty of it!"[192]

— Revealed by Nyangral Nyima Özer

Faced with such an overwhelming presence and display, deep faith was born in the Tibetan disciples. They could not help but prostrate to the Mahaguru and express their devotion, and so they proved their worth as recipients of the Dharma. And indeed, as a kind of reminiscence of the Guru's blessings, later, in the 14th century, gold was discovered in the soil of western Mangyul, which only increased its prosperity further.[193]

The Mahaguru led these Tibetans to a cave behind the mountain where the Arya Vati Zangpo temple stands. There, the Mahaguru initiated them into the Vajrayana. These intrepid envoys—Kawa Paltsek, Nanam Dorjé Düdjom, and Chokro Lu'i Gyaltsen—thus became the first Tibetan disciples to receive Vajrayana teachings from the Mahaguru. In remembrance of this momentous occasion, this cave was given the name Ngödrup Phuk (Cave of Siddhis).[194]

Taming the Demons of Tibet

The Mahaguru's arrival could not have come sooner, as Tibet now found itself in the direst of situations. Gods and demons were laying waste not only to Samye monastery, but also to the sacred sites established by earlier generations. The great Jowo Rinpoche statue, brought to Tibet by Queen Wencheng, was under such threat that it had to be removed to this Mangyul borderland until such time as Guru Rinpoche had fully tamed the rampaging spirits.[195]

Thus, while King Trisong Detsen awaited the Mahaguru's arrival with both longing and despair, Guru Rinpoche and his first Tibetan disciples were setting out on their journey to Central Tibet. Even as their journey began, the Mahaguru set to work. He began taming the powerful spirits of the mountains and valleys, who, overwhelmed at his mastery, offered their very life force as a pledge to abandon their harmful ways and instead act only in accordance with the Dharma. The party had only got as far as Palkü Tso (Lake of Glory), just beyond the Gungthang Pass on the outskirts of Mangyul, when yet another troublesome spirit showed up, in all her fury:

> As they descended to northern Namtang (Sky Plain), suddenly Namen Karmo (White Sky Lady), started sending down bolts of lightning. The Mahaguru stretched out his left palm, in which there was mirror-like water, and drew the lightning bolts into the water until they were shrunken and dry, the size of seven peas. The Lady took fright at the sight and fled to Palmo Paltso (Glorious Lake of the Glorious Lady). The Master then made a threatening gesture, and the lake became an inferno. As the lake began to boil, the Lady's flesh began falling from her bones, and again she fled.
>
> The Master then flung his vajra and hit her in the right eye, at which she pleaded, "Successor of the Teacher, Dorjé Tötreng Tsal, please don't make any more obstacles for me, please accept my apologies!" She then offered him the essence of her life-force and was bound

under oath, taking the name Gangkar Shamé Dorjé Chenchikma, (Fleshless One-Eyed Vajra Lady of the White Glaciers).[196] ፨

— Revealed by Nyangral Nyima Özer

This encounter was not the Mahaguru's first with the notorious Tenma goddesses. He had already encountered them while in retreat at the Asura Cave in Nepal. As he would explain to Dharma King Trisong Detsen later on, some spirits need to be subdued more than once, and often three times, before they become completely obedient and willing to dedicate their lives to the service of the Dharma and those who uphold it.[197] Through these multiple encounters, the Tenma goddesses were eventually installed as steadfast guardians of the Vajrakilaya mandala, bound to protect practitioners from all obstacles to the Dharma. The Mahaguru gave Gangkar Shamé the secret name Dorjé Yüdrönma (Turquoise Lamp, Fleshless Vajra Lady).[198] To this day, these twelve goddesses of Mangyul are still invoked for protection, and this particular episode of taming is still celebrated by the people of Mangyul, who travel to the shores of Palkü Tso to pay homage.

So, as Guru Padmasambhva's party proceeded towards the heart of Tibet, the gods and spirits of the land were subdued, one by one. Although many of the spirits tried to defeat the Mahaguru with their elemental powers, or alternatively fled in terror, none would manage to escape. Guru Rinpoche, the Buddha's regent in this Snowy Land, would bind them all and make them swear allegiance to the Dharma. The road ahead still swarmed with a host of such spirits, and the final taming would take place high above Samye, on the summit of Mount Hepori.

The Wisdom Dakini's Journey

Khandro Yeshé Tsogyal and Belbang Kalasiddhi

Meanwhile, a manifestation of Vajravarahi's enlightened qualities had been born into a local family of weavers in Nepal,— a little girl named Dakini. Tragically, when Dakini's mother died in childbirth, mother and child were left together in a nearby cremation ground, completely abandoned. But Lhacham Mandarava, Guru Padmasambhava's disciple and consort, found the child there and could see that she was clearly destined for the practice of Vajrayana. She raised the infant Dakini herself, nourishing and caring for her with a mother's love, and when the time came, she introduced her to Guru Rinpoche. Upon initiation, the girl received the name by which she would gain wide renown: Belbang Kalasiddhi (Kalasiddhi of the Weavers). [199]

Mandarava and Guru Padmasambhava continued on their travels, but Kalasiddhi remained in Nepal. Many years later, Khandro Yeshé Tsogyal—by now the Mahaguru's foremost disciple—arrived in Nepal with six disciples of her own, on a mission to spread the teachings. By seeming happenstance, they encountered Kalasiddhi one day. Yeshé Tsogyal immediately recognized this now full-grown woman as a fellow practitioner and took her under her wing, becoming her guide and teacher.

Eventually, Belbang Kalasiddhi and the other six disciples accompanied Khandro Yeshé Tsogyal to Mangyul, where they remained for a year. During this time Khandro Yeshé Tsogyal gave many teachings, including the sacred practice of Guru Yoga, through which Kalasiddhi and the other disciples all gained deep realization. Then, at the invitation of King Mutri Tsenpo of Tibet, Khandro Yeshé Tsogyal and Belbang Kalasiddhi left Mangyul and traveled to Samyé Monastery, where they were welcomed with great reverence and joy. [200] Many years later, when they returned once more to Mangyul, Khandro Yeshé Tsogyal taught the Dharma, led feast offerings, hid *terma* treasures, and blessed the land. [201]

Later still, Yeshé Tsogyal would offer Kalasiddhi to Guru Padmasambhava as a personal consort, and together the wisdom dakinis would reveal the mandala of the *Lama Gongpa Düpa* (*The Guru's Wisdom Assembly*). Belbang Kalasiddhi assisted the Mahaguru in his activity of concealing *terma* treasures throughout Tibet, and she continued to follow Khandro Yeshé Tsogyal as her lifelong teacher. [202]

The Mahaguru's Legacy

The Discovery of Hidden Valleys

> *I, the Lotus King of Uddiyana, have concealed blessed*
> *treasures in the safe valleys and territories of even the small*
> *regions, in order to tame the landscape. I have appointed path-*
> *finders, gate-keepers, and attendants. For that reason, every*
> *hidden land, every meditation cave, and all the great sacred*
> *places are symbols of my teachings. Leave them undisturbed.*
> *Without hesitation, go seek my blessed meditation*[203] *caves,*
> *like a son inheriting his father's palace...* ༔
>
> — *Revealed by Rikdzin Gödem*

Among its many sacred features, Mangyul encompasses a *beyul* (hidden valley)—foretold in prophecy and blessed by Guru Padmasambhava.[204] *Beyuls* are valleys or areas of land (*yul*) that are hidden (*bé*) not only because of their secluded, largely inaccessible locations, but also because they are guarded by the Mahaguru himself. By concealing their spiritual qualities, Guru Padmasambhava has kept these locales pure and protected from the many ways that humans contaminate sacred space. *Beyuls* are therefore treasure-safes that keep sacred environments hidden for generations until their time ripens, thereby ensuring that their blessings remain alive and vibrant.[205]

In the *Pema Kathang*, the Mahaguru names four *beyuls* in particular, hidden for his future disciples and awaiting their future discovery.[206] One of the greatest revealers of *beyuls* was Rikdzin Gödem (1337–1409), an emanation of one of the Mahaguru's first disciples, Nanam Dorjé Düdjom.[207] Rikdzin Gödem revealed prophetic guides and provided keys for three of the four *beyuls* mentioned in the *Pema Kathang*, and discovered another four[208] besides. By following the guides and keys, the *tertön* opens the *beyul* in order to unlock its spiritual qualities. This involves the treasure-revealer taking a journey to the *beyul's* spiritual center and performing a specific set of rituals on a specific auspicious day. In Mangyul, Rikdzin Gödem discovered and opened *beyul* Kyimolung, (Valley of Happiness).[209]

Rikdzin Gödem spent a significant amount of time in Mangyul and soon formed a close connection with the lord of this realm, Trigyel Chokdrup Dé, King of Gungthang. The King requested that Rikdzin Gödem accept him as a personal disciple, offering him the monastery at Riwo Palbar (Blazing

Mountain)—a sacred mountain where the Mahaguru had hidden treasures in the past, and where the great saint and adept Jetsün Milarepa (1040–1123) had practiced in retreat. In turn, Rikdzin Gödem offered the King the dagger known as the Sisum Düdul Phurpa (Demon Tamer of the Three Worlds), which the Mahaguru had previously used at the Asura Cave in Nepal. Thus he introduced the King to the Vajrayana.[210]

As mentioned above, Rikdzin Gödem opened the hidden valley of Kyimolung, (Valley of Happiness), at the Mangyul border with Nepal. Subsequently, the great *tertön* Tenyi Lingpa (1480–1536), during his time in this Mangyul-Gungthang region, emphasized the importance of further establishing the hidden valley of Kyimolung.[211] The task finally fell to Rikdzin Gödem's own reincarnation, Garwang Dorjé (1640–1685), who went on retreat in Kyimolung, re-opened the sacred valley, and re-discovered from a rock shaped like a lion's face the *Dorsem Tukyi Melong* (*Mirror of the Enlightened Mind of Vajrasattva*)—a teaching on the six yogas, hidden there by Rikdzin Gödem himself.[212] Thus, Mangyul remains a treasure site of great blessings, where the Mahaguru's influence continues into these present generations, providing an ideal refuge where the Dharma still flourishes amidst the Himalayan peaks—a gateway to the land of Tibet.

SHONGPA LHACHU

Arriving at the Tolung Valley, you conjured the Shongpé Lhachu Spring,
And on the riverbank at Zurkar you first met with the Dharma King.
His retinue was with him and, when he failed to bow,
You sang vajra verses and displayed wondrous miracles,
Inspiring great faith in his mind. Homage to you![213]

— *Jamyang Khyentsé Wangpo*

Introduction

Guru Padmasambhava continued over hill and dale, from the borderlands of Mangyul toward the heartland of Tibet, taming all manner of haughty spirits along the way. Finally, the Mahaguru reached the Tolung valley, just outside the city of Lhasa, in Central Tibet. Getting wind that his new guest had arrived, King Trisong Detsen sent a welcome party to greet the Mahaguru and guide him back to the palace in Drakmar. Thus, it was here in Tolung that the King's envoys met the Mahaguru—and found themselves without water to serve their guest tea. Guru Rinpoche thereupon plunged his staff into the earth and water came shooting forth, giving the place its name, Shongpa Lhachu (Divine Spring). This was yet another sign that the Tibetans had welcomed no ordinary visitor into their kingdom; it was a harbinger of the many miracles to come.

Approaching the Sacred Site

The Divine Spring of Shongpa is today a clear pool of water set in a sanctuary of willows in the Tolung Valley of Central Tibet. When Kathok Situ Chökyi Gyatso visited in the early 20th century, he noted the many fish filling this sacred pool—as they do today—and seeming to survive through the cold winters without even needing to hibernate. These divine waters, the result of Guru Rinpoche's miracle for the King's welcome party, still serve the nearby villages and are hailed as purifying illness and waashing away sin.

The nearby monastery of Kyimolung was founded in recognition of the site's amazing qualities and, at the time of Kathok Situ Chökyi Gyatso's visit, there was a four-pillar temple to Guru Padmamsambhava's eight manifestations, immediately north of the spring. Statues of these eight unique forms were housed in this temple, along with Guru Padma's staff, the most revered treasure object of all. Although this temple was destroyed in the mid-20th century, it was rebuilt and the spring restored in the 1980s, so that its waters again flow unhindered.

The *Kathang Denga* says this, of these amazing waters:

> While there are many kinds of water that flow in this world, those that have been blessed by the practice of Padmasambhava, and particularly these Divine Waters, have special qualities. Whoever washes with them, or drinks from them—their evils and obscurations will be purified, they will gain an altruistic and meritorious mindset, their heart's wishes will be fulfilled, and they will gain all the enjoyments desired by worldly people too.[214] ༈

— *Revealed by Orgyen Lingpa*

Today there are a number of caves in the Tolung valley that are associated with Guru Padmasambhava, including the Nechen Drubpuk (Sacred Site Practice Cave), located above Zangmo village in Yabda, and the Shelkar Drupuk (White Crystal Practice Cave) on Shunkyi Drak Mountain. According to one scholar, these may have been sites where the Mahaguru practiced and tamed local spirits, as he did in Yari Gong[215] and Kaladrak, as mentioned in the stories of the Tolung Valley that we will read below.[216]

The Mahaguru's Journey

A Royal Procession

Guru Padmasambhava and his party were fast approaching Central Tibet. In accordance with ancient royal custom, Dharma King Trisong Detsen sent out a grand welcoming party to meet them, twenty-one envoys in all. They met in the Trambu forest of Tolung Valley, and the envoys carried this message from the King:[217]

> The time has come to gather, in Tolung's Trambu Forest. ༈
> Powerful and triumphant, great King that I am, ༈
> I have sent many envoys; I alone have not come."[218] ༈

The time for their meeting was approaching, but there was still more work to be done. The Mahaguru spent the next several months in Tolung, binding local spirits and entrusting them with *terma* treasures:

> For a winter and a month, the Guru stayed on Mount Kaladrak, ༈
> Binding the *tsen* spirits and entrusting them with treasure. ༈
> Next, the Guru stayed at the Kyangbu forest in Zulpuk, ༈
> Taming planetary demons and *damsi* spirits, ༈

Entrusting them with treasure. §
Then, in the springtime, the Guru stayed in Yari Gong, §
Taming the *gongpo* of Jarong and the *damsi* of Sosha.[219] §

King Trisong Detsen was becoming increasingly worried. His plans to bring the Mahaguru to Drakmar and establish Samye Monastery were by now massively delayed, for reasons he did not understand. So the King decided it was time to call in his army. From his encampment on the banks of the Tsangpo River, he dispatched his esteemed royal minister Lhasang Lupel, along with five-hundred iron-clad horsemen, to find out what was happening in Tolung. They arrived, but soon an obstacle arose:

> After finally meeting at the bottom of the Tolung Basin, §
> They were unable to find water to make the ceremonial tea. §
> So Padmasambhava, Uddiyana the Great, §
> Set his staff into the depths of a Tolung well, saying: §
> "There you are, Lhasang! Water is now flowing. Gather it in a basin!" §
> Thus it gained the name Divine Waters of the Basin.[220] §
>
> — *Revealed by Orgyen Lingpa*

Lhasang, the King's high minister, had been rendered powerless for want of one simple, yet crucial element: water. This situation posed no difficulty to the Mahaguru, however. In full view of the King's massive army, Guru Padmasambhava performed a miracle that brought forth healing waters, while establishing the minister firmly in his service. Meanwhile, the Tibetans could now properly welcome this visitor to their kingdom, and take him to meet their King.

The Mahaguru's Legacy

Jamyang Khyentse Wangpo's Vajra Song

When Jamyang Khyentsé Wangpo arrived on pilgrimage at this Divine Spring of Tolung, he made one hundred feast-offerings to Guru Padmasambahva. As he prayed fervently to the Mahaguru, the following vajra song arose within the space of his awareness:

> *Aho! You who perform the activity of all buddhas*
> *Of the past, the present, and the future,*
> *Protecting the land of Tibet and all its inhabitants—*
> *Lord Padmasambhava, you of kindness beyond measure,*
> *Please watch over us with compassion. To you, I pray!*[221]

ZURKHAR DO

At Drakmar's Tamarisk Grove, the King came forth to greet me. ⸘
Although he was emperor, Manjushri's emanation, ⸘
The veil of his human birth was dense in the extreme, ⸘
And so he failed to see my qualities in full. ⸘
High and mighty, full of pride, the King's attitude was offensive. ⸘
I sang a song then of my greatness and displayed my magic. ⸘
The emperor's faith was kindled; he bowed down low ⸘
And presented a throne of gold and gifts in great abundance. ⸘
All Tibet's gods and humans then came to pay their respects.[222] ⸘

— Revealed by Chokgyur Dechen Lingpa

Introduction

After repeated invitations and many months of waiting, King Trisong Det-sen finally met Guru Padmasambahva for the first time here at Zurkhar Do (*Confluence of the Twin Castle*). However, when the Tibetan King approached the Mahaguru, it was with a royal air of haughtiness, and the exchange that followed indicates a crucial moment of taming—where the teacher humbles his student's pride and so prepares the field of his mind for the planting of potent seeds of Dharma. To atone for his initial lack of respect, Dharma King Trisong Detsen commissioned five stupas to be built at Zurkhar—the Riknga Chorten (Stupas of the Five Families), symbolizing the transformation of the five negative emotions into the five wisdom buddha families.[223] Later, these stupas would hold treasures hidden by Guru Rinpoche himself. Just to the west of where Samye's foundations were laid, the stupas remain as a landmark for this historic encounter between Padmsambhava and Trisong Detsen, the Tantric Master and the Dharma King.[224]

Approaching the Sacred Site

Zurkhar Do lies at the foot of a valley running parallel and west of Samye, on the banks of the mighty Tsangpo River, in Drakmar. This prime location has made it a traditional landing and launch point for ferries across these waters. Long ago, however, even before Samye's foundations were complete, this was the site of a royal palace, the Twin Castle. Today, there are five white stupas, the Riknga Chorten, rising high above the river's edge, on a dry, rocky rise. Just to the east, between Zurkhar Do and Samye monastery, in what is now a

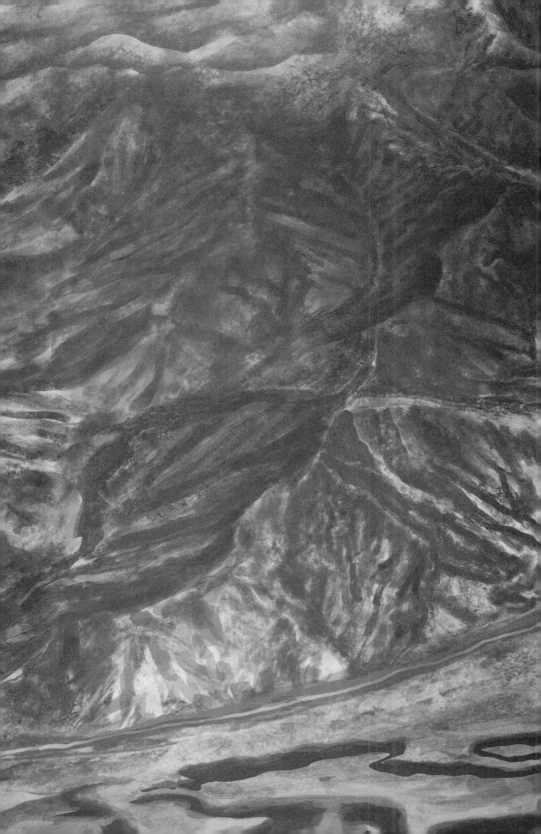

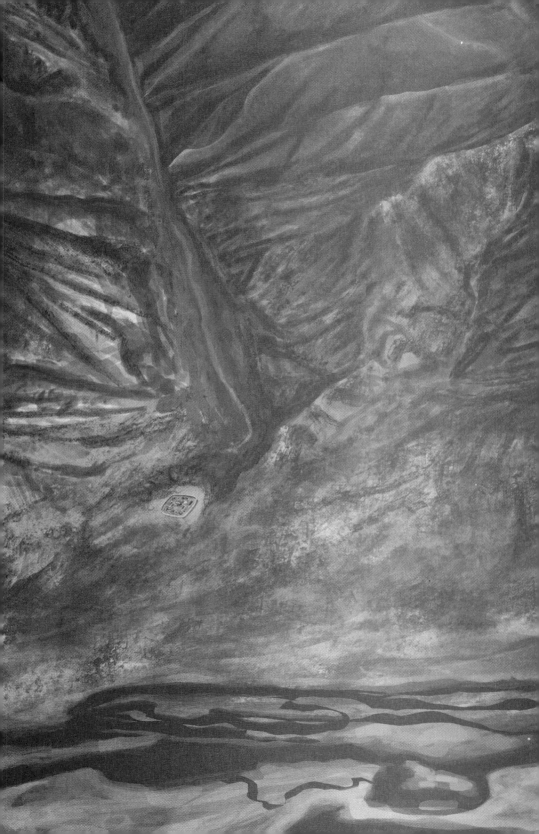

willow grove, there once stood a beautiful peach and walnut forest—an area once known as Önpuk Drakmar (the Tamarisk Grove of Drakmar). This once verdant landscape, the very heart of the Tibetan empire, hosted the King and his court, as they awaited the arrival of the Mahaguru into their midst.

The Mahaguru's Journey

A Grand Royal Reception

As the grand welcome party approached from Tolung, Dharma King Trisong Detsen looked out from his residence at the Twin Castle, surrounded by his dearest queens and most trusted ministers, all assembled amid music bright and loud to receive the Great Master of Uddiyana.[225]

> The King of Tibet stood tall, surrounded by his men, ᠅
> Quivering and bright like a brood of pigeons. ᠅
> Both queens, too, were surrounded by their ladies, ᠅
> Quivering and iridescent, like a silken tent, ᠅
> And all to sound of drums, songs, and dances of welcome.[226] ᠅

> — *Revealed by Orgyen Lingpa*

The emotions coursing through King Trisong Detsen might have been a mix of nervousness and excitement as he waited to receive Guru Padmasmabhava under the cool shade of the tamarisks, his retinue crowded about in their finest attire. The Mahaguru came into view and approached, as the many attendants looked on. The time had come for their meeting, but who would pay their respects to whom? The Mahaguru stood tall, knowing it would be inappropriate for a representative of the Buddha to bow before the mundane authority of the King, while King Trisong Detsen stood in rumination, reflecting on his status as overlord of the land, in the expectation that Guru Rinpoche should bow down before him just as Shantarakshita had done.

So the two stood there, eye to eye, neither offering obeisance to the other. Then suddenly, to the surprise of the King and everyone else, Guru Rinpoche broke into song, a display of his true character and greatness, and a rebuke of the King's pride:

> I shall sing a song of the greatness and might of this Master, ᠅
> For while buddhas of past, present, and future come from the womb, ᠅
> And gather the two accumulations for three countless eons, ᠅
> I am Padmasambhava, the Buddha Lotus-Born, ᠅

I hold pith instructions on the view that over-arches all, ⁝
I've trained in the teachings of the sutras and tantras, ⁝
And can explain all the vehicles completely, unmixed. ⁝
I am Padmsambhava, the Sacred Dharma Lotus-Born, ⁝
I hold pith instructions on the conduct that undergirds all. ⁝
Externally I possess the ways of a saffron-robed monk, ⁝
While internally, unsurpassed, I practice the yoga of Secret Mantra. ⁝
I am Padmsambhava, the Sangha Lotus-Born. ⁝

The Mahaguru continued with his song, singing of his mastery of all knowledge and all things both spiritual and mundane, and finally addressed the King:

You now, you are King of Tibet, a land uncivilized, ⁝
A King in a land of non-virtue... ⁝
Your chest is swollen with royal pride, ⁝
Your belly smug with grand dominion; ⁝
You stand so high and mighty, ⁝
Drunk in your machismo, scepter in hand. ⁝
I will not prostrate to you, King! ⁝
And yet, our connection made through past aspirations ⁝
Has brought me here to the heart of Tibet. ⁝
O Great King, have I not come?[227] ⁝

— *Revealed by Orgyen Lingpa*

The King and his retinue were shocked and affronted at this disrespectful response. Guru Rinpoche then made a slight hand gesture, unleashing flames from his fingers and burning the King's fine clothes to a crisp. Unable to take any more, every single one of them—King, queens, ministers, and retinue—fell to the ground, prostrating before the Mahaguru, and King Trisong Detsen immediately offered his apologies:

Now, with shame and regret I offer prostrations, homage, and respect! ⁝
I did not treat you as you should be treated, as one to be revered. ⁝
Cleanse my veils of evil, wrought by what I have done! ⁝

The Master then commanded:

Emperor, listen now to what comes from the lips of this Master: ⁝
In order to repair your broken samaya with awakened form, ⁝
Build five wondrous stupas of stone, and thus be cleansed![228] ⁝

As instructed, the King ordered five stupas to be built at Zurkhar Do, symbolizing the transformation of the five negative emotions.[229] The stupas were carved out of the rock, painted white, and each adorned with a lotus. Upon their completion, Guru Padmasambhava hid sacred *terma* treasures within.

Soon after their meeting, the King then guided the Mahaguru up to his residence, the palace of Drakmar. The Mahaguru performed a consecration of the Drinzang temple there, inviting all the statues to join them in a great feast that he had arranged in front of the temple. Miraculously, that night all the statues left the temple and, even after returning to their former places, continued feasting until the following morning. The butter lamps and incense had lit themselves and music was heard resounding everywhere.[230] Such was the beginning of this auspicious relationship between the King and the Guru.

Among King Trisong Detsen's retinue at this time was the young queen, Khandro Yeshé Tsogyal. The moment she laid eyes on the Mahaguru, as he was being welcomed by the royal party, deep faith and devotion arose within her heart. She knew that her karmic connection was ripening; she had met her root teacher. So with great joy she joined in all the welcome ceremonies, knowing that the Mahaguru's arrival healded a new era for Tibet, a golden age for spiritual seekers like her. Thus, when the Mahaguru retired to the Samye Chimpu caves, Yeshé Tsogyal eagerly awaited an opportunity to approach him and request Dharma teachings.

The Mahaguru's Legacy

Gyalwa Longchenpa's Transmission of the Nyingtik Teachings

> The graveyard of Zahor will be placed in the region of Ü. ჻
> A dog will bring forth a skull from under a stupa. ჻
> This treasure, hidden in Samye Chimpu, ჻
> Will come with this sign that it must be revealed. ჻
> Thus the treasure revealer Drimé Öser shall be born.[231] ჻
>
> — *Revealed by Orgyen Lingpa*

Longchen Rabjam Drimé Özer (1308–1364) appeared in Tibet as yet another buddha, an omniscient master of the Dzokchen teachings of the Great Perfection. Gyalwa Longchenpa, as he is known, thus ranks among the most significant figures of the Nyingma tradition, just after Guru Padmasambhava himself.[232] His profound realization as a yogi traversing the path to enlightenment, coupled with his prolific scholarly gifts, was encapsulated in a large collection of writings still treasured throughout the world today. Longchenpa is most widely known for elucidating the Dzokchen teachings of Padmasambhava (*The Khandro Nyingtik*) and Vimalamitra (*The Vima Nyingtik*), and for combining the two by adding his own revelations and commentaries into a compendium of teachings known as the *Nyingtik Yapzhi* (*The Fourfold Heart Essence*).[233] In particular, after having practiced the *Nyingtik* teachings at Samye Chimpu,[234] Longchenpa stayed near the stupas of Zurkhar, and there taught the priceless *Khandro Nyingtik* teachings to his disciples for the very first time.[235]

Orgyen Lingpa's Revelations

Orgyen Lingpa (b. 1323), the great revealer of the *Pema Kathang*, was himself an emanation of Dharma King Trisong Detsen. While his treasure revelations were vast in scope and beyond imagining, and filled a hundred volumes, only a few of these precious works are still accessible to us today. One of these was revealed from the stupas of Zurkhar—a practice cycle focused upon Avalokiteshvara entitled *Mahakarunika: Supreme Light of Wisdom*. Another was *The Glorious Protector: Tiger Rider*.[236]

Jamyang Khyentse Wangpo's Vajra Song

When Jamyang Khyentse Wangpo visited this sacred site on pilgrimage, he offered one hundred feasts to the Mahaguru, and, as a result of his fervent prayers, spontaneously composed the following vajra song:

> *Aho! Universal Lord of the Four Kayas,*
> *Always you reside in the bindu at my heart's center.*
> *Great Guru, to you I prostrate; devotion fills my body, speech and mind.*
> *To you I offer this song of experience and realization!*[237]

MOUNT HEPORI

On Palmothang's glorious plain ⁝
You gave the twelve tenma goddesses their binding oath; ⁝
High on the Khala pass of Central Tibet ⁝
You bound the white snow goddess Gangkar Shamé; ⁝
In the Damshö marshlands beneath Mount Lhabüi Nying ⁝
You swore Thangla Yarshu to a solemn vow; ⁝
And high up on the peak of Mount Hépori ⁝
You placed all the devas and rakshasas under oath. ⁝
Then, of all these mighty gods and demons, ⁝
Some offered the very essence of their life force, ⁝
Some became guardians of the teachings, ⁝
And some took the pledge to be your servants.[238] ⁝

— *Revealed by Chokgyur Dechen Lingpa*

Introduction

From his vantage point atop Mount Hepori, Guru Padmasambhava enacted a grand subjugation of the evil forces that were preventing the construction of Samye Monastery, King Trisong Detsen's most cherished aspiration. The Mahaguru offered the cleansing smoke of *sang* and then flew high into the sky, where he performed a vajra dance of taming, thereby overpowering the troublesome spirits of the region and making them swear allegiance to the Dharma. It was through this amazing feat at Hepori that the path to building Samye was cleared. The demons of Tibet were now protectors, helping to transform the Land of Snows into a haven for the Dharma.

Approaching the Sacred Site

Located in the Drakmar Valley, Mount Hepori rises above the mandala of Samye Monastery, close to its southeast. This boulder-strewn ridge, dry and sandy, sits in contrast to the lush green fields and trees that surround the monastery itself, and the peak provides a marvellous view of the entire Samye mandala. There had long been a tradition of making smoke offerings on Hepori, and the Mahaguru adopted this ritual even as he was being welcomed by King and retinue, transforming it into a Dharma practice of cleansing, offering, and taming. To commemorate this occasion, a protector shrine was built and at one time adorned the top of the mountain, along with stupas containing relics of Abbot

Shantarakshita, the disciples Kawa Peltsek, Yeshé Dé, Chokro Lu'i Gyaltsen, and the mother of the great translator Vairocana. All these stupas were positioned in the cardinal directions along the slopes of Hepori. A shrine for cleansing smoke offerings (*sang*) has now been re-built, so that today's practitioners can continue to connect to the blessings which imbue this sacred mountain.[239]

The Mahaguru's Journey

The King's Plea

Once the festivities hosted by Tibet's Dharma King Trisong Detsen had concluded in their miraculous display, the Mahaguru of Uddiyana retired to the Chimpu caves, above the site where the monastery was to be built—the echoes of this momentous welcome still ringing throughout the land.[240] With the first day of the autumn moon, however, the time for Guru Padmasambhava's activity had come. The King invited the Mahaguru down to the palace and invited him to take a seat upon a throne of gold. At his side was the Abbot Shantarakshita, and both were offered food and drink, along with myriad gifts to please the senses. After offering these and many more, King Trisong Detsen spoke:

> Myself, I am chief of the virtueless, lord of the red-faced ones, ༔
> And the Tibetan people are coarse, hardened by affliction. ༔
> Tame us, so hard to tame, and establish a support for Dharma! ༔
> Incarnate Buddha, please bless this ground! ༔

Guru Padmasambhava, delighted at the King's request, replied:

> O Great Ruler, protector of the Tibetan realm, ༔
> Your barbarous kingdom is a land of demons, ༔
> And on my way here I tamed many terrible spirits. ༔
> Yet now, to tame Tibetans, worse even than monkeys, ༔
> The King constructs a temple. How amazing![241] ༔
>
> — *Revealed by Orgyen Lingpa*

Subduing Negative Forces

To realize this project, the Mahaguru instructed the King to build a nine-storey temple upon the heart of the Demoness of Lowo, a wild local spirit who lay giant andsupine across the Tibetan landscape. A stupa would also have to be built upon her navel, a black mound upon her head, and one hundred and eight stupas upon all four of her limbs. This would all add to what had already been erected five generations earlier, during the reign of King Songtsen Gampo, to suppress this endemic force of hindrance.

Another principal source of obstruction, as Guru Rinpoche explained, was the naga king Manasvi, who wielded great power over Tibet. In an instant, the Mahaguru covered the distance to Manasvi's residence, a lake in the valley of Maldro, and there performed a ritual of confession to mend vows and place a naga treasure within a shrine.[242] Thus the nagas became oath-bound, their troublesome ways supressed, at least for a time.

Finally, Guru Padmasambhava climbed Mount Hepori and set out offerings of food and drink at the top. On the mountain's four ridges he placed four treasures, and on its four slopes he lit four purifying fires. Where the mountain was shaped like the head of a turtle, he placed an image of Hayagriva, and then proclaimed:

> *Hung*! Listen! ?
> Listen, spirits and demons, to the words of Padmasambhava! ?
> My awakened form, this emanation, ?
> Is unmatched throughout the world. ?
> I am Tsokyé Dorjé, Lake-Born Vajra, never tainted by birth. ?
> Nothing can harm my body, for I have realized deathlessness! ?
>
> The samsaric suffering of beings in the six classes is frightening— ?
> Their lives are short, these barbarous beings, and their distractions great. ?
> The construction of a temple by Trisong Detsen ?
> Is like the raising of a victory banner, topped by a jewel. ?
>
> Once the Buddha's teachings are established in Tibet, ?
> Your displeasure will make no difference, you spirits and demons! ?
> This, the invitation of the Great Pandita of India, ?
> Is like a lamp held aloft in the midst of darkness. ?
>
> Once the holy Dharma suffuses Tibet with happiness, ?
> Your leaving will make no difference, all you spirits and demons! ?
> Enjoy these gifts, therefore, grant permission for this land, ?
> And fulfil the aspirations of King Trisong Detsen! ?
> Build the temple, spirits and demons! Assemble for the work! ?
> Do not transgress the command of Padmasambhava, ?
> Wielder of mantras![243] ?
>
> — *Revealed by Orgyen Lingpa*

With these powerful words, the Mahaguru then flew into the air and performed a wrathful vajra dance, uttering his fierce refrain to the spirits and demons of Tibet. In response, stones and earth from the surrounding hills and valleys began rolling down to the site at Samye. The once-terrible forces of nature had accepted the Mahaguru's command, and were now in the service of the King. Together, they would accomplish the building of Samye Monastery.

Thus it was at Mount Hepori, above Samye, that Guru Rinpoche subjugated the negative forces that were impeding the initial construction of the monastery, and it was from here that he performed the consecration of the temple site. Later, he arranged for a small *sang* and protector temple to be built on the mountain top, in order to keep the local spirits appeased. Guru Rinpoche thus started the tradition of always making a *sang* offering before beginning any great task—such as building a temple, consecrating a shrine, or performing a *drupchen*.[244] The main purpose of offering *sang* is to remove all obstacles and thus secure success in the undertaking. The *sang* practice that Guru Rinpoche performed on the peak of Hepori was later inscribed on the original walls that surrounded Samye Monastery, and can still be practiced today.[245]

The Mahaguru's Legacy

The Nanam Lineage of Vajrakilaya

> *Emaho! Sovereign and 'sole deity'*
> *of the Land of Snows was Lord Trisong Detsen.*
> *You were his Dharma minister, born into the Nanam clan,*
> *always loved by Orgyen Padma, throughout your many lives—*
> *master of mantras, Dorjé Dudjom, to you we pray!*[246]
>
> — Tertön Drimé Ösel Lingpa

In a previous age, in Nepal the Tibetan minister Nanam Dorjé Düdjom had been the fourth brother, younger than the trio who became the Great Abbot, Dharma King, and Mahaguru. All four brothers had made aspirations in front of the Great Jarung Kashor Stupa. At that time, the youngest also planted potent karmic seeds—to be reborn as a powerful minister who would facilitate the reunion of his brothers in the future. Thus, when these seeds ripened, he took birth in the 8th century within the Nanam clan. His parents named him Dorjé Dudjöm and his destiny carried him into the presence of Dharma King Trisong Detsen, as a young servant of the royal court. Showing great skill in both religious and worldly matters, he soon became one of the King's most trusted advisors.

Nanam Dorjé Düdjom was renowned for accomplishing every task that he was set, and so it was that the Dharma King eventually entrusted him with the task of leading a party to invite the Mahaguru to Tibet. They were successful and, in Mangyul, Dorjé Düdjom became one of Guru Rinpoche's first Tibetan disciples. At the behest of his guru, he initially practiced *Jikten Chötö*, associated with the taming of worldly spirits, and then focused on the mandala of Vajrakilaya. Through following these instructions, Dorjé Düdjom eventually became an extremely accomplished yogi. He was known to display miraculous abilities such as moving freely through solid rock and flying like wind through the sky.

One day, while he was practicing Vajrakilaya on Mount Hepori, he left a clear indent with his *kila* dagger in the rock wall outside his hermitage, a mark that can still be seen. Later, along with King Trisong Detsen and Khandro Yeshe Tsogyal, Dorjé Düdjom was one of the three disciples entrusted by the Mahaguru with the Vajrakilaya teachings, such was their accomplishment of this practice. The teachings that were especially entrusted to Dorjé Düdjom became known as the *Nanam Lineage of Vajrakilaya*, a tradition that is still alive today, in the revelatory activities of Tertön Sogyal Lerap Lingpa (1856–1926).[247]

Revelation of Takyung Barwa

> *To Orgyen Dorjé Chang, you who embody all the conquerors,*
> *You who appear so wild and wrathful*
> *to all recalcitrant opponents—*
> *To you and all the deities in the Wrathful*
> *Guru Takhyung mandala,*
> *I pray: Bestow the fruition of liberation!*[248]
>
> — Namkha Tsewang Chokdrup

In the year 1795, when Rikdzin Jikmé Lingpa climbed upon the peak of Mount Hepori to offer the cleansing smoke of *sang*, he received a stunning vision. This event would eventually lead to the revelation of *Lama Drakpo Takhyung Barwa* (*Blazing Wrathful Guru, Hayagriva and Garuda*), a practice of the Mahaguru in his wrathful form, especially powerful for subjugating negative forces and overcoming diseases. Jikmé Lingpa shares his astonishing story in a letter to Derge's Queen Tsewang Lhamo (d. 1812):

> The government had asked me to perform a smoke offering (*sang*) at Mount Hepori. As I did the practice, I had a vision that many beings of the eight classes of spirits were convening. In particular, Dorjé Lekpa appeared in the form of a monk and offered me a kila dagger that emitted sparks of fire. He said that this kila dagger was the one used by the great master Padmasambhava to tame the naga at Maldro. Later, in the afternoon, the monk Gedön and I visited the site where the stone statue of the Buddha was unearthed.[249] He asked me many questions about meditation, which caused my mind to lose all sense of reference. In that state, I came across a boulder under which there grew a tuft of grass. I lifted it to reveal some charcoal and piled up stones. In the midst of the pile was this kila, firmly stuck. I was absolutely sure, without any doubt, that it was made of a kind of bronze alloy no different from the very fine *zikhyim*[250] that contains meteoric iron, with the nature of the eight classes of spirits.[251]

In the winter of that same year, Jikmé Lingpa fell seriously ill and his life was in great danger. It was at that point that he had a vision of the Mahaguru:

> Just as the Great Master Padmasambhava had prophesied, I had fallen sick and there were dangers to my life. I had an intense feeling that a damsi spirit clothed in rags was cutting my waist with a sword. Unable to take my eyes off the form of the great master Padmasambhava, my mind was filled with great devotion. Then, through the blessings of Padmasambhava, the damsi spirit became embarrassed and full of regret and asked for forgiveness. Padmasambhava then imparted to me the following spiritual instruction...[252] ༔

The instruction imparted to him by the Mahaguru was none other than *Blazing Wrathful Guru, Hayagriva and Garuda*. Through its practice, Jikmé Lingpa was able to overcome all obstacles and swiftly regain his full health and strength. To this day, the practice is treasured as a powerful method for overcoming demons and disease, and it all began with the offering of *sang*, and with profound visions upon the peak of Mount Hepori.

THE SACRED DHARMA
TAKES ROOT IN TIBET
Samye Monastery

On the tenth day of the Rat month, you tamed Tibet's gods and spirits.
You built Samye to perfection, lit the flame of the sacred Dharma,
And ripened and liberated your fortunate disciples—the King and subjects.
Padmasambhava, to you we pray:
Grant your blessing, that idle chatter, harsh words, lies and slander,
Impairments of the shravaka's vinaya discipline and of the bodhisattva precepts,
All breakages of samaya vows, wrongdoing and downfalls—
That all may be healed, and our whole being transformed and purified.[253]

— *Jamgön Kongtrul Lodrö Thayé*

With his heroic taming of Tibet's malicious gods and spirits, Guru Padma-sambhava had now cleared the spiritual ground for the firm foundations of the sacred Dharma to be laid in the Land of Snow. The goal was clear: to establish a grand monastery dedicated to the way of Buddha Shakyamuni, where the sacred Dharma would be taught and the tradition of the monastic Sangha faithfully upheld. By the blessings of the Mahaguru, the construction of Samye monastery with its surrounding temples, sanctuaries, and stupas thus began with rapid speed. The heart-wish of Dharma King Trisong Detsen was finally being fulfilled. Establishing such a sanctuary, as sacred as it would be, was not enough, however. The teachings of the Buddha were at this point only accessible through the instructions of Guru Padmasambhava and Abbot Shantarakshita; the scriptures themselves remained in foreign tongue. Translation into the Tibetan language was still of primary importance, for only then would the full scope of the Dharma be made available to the Tibetan people and permeate the culture for the benefit of future generations. Thus, the brightest and most promising youths were assembled, trained, and sent to Greater India, to bring back not only precious scriptures, but also siddhas and panditas in order to deepen their understanding of the Buddha's words. The Snowy Land of Tibet was awakening to the Dharma and, although many obstacles and challenges had to be overcome and mastered, the Tibetans persisted. They pursued this virtuous path and eventually rose victorious to establish the Buddha's teachings on a truly vast scale. So vast a scale, in fact, that we are still reaping the fruits today—a path of practice that leads us, too, to realize the wisdom, love, and dignity of Guru Padmsambhava, the Second Buddha of our age.

SAMYE MONASTERY

When you planted the teachings of the sublime Dharma,
As if hoisting a victory banner,
Samye was completed spontaneously, no need to be built,
And the entire vision of the King was fulfilled.
Then, you bore the names of three supreme beings—
One was Padmakara, 'Lotus-Born',
One was Padmasambhava,
And one was Tsokyé Dorjé, 'Lake-born Vajra'.
O Dorjé Drakpo Tsal, we invoke you now by your secret name!
With your compassion, inspire us with your blessing!
With your love, guide us and others along the path!
With your realization, grant us siddhis!
With your power, dispel the obstacles facing us all!
Outer obstacles – dispel them externally!
Inner obstacles – dispel them internally!
Secret obstacles – dispel them into space!
In devotion, I pay homage and take refuge in you![254]

— *Revealed by Chokgyur Dechen Lingpa*

Introduction

Dharma King Trisong Detsen's greatest aspiration was to found the monastic institute known as Samye (The Inconceivable). Hailed by those who followed as the "unchanging, spontaneously accomplished temple," Samye's importance to the history of Tibet cannot be overstated, for here the Tibetan Buddhadharma was established, tested, defended, and upheld for well over a millennium.[255] The story of its founding is the story of the introduction of the Dharma to Tibet, which was met with bitter contention not only by native demons and spirits, but also by ministers and minor royalty who feared their ancestral traditions would be overshadowed by the coming of the Buddha's teachings. The coming of Guru Padmasambhava was thus vital to this story of transformation, for through the force of his fiercely compassionate wisdom he could tame the obstructors, such that they could remain as forces for good. With these ancient and elemental powers brought under the sway of the Buddha's teachings, Tibetans—both human and non-human—quickly fulfilled the King's aspiration. Only then could the work of Shantarakshita, that great Abbot of Zahor, truly begin: the first Tibetans were ordained into his flawless monastic lineage, and youngsters were trained in translation and dispatched to India—their mission, to bring back masters of the Dharma to complete the project of translating the Buddha's words into their native tongue. In this way, the transmission of realization handed down from Shakyamuni Buddha, through Padmasambhava, was able to flow into these disciples, whose efforts would set the stage for a cultural transformation that still shapes the world today.

Approaching the Sacred Site

Samye was established in the mid-eighth century above the northern shores of the Tsangpo River, in the Drakmar Valley, ancestral home of King Trisong Detsen. The complex itself was modeled after the Indian monastery of Uddandapura, and as such, it was laid out as a mandala, or world-system, conforming to the principles of sacred Buddhist cosmology.[256] At its center was Samye's main temple, the Ütsé (Central Peak), a symbol for Mount Meru, the navel around which the universe revolves. For the construction of this grand mandala, King Trisong Detsen assembled the very best artisans of Nepal, China, and Tibet, inviting them to work together. And so it was, that the original central temple featured a top storey in the Indian style, a middle storey in the Chinese style, and a foundational storey in the Tibetan style.[257] Thus the full name for the main temple was, in fact, the Ütsé Riksum (Central Peak of Three Styles).

In the four cardinal directions were temples representing the four continents. The eastern temple was that of Noble Manjushri, and the southern, western, and northern temples were dedicated to Aryapalo (Hayagriva), Maitreya, and Avalokiteshvara, respectively. These were surrounded by eight temples for the eight subcontinents, and various buildings dedicated to the awakened forms of the Buddha and the Dharma protectors. There were other buildings too, for the use of translators and visitors from other lands. Four Varjakilaya stupas were built, as well as further stupas—white to the southeast, red to the southwest, black to the northwest, and blue to the northeast— each unique in style, and with an additional fifth stupa to pacify mischief-making spirits. Surrounding all of this was a wall adorned with 1,008 stupas, representing the iron mountains that ring this world-system, and on four stone columns, standing guard over this magnificent mandala, were four copper dogs.[258]

Samye thus became the center of the Dharma's spread in Tibet, and a site of great treasure and revelation. Here is where, for instance, the great Orgyen Lingpa revealed a companion treasure volume to the *Pema Kathang*—the

Kathang Dé Nga (Five-Part Chronicles), a text which elaborates on various episodes and key figures in Guru Padmasambhava's life.[259] With the passing of the centuries, the temples themselves have undergone many waves of reconstruction, most recently by Kyapjé Dilgo Khyentsé Rinpoche in the 1980s, but the complex itself still retains the character of a grand mandala just as prescribed by the Abbot and Mahaguru, and thus still beats as the very heart of the Dharma universe that is Tibet.

The Mahaguru's Journey

Establishing the Support for Enlightened Body

> *When you travelled north to help the King,* §
> *You bound all the harmful forces of Tibet under oath.* §
> *In consecrating Samyé, you fulfilled the vision of the King,* §
> *Filling every corner of Tibet with the Dharma.* §
> *To the nirmanakaya Padmakara, we pray!* §
> *To the Lotus-Born Guru of Orgyen, we pray!*[260] §

> — *Revealed by Tulku Zangpo Drakpa*

Building Samye Monastery

Since Guru Rinpoche had by this time brought Tibet's gods and demons under his command, the spirits, rather than presenting further obstacles, joined in the construction work instead, continuing at night what the humans built by day.

> Sixty thousand workers prepared the clay bricks §
> And, once courses were laid and the work got harder, §
> The ministers called on the spirits and demons to take up the task. §
> Thus, Brahma and Indra became bricklayers, too, §
> And the Four Great Kings became supervisors. §
> All the spirits and demons, male and female, §
> Chattered together as they laid the bricks. §
> Compared to what flesh-bound humans built by day, §
> The spirits and demons—all eight classes— built even more by
>   night.[261] §

> — *Revealed by Orgyen Lingpa*

With all of this construction taking place, materials were soon in short supply. Accordingly, the royal naga prince Manasvi of Maldro arrived before the King in a vision and made him an offer: he would provide them all the resources they needed to complete their temple, but the King would have to interrupt the Mahaguru's meditation. The Mahaguru had by this time retired to the caves of Samye Chimpu to subdue the remaining untamed nagas of the land. The Dharma King made his way up to his teacher's residence, where he met a great garuda bird with a serpent in its beak. At his proclamation, "Relax your meditation, I've attained a siddhi!" the garuda instantly transformed into Padmasambhava, the serpent escaped, and just as quickly came the reply, "What kind of siddhi is that?" "All I can see is wood!"

The Mahaguru then chastised the King, who did not yet fully understand the extent of the Guru's abilities. He explained that it was still dangerous to bend to the ways of the untamed nagas, and merely for resources at that. Rather, they should form an alliance. So Guru Padmasambhava led the King and his retinue to the great lake of Maldro, where the Mahaguru erected a tent and hid his entire company. For three days he meditated there, until finally a ravishing woman appeared, saying, "What is the Master doing here by the lakeside?" To which he replied:

> "I come to form an alliance between ༔
> Trisong Detsen, King of humans, ༔
> And Nanda, king of the nagas! ༔
> Since the King's monastery is still not complete, ༔
> send a message to the nagas: tell them to share their wealth!"[262] ༔

> — *Revealed by Orgyen Lingpa*

Only few days later, with all these blessings, a large serpent appeared and gold began washing up on the shore. The King's ministers collected the gold; they now had all the resources they needed to complete the construction of Samye.

A Grand Offering

Guru Padmasambhava had not only shown immeasurable kindness in coming to Tibet and promising to support the building of Samye, but he had also displayed his great miraculous ability and strength in binding the gods and demons to his service. To the King, the Mahaguru meant everything. Thus, it was during these early days that King Trisong Detsen invited Guru Rinpoche to his palace and demonstrated his devotion in a most extraordinary way. In front of the entire assembly, the King offered his entire kingdom and a sumptuous display of material offerings laid out to perfection. He then presented the Mahaguru with a golden mandala, representing the entire universe and all within it, and formally requested him to become the principal guide of the Tibetan people, to teach the Dharma and remain with them to help establish Samye Monastery.[263] With this request, the King recited this famous verse of offering:

> The ground is purified with scented water
>   and strewn with flowers.
> It is adorned with Sumeru, king of mountains, and the four
>   quarters of the universe, and the sun and moon.
> Thinking of it as a blessed buddhafield, I offer it.
> By virtue of this offering, may all beings here and now
>   attain the happiness of that pure land! [264]

Further, the King was well aware of his queen Yeshe Tsogyal's devotion and longing for the Dharma. And so, he offered her as well, as a disciple to the Guru, fully releasing her from all worldly ties. She was not only his own beloved queen, but Tibet's most promising Dharma student. With joy the Mahaguru accepted the King's request, and promised to teach the Dharma and remain in Tibet until Samye was complete.

And while Guru Rinpoche symbolically accepted the King's offering of his kingdom, he did not accept worldly domain, for this would only interfere with his spiritual endeavor. The Mahaguru did, however, foresee the vast and unimaginable benefit that Khandro Yeshe Tsogyal would bring to the Dharma, and so accepted her as his spiritual disciple and consort.[265] Yeshe Tsogyal, for her part, was overjoyed to leave behind the worldly ways of the royal court. She joined the Mahaguru, now finally able to enter the path of spiritual awakening.

Furnishing Samye with Statues and Relics

One night, while the King was fast asleep, a dream came to him. Divine beings were telling him that the time had come to prepare sacred images for Samye. The place itself had been blessed by Noble Lady Tara, and lying hidden in nearby Hepori were several statues of the Buddha and bodhisattvas that had been blessed by Shakyamuni Buddha himself. The next morning, King and retinue climbed the mountain. They soon found, just beneath the soil, the *ushnisha* crowning the head of a large self-arisen statue of Shakyamuni Buddha—a statue later renowned as the Jowo Jangchup Chenpo (Lord Mahabodhi). A further twelve images—ten bodhisattvas and two door guardians—were excised from the rock that day, and all thirteen images were brought to the main temple, where they became supreme objects of devotion at Samye.

While these statues, blessed and naturally-arisen, had lain hidden until the time for the Dharma to be established in Tibet, many more were needed. Under the guidance and supervision of both the Mahaguru and the Abbot, it was now particularly the job of the skilled Newar craftsman to carve, mold, and sculpt the remaining statues required for all the various temples that formed the Samye mandala.[266] When it came to filling the statues with sacred substances, the Mahaguru and Abbot offered many relics that they themselves had brought to Tibet. They also advised the many artisans gathered there in the art of preparing the mantras, *dharanis*, medicines, and sacred substances that were needed to fill the statues.

As the project proceeded, the Mahaguru one day told the King that, in order to secure the establishment of the Dharma at Samye, it was absolutely necessary to enshrine there some relics of Buddha Shakyamuni—the buddha who brought the Dharma to this world. Thus, the Mahaguru sent the King on a mission to retrieve the Buddha's relics, specifically from Lotus Essence Stupa in Rajgir. Aware of the potential difficulties this posed, and thinking that brave and strong men would be necessary to accomplish the task, the King called upon his very best soldiers. And so, accompanied by two regiments of his Tibetan cavalry, Dharma King Trisong Detsen began the long journey south to India.

As the Tibetan army entered the Indian plains, the people were shocked by the appearance of these fierce-looking warriors. Thinking that it might be a scouting mission for a large-scale invasion, they either fled in terror or bowed in fear. When the party finally arrived before the Bodhi Tree in Bodh Gaya, they made vast aspiration prayers for the Dharma to spread in Tibet, accompanying this with all the most elaborate offerings. They then continued on to the Lotus Essence Stupa in Rajgir, just as the Mahaguru had prescribed. Opening the stupa, they took out a portion of the relics, and afterwards sealed the stupa again. While on their way home, the Tibetan cavalry set up an iron pillar beside the River Ganges as a testament to Tibet's far-reaching dominion. Upon their arrival back in Drakmar, the Tibetans held celebrations and placed these most precious relics inside the five main stupas at Samye—where they would provide for the Dharma to spread freely for the generations to come.[267]

The Guardian of Samye

As the temples of the Samye mandala were gradually completed, and as the temples themselves grew full of precious statues and relics, the King began to perceive an urgent need for a guardian to protect the complex from threats posed by enemies, both human and non-human. The King thus approached the Abbot and, upon brief discussion, it became clear that they should consult the Mahaguru. They approached the Mahaguru, and the Abbot spoke:

> If we entrust it to a demon, that's like trusting a murderer; ఠ
> The planets, meanwhile, are fierce; nagas are hostile; ఠ
> *Tsen* spirits peaceful; and *mamos* simply dangerous... ఠ

Guru Padmasambhava then replied:

> A demon incarnation will appear before the King; ఠ
> Disease will enter his heart, making him unfit and unreliable. ఠ
> The one known as Marici will become distraught; ఠ
> A demonic emanation at that time will cause harm. ఠ
> One hundred and ten generations hence, ఠ
> the Mongolian King Namte'u Karpo will come ఠ
> and bring all of Tibet under his domain. ఠ
> The ancestral Mongol deity is Namlha Jangchup— ఠ
> Therefore you should invite Gyalpo Shing Chachen! ఠ
> If you entrust it to them, your temple will not be destroyed![268] ఠ

> — *Revealed by Orgyen Lingpa*

Thus the Mahaguru in his clairvoyance knew the answer was to install Gyalpo Shing Chachen (Wood Bird King) as protector of Samye. He was the main ancestral spirit of the hostile Mongols and neighboring tribes, and the Mahaguru could see his dark schemes to bring Tibet under his sway by influencing the Mongol rulers. He knew therefore to turn the potential attacker into a defender.

And so, with the dual purpose of protecting Samye and preventing future invasions of Tibet by hostile neighboring tribes, the Guru sent Prince Murub Tsenpo, King Trisong Detsen's son, accompanied by an army, to the Mongolian encampment of Bhata Hor.[269] Their mission was to provoke Shing Chachen into action. To this end, Murub Tsenpo and his men stole the possessions that Shing Chachen had sworn to protect. Shing Chachen had no choice but to pursue the invaders back to Tibet, where Guru Rinpoche was already awaiting their arrival. The moment that Shing Chachen was in sight, the Guru bound him under oath and placed him in charge of Samye monastery. Shing Chachen was thus invited to take up residence in Samye's Pehar Kordzö Ling (Sanctuary of the Vihara's Treasury), from which time he became known as Gyalpo Pehar, named after the protector's new residence—a *vihara*, or monastery.[270]

Consecrating Samye Monastery

Within five years, Samye's construction was complete.
Thereupon, with Shantarakshita,
by means of the mighty Vajradhatu mandala,
You performed the consecration, tossing multitudes of flowers,
And revealed the amazing wonder that is Samye.
Homage to you![271]

— *Jamyang Khyentsé Wangpo*

The spirits of the land were now under control, resources were flowing in, and the site was protected, all through the force of Guru Padmsambhava's presence. Construction proceeded at a rapid pace, so that in the Fire Horse Year of 766, after a mere five years of work, the construction of "glorious Samye— the inconceivable—the unchanging, spontaneously accomplished temple" was complete.[272] Towards the end of that same year, on the astrological day of the victory star, Guru Padmasambhava and Abbot Shantarakshita met at Samye to perform the consecration of the temple and scatter flowers of auspiciousness. Then, in the following year, Guru Rinpoche sat down at the eastern door of Samye's three-styled temple and opened the *Vajradhatu* mandala. After practicing for seven days, the Mahaguru bestowed empowerment upon the King and then blessed Samye in a most extraordinary way:

Guru Padma then threw the flowers of consecration, ⸪
And as the flowers were falling on the three-styled temple, ⸪
The statues within started to leave through the eastern door, ⸪
Holding their implements aloft and waving them about. ⸪
The King wondered whether they shouldn't be put back, ⸪
But the statues made three rounds of the temple and stupas, ⸪
And once again returned to their places within.[273] ⸪

— *Revealed by Orgyen Lingpa*

Such was the power of Guru Rinpoche's blessing at this time, and such was the amazing spectacle of Samye's consecration! Not only did the statues of the main temple show that they were alive with the activity of the deities, but the protectors too arrived, and the whole region was enveloped with signs of auspiciousness:

> All the temples were consecrated, flower petals strewn, ॰
> And wisdom deities descended into the statues, for all to see. ॰
> Rays of light blazed forth and music resounded. ॰
> The gods showered down a rain of flowers, ॰
> And the nagas came with gifts of precious gems. ॰
> And so the world was filled with every auspiciousness. ॰
> Male and female protectors arrived, flanking the temple's sides. ॰
> The stone pillars shot forth flames, and the dogs on top of them
>   growled and barked. ॰
> Three times arura fruits were showered down like rain. ॰
> Over all Tibet and Kham auspicious signs and goodness reigned. ॰
> Gods and men were filled with joy, again and yet again— ॰
> and so the banner of renown unfurled across the land.[274] ॰

> — *Revealed by Chokgyur Dechen Lingpa*

Amongst these and many more miraculous signs, Samye monastery was consecrated. The whole of Samye was transformed into a sacred place that grants liberation upon sight, such that connecting in even the smallest of ways would garner the greatest spiritual riches, not only for Dharma King Trisong Detsen, but for all future pilgrims as well:

> Samye is equalled only by the Vajra Seat of India, ॰
> Unrivaled by anything under the sun. ॰
> Seeing it with your own eyes closes the doors to the lower realms. ॰
> Whoever circumambulates around it ॰
> Will be reborn in the heavenly realms, even if they're a butcher. ॰
> Whoever prostrates in homage to Samye ॰
> Will ordinarily become a great and magnificent king. ॰
> And, whenever this story of Samye is told to others, ॰
> The one who hears will be freed from all their karma.[275] ॰

> — *Revealed by Chokgyur Dechen Lingpa*

And thus, Samye's construction had established a wish-fulfilling gem in the heart of Tibet. With a physical support for the Dharma now in place, the heart-wish of King Trisong Detsen was finally being fulfilled. There was still much to accomplish, however, for the Buddha's teachings require students to uphold them and a culture dedicated to preserving and spreading their essential message. Only the Mahaguru was fit to undertake such a task.

Establishing the Support of Enlightened Speech

Turmoil at the King's Court

> *Having successfully turned the Wheel of Dharma,*
> *The two of you, the Masters, announced your return to India.*
> *The King, heartbroken, begged you to stay,*
> *And in your great kindness you agreed to remain.*
> *Homage to you![276]*
>
> — *Jamyang Khyentsé Wangpo*

The Guru and Abbot had fulfilled the King's request, not only in the building of Samye monastery, but also in terms of instructing Tibetan disciples. This, however, had met with harsh criticism among the royal ministers, who were opposed to the shaping of native minds by these foreigners. Struck by the vehemence of their opposition, the Mahaguru and Abbot began to wonder whether it was actually time to return home:

> This kingdom of Tibet is a land of savages; ༔
> They don't know good from evil, ༔
> So how can Dharma's truth be taught? ༔
> Since these Tibetan ministers are all puffed up with jealousy, ༔
> Let's give up and go home, once the King's wishes are fulfilled.[277] ༔
>
> — *Revealed by Chokgyur Dechen Lingpa*

King Trisong Detsen was heartbroken when he caught wind of their plans. Shedding many tears, he approached his teachers, offered them a lavish mandala of gold, and made the following request:

> Although I have built shrines for awakened body, speech, and mind ༔
> And brought the Dharma of Sutra and Tantra to Tibet, ༔
> It still needs to spread through study, practice and meditation. ༔
> So, masters, please ensure that this takes place! ༔
> Abbot, Master, I beseech you—don't leave, but stay here, in Tibet![278] ༔
>
> — *Revealed by Chokgyur Dechen Lingpa*

The King was now more dedicated than ever to ensuring that the Dharma would take firm root in his kingdom. Master and Abbot could see that his devotion and commitment were unwavering and actually a reflection of a large swathe of Tibetans, especially the Mahaguru's own Tibetan disciples, who also longed for the Dharma and were eager to embrace it, whatever the evil-minded ministers might say. In light of this sincerity, the Mahaguru and Abbot decided to prolong their stay. They would remain to train the next generation of Tibetans to promulgate the lineage of the Buddha.

Training Tibetan Translators

The King ruled according to the two systems.
As foretold, he sent out invitations
To Vairocana, Kawa Paltsek, and Chokro Lu'i Gyaltsen.
Trained as translators, they became rare scholars
And pioneered translations of Sutra and Tantra.
Homage to you![279]

— *Jamyang Khyentsé Wangpo*

While the physical foundations were a necessary basis for the Dharma, it needed to be accessible to everyone in their native language if it was to remain and spread. So it was decided by Mahaguru, King, and Abbot that they would embark upon a project to translate the vast corpus of Buddhist literature from Sanskrit and other scriptural languages into Tibetan. For this, skilled translators needed to be trained. Thus began the establishment of the support of enlightened speech—the translation of the myriad Buddhist teachings extant in India into the language of the Snowy Land of Tibet.

While King Trisong Detsen was overjoyed at the prospect that the Guru and Abbot had decided to prolong their stay and oversee the translation project, his mind filled with worry. He could see that Sanskrit was a complex and difficult language, and wasn't sure that the Tibetans would be able to master it, or even be able to utter the three lines of refuge to Buddha, Dharma and Sangha in it. But the Mahaguru and Abbot consoled him, saying:

We can see all those Tibetan children of noble birth ⁏
Appropriate for the task, and we will teach them how to translate. ⁏

— *Revealed by Chokgyur Dechen Lingpa*

Through their clairvoyance, these masters knew that Buddha Shakyamuni's own disciples had taken rebirth in Tibet. If found and trained, they would be destined to bring the texts of the Buddhadharma from India and translate them for the benefit of the entire kingdom, and for future generations.

Guru Rinpoche directed the search, advising the King first to seek out an eight-year-old child, the reincarnation of Shakyamuni Buddha's close disciple Ananda. This child was to be brought to him in the capital for training in translation, and his name was Vairocana. Vairocana joined other prophesied translators, including Chokro Lu'i Gyalsten, Kawa Peltsek, and Yeshé Dé, and they all received extensive explanations on the systems of Sutra and Tantra from the two great masters, who themselves provided guidelines for the work. Additionally, one hundred and eight children of the highest intelligence were gathered, and likewise trained in the arts of translation.

It was from among this esteemed group that Abbot Shantarakshita ordained seven into the Mulasarvastivadin lineage of the Vinaya, thus establishing the ordained Sangha of monks and nuns in Tibet.[280] Later, after these first monastics proved themselves capable, the Abbot went on to ordain many more monastic aspirants, and thus the ordained Sangha grew. Not everyone who wanted to study the Dharma wished to take on the vows of ordination, however, and the task of establishing the Sangha of lay tantric practitioners fell to Guru Rinpoche. The two core groups of the Sangha present in India were now taking shape in Tibet, two pillars that had existed from ancient times and continue to the present day.

Once fully trained, the Tibetan translators were sent by Guru Padmasambhava and Shantarakshita to India to seek out great teachers and siddhas who could assist in their task. On the recommendation of both Guru and Abbot, the translators took as their prime destination the great monasteries of Nalanda and Vikramashila, the very lifeblood of Buddhist practice in India.[281] The monasteries' resident siddhas and panditas were well aware of the Guru and Abbot's great contributions to their monastic establishments and, upon hearing of their mission to establish Buddhism in Tibet, they welcomed the Tibetan translators into the halls of their venerable institutions. There, the Tibetans had not only shelter and food, but access to a vast number of scriptures and to Indian scholars with whom they could work side by side. Some of them not only explained the scriptures to the Tibetans, but also actively participated in the translation process.[282] As a result of their training in both Tibet and Greater India, these translators become renowned as *lotsawas*.[283] After their sojourns in India, the lotsawas returned to Tibet, often accompanied by their supportive Indian siddhas and panditas, and bearing heavy loads of many scriptures, to take up residence at Samye, where the translation process could continue under the patronage of King Trisong Detson.

In particular, the Dharma King had sent three of his best translators to King Indrabhuti of Uddiyana. Laden with lavish gifts, these three had requested the very best of the King's five hundred panditas—one who was learned in the highest tantras. King Indrabhuti kindly granted their request, offering them the mahapandita Vimalamitra.[284] Furthermore, Buddhaguhya, the scholar renowned for his mastery of the *Guhyagarbha* tantra, and one of Guru Padmasambhava's own root teachers, was also in residence at King Indrabhuti's court when the Tibetan translators arrived to request Indrabhuti's help. While Buddhaguhya initially stayed behind to help the Dharma flourish in Uddiyana and farther afield, he later went on pilgrimage to Tibet, and taught the Dharma there.[285] Likewise, other great masters, such as the vidyadhara Humkara, and the Newar masters Shilamanju and Vasudhara, accepted King Trisong Detsen's invitation and made their way north to Tibet, staying awhile and practicing with the Tibetan disciples in the caves above Samye and elsewhere, helping to guide the people of Tibet to ever greater levels of realization.[286]

Translating the Dharma into Tibetan

> *Translations were made of everything beneficial,*
> *Such as scientific texts on medicine and astrology.*
> *The complete and perfect volumes of the teachings thus unfolded,*
> *Streaming forth a garland of the Buddha's words,*
> *Held in highest reverence, installed and established,*
> *And consecrated all around with flowers.*
> *Auspiciousness and virtuous signs increased in great abundance.*
> *Homage to you!*[287]

> — *Jamyang Khyentsé Wangpo*

King Trisong Detsen now requested Guru Rinpoche to take his seat upon a golden throne in Samye's Hall of Translations, flanked by the Abbot Shantarakshita and the Master Vimalamitra, before the array of siddhas, panditas, translators and scholars. The King proceeded to offered lavish gifts to each of the assembled, setting in motion the translation of the Dharma into Tibetan:

Countless teachings of Sutra and Tantra ༔

Were, day and night, translated, studied, explained, §
Throughout the Tibetan kingdom Dharma schools were established, §
And sutras and tantras compiled in myriad volumes. §

Over the course of the next thirteen years, scholars and translators worked together to bring the Dharma of Sutra and Tantra, along with the other traditional sciences, into the Tibetan language, and to provide detailed explanations of this vast ocean of wisdom. This immense undertaking would provide a stable basis for the Dharma to truly flourish in the Land of Snows, an unrivaled offering that has meant that all the Buddha's teachings are available to practitioners today.

Once complete, all the scriptures were installed in the middle storey of Samye's main temple. Then, the great masters and translators gathered at Samye received yet more gifts from King Trisong Detsen. In his gratitude, he gave to each a golden mandala and a brick of solid gold.

Then the great Indian panditas, each escorted by their lotsawa, §
Embarked upon the journey home to their own lands. §
Like the rising sun, the Dharma now shone upon Tibet.[288] §

— *Revealed by Chokgyur Dechen Lingpa*

The assembly of pandits returned home, but the Mahaguru and Abbot stayed behind in Tibet. Guru Padmasambhava took up residence at the nearby Samye Chimpu caves, while the Abbot stayed at Samye's Jangchub Ling (Temple of Awakening). They had carried out a great work, for the Tibetan people now had a host of learned scholars who could understand and interpret the sacred teachings of the Buddha. The age of the *lotsawa* had arrived.

Subduing the Bön Opposition

Another hundred great panditas were invited to Tibet,
Including, among others, the great master Buddhaguhya.
Their mission was to quell the teachers of Bön.
In debate and feats of power, they soundly crushed these opponents,
Allowing the pure brilliance of the Dharma to shine.
Homage to you![289]

— *Jamyang Khyentsé Wangpo*

At the time of King Songtsen Gampo, the Dharma of Buddha Shakyamuni had begun to spread in Tibet alongside another spiritual tradition, *Bön*, which had been introduced by the enlightened being Miwo Shenrab long before. Both, in fact, showed a spiritual path that would eventually unveil ultimate reality and liberate beings, and both were harmoniously practiced side by side. But soon after the passing of King Songtsen Gampo, and long before Trisong Detsen became King, some Bön priests obsessed with power pushed aside the values of their tradition and promoted a new form of Bön, the *Gyu Bön*, which promised wealth and worldly power. They began worshipping the most powerful of the local gods and spirits through black magic and blood sacrifices, in the hope of acquiring their demonic influence and power.

Thus, while more Tibetans than ever were versed in the Buddhist teachings, there were still those who clung to rites and beliefs that lay completely counter to the path of virtue. King Trisong Detsen and others were well aware of the threat imposed by the Gyu Bön, yet certain high-ranking courtiers still supported their practices, either in public or in private. With the arrival of Guru Padmasambhava, the Gyu Bön priests were increasingly called upon to obstruct his activity—often by these evil-minded royal ministers—which in turn increased doubt among the Tibetan people regarding the King's endeavors to establish Buddhism in Tibet. In the face of these intransigent forces of harm, Dharma King Trisong Detsen consulted Guru Rinpoche on the best course of action. The Mahaguru declared that a public debate would be held between the Buddhist and Gyu Bön priests. Following the traditional rules of Indian debate, the winning side would become the official religion of the kingdom, while the losers would have to give up their beliefs for good.

A date was set and the greatest scholars from both sides assembled in front of Samye. Crowds thronged the stage and, with a marvelous display of learning, accomplishment, and even a miraculous display of powers, the Buddhist side excelled in every way possible, leaving the Gyu Bön priests and ministers devastated in their wake. The contest served to quell doubt in the audience, and the Tibetan people could now confidently embrace the Dharma. Several ministers who had supported the evil Gyu Bön path were physically banished to the hinterland, while others completely lost the trust of the Tibetans and were relegated to obscurity—their scriptures heaped up and burned. Meanwhile, the path of traditional Bön was restored, and in support Guru Padmasambhava himself hid many Bön scriptures as *terma* treasures, so that the authentic Bön tradition would last long into the future.[290] Safe now, too, were the Buddha's teachings, which could be propagated without the danger of undue interference. The Dharma had found its footing in the Snowy Land of Tibet.

Establishing the Next Generation

The King's Final Retreat

> *In the center of the three-storey temple of glorious Samye*
> *You accomplished Amritakundali, as Vajra master of the assembly.*
> *To you, King Trisong Detsen, with your unwavering samadhi,*
> *We pray: please grant your blessings![291]*
>
> — *Changdak Tashi Topgyal*

The Dharma was now flourishing in Tibet, which brought long-awaited peace to the mind of King Trisong Detsen. His heart filled with appreciation, for after years of hard work in the face of countless, insurmountable obstacles, his deepest aspirations and wishes had been fulfilled. Thus, the King began a slow retreat from his royal obligations, longing to devote his remaining years to spiritual practice. The Mahaguru, at his cave residence above Samye, had initiated the King into the practice of the deity Amritakundali, also known as Chemchok Heruka.[292] With these heart instructions, the King then retreated into a chamber within one of the temples at Samye, where he dedicated himself one-pointedly to the practice of Chemchok. His meditation become totally unwavering, and through it the King realized the very essence of this enlightened form of awakening.[293] After this, his very body was a mandala of deities, and he was able to journey to any pure realm he wished.[294]

And yet the duties of his royal office still called. It was the year 801, and preparations for the Tibetan New Year festivities were underway. That particular year, however, the Mahaguru approached the royal court and advised against proceeding with the festivities. Obstacles were bound to follow. But his advice was neglected, and the festivities soon began. King Trisong Detsen, meanwhile, was dressed in his finest robes in preparation for the annual horse race. When the race began, the King galloped down the field, far ahead of the competition, when suddenly an errant arrow struck the King down. Royal guards quickly rushed onto the course and carried the King back to his chambers. Despite their best efforts, there was nothing to be done: King Trisong Detsen passed away from the injury, merely fifty-nine years of age. The spectators were told that he had suffered only a minor injury and was going to retreat from his royal duties while he recovered. For another ten years the King's passing was kept a secret, during which time the Mahaguru guided the kingdom, ensuring the Dharma would remain and continue to spread.

Teaching Prince Mutik Tsenpo

Shortly after Dharma King Trisong Detsen's passing, the Mahaguru guided his son, Prince Mutik Tsenpo, to Mount Hepori.[295] The spacious view afforded by the mountain gave the prince an immediate feeling of ease and release. After a short pause to let the scenery work its way into the heart of the grieving prince, the Mahaguru uttered these words of consolation:

> If, once born, people didn't die, the earth could no longer hold us. ༚
> This wouldn't be good for anyone, nor for your father. ༚
> All are born, and all at some time pass away. ༚
> This body of wealth and freedom, feeble as it is, ༚
> Has many causes of destruction, few of survival. ༚
> It cannot stand a moment's touch too hot or cold. ༚
> And the bloom of youth is taken by harbingers of disease. ༚
> Radiant health can be stolen by any sudden condition. ༚
> It's like a dew drop upon a blade of sacred kusha grass ༚
> Which, suddenly, under the intensity of the rising sun, ༚
> Evaporates, and is no more. ༚
> Your human life of wealth and freedom is just like that![296] ༚

> — *Revealed by Orgyen Lingpa*

The grieving prince thus confronted the truth of impermanence, for death comes to us all. In the face of this reality, he could draw inspiration from his father's legacy, and he too decided to pursue the spiritual path, for only the Dharma mattered to him now. Thereupon Mutik Tsenpo and the Mahaguru returned to Samye, and, in the grand middle storey of the main temple, the new monarch formally requested Guru Padmasambhava to bestow upon him the higher teachings of the Vajrayana path, up to the very pinnacle of the Great Perfection. Receiving this incredible transmission, King Mutik Tsenpo then proclaimed:

> These essential points have not once been uttered— ༚
> Not by buddhas past, present, nor to come. ༚
> Never have they been taught, nor will they ever be taught. ༚
> I will make use of all of your pith instructions, ༚
> For the teaching of such advice is totally unheard of![297] ༚

> — *Revealed by Orgyen Lingpa*

Guru Padmasambhava thus guided the prince to become a great King capable of guiding his kingdom in both worldly and spiritual matters. Then, ten years after the passing of Dharma King Trisong Detsen, the Mahaguru publicly enthroned Prince Mutik Tsenpo as successor to the throne. During this transition period, the Abbot Shantarakshita passed away at his residence, the Temple of Awakening at Samye. The Mahaguru and Mutik Tsenpo wrapped his holy remains in silk and performed the final rites for the Great Abbot.[298] It was the ending of an era. The transmission of the Dharma was not complete, however, for there was a new generation of practitioners taking up the Dharma, following the Mahaguru's instructions with all their heart. The transmission of the Mahaguru's realization was still very much underway.

The Mahaguru's Legacy

The Homeland of Gyalwa Longchenpa

The life story of the great Longchen Rabjam Drimé Özer is deeply tied to Samye. As a child, Longchenpa's family moved close to the monastery and, by age twelve, he was ordained there as a novice monk, taking the name Tsultrim Lodrö. Just two years later, he wrote his first commentary on the Vinaya, the monastic code. Later, at Yartokham, in the Samye uplands, Longchenpa eventually met his root guru, Rigdzin Kumaraja.[299] Throughout the course of his life, Longchenpa would return many times to Samye, so much so that he became known as *Samyepa* (*The One From Samye*).

At the age of fifty-six, after pilgrimage abroad, Longchen Rabjam finally returned for the last time to Samye, where he bestowed empowerment upon a large group of people. It was here that Gyalwa Longchenpa then passed into parinirvana amidst wondrous signs. As Kyapjé Nyoshul Khen Rinpoche writes:

He adopted the dharmakaya posture and passed into the primordial state of resolution. At that time, the clear sky filled with canopies of rainbow light and a rain of flowers fell. Wild roses and other flowers began to bloom. Some people experienced the stable realization of utter lucidity.[300]

Revelation of the History of the Great Jarung Kashor Stupa

One of the most beloved and elaborate accounts of the story of the Jarung Khashor, or Boudha Stupa, was discovered here at Samye. This treasure revelation, entitled *Liberation Upon Hearing: The History of the Great Jarung Kashor Stupa*, records the words of Guru Padmasambhava himself as he elaborates on the brief history of the stupa, as recounted in Chapter 58 of the *Pema*

Kathang.[301] In particular, it highlights the great aspirations made by four brothers, lifetimes ago, which, as we have seen, changed the face of the Buddhist landscape in the generations that followed.

A treasure hidden in the recesses of the Red Stupa at Samye monastery, it was discovered by the great Buddhist teacher Ngakchang Shakya Zangpo, while on pilgrimage during the 15th century. This treasure account begins by detailing the auspicious circumstances in which the Mahaguru revealed the history:

> It was on the tenth day of the Monkey month of the Male Fire Monkey Year, in the middle storey of the great monastery of Glorious Samye, the Unchanging, the Spontaneously Accomplished. A grand empowerment for *The Guru's Utterly Secret Heart Practice* was being conferred on the Dharma King and the twenty-five disciples. On this occasion, the disciples requested the Precious Master of Uddiyana to take a seat upon nine brocade cushions... §

> They presented five measures of gold dust, seven gold bricks, one hundred bolts of fine silk, and countless other goods and enjoyments. The King, Trisong Detsen, then prostrated one hundred times, and requested ... §

> Pray, tell us how, during the time of the Tathagata Kashyapa's teachings, in the Maguta district of Nepal, teacher and disciples alike were born as the four sons of a poor poultry-woman, and how they built the Jarung Kashor Stupa. How did they[302] come to build the stupa, and what aspirations did they make? §

The Mahaguru's heart disciple Khandro Yeshé Tsogyal recorded the Mahaguru's words, and afterwards she hid them as a treasure at Samye, as the scripture itself goes on to reveal:

> Khandroma Yeshé Tsogyal recorded in writing what the Guru of Uddiyana had spoken. Together with the cycle of teachings on *The Guru's Utterly Secret Heart Practice*, this teaching was then hidden as a *terma* treasure behind the statue of Mahavairocana in the upper storey of the great temple at Glorious Samye, the Unchanging, the Spontaneously Accomplished. Aspiration prayers were made that it would be found in future by someone with the right karmic connection.[303]

The treasure's colophon further reveals that it was the great treasure-revealer Lhatsün Ngönmo who initially revealed it. However, because it was not yet the proper time to spread this treasure, she once again hid it:

> I, the treasure-revealer Lhatsün (Lhawang Gyatso Drolo) Ngönmo, having discovered this *terma* behind the statue of Mahavairocana, copied down this history as spoken by the precious Guru of Uddiyana. In accordance with the prophecy instructing me to reconceal the actual *terma* in a treasure site, I left a yellow parchment behind and hid the copied text within the southwestern side of the lion throne on the red stupa at Samye. As I did so, I made this aspiration prayer: "May it be discovered in the future by someone with the right karmic connection!"

In the year 1512, this same treasure was rediscovered and propagated by Ngakchang Shakya Zangpo, who had been assisting with renovations at Samyé. He briefly signed the revelation, as follows:

> I, Ngakchang Shakya Zangpo, through the compassionate blessing of the Guru of Uddiyana, received a prophecy in my dreams. Thus I discovered this *terma* treasure in the year of the Male Water Monkey, on the eighteenth day of the Sheep month. May it benefit all sentient beings![304]

Revelation of the Guru Tsokyé Nyingtik

> *Through devotion's power,*
> *may our bodies and minds be freed from bondage,*
> *So that we meet the Lake-Born Guru, self-awareness, in person,*
> *And then establish all beings, infinite as space,*
> *In the state of indestructible great bliss![305]*
>
> — *Jamgön Kongtrul Lodrö Thayé*

Jamgön Kongtrul Lodrö Thayé relates how Jamyang Khyentse Wangpo decoded the cycle of the *Guru Tsokyé Nyingtik, The Heart Essence of the Lake-Born Guru*,[306] and subsequently received the transmission and empowerment from the Mahaguru, all at Samye:

> At the age of twenty-nine, while travelling the north road (from Kham) on his way back to the Ü province of Central Tibet in the

Earth Monkey Year (1848), he [Jamyang Khyentse] was passing through the Gégyel region (in western Nangchen) when the tenth day of the eighth month came around. He performed the *Lama Sangdü* (*Secret Assembly*) offering ceremony and entered a state of mental exhilaration. Upon going outside, he came upon a lovely south-west-facing cave, went in, and in joyful mood performed a guru yoga practice. Toward the end, he became a little drowsy and was startled awake by a loud noise, whereupon he beheld in the sky before him, actually there, the Guru—in his *Zahorma*[307] form, flanked by two consorts. Having granted their blessing, they dissolved into him, and thereafter the basic *Tsokyé Nyingtik* cycle shone vividly in his mind, the practice manual for which he transcribed right there and then.

Then, at Samyé, on the fifteenth day of the ninth month, he was making extensive offerings before the Guru Tsokyé Dorjé statue in the local governor's residence (Samyé Dzong). The statue was a *terma* revealed by Nyangral Nyima Özer and, as he performed the practice from the transcribed manual, he saw the image turn into Tsokyé Dorjé himself, grant the empowerment and instructions, and dissolve into him. The subsidiary cycles also manifested clearly in the expanse of his awareness, but he placed them under seal for a long time to come.[308]

Jamyang Khyentse Wangpo himself composed the following vajra song, which begins:

> *Embodiment of all sources of refuge, Lake-Born Vajra,*
> *With a heart full of devotion, I pray and sing this song:*
> *May you establish all beings within the primordial palace!*[309]

A Feast Offering to the Guru Ngadrama

During his stay at Samye, Guru Padmasambhava was once presented with a statue which he declared to be a faithful likeness. He thus gave it his blessing, declaring it to be inseparable from himself. It became known as the Guru Ngadrama (Looks-Like-Me Guru), and was enshrined in the middle storey of the main temple at Samye, holding the presence of the Mahaguru there for the generations that followed.

When in the 20th century Kyapjé Jamyang Khyentse Chökyi Lodrö arrived on pilgrimage at Samye, he was met with a brilliant rainbow circling the central tower of the main temple and a gentle rain beginning to fall. Ascending to the middle floor, Khyentse Chökyi Lodrö performed more than one hundred thousand tsok offerings from the *Tukdrup Barché Kunsel* (*The Heart Practice, Dispeller of All Obstacles*), along with many other elaborate offerings, all in front of this particular image. When night fell, everyone could see fire blazing from the stupa for about an hour. It was during this period, either soon before or after, that the Queen Mother of Sikkim, Gyalyum Kunzang Dechen (1906–1987) took a black and white photograph of the image, which still captures its presence. The image, also known as "Looks Like Me," is now popular the world over, and has been the basis and inspiration for countless statues and paintings of Guru Rinpoche.

THE MAHAGURU'S EXILE

Zhotö Tidro

It was in the midst of Samye's construction that Guru Padmasambhava was offered the sublime Khandro Yeshé Tsogyal as spiritual consort, and that was when she began her training. As the walls of Samye continued to rise and the temples were being furnished, the Mahaguru and his disciple went up to the caves of Samye Chimpu and Drakmar Yamalung, where the foundational teachings of the vehicles of Sutra and Mantra were introduced, including the essential points of the samaya vows, culminating in Yeshé Tsogyal's first empowerment into the Vajrayana.[310] The noble lady had quickly mastered the Dharma as presented by her teacher, and was already becoming one of the most realized of Tibetans.

In the meantime, however, affairs at Samye were taking a very different turn. Soon after the Guru and his disciple had gone into retreat, King Trisong Detsen's ministers began to inquire about the fair queen's absence. The kingdom was rapidly shifting in favor of the Dharma, a threat to their own entrenched status and power. When the King finally disclosed to them that he had in fact offered his queen to Guru Rinpoche, these evil-minded officials took up the affair as a sign of royal weakness, immediately using this information to their advantage and launching an attack on Buddhism itself—a foreign religion that undermined the strong traditions of yore. An Indian yogi couldn't simply wander off with the queen. Thus, they declared that Guru Rinpoche and Yeshe Tsogyal had betrayed the kingdom of Tibet, and demanded that the couple should be expelled from the country entirely. Furthermore, if their demands were not met, they would force the King to step down.

Faced with this dilemma, King Trisong Detsen sent a message in secret to Drakmar Yamalung, where the Mahaguru was in residence.[311] So as not to cause any further obstacles for the King, Guru Rinpoche and Yeshe Tsogyal agreed to comply with the demands, but only as a show.[312] The Mahaguru was thus relieved of his responsibilities at Samye, but, instead of leaving the country, he travelled with Khandro Yeshe Tsogyal and many other disciples throughout Tibet, blessing the land, practicing in retreat, and hiding sacred treasures. Once he had introduced these heart-disciples to the Great Perfection at Samye and Samye Chimpu,[313] Guru Rinpoche then settled at Zhotö Tidro, where he transmitted the instructions of Atiyoga, the very pinnacle of the Buddhadharma, to Khandro Yeshe Tsogyal, his foremost disciple. As we will see in the subsequent chapters, Guru Rinpoche also travelled to other caves, eight in particular, which became his main sites of practice during his journey through Tibet. Eventually the Mahaguru would be invited back to Samye, where he would defeat the forces opposed to the Dharma, consecrate the monastery, and provide a blessed space for the Buddha's teachings to be transmitted in full.

ZHOTÖ TIDRO

When engaged in secret practice with the Lady Tsogyal
You opened the secret door of Body, Speech, and Mind
According to the lineage of oral instructions.
Urgyen, you who ripen and liberate disciples, I remember you now,
And I pray to you, O Precious One of Uddiyana:
Grant us empowerment, bestow your blessings![314]

— *Nyangral Nyima Özer*

Introduction

The King's wicked court officials were unrelenting in their demands: Guru Padmasambhava had to go, as did the wisdom consort, Khandro Yeshé Tsogyal. However, Dharma King Trisong Detsen had received his answer; he knew that if he offered gold for their journey into exile, the pair would in fact remain, albeit in the secrecy of retreat. So the Mahaguru and his consort received the royal command at their residence in Yamalung. They came down from the mountain in full view of the watching ministers, seemingly bound for somewhere beyond the kingdom's borders. Instead of leaving Tibet, however, the two made their way to the caves of Zhotö Tidro, far to the northeast of Samye. Rather than exile, they would enter retreat.

Thus, Guru Rinpoche used this apparent obstacle as an opportunity to impart further guidance to Khandro Yeshe Tsogyal on the most cherished of teachings—the innermost heart essence of the awakened mind, the priceless *Nyingtik* (*Heart Essence*) teachings. Yeshé Tsogyal was now blossoming as a wisdom dakini, a lineage holder of the heart of the Dharma. Her devotion and realization were already unparalleled, and yet, to reach the height of her potential, the Mahaguru instructed her to travel alone to Nepal to find her own predestined spiritual consort, the young Arya Salé. After much hardship, Yeshé Tsogyal finally met this partner in practice, and together they returned to Zhotö Tidro, to enter retreat together and achieve ever deeper levels of spiritual realization.[315]

Approaching the Sacred Site

Zhotö Tidro lies in the Drikung Valley, to the northeast of Lhasa. Limestone mountains rise from rivers to form a natural sanctuary, lending it the later name of Terdrom (Treasure Chest). In the lower part of this valley, at the confluence of two rivers, one finds medicinal hot springs and a vibrant nunnery, while in the upper valley the retreat cave used by Guru Padmasambhava and Khandro Yeshé Tsogyal can still be reached.[316]

This treasure chest of blessings is today considered a jewel-like gathering place of the dakinis, yet when Guru Rinpoche initially visited Zhotö Tidro he found a noxious lake inhabited by malicious spirits. Knowing that it would pose a threat to future yogins and yoginis who would come to meditate there, the Mahaguru split the rock and drained the lake, assisted by an emanation of Vajrayogini.[317] Guru Rinpoche then tamed the local spirits and blessed the lake's remaining pools, transforming it into medicinal hot springs that would heal all those who bathed there. The Mahaguru further recognized the site as particularly potent for the accomplishment of wrathful activities.

Later, the Mahaguru returned to Zhotö Tidro with Khandro Yeshé Tsogyal, to the spiritual center of the site, the Khandro Tsokchen (Great Hall of Dakinis), a large cave where he entrusted his spiritual consort with the Nyingtik teachings, some of which she hid in the immediate vicinity of the cave. From this precious treasure cache, Pema Ledrel Tsel later discovered parts of the *Khandro Nyingtik*, and Jé Rinchen Phuntsok (1509–1557) revealed the *Gongpa Yangzap* (*Most Profound Realization*)—now the main practice of the Terdzom nunnery, where this wisdom-dakini activity is still a thriving and active presence.[318]

The Mahaguru's Journey

A Dangerous Departure

> By miraculous means, the two of you sped to Zhotö Tidro.
> In the assembly hall there, you offered the Guru the great bliss mandala.
> Thus were you granted the four secret empowerments,
> Maturing in you the enlightened body, speech and mind
> And refining your pure perception of the master. To you, we
> pray![319]
>
> — Jamgön Kongtrul Lodrö Thayé

Even after the formal departure of the Mahaguru and his royal consort from the Tibetan realm, there were ministers who continued to conspire. "That tantric yogi is powerful! If we do not kill him now, he will surely cast a curse upon Tibet." Secretly they sent out assassins on horseback in pursuit of Guru Rinpoche, his consort, and their escorts. As the party arrived at the Tibetan border, the Mahaguru spoke a warning to his escorts: "When morning comes, we will encounter harm-doers."

The following day, just as predicted, the assassins arrived at their camp, weapons in hand. As they were about to strike with deadly force, Guru Rinpoche suddenly made a subtle gesture and they froze—motionless as clay statues, unable to utter a single word. Handing his escorts a handful of mustard seeds, the Mahaguru instructed, "Throw these at the assassins. I'm off to tame the demons on the southwest border." Everyone witnessed his departure—flying into the sky on his horse, his Dharma robes flapping and his staff clattering. The escorts headed back to camp and threw the mustard seeds at the petrified assassins, who quickly regained consciousness[320] only to find that the Mahaguru of Uddiyana had already left. He hadn't gone to the southwest, however, as the escorts informed them, but to the caves of Shotö Tidro, far to the northeast of Samye, there to enter retreat with his most trusted disciple, Khandro Yeshé Tsogyal.

The Heart Essence of the Dakinis

In the great assembly hall of Zhotö Tidro,
To the foremost of dakinis, Tsogyal of great bliss,
From a state of fourfold joy and ecstasy, I pray:
Inspire me to find freedom in the exhaustion of phenomenal reality.[321]

— *Jamyang Khyentsé Chökyi Lodrö*

This exile in the face of intense pressure from the King's royal ministers had, in fact, presented a precious opportunity to Guru Rinpoche and Khandro Yeshe Tsogyal, for now they could enter retreat unperturbed by anything or anyone. The Mahaguru and his most trusted disciple did not let this precious opportunity slip away. For her part, Khandro Yeshe Tsogyal had already demonstrated the deepest devotion to her Guru and his teachings. Aware of the extraordinary aptitude of his Tibetan disicple, Guru Rinpoche began to transmit to her, step by step, all the teachings that he had received over the long course of his spiritual path. Khandro Yeshé Tsogyal thus received from the Mahaguru the outer, inner, secret, and innermost empowerments, along with detailed instructions, putting immediately into practice whatever she had received. Diligently meditating both day and night, she swiftly progressed along the path.

One day, while the Mahaguru and Yeshé Tsogyal were in their retreat cave at Zhotö Tidro, some wisdom dakinis arrived before the lady, with the following exhortation:

This great master, this nirmanakaya emanation, holds in his mind the profound transmission of the *Nyingtik* teachings of direct experience, through which one awakens to buddhahood in three years, and which cause the physical body to vanish in this very lifetime. You should therefore beseech him to give you these instructions.

Khandro Yeshé Tsogyal therefore prepared a grand feast offering and, along with many prostrations and circumambulations, presented it to the Mahaguru with this request:

Great master, I humbly ask that you bestow on me the sacred transmission of the *Nyingtik* teachings of direct experience, which bring about awakening to buddhahood and cause the body to vanish in this very lifetime.

Pleased, Guru Padmsambhava answered:

Tsogyal, your request is an excellent one. This advice is quite unlike any other you have received previously. It represents the pinnacle of all the developmental stages of the nine spiritual approaches. Perceiving its key point nullifies any view and meditation that involve intellectual speculation. The paths and levels of realization are perfected without any need for effort. Negative emotions are freed in their own place without the need for contrivance, transformation, or antidotes. Without being created by causes, the fruition is perfect in itself. Spontaneously present enlightened intent arises in an instant. In this very lifetime, the body of flesh and blood is freed as sambhogakaya, a state of utter lucidity. Within three years, one can journey to the pinnacle realm of Akanishtha and reach the dharmakaya, the ongoing state of genuine being, the precious pure realm of spontaneous presence. Such advice is to be found in the *Khandro Nyingtik* (*Heart Essence of the Dakinis*), and I will impart it to you."[322]

Seeing that Khandro Yeshe Tsogyal showed extraordinary potential, and foreseeing that she would become the main upholder of his lineage and teachings in Tibet, the Mahaguru agreed to fulfill her request. Opening the mandala of the peaceful and wrathful deities in the Khandro Tsokchen (Great Hall of Dakinis), the Mahaguru began to transmit to Yeshe Tsogyal the innermost pith instructions of the Great Perfection, in their entirety. A hundred-thousand wisdom dakinis gathered as Guru Rinpoche taught the *Khandro Nyingtik* (*Heart Essence of the Dakinis*) and the eighteen tantras of the Great Perfection.[323]

Among the many pith instructions given there, Guru Padmasambhava gave Khandro Yeshe Tsogyal this heart advice, on overcoming obstacles that hinder recognition of the mind's deepest nature:

> Tsogyal, the empty essence of your awareness is not created by anyone. Without causes and conditions, it is originally present. Don't try to change or alter awareness. Let it remain exactly as it is! Thus will you be free from straying; thus will you awaken within the state of primordial purity.[324] §
>
> In the same way, your cognizant nature is originally and spontaneously present, indivisible from emptiness. Its expression, the unconfined capacity of whatever arises, has no concrete existence. Recognize that all three aspects [of awareness] are a great indivisible unity. Thus will you awaken as the indivisibility of the three kayas. §

> — *Revealed by Pema Ledrel Tsel*

It was in Tidrö that Khandro Yeshe Tsogyal was appointed as the Mahaguru's ultimate heir and lineage holder. Together, Mahaguru and Khandro compiled and arranged all these innermost pith instructions, hiding them as *terma* treasures—including the *Khandro Nyingtik* teachings, which he had only ever transmitted once before, at Samye Chimpu, to the young Princess Pema Sal as she was passing away.[325]

Reaping Great Siddhis

> *You exchanged teachings with Vasudhara, Shakyadema and others,*
> *And made your way back to Tidro.*
> *You cultivated the four joys, attained the siddhi of the vital essence,*
> *And brought the five elements under your control. To you, we pray!*[326]

> — *Jamgön Kongtrul Lodrö Thayé*

Khandro Yeshé Tsogyal, for her part, had displayed an incredible mastery of these highest teachings. The Mahaguru now counselled that, in order to fulfill her full spiritual potential, she would have to seek out another partner for practice. So Yeshe Tsogyal left for Nepal, while Guru Rinpoche moved to other sacred caves, where he gave teachings to his other Tibetan disciples.[327] In Nepal, Yeshé Tsogyal met fellow disciples of the Mahaguru, such as Vasudhara and Shakyadevi, and, after much hardship, eventually found her companion in Arya Salé, a young servant whom she freed and who could now take up the path of Secret Mantra under the guidance of Guru Rinpoche's foremost student.[328]

When Khandro Yeshe Tsogyal returned to Tibet, it was with Arya Salé at her side. Together they travelled to Zhotö Tidro to begin their retreat. As the 10th day of the lunar month arrived, they offered a great feast, and miraculously Guru Padmasambhava appeared before them, granting empowerment and blessings. Over the months that followed, Khandro Yeshe Tsogyal attained complete mastery over the five elements. She could now pass unhindered through rocks and buildings, and she was no longer subject to ageing, sickness and death.[329] Her retreat with Arya Salé had garnered great rewards, and on its completion Guru Rinpoche returned to them in person, in Zhotö Tidro, and gave them further teachings and instructions, refining their already great realization of the Dharma.[330]

The Mahaguru's Return to Samye

During this period of exile and retreat, King Trisong Detsen had been kept informed of the whereabouts of the Mahaguru and Yeshe Tsogyal, for his faith was undiminished, despite the circumstances. He could see too that his Tibetan subjects' interest in the Dharma was growing, and accordingly sent three translators with offerings of gold to Zhotö Tidro, with a message that the time was ripe for the pair to return to Samye. And so it was that Guru Rinpoche, Yeshe Tsogyal, and Arya Sale left Zhöto Tidro and returned from exile.[331]

The hostile ministers heard about the Mahaguru's imminent return and were furious, but even so, they joined the welcoming party, filled as they with fear and apprehension. And so it was that King, Abbot, and the entire Tibetan people gathered together in welcome. When the Mahaguru finally arrived, everyone prostrated and paid their respects. But to the King's surprise, he could only see the Mahaguru and what appeared to be his Indian servant. He anxiously inquired what had happened to his queen, at which point the Mahaguru gave a broad smile and tapped his *katvanga* (trident), instantly transforming it into Khandro Yeshé Tsogyal.

Everyone was amazed and inspired by this display of magic—including the evil ministers who had plotted against him; their awareness was now growing that the Mahaguru was truly no ordinary being. For them, fear was now the dominant emotion, as they worried that there might be a similar fate in store for them remembered what had happened to their hired assassins and so they decided to put aside their evil schemes, if only for the time being.[332] The Mahaguru, for his part, took up residence at the nearby Samye Chimpu caves, from which vantage point he could oversee the remaining construction of Samye Monastery.

Accomplishing the Practice of Atiyoga

> Having accomplished the Guru practice at Tidro,
> You received great blessings,
> And all appearances arose as the Guru's great display.
> In visions you travelled to Uddiyana, land of the dakinis,
> And to other lands supreme among all realms.
> And so it was that you beheld marvelous signs. To you, we pray![333]
>
> — Jamgön Kongtrul Lodrö Thayé

Much later, when Samye was complete and the time had come to leave Tibet, Guru Rinpoche took his leave at the Gungthang Pass, with Khandro Yeshé Tsogyal at his side. Riding on rays of light, they touched down in Tsawarong in Nepal; and there in a secret cave the Mahaguru granted her the final teachings on Atiyoga and the Great Perfection, with instructions on how to continue her practice. Then, while Guru Padmasambhava continued southwest to the land of the *rakshasas*, Yeshé Tsogyal returned to Zhotö Tidro where she practiced for a further six years until her awareness reached the ultimate extent of realization, the full fruition of the practice of the Great Perfection.[334]

As Khandro Yeshé Tsogyal's retreat came to an end, an invitation arrived from the new King of Tibet, Mutri Tsenpo, asking her to come back to Samye and guide the Tibetan people in the Dharma. So Yeshé Tsogyal took up residence at Chimpu and for six years turned the Wheel of Dharma for the King, royal court, and resident practitioners and translators.[335] Zhotö Tidro, however, remained one of Khandro Yeshé Tsogyal's personal retreat places. Over the course of her incredible life, this wisdom dakini returned to the caves of Zhotö Tidro numerous times, practicing the entirety of the Buddhist path, from the austerities of the lower vehicles, to the inner practices of *tummo* fire, up to and including the ultimate teachings of the Great Perfection. Further, as a result of her time there with the Mahaguru, she hid a vast number of *terma* treasures, including parts of the *Khandro Nyingtik*, scattered in and around the treasure-like mountains of Zhotö Tidro.[336]

The Mahaguru's Legacy

Gyalwa Longchenpa's Blessings

Gyalwa Longchenpa was naturally drawn to Zhotö Tidro, given its history as the place where the *Nyingtik* teachings were first imparted to Khandro Yeshé Tsogyal. When he approached the sacred site on pilgrimage, a welcoming party of dakinis greeted him and offered him the sacred site. From then on, Longchenpa would stay for long periods of retreat at Tidrö, blessing the caves in the surrounding area and experiencing vivid visions of the Mahaguru surrounded by dakinis. Due to this practice at Tidrö, the resident dakinis became Longchenpa's personal guardians, granting him protection and prophecy throughout his spiritual career.[337]

Revelation of the Dorsem Nyingtik

> *When Kharak and Lakha take to spying on one another,* ⸭
> *It is a sign that the time has come* ⸭
> *To reveal treasure from within the White Stupa.* ⸭
> *Thus, Urgyen Kunkyong Lingpa will appear.*[338] ⸭
>
> — *Revealed by Orgyen Lingpa*

Kunkyong Lingpa (1396 –1477) or (1408 –1489) was a reincarnation of the great Lotsawa Vairocana, and the direct reincarnation of Dorjé Lingpa (1346–1405). Kunkyong Lingpa was likewise drawn to Zhotö Tidro by the profound blessings of the Mahaguru's transmission of the *Khandro Nyingtik* to Khandro Yeshé Tsogyal there. This pilgrimage created the auspicious conditions for him to reveal a prophetic guidebook, the contents of which would lead him to sacred caves where, among many other profound treasures, he would reveal the *Dorsem Nyingtik* (*Heart Essence of Vajrasattva*).[339] This priceless treasure constitutes pith instructions received by Guru Padmasambhava directly from Garap Dorjé on the practice of the Great Perfection—instructions that the Mahaguru had in turn given to the great Lotsawa Vairocana, while in retreat on Juniper Ridge in southern Tibet.[340] An identical version of this treasure was later revealed by Taksham Nüden Dorjé (1655–1708), a reincarnation of Vairocana's scribe— and the one who revealed the precious biography of Khandro Yeshé Tsogyal.

In the 17th century, another of Vairocana's incarnations, Pema Dechen Lingpa, gathered all these streams of instruction and fused their blessings into one, in a lineage that still continues due to Jamgön Kongtrul's farsightedness in including it as an important treasure in his *Rinchen Terdzö* (*Treasury of Precious Termas*).[341] As predicted, Kunkyong Lingpa revealed many more treasures, including from the White Stupa at Samye. However, since the time for these to be distributed was not yet ripe, he re-concealed many of them again.[342]

Revelation of the Gongpa Yangzap

The *Gongpa Yangzap* (*The Most Profound Realization*), which combines Mahamudra and the Great Perfection, was a treasure teaching initially entrusted by Guru Rinpoche to Prince Mutik Tsenpo and Khandro Yeshé Tsogyal. Transcribing these teachings onto six yellow scrolls, Yeshé Tsogyal later hid them in Keru Yongdzong, the upper sanctuary of the Khandro Tsokchen cave.

Following prophecies, Jé Rinchen Phuntsok, a reincarnation of Prince Mutik Tsenpo, went with his spiritual consort to Zhöto Tidro on the tenth day of the eighth lunar month in the Dog Year (1538). There they practiced together, repeatedly invoking the Mahaguru. Finally, on the twenty-fifth lunar day, the day of the dakinis, Jé Rinchen Phuntsok retrieved the *Gongpa Yangzap*, an outstanding treasure that became the basis of practice in that region, right up to the present day.[343]

Transmission of the Nyingtik

Jamyang Khyentsé Wangpo arrived at Tidro in the fifth month of the Iron Mouse Year (1840), at only twenty-one years of age. Through the powerful blessings of the site, Khyentsé Wangpo's ordinary state of mind immediately fell away and he entered into the flow of non-conceptual wakefulness. Ascending into the Khandro Tsokchen cave, he offered up a great feast, and both Guru Padmasambhava and Khandro Yeshé Tsogyal appeared before him in a vision. They bestowed on the young Khyentsé Wangpo the entire *Khandro Nyingtik*, the heart essence of the Great Perfection as transmitted to Khandro Yeshé Tsogyal herself.[344] In a deep state of reverence and devotion, he expressed his resulting realization in a vajra song, which begins with the following lines:

> *Aho! Within the natural state, primordially pure,*
> *The four visions of luminosity are complete!*
> *In the presence of the great, spontaneous three kayas,*
> *I pay homage to you, the ultimate Guru!*[345]

THE EIGHT CAVES OF ACCOMPLISHMENT

*Samye Chimpu, Drak Yangdzong, Lhodrak Karchu,
Yarlung Sheldrak, Sengé Dzong, Yarlha Shampo,
Paro Taktsang and Drakmar Yamalung*

Over the course of Samye's construction, and in the years that followed its miraculous consecration, the Mahaguru travelled the entire length and breadth of the Himalayan plateau, so that not a single piece of earth remained untouched. Through his presence and grace, his teaching, retreat, and treasure concealment, the Mahaguru blessed innumerable sacred sites throughout the vast territory of Greater Tibet. But among them all, eight caves have been variously identified as exceptional for the practice of Vajrayana. The Mahaguru took special attention to unlock their sacred power, reveal their sacred features, and instruct his own disciples to practice there, so as to bless them further for the generations to come.

Located in Bhutan, and in Central and Southern Tibet, these eight caves hold the refined nectar of Guru Rinpoche's legacy. They are unique, in that each cave was infused with a particular blessing, becoming physical embodiments of Guru Padmasambhava's awakened body, speech, heart, qualities and activity, and listed as follows in the *Pema Kathang*:[346]

1. Drak Yangdzong, representing the Guru's awakened body
2. Samye Chimpu, representing the Guru's awakened speech
3. Lhodrak Karchu, representing the Guru's awakened heart
4. Yarlung Sheldrak, representing the Guru's awakened qualities
5. Sengé Dzong, representing the Guru's awakened activity

Three additional caves complete the network of eight:

6. Yarlha Shampo
7. Paro Taktsang
8. Drakmar Yamalung

In ancient India, the prime locations for Vajrayana practice were the charnel grounds, especially the mandala of the eight great charnel grounds. Prior to his journey into Tibet, Guru Rinpoche had practiced at length in these eight charnel grounds—binding spirits to oath, unlocking the higher stages of the Vajrayana path, and displaying unique manifestations.[347] One of his greatest acts in Tibet was this instilling of the powerful blessings of ancient India into this wild highland plateau. The Mahaguru said of this activity:

> The celestial abodes of the dakinis were transferred ⸭
> To our world and are found in India, ⸭
> And only branches of these [abodes] have appeared in Tibet, ⸭
> And siddhas are therefore few and far between. ⸭
> Therefore, I, the Lotus-Born, ⸭
> Have practiced at and blessed ⸭
> All of Tibet's most marvelous and vital sites. ⸭
> I invited the vidyadharas and dakinis ⸭
> From the celestial abodes, the sacred sites, ⸭
> And the charnel grounds of India, ⸭
> And have dissolved them into each ⸭
> And every one of these supreme sacred sites. ⸭
> Thus they are now indivisible from the celestial realms. ⸭
> The inventories to these sites, I have hidden as treasures.[348] ⸭
>
> — *Revealed by Jamyang Khyentsé Wangpo*

Rather than charnel grounds, as in India, the supreme sites of the Mahaguru's practice in Tibet were chiefly caves. From a spiritual perspective, however, these rugged, wild, and secluded grottos were already guarded by spirits and other beings—something they had in common with India's charnel grounds. Indeed, several of these cave sites had also served as burial grounds.[349] The cultural taboos surrounding Indian charnel grounds had traditionally provided ample seclusion for spiritual seekers, and the shade of their trees, the coolness of their river banks, created ideal conditions for practice. In the unforgiving climate of Tibet, however, spiritual practitioners would naturally seek the weather-proof conditions of caves, high in the mountains and away from society. Thus, while in Tibet, Guru Rinpoche blessed eight caves, one for each of the eight Kagyé deities and the principal yidam practices of the Nyingma tradition, as handed down from the great vidyadhara masters of India.[350] Due to the Mahaguru's blessings, the caves listed above became, respectively, the sites for these fierce embodiments of awakening:

1. Yamantaka
2. Hayagriva
3. Yangdak Heruka
4. Chemchok Heruka

5. Vajrakilaya
6. Mamo Bötong
7. Jikten Chötö
8. Möpa Drakngak

While the Kagyé mandala features eight wrathful deities, Guru Padmasambhava's students both at that time and in later generations would receive teachings on just one or another of these eight, depending on their karmic propensities. As their main deity, however, disciples would often receive Vajrakilaya, owing to the unique and profound connection the Mahaguru had formed with this practice, springing from his own supreme realization at Asura Cave in Nepal.

As we will see in the following pages, each yidam deity carries a unique blessing and a particular set of pith instructions that allow the practitioner to achieve accomplishments such as pacifying circumstances, increasing wealth, magnetizing siddhis, or clearing obstacles. While the Mahaguru originally did these practices in distinct locations, he knew that future disciples might not be able to do the same, and he thus condensed these pith instructions into pieces of heart advice which he shared with his students and hid as *terma* treasures. It is in this way that we may already, unknowingly, be practicing many of the original teachings connected with the Kagyé deities, distilled and filtered through generations of practitioners.

In addition to Guru Padmasambhava, a further eight sublime beings are renowned for practicing these Kagyé deities and thereby attaining realization in the eight great charnel grounds. Once they reached great accomplishment, they were known as the eight vidyadharas of India. All eight were both teacher and student to the Mahaguru, and all focused their practice upon a particular Kagyé deity, with the result that each is associated with the mastery of a specific practice. These vidyadharas, corresponding with the list of Kagyé deities above, are:

1. Manjushrimita
2. Nagarjuna
3. Humkara
4. Vimalamitra
5. Prabhahasti
6. Dhanasamskrita
7. Rombuguhya
8. Shantigarbha

In Tibet, from amongst all the disciples he had gathered since first setting foot on Tibetan soil, Guru Rinpoche selected eight karmically destined students to practice a Kagyé deity in each of the eight great caves. Due to the unique blessing of each cave, the disciples' progress was accelerated and they all reached accomplishment swiftly and without hindrance. As a result, these students became renowned as the eight vidyadharas of Tibet, and with this, the transmission of the Dharma of realization, the establishment of the enlightened mind, was complete. As time went on, not only these sublime beings, but many more besides, went on to practice in these sacred caves and reach the same great accomplishment. Nevertheless, the eight vidyadharas of Tibet are held aloft as supreme examples of accomplishment, and they correspond with the above-mentioned caves and Kagyé deities as follows:

1. Nupchen Sangyé Yeshé
2. Gyalwa Chokyang
3. Namkhé Nyingpo
4. Dharma King Trisong Detsen and Nyak Jñanakumara[351]
5. Khandro Yeshe Tsogyal
6. Palgyi Yeshé
7. Palgyi Sengé
8. Vairocana

These disciples of the Mahaguru later hid treasures of these practices within the walls, rocks, natural springs, and spaces of these magnetizing caves, and many of today's most cherished teaching cycles materialized within these very spaces.

Thus, like the eight great charnel grounds of India, these supreme cave sites became the gateways through which the Vajrayana entered Tibet. Regarded as the most sacred sites of the Mahaguru, not only do they embody his very being, but they have been continuously maintained throughout the history of Buddhism in Tibet, up to the present day. Over the many centuries, many thousands of practitioners have reached accomplishment in these caves, revealed treasures from within them, and met the Mahaguru in visions, and incalculable numbers have been suffused with the Mahaguru's blessings. Within the Himalayan regions, the eight great caves of accomplishment are considered to be the most sacred of all of Guru Rinpoche's sacred sites, and first and foremost among them is Samye Chimpu.

SAMYE CHIMPU

When you practiced at Samye Chimpu, ⚬
You repelled all harmful circumstances and granted siddhis. ⚬
You set the King and ministers on the path to liberation, ⚬
Destroying those Bönpo teachings that conjure evil spirits, ⚬
And showing the dharmakaya, precious and immaculate. ⚬
O Kalden Drendze, you lead us fortunate ones to Buddhahood: ⚬
With your compassion, inspire us with your blessing! ⚬
With your love, guide us and others along the path! ⚬
With your realization, grant us siddhis! ⚬
With your power, dispel the obstacles facing us all! ⚬
Outer obstacles – dispel them externally, ⚬
Inner obstacles – dispel them internally, ⚬
Secret obstacles – dispel them into space! ⚬
In devotion, I pay homage and take refuge in you![352] ⚬

— *Revealed by Chokgyur Dechen Lingpa*

Introduction

Central to the mandala of the eight great caves is Samye Chimpu, representing the Mahaguru's awakened speech. Located in close proximity to Samye, it served as an ideal residence for the Mahaguru during the construction of Samye monastery. While the other seven caves served primarily as retreat locations, Chimpu became a sacred site for the transmission of Dharma teachings. While their blessings are equally great, the Mahaguru mostly refrained from giving detailed instructions to his disciples at these other locations, instead advising them to follow his example in using them as strict retreat locations. Thus, it was at Chimpu that the Mahaguru initiated his closest students, known as the Twenty-Five Disciples, into the Kagyé mandala, and transmitted to them countless teachings and practices. What began at that time has inspired a thousand-year long tradition, where many of the greatest Tibetan masters have likewise joined the disciples of the Mahaguru and entered retreat at these sites. This activity has led to profound realization and some extraordinary revelations of treasures and teachings, and the selfless upholding of the lineage, teachings, and traditions of Guru Padmasambhava. Thus, today's great Nyingma masters respect these eight caves as absolutely essential to any devoted follower of the Mahaguru.

Indeed, Samye Chimpu is widely praised as the premier residence and retreat site of Guru Padmasambhava himself, over the course of his time in Tibet— equal in power to the great charnel grounds of Ancient India. Long before the Mahaguru's arrival, the caves of Chimpu had served as ancient burial sites, attracting a similar spiritual energy to that of the cemeteries where he had roamed in India, attaining ever deeper levels of realization. Furthermore, these caves, although in the vicinity of Samye monastery, also provided ample seclusion from the day-to-day business of its construction, and so the Mahaguru settled here, spent extended periods in retreat, and taught and transmitted the Dharma to his students in myriad ways. In particular, the Mahaguru recognized the Chimpu caves as vital for safeguarding and maintaining the blessings of Samye Monastery.[353] Just as the Sitavana charnel ground served as one of the main sites for revealing and transmitting the Vajrayana in India, the transmission of the essence of the Mahaguru's realization, his mind of enlightenment, has it source at Samye Chimpu, earning it a legacy of pilgimage and praise, as one of Tibet's most sacred sites.[354]

Approaching the Sacred Site

"The valley of Chimpu is like a blossoming lotus."
Outwardly, it is shaped like open petals;
Inwardly, it is Vajravarahi's dharmadayo, of the three liberations;
Secretly, it is the expanse of the Vajra Queen's bhaga.
At its center is Drakmar Ke'u-tsang, the Red Rock Treasure Nest,
Which rests on mountain slopes that rise like a victory banner.[355]

— *Rikdzin Jikmé Lingpa*

Replete with aromatic herbs and shrubs, the highlands of Samye Chimpu rise up to form the head of Drakmar Valley. The *Pema Kathang* hails it as akin to a blossoming lotus, an image later masters like Jigmé Lingpa evoked in their own guides to this sacred site. The caves themselves are perched high on the mountainside, overlooking the entire valley, and from these slopes rivers flow down to Samye monastery. At Samye Chimpu there a not just one, but a whole complex of caves, each of which has its own, unique history. The spiritual center of Chimpu, however, is the cave of *Drakmar Ke'u Tsang*, the *Treasure Nest of Drakmar*. This is where Guru Rinpoche first initiated his disciples into the Vajrayana, and where over many years he transmitted the very heart essence of the Buddhadharma. Surrounding *Drakmar Ke'u Tsang* are several more caves where Guru Rinpoche practiced and accomplished specific activities. The Mahaguru's closest disciples likewise entered into solitary retreats in the Chimpu caves, and as a result attained incredible realization, as did the many great masters who followed. The miraculous traces of their awakened activities—syllables, images, handprints and footprints, etched and engraved in and around the Chimpu caves—can still be seen today.[356]

The Mahaguru's Journey

Ascending to Chimpu

> *When your body was residing there,*
> *Uttering 'hung' with your speech, you averted an avalanche*
> *And blessed the site with this syllable of your unchanging mind.*
> *To you we pray: Please grant your blessings![357]*
>
> — *Changdak Tashi Topgyal*

Soon after he was welcomed to the Drakmar Valley by King Trisong Detsen, Guru Padmasambhava surveyed the area for a suitable retreat place, one that could become his personal residence. Intuitively, the Mahaguru was drawn to the ancient burial ground of Chimpu and its associated caves, high above the foundations where Samye Monastery was to be built. When Guru Rinpoche first ascended the hill to the Chimpu caves, though, the local spirits tried to bury the Mahaguru with rocks and boulders sent tumbling down the mountainside. As the stones were careening toward him, Guru Rinpoche forcefully uttered *hung*, catching the stones in midair and sending them right back whence they came, now assembled in the shape of the syllable *hung*. To this day, a *hung* syllable is clearly visible in the cliff where the cascade began.[358]

Forging an Alliance between Humans and Nagas

> *At Samyé Chimpu, in your wisdom you tamed the nagas,*
> *Thereby forging a connection between the nagas and the King.*
> *The nagas, in turn, offered quantities of gold.*
> *Under your guidance, the temple bell was hung, and*
> *You delegated spirits as the monastery's guards. Homage to you![359]*
>
> — *Jamyang Khyentsé Wangpo*

Shortly after putting an end to the spirits' evil scheming, the Mahaguru was practicing at the Chimpu caves. While previously he had pacified the nagas

156

and their King Manasvi by building a naga temple at the Maldro lake, he saw that although the nagas had obeyed his orders, their minds were still untamed and they continued to harm other beings whenever they got the chance.[360] So the Mahaguru, visualizing himself as Garuda, focused his meditation on subduing the nagas. Feeling the immediate impact of the Guru's practice, the nagas rushed to the Dharma King, promising to supply especially the necessary timber for building Samye, if the King would only stop Guru Rinpoche from suppressing their kind. The King agreed and went to the Mahaguru's meditation cave, where he called out to the Guru "Pause your meditation and I will surely benefit!" Surprised, the Guru asked, "What is the benefit that you will gain from this?" "I will receive timber from the nagas," the King replied. The Guru pointed out that, rather than bending to the nagas' wishes, it would be more helpful to form an alliance between the Tibetan King and the king of the nagas.[361] The Mahaguru then returned to Maldro, the lake and residence of the naga king Manasvi. There he meditated and summoned the naga king. Eventually, Maldo Zichen appeared and announced:

> "Above ground, King Trisong Detsen is the greatest.
> Below ground, I am the greatest. We two should become allies."[362]

Following this encounter, gold washed up onto the shores of the lake, and from then on, the nagas provided the material necessary for building Samye monastery. Subsequently the particular cave in which the Mahaguru had been meditating was named the Ludül Puk (Naga-Taming Cave).

Awakened Speech

> *The blessing of the wisdom mind of Padma Heruka*
> *Descended to Indradevi and Nagarjuna,*
> *And down to Padmakara.*
> *To the masters past, present, and future*
> *Of the wisdom-speech lineage, we pray!*
> *To the Lotus-Born Guru of Orgyen, we pray!*[363]
>
> — *Revealed by Tulku Zangpo Drakpa*

Among the eight caves of accomplishment, those of Chimpu became especially connected with the Mahaguru's awakened speech. Here, Guru Rinpoche entered retreat focusing on Hayagriva, also known as Padma Heruka, for three months and three days.[364] Hayagriva emerges as the wrathful form of Amitabha,

Lord of the Lotus Family who embodies the speech of all buddhas. Thus, Hayagriva's special qualities are related to magnetizing, for he greatly enhances the power of speech, enabling the practitioner to become both eloquent and persuasive. As part of the Lotus Family, he is also connected to Amitayus, Buddha of Infinite Life, and can therefore bestow the siddhi of vidyadhara with power over life, extending the practitioner's lifespan indefinitely.[365] Hayagriva is further renowned for his ability to defeat vicious spirits and thereby cure all sorts of spirit-related diseases. And Guru Padmasambhava, being himself an emanation of Buddha Amitabha, is in his very essence Hayagriva. This we see reflected in the fact that when the demon Madram Rudra was poised to overtake the entire universe, the Mahaguru intervened by appearing in the wrathful form of Hayagriva to liberate Rudra from his terrible ego-driven schemes of domination.[366]

The teachings on Hayagriva were first revealed by the great vidyadhara Nagarjuna, that great Mahayana scholar who had much earlier revealed the *Prajñaparamita* scriptures. While Nagarjuna was outwardly a great master of the Sutra tradition, he was also a practitioner of Tantra, and in particular the mandala of Hayagriva. Many years earlier, the Mahaguru had helped the young Nagarjuna retrieve the *Prajñaparamita*, and the two had shared an intimate teacher-student relationship from that time on. Thus, when they met again, much later, at the Sitavana charnel ground, it was with great joy that Nagarjuna bestowed his heart-teachings on Hayagriva to Guru Rinpoche.[367] Then, with the blessings of the Dakini Karmendrani, they revealed the Hayagriva teachings there together.[368] Thus, as well as being already indivisible from this deity, the Mahaguru received the transmission in full while in India, and chose the Chimpu caves as the place to establish the practice in Tibet.

By means of empowerment, teachings, and oral transmission, Guru Rinpoche entrusted the practice of Hayagriva to his disciples, while rendering the site itself identical to his awakened speech. And during the *Kagyé* empowerments at Samye Chimpu, the Mahaguru entrusted these teachings in particular to Gyalwa Chokyang, who later practiced at Chimpu, accomplishing the great siddhi of magnetizing wrath.

Establishing the Support of Enlightened Speech

Transmission of the Kagyé Teachings

> *In the Red Rock Cave at Samye Chimpu,* ⁞
> *You matured those fortunate ones, the King and subjects,* ⁞
> *Empowering them into the mandala of the Secret Mantrayana,*
> *The great sadhanas of the Kagyé.* ⁞
> *You made the resultant vehicle of secret mantras spread far and wide.* ⁞
> *To you, whose kindness is beyond all imagining, we pray!* ⁞
> *To the Lotus-Born Guru of Orgyen, we pray!*[369] ⁞

> — *Revealed by Tulku Zangpo Drakpa*

On his journey through the Indian subcontinent, Guru Padmasambhava had gathered the most priceless Buddhist teachings yet to appear in our human realm. Among these were eight extraordinary sadhanas, collectively called the *Kagyé* (*The Eight Instructions*), received from eight accomplished masters known as the eight vidyadharas of India. The Mahaguru first received and practiced these sadhanas while in individual training with each of the eight vidyadharas in the eight great charnel grounds. Later, the Mahaguru also received these sadhanas at a gathering of the eight vidyadharas in the Sitavana charnel ground near Bodh Gaya.[370] These sadhanas form the very basis of the generation stage in Mahayoga, and thus they also serve as the foundation for the higher practices of Anuyoga and Atiyoga. For his Tibetan disciples to make any meaningful progress on the Vajrayana path, the foundational sadhanas of the *Kagyé* therefore needed to be transmitted. And so, upon Dharma King Trisong Detsen's sincere request, Guru Rinpoche bestowed the complete empowerments of the outer, inner, and secret mandalas of the *Kagyé* to the King and the twenty-five disciples, all of whom had gathered at Chimpu's Drakmar Ke'u Tsang cave. Moreover, Guru Padmasambhava also arranged and composed a variety of auxiliary sadhanas and instructions to these practices, which he entrusted to these students according to their karmic connections.

Among the many students that received the *Kagyé*, eight in particular showed particularly promising signs of accomplishment. These were Nubchen Sangyé Yeshé, Gyalwa Chokyang, Namhké Nyingpo, Dharma King Trisong Detsen, Khandro Yeshé Tsogyal, Palgyi Yeshé, Palgyi Sengé, and Vairocana. To determine which of the eight Kagyé deities would become their main practice, the disciples were asked to throw a flower into the mandala of the deities. Depending where, on which deity, their flower landed, they each received a specific yidam practice. As it happened, each of these eight disciples' flowers fell upon a different Kagyé deity. Guru Rinpoche sent them out, each to a different cave, in order to accomplish their karmically appropriate deity in these eight great caves that he had already blessed with his own meditation.[371] By entering into intensive retreat until they reached accomplishment, these eight gained renown as the eight vidyadharas of Tibet, each of them displaying unique and miraculous abilities as visible signs of their realization.[372] The *Kagyé* teachings were eventually hidden as *terma* treasures by Guru Padmasambhava and his disciples, throughout Tibet. King Trisong Detsen, because of his auspicious request, was entrusted with the main body of *Kagyé* teachings for safeguarding. This connection lasted long into the future, since the *Kagyé* teachings were later revealed as *terma* treasures by King Trisong Detsen's subsequent incarnations, namely Nyang Ral Nyima Özer (1124–1192) or (1136–1204), Guru Chöwang (1212–1270), Rigdzin Gödem (1337–1408), Orgyen Lingpa (b. 1323), and Jamyang Khyentse Wangpo.[373]

Requesting the Transmission of the Great Perfection

Despite such a momentous transmission, Guru Rinpoche would still not even utter the word *Dzokpachenpo* (Great Perfection) in public.[374] King Trisong Detsen, however, had become aware that these teachings existed and, in his great yearning for the Dharma, sent messengers to Mount Kailash to ask the great master Buddhaguhya to come and teach on the Great Perfection in his kingdom. Instead of visiting, Buddhaguhya sent the King a gift—the *Gyütrul Lamrim* (*The Gradual Path of the Mayajala*), a commentary that he had written on the *Guhyagarbha Tantra*—with the reply:

> I am practicing on Mount Kailash and will not be going to Samye. However, in our country, the Land of the Noble Ones, there is no Mahasiddha greater than Guru Rinpoche, Padmasambhava. He has received the *rikpé tsal wang* (the utmost precious empowerment of the display of awareness), and has gained complete mastery over all appearance and existence, samsara and nirvana. Basically, he has fully mastered Dzokchen. And as he is already with you in Tibet, there is no reason for me to come.[375]

Shortly thereafter, a grand ceremony was arranged to commemorate the advent of the Horse Year and mark the Dharma King's forty-ninth year. This elaborate event gathered a distinguished assembly of panditas and masters, with

Guru Rinpoche himself presiding over the gathering. In the presence of these esteemed wisdom-holders, the Dharma King humbly prostrated himself and spoke the following words:

> Today is the beginning of a crucial year for Tibet. Buddhaguhya says that you are a master of the Clear Light Dzogpachenpo teachings and that your mind holds dominion over all that appears and exists in the whole of samsara and nirvana, which means you must have teachings to give us. Please, grant us these teachings, here in Tibet, on this very special occasion of the New Year.[376]

The King, acting as the representative of all of Guru Rinpoche's devoted heart disciples, humbly implored Guru Rinpoche to grant them the profound teachings of the Great Perfection, the highest pinnacle of spiritual wisdom. "If you cannot," he said, "then at least give us the essential instructions. If you cannot even do that, Buddhaguhya told us that you have received the *rikpé tsal wang*, so such an empowerment must exist. Please grant that to us at least!"[377]

Then, still before this grand assembly, King Trisong Detsen asked the Mahaguru for the name of his own root teacher, the one who had granted him the final introduction to the nature of mind, but Guru Rinpoche remained totally silent on these deeply precious matters.

Subsequently, Dharma King Trisong Detsen came across Guru Rinpoche, Vimalamitra, and a few other lotsawas, all engaged in the translation of teachings at Dragyur Ling, the translation center at Samye. Once again, the King approached Guru Rinpoche and inquired about the identity of his root guru. Vimalamitra, hearing the question, remained silent, leaving it to Guru Rinpoche to respond. However, Guru Rinpoche chose not to answer the King's question and instead abruptly ceased his activities and departed. Despite continuous efforts, even by Khandro Yeshe Tsogyal, to uncover the identity of Guru Rinpoche's teacher, and using various skillful means, he steadfastly refused to provide even the slightest hint.

After three years had elapsed, a significant moment arrived during the auspicious Monkey month of the Monkey Year. It happened on the Tenth Day, in the early morning, as Guru Rinpoche arose at the temple of Butsar Sekar Ling in Samye. As he was preparing to depart, Khandro Yeshe Tsogyal and the others inquired about his intended destination. "Everyone in Tibet, from King Trisong Detsen and his court down to the most ordinary citizen, is desperate to discover the name of my root teacher," he said. "You'd think they were all dying of thirst! So now I will reveal it. Follow me."

Guru Rinpoche walked ahead with everyone eagerly following behind. He guided them up to the sacred site of Samye Chimpu and halted in front of the entrance to Drakmar Ke'utsang. There, he turned to face the gathering and spoke the following words: "You want to know the name of my root teacher, right?" There was a breathless silence. "My root teacher is the glorious Heruka, the Fearless Vidyadhara Shri Singha!" As Guru Rinpoche uttered these words, he joined his palms together above the crown of his head in a gesture of reverence. In that very moment, the sky was adorned with an array of enlightened beings, and every sentient being—human and non-human, as well as the mountains, rocks, and trees of the Land of Snows and Samye Chimpu—bowed in deep homage toward the sacred land of India, paying homage to the great master Shri Singha.[378] That momentous occasion marked the very first time that the Mahaguru revealed the name of his esteemed root guru.

Once again, the Dharma King and disciples, while offering an immense mandala of riches, pleaded to be given the teachings that had been taught by his root teacher, but the Mahaguru would not budge. Later, however, after returning to Samye, the Mahaguru did grant his disciples the *rikpé tsel wang*, and transmitted the empowerments and liberating instructions that he had received from Shri Singha, all of this taking place in the middle chamber of the main temple. At this point, Guru Rinpoche revealed only a few key points of the Great Perfection teachings. Soon, however, a suitable vessel for these pinnacle teachings would emerge.[379]

Entrusting Princess Pema Sal with the Great Perfection Teachings

Guru Padmsambhava returned to Chimpu, where he continued to teach his fortunate disciples. King Detsen was in the midst of sponsoring one hundred and eight feast offerings, when, in the middle of the night, he received troubling news: his daughter, nine-year old Princess Pema Sal, had fallen gravely ill. She was led up to Chimpu on a white horse, to gain blessings from the Mahaguru. It was too late however, and the young princess passed away before they got there.

The party finally arrived and laid the princess down upon on a rock before the Mahaguru. The King, seeing his beloved daughter's lifeless body, was overcome by grief and fainted on the spot. When he came to consciousness again, the Mahaguru consoled his dear disciple, explaining that his daughter's death was itself a powerful teaching on the nature of impermanence:

Listen, your majesty— ⸸
In general, all mundane pursuits are like dreams. ⸸
The mark of composite things is that they are like magical illusions. ⸸
Your kingdom is like last night's dream. ⸸
Your wealth and subjects are like dew drops on a blade of grass. ⸸
This fleeting life is like bubbles upon water. ⸸
All composite things will perish. ⸸
Meeting ends in separation. ⸸
All composite things are like this. ⸸
There is not a single thing that is stable and lasts. ⸸
Do not cling to the impermanent as being permanent. ⸸
Train in the non-arising nature of dharmakaya.[380] ⸸

— Revealed by Gyalwa Longchenpa

At these words of uncompromising truth, King Trisong Detsen began to gain some distance from his terrible suffering. The Mahaguru continued, explaining that Princess Pema Sal had, in a past life long ago, amassed a great store of merit at the Boudha Stupa in Nepal. She had in fact been an insect, accidentally killed during the consecration ceremony, and was reborn in this present time as Princess Pema Sal due to aspirations made on her behalf.[381] In a miraculous gesture, Guru Rinpoche then summoned her consciousness by drawing a red syllable *nri* on her heart, spoke her name aloud, and so brought the Princess back to life, before the eyes of her distraught father and all those gathered there. The Princess slowly regained consciousness and, once she was able to listen and speak again, the Mahaguru entrusted her with the *Khandro Nyingtik* (*The Heart Essence of the Dakinis*), the very essence of the Great Perfection, while allowing not another soul to listen. This transmission complete, her karma took its hold, and again, finally, she passed away. Where her body had been placed on the rock, a vivid imprint appeared in the shape of a triangle, symbolic for the *dharmodaya*, the source of all phenomena.

The Mahaguru then offered a prophecy to the Dharma King. Centuries later, Princess Pema Sal would reincarnate as the master Pema Ledreltsal (1291–1315), who would reveal this *Khandro Nyingtik* cycle that he had just whispered to the Princess (and would later teach to Khandro Yeshé Tsogyal in her retreat at Zhotö Tidro).[382] Pema Ledreltsal's next rebirth, in turn, was predicted to be the omniscient Longchen Rabjam. At the Master's words, although his daughter was no longer physically with him, the King realized that not only was she brought onto the spiritual path in a most extraordinary way, but she would also benefit beings in the future on a truly vast scale. Thanking the Mahaguru, his heart and mind were finally at ease. The transmission of Great Perfection was thus preserved, to be assisted by the activity of yet another peerless master, the Great Vimalamitra.[383]

Khandro Yeshé Tsogyal Takes Residence at Chimpu

While Khandro Yeshé Tsogyal had accompanied the Mahaguru to Samye Chimpu on numerous occasions, her role in upholding his lineage of teachings and practices became even more prominent after the Mahaguru's departure from Tibet. As the Mahaguru's main heir, Khandro Yeshé Tsogyal took on the responsibility of continuing his legacy. She was regularly invited to Samye monastery, where she would turn the Wheel of the Dharma and transmit the profound teachings that she had received directly from the Mahaguru.

On these significant occasions, the revered wisdom dakini, following in the footsteps of her guru, chose the Chimpu caves as her primary abode. It was during this time that the Dharma King, the royal court, and the resident practitioners and translators began to seek the presence of the wisdom dakini at the Chimpu caves. There, she imparted to them the highest teachings on the Great Perfection. In moments of deep devotion and collective invocation of Guru Padmasambhava, the Mahaguru himself would manifest before them in a radiant aura of light, granting them empowerments and teachings.[384]

The Mahaguru's Legacy

Master of Hayagriva, Gyalwa Chokyang

> *Bhikshu born in Uru, into the Nyenlam clan,*
> *At Wentsa you accomplished Hayagriva, Mighty Lotus.*
> *To you, Gyal Chok Yang, you who neigh from the crown,*
> *We pray: Please grant your blessings![385]*
>
> — *Changdak Tashi Topgyal*

Gyalwa Chokyang was born into the Nyenlam clan in Uru and ordained by Abbot Shantarakshita, one of just seven in the very first group of Tibetan monks to receive ordination. Already, from a young age, he was known for his disciplined life.[386] During the *Kagyé* empowerment at Chimpu, Gyalwa Chokyang's flower fell on the mandala of Hayagriva. Consequently, he was instructed to remain in Wentsa, close to the Chimpu main caves, and practice

Hayagriva. The cave where Gyalwa Chokyang engaged in his retreat became known as Tamdrin Phuk (Hayagriva Cave). Upon accomplishing Hayagriva, Gyalwa Chokyang transformed into the deity, and the neigh of the horse on the crown of his head could be heard far and wide. Gyalwa Chokyang also attained the siddhi of "control over life" and thus could heal those at the brink of death. Gyalwa Chokyang's family descendants became the custodians of Samye Chimpu.[387] From the paternal side, Gyalwa Longchenpa was a descendant of Gyalwa Chokyang (1308–1364),[388] and his reincarnations include the Second Karmapa, Karma Pakshi (1204–1283).[389]

The Transmission of the Vima Nyingtik

> *Vimalamitra was waiting, crown jewel of five hundred scholars,*
> *And, with royal assent, he set off without delay.*
> *Arriving at Samyé, he conjured wondrous miracles,*
> *Inspiring tremendous faith in the Dharma King.*
> *They showered him with offerings and a joyous royal welcome.*
> *Homage to you!*[390]
>
> — *Jamyang Khyentsé Wangpo*

Late into his thousand-year stay in Greater India, the Mahaguru met a young boy who would become a future master of the Great Perfection. Vimalamitra was still a child, but the Mahaguru immediately perceived and encouraged his extraordinary potential.[391] Inspired thus by the Master, the young Vimalamitra travelled from his homeland of Kashmir to the Vajra Seat of Bodh Gaya, where he studied Dharma under the tutelage of Buddhaguhya and composed scriptural commentaries, in particular on the *Guhyagarbha Tantra*.[392]

Upon receiving a vision, Vimalamitra then sought out and eventually found the renowned teacher Shri Singha, from whom he received all the *Nyingtik* teachings of the Great Perfection. These he safeguarded and preserved, serving also as a spiritual advisor to several kings over the course of the following decades. It was during this time that Vimalamitra reconnected with Guru Rinpoche, to exchange teachings and engage in their combined enlightened activity, including the revelation of the *Kagyé* teachings whilst in retreat at the charnel ground of Sitavana.[393]

Later, Vimalamitra moved to the court of King Indrabhuti of Uddiyana. While he was there, King Trisong Detsen, on the recommendation of his clairvoyant minister Nyang Tingdzin Zangpo, sent the two translators Kawa Paltsek and Chokro Lu'i Gyaltsen to India to invite this esteemed scholar to Tibet. Vimalamitra was two hundred years of age, the very best of the Uddiyana's five hundred panditas, and when they came bearing lavish gifts for King Indrabhuti and made their sincere request, they received consent. But as had happened with the Mahaguru, evil-minded Tibetan ministers were already sowing doubt in King Trisong Detsen's heart, calling Vimalamitra a black magician and a danger to the kingdom. When the King, as a result, refused meet the master on arrival, Vimalamitra decided to perform a series of miracles before the eyes of the Tibetan court, including emanating a colossal image of Buddha Vairocana that filled the whole of Samye with the lights of the five wisdoms.

In the wake of this display, awe and faith grew in the King, who bowed before this master, requesting him to expound the Dharma and guide the translation of the Buddha's teachings into Tibetan. And this Vimalamitra did, teaching the sutras by day, and the tantras and pith instructions to a select few disciples by night. After thirteen years in Tibet, he left for the five-peaked mountain of Wu Tai Shan in China. There this supreme sidddha remains until the end of this age, in the deathless state of the rainbow body, sending an emanation to Tibet every one hundred years, thus keeping the transmission of the Great Perfection alive and flourishing.[394]

Vimalamitra thus transmitted the Great Perfection teachings, which became known as the *Vima Nyingtik*, in countless ways. One of the principal lines of transmission was through his closest students, Dharma King Trisong Detsen and Nyang Tingdzin Zangpo, who entered retreat in the Upper and Lower Caves of Nyang at Samye Chimpu, to practice the instructions they had received.[395] Nyang Tingdzin Zangpo, in particular, later concealed the *Vima Nyingtik* in the temple that he built—the Zha Lhakang in Uru. A hundred years or so later, these treasures were retrieved and realized by Dangma Lhundrup Gyaltsen (10–11th century), who then passed them on to Chetsün Senge Wangchuk (11–12th century). Guided by a vision of Vimalamitra, Senge Wangchuk in turn travelled to Samye Chimpu, where he received the *Nyingtik* teachings previously hidden by Vimalamitra, offered by a woman with conch teeth and turquoise eyebrows. After further visionary guidance, Chetsün Senge Wangchuk combined the treasures he had received from his teacher Dangma Lhundrup Gyaltsen with those that he retrieved from Chimpu. Meditating upon these combined instructions for seven years, Senge Wangchuk attained the rainbow body, so that his entire physical body was transformed into the light of wisdom.[396] In this way, the transmissions of the *Vima Nyingti*k in particular were passed down the generations, reaching their most prolific and influential upholder in the omniscient Longchen Rabjampa.

Transmission of the Nyingtik Teachings

As mentioned above, the Great Perfection teachings had been given directly to Dharma King Trisong Detsen's daughter, Lhacham Pema Sal, just as she was on the verge of passing away. The fortunate princess then reincarnated as Pema Ledrel Tsel (1291–1315) who, at the age of twenty-three, discovered these pith instructions, the *Khandro Nyingtik*, at Danglung Tramodrak in Dakpo. Pema Ledrel Tsel practiced the teachings in secret, later transmitting some of them to his heart disciples. He soon re-concealed them, however, knowing that the time for propagating these teachings lay in the future. Shortly thereafter, the *tertön* passed into parinirvana, at the age of twenty-five.

As prophesied by the Mahaguru in the *Pema Kathang*, Pema Ledrel Tsel's immediate reincarnation was none other than the legendary master Gyalwa Longchenpa. Longchenpa, originally ordained by Samdrup Rinchen at Samye Chimpu, spent extended periods studying, meditating and teaching at Chimpu's Rimochen cave, and later at his hermitage at Kangri Tökar. His main root teacher, Rikdzin Kumaraja, would later grant him the *Vima Nyingtik* teachings, but only after much hardship. When Longchenpa entered into retreat to practice these teachings, his past karmic propensities began to ripen, and soon he realized that the *Khandro Nyingtik*, re-concealed by his predecessor Pema Ledrel Tsel, still lay hidden, awaiting his discovery.

At the age of thirty-one, Longchenpa sent one of his students, Özer Gocha, to retrieve the *Khandro Nyingtik*. After much hardship, Özer Gocha successfully returned with the scriptures and offered them to Longchenpa for inspection. At the same time, Longchenpa had a vision of the Dharma protectress Shenpa Sokdrubma, who presented him with a volume of the very same text. At thirty-two, while in retreat at the Rimochen cave at Chimpu, following visions of the Mahaguru and Khandro Yeshé Tsogyal that lasted for six days, Longchenpa gave his first transmission of the *Nyingtik* teachings to eight fortunate disciples, including Özer Gocha.[397] During the empowerments, the protectress Ekajati entered one of Longchenpa's female students and gave prophecies. Further, in visions, Guru Padmasambhava and Khandro Yeshé Tsogyal transmitted the full *Nyingtik* teachings to Longchenpa. The Mahaguru granted him the name Drimé Özer (Stainless Light), while the wisdom dakini named him Dorjé Ziji (Blazing Vajra). It was during these *Nyingtik* transmissions that Longchenpa sang this vajra-song:

> O yogis, I am so very happy and joyous!
> Tonight, we are in the pure land Unexcelled.
> In our bodies, the palace of Peaceful and Wrathful Deities,
> Flourishes the assembly of Buddhas,
> The union of clarity and emptiness.
> Buddhahood is not somewhere else, but in us.
> O meditators, you who hold your minds one-pointedly,
> Don't hold your mind in one place, but let it go at ease.
> Mind is emptiness or openness, whether it goes or stays.
> Whatever arises in the mind is the mere play of wisdom.[398]

Additionally, during his retreat at Chimpu, Longchenpa discovered three *terma* scrolls, including one for the *Drönzhi Ösel* (*The Luminosity of the Four Lamps*).[399] By combining the *Vima Nyingtik* with the *Khandro Nyingtik,* and adding his own revelations and commentaries, Longchenpa went on to create the sublime compendium of teachings known as the *Nyingtik Yapzhi* (*The Four Seminal Heart Essences*).

After a lifetime of practicing, realizing, and synthesizing the *Nyingtik* teachings, Longchenpa at one point knew that his wisdom mind was soon to part from his physical body. He journeyed once more back to Samye Chimpu and, arriving, famously declared:

> This place is just like the Sitavana charnel ground in India.
> I would rather die here than be born elsewhere.
> Here I will leave this worn-out, illusory body of mine.[400]

Though Longchenpa intended to pass away at this site, he was requested to bestow empowerments to a large group of people waiting below at Samye Monastery, which is where he would leave his body several days later. While this would be his final visit in his physical human form to the great meditation cave of Chimpu, he would return many times in visions there, to his own emanation, Rikdzin Jikmé Lingpa.

Revelation of the Longchen Nyingtik

Emanations of the Mahaguru's disciples continued at Chimpu with the great visionary and treasure revealer Rikdzin Jikmé Lingpa (1730–1798).[401] During his first three-year retreat at the age of twenty-eight, Jikmé Lingpa had been on a visionary journey to the Jarung Kashor stupa in Nepal and received the renowned mind treasure the *Longchen Nyingtik* (*The Heart Essence of the Vast Expanse*).[402] At thirty-one, he started a second three-year retreat, this time at Chimpu. Jikmé Lingpa focused on studying the writings of Longchenpa, perceiving him as the Buddha.[403] He began his retreat in the Upper Cave of Nyang, later moving to the Lower Cave, where King Trisong Detsen had received the *Nyingtik* teachings from Nyang Tingdzin Zangpo.

It was during this retreat that Rikdzin Jikmé Lingpa recieved three visions of Longchenpa's wisdom body, causing his realization of the Great Perfection to unfold to the full. In the Upper Cave he received the first vision, in which Longchenpa's vajra body appeared, bestowing complete understanding of his writings. The second and third visions occurred in the Lower Cave. In the second, he received the blessing of Longchenpa's vajra speech, empowering him to uphold and propagate these teachings. In the third, he received the blessing of Longchenpa's wisdom mind, transferring to him the timeless awareness of Longchen Rabjam.[404] Thus, his realization of the lineage of the Great Perfection, as passed down by Guru Rinpoche, Vimalamitra, and Longchenpa, was unsurpassed.[405] Rather than studying and practicing, Jikmé Lingpa received everything he needed directly, through the power of his unsurpassed devotion.

Later, at Samye Chimpu, Jikmé Lingpa gave the liberation and ripening empowerments of the *Longchen Nyingtik* for the first time, to fifteen select disciples.[406] It was also here at Chimpu that he wrote the profound and moving prayer, *Training in the Pure Realms of the Three Kayas*:[407]

> *Kyema Kyihü! O Lotus-Born, Master of Pure Awareness,*
> *Sentient beings like me, in this degenerate age,*
> *We are riddled with evil karma.*
> *When I yearn for happiness, yet contrive to create only suffering,*
> *When my every effort is completely wrong, who can I turn to?*
> *Look on me with compassion, you who dwell in Ngayab Ling—*
> *Care for me, guide me, inspire me, make me one with you.*
> *Lead me, right now, to the Copper-Coloured Mountain of Glory!*[408]

In the prayer's colophon, Jikmé Lingpa gives us a glimpse into how an awakened master perceives the sacred landscape, and what kind of transformation this wrought upon him:

> *Once I was alone in solitary retreat in the divine Ke'u Tsang Vajra*

Cave, a hermitage blessed by the naturally-arising enlightened speech of Padmasambhava. One morning, I caught sight of Mount Hepori and thought: "Wait...It was on that very hilltop just over there that Abbot Shantarakshita, the master Padma, the King and the disciples once walked, subjugated gods and ghosts, and relaxed. Many are the tales that appear to that effect. But now, apart from their names, not a single trace of them remains." I was gripped by a conviction that in the very same way, everything is transient, impermanent. And although I had reckoned on staying alive, and not dying, for a few years more, what certainty was there that I would not leave for my next life the very next day? This train of thought filled me with haunting sorrow and aching weariness, and a sense of renunciation that was boundless. The memory of Guru Rinpoche, the King, and the disciples plunged me into floods of tears. And this was why, at that moment, I, Chatral Khyentsé Özer, wrote this "Prayer and Aspiration to Training in the Pure Realms of the Three Kayas"...[409].

Jamyang Khyentsé Wangpo's Three Vajra Songs

For Jamyang Khyentse Wangpo too, Samye Chimpu was one of the single most sacred sites in all of Tibet.[410] We can see from Khyentse Wangpo's accounts of his visits, both on pilgrimage and in visions, that this sacred site had a profound impact on him too. On his great pilgrimage through Central Tibet, he offered a thousand feasts in the *Drakmar Ke'u Tsang* cave and, as a result of his fervent prayers, composed the following vajra song to the eight great vidyadharas of India, which begins as follows:

> *Hail to Wrathful Guru Padma!*
> *The yoga of dissolving the winds into the avadhuti*
> *Evokes this melody of the indestructible nada.*
> *A symbol of the speech of all the buddhas,*
> *Reflecting the indivisible vajra,*
> *This springtime glory of the luminous essence pervades all creation.*
> *And so, to a rain of flowers,*
> *I praise unexcelled Samye Chimpu all day long.*[411]

This profound vajra song of praise concludes with the following prayer:

> *The emergence of the eight consciousnesses from temporary confusion*
> *Is established as the mandala of the eight great glorious herukas.*

O Vidyadhara Padmasambhava,
Arising from the major and minor marks on the nine expanses of
Wisdom—From the bottom of my heart, I remember you now:
Please bless me that I may accomplish the indivisible four kayas![412]

On the 10th day of the month, Khyentse Wangpo moved to the Wentsa cave, where Gyalwa Chokyang had realized the deity Hayagiva. Here, he offered another grand feast to the Mahaguru and composed the following vajra song:

Aho! The magical manifestation of discriminating wisdom,
Devoid of all attachment,
Appears in youthful form, unimpeded, as the Wrathful Lotus.
Liberating the illusory foe, afflictions, into the dharmadhatu,
To the mandala of the mighty play of Hayagriva, I bow![413]

Jamyang Khyentse Wangpo continued his retreat, offering a feast at the Rimochen Cave where Gyalwa Longchenpa had practiced in retreat for three years. There, in a vision, he received the *Khandro Nyingtik* teachings directly from the Mahaguru. It was here that Khyentsé Wangpo spontaneously composed the following vajra song invoking Gyalwa Longchenpa:

Aho! While awakening has always lain within the bindu of our heart,
You appeared as a saffron illusion in order to spread the ultimate teachings.
Omniscient King of Dharma, from the depths of my heart
I pray to you, evoking this music of a vajra song![414]

Later, when Jamyang Khyentse Wangpo was transmitting the *Khandro Nyingtik* to the Queen Mother of Dergé, and to Gyalyum Chöying Zangmo (d. 1892) and others, he had a profound vision, in which he travelled back to Chimpu to receive the entire *Nyingtik Yabzhi* from Gyalwa Longchenpa directly.[415] Thus, Samye Chimpu has been, and still remains, a source of profound inspiration for generations of the Mahaguru's descendants. The pinnacle of his teachings, the Great Perfection itself, has been resounding within these cave walls, echoing into the hearts of devoted practitioners, right up to the present day.

DRAK YANGDZONG

The awakened body of blazing vajra-wisdom,
Destroyer of confused, dualistic minds,
Instantly appears, peaceful and smiling,
Granting relief to the ocean of beings—
Glorious Heruka, Vanquisher of Time,
Your splendor is like the morning sun rising,
A pleasure grove, replete with all inner and outer excellence,
To delight the vidyadharas.[416]

— *Jamyang Khyentsé Wangpo*

Introduction

The caves at Drak Yangdzong[417] (Clifftop Fortress) were blessed by the Mahaguru's practice of Yamantaka, the wrathful aspect of Manjushri, thus rendering the site identical to the awakened body of the buddhas. After staying here in retreat, the Mahaguru also hid several *terma* treasures at the site. Later, the Mahaguru's heart disciple Nupchen Sangyé Yeshé took Drak Yangdzong as his main retreat hermitage, likewise practicing Yamantaka until he attained total accomplishment of this wrathful deity's essential wisdom.[418]

Approaching the Sacred Site

From Zurkar Do, the pilgrim travels west along the northern shore of the Brahmaputra River, eventually reaching the Drak Valley, a dry inland area studded with willow groves. Moving north into the valley, the pilgrim first arrives at Dramda village, the birthplace of Nupchen Sangyé Yeshé. The highlight of the village is a temple dedicated to Nupchen, which houses a stupa that holds his relics. Further north is Tsogyal Lhatso, birthplace of Khandro Yeshé Tsogyal.[419] Continuing on, the pilgrim comes to the sacred Guru Rinpoche sites of Drak Yangdzong (Clifftop Fortress) and Dzong Kumbum (Fortress of a Hundred Thousand Deities).

High above a tributary of the Brahmaputra River, above slopes of rhododendron and juniper, is Drak Yangdzong, also known as Shinjé Rolpé Phodrang (Palace of Yamantaka's Display). Its two large, linked caverns are at the center of a network of caves and tunnels which have been home to practitioners for centuries upon centuries. Like Samye Chimpu, Drak Yangdzong is an ancient funeral site, and the juniper-covered hill southwest of the caves is much like the Kula Dzokpa charnel ground of South India.[420] Some hold that the Yang-dzong itself looks like Yama, Lord of Death—the very deity overcome through the practice of Yamantaka—the ridge's spires, his horns; the lower cave, his jaw.[421] The spiritual center of Drak Yangdzong is the Zhinjé Rolpé Drupné (The Practice Cave of Yamantaka's Display). This is the inner sanctuary in which the Mahaguru accomplished Yamantaka's mandala, now dissolved into the living rock.

The Mahaguru's Journey

Awakened Body

> The blessing of the wisdom mind of Manjushri Yamantaka ༔
> Descended to the great master Manjushrimitra, ༔
> And all the way down to the 'zombie' Vetalasukha. ༔
> To the masters past, present, and future ༔
> Of the wisdom body lineage, we pray! ༔
> To the Lotus-Born Guru of Orgyen, we pray![422] ༔

— *Revealed by Tulku Zangpo Drakpa*

The Drak Yangdzong caves are those that represent Guru Rinpoche's awakened body. Here, the Mahaguru entered retreat, focusing on the yidam deity Yamantaka.[423] Yamantaka is the wrathful form of Manjushri, the actual body-essence of all the buddhas. Being a form of Manjushri, the embodiment of wisdom, Yamantaka is known for greatly accelerating a practitioner's wisdom and intelligence. The very name Yamantaka—"Slayer of Yama (the Lord of Death)"— suggests how the practice is also a powerful means for extending the practitioner's life. Moreover, it contains a unique set of pith instructions on mantras particularly powerful in overcoming fierce enemies.

The teachings on Yamantaka were revealed by the vidyadhara Manjushrimitra, who was himself a heart disciple of Garab Dorjé. He revealed them on Mount Malaya as a golden ritual text, written in ink of crushed beryl. Manjushrimitra used the practice of Yamantaka as a means to subdue rulers who were threatening to destroy the Dharma. He later concealed this book on the Indian mainland, at a secret location to the north of Bodh Gaya.[424] It was on Mount Malaya and from Manjushrimitra that Guru Rinpoche received the outer and inner teachings on Yamantaka, then practicing them in retreat until receiving a direct vision of Yamantaka.[425] These two masters thus formed an intimate student-teacher relationship, and together they would later reveal the Yamantaka teachings as a treasure text at the Sitavana charnel ground.[426]

Guru Padmasambhava transmitted the Yamantaka teachings to King Vasudhara of Nepal, and to many other disciples in that land,[427] and, once he reached Tibet, he chose the caves of Drak Yangdzong as the sacred site where Yamantaka's blessings would especially reside. By one-pointedly practicing Yamantaka there himself, he not only introduced this practice tradition to Tibet, but also blessed the site as being identical to his own awakened body. Later, when he gave the *Kagyé* empowerments at Samye Chimpu, these Yamantaka teachings were entrusted to Nupchen Sangyé Yeshé, who then practiced them at Drak Yangdzong at the Mahaguru's command.

It was at this time that Guru Rinpoche and Khandro Yeshé Tsogyal concealed many *terma* treasures in the caves and surrounding area. Specifically, the Mahaguru hid a longevity vase bearing extraordinary instructions, and a skull cup, at Drak Yangdzong's Crystal Cave, with the following aspiration:

> *When the time of the last five-hundred years arrives, my emanation will appear— wrathful, fierce, and powerful, with a black mole at his heart center in the shape of a vajra. He will open the door to this treasure of my heart. He will take out this life-vase and the miraculous terma instruction and, having attained the vidyadhara level of longevity, he will subdue with magical armies all demons and heretics.*[428]
>
> — Revealed by Nyangral Nyima Özer

There were many who eventually followed the Mahaguru's example and went into retreat at Drak Yangdzong, with fifty-five of them reaching especially profound accomplishment, becoming collectively known as the Fifty-Five Yogis of Yangdzong.[429]

The Mahaguru's Legacy

Master of Yamantaka, Nupchen Sangyé Yeshé

> *Coming from the valleys in the land of Nup,*
> *At Drak Yangdzok you accomplished Yamantaka, Death-Lord Slayer.*
> *To you, Sangyé Yeshé, who pierce solid rocks with your phurba,*
> *We pray: please grant your blessings!*[430]
>
> — Changdak Tashi Topgyal

Nupchen Sangyé Yeshé was born into a family descending from two highly respected Tibetan clans, the Nup and the Chim, in the Drongmoché village of Drak Valley.[431] Leading up to his birth, a sandalwood tree grew miraculously from the grounds where his ancestors were buried, and signs showed that he would be a saintly emanation. From a very young age, Nupchen Sangyé Yeshé showed great interest in the Dharma and, after receiving ordination from Abbot Shantarakshita, he studied the Dharma and the Indic language extensively.[432] Later however, Nupchen renounced his celibate lifestyle and joined the Mahaguru's lay community of white-robed yogis. Nupchen Sangyé Yeshé became a student of Guru Padmasambhava, and was instructed to practice Yamantaka in particular. Having received teachings on Yamantaka from the Mahaguru on various occasions, he stated:

> The Mahaguru then bestowed
> Upon this humble monk
> The nine tantras of fierce mantra,
> A variety of ways to practice them,
> And all their minor activities and necessities.[433]

Already a bright student, Nupchen's practice of Yamantaka, a form of Manjushri, only further enhanced his intelligence, so that he became incredibly learned in the Dharma and mastered Sanskrit and its vernaculars with ease. At Samye Monastery, he studied with the Newar prince Vasudhara—one of the Mahaguru's main Newar students, and himself an adept of the practice of Yamantaka, who, when he heard that the Mahaguru intended to establish Buddhism in Tibet, also made his way to Samye to support this endeavor.

Following the advice of his teachers, Sangyé Yeshé visited India and Nepal several times, receiving teachings and empowerments from the greatest masters of the day, including Shri Singha, Vimalamitra, and Shantigarbha. Making his way to Gilgit, he studied too with the Anuyoga adepts Dharmabodhi and Dhanarakshita, and the lotsawa Ché Tsenkyé.[434] Sangyé Yeshé also studied and received many pith instructions from the Mahaguru's esteemed lotsawa and student Nyak Jñanakumara.[435] Later he stated, regarding his teachers:

> These pith instructions were bestowed upon me
> By the Indian adept Vimalamitra,
> By the master of Uddiyana, Padmasambhava,
> By the Newar adept Vasudhara,
> And by the Tibetan adept Jñanakumara.[436]

Throughout his life, the caves of Yangdzong were Sangye Yeshe's main retreat place. Here, in his homeland of Drak, Nupchen Sangyé Yeshé practiced with his own disciples, transmitting to them the many teachings that he had received from his esteemed teachers. He continued to focus especially on the practice of Yamantaka over the course of these retreats, and swiftly gained accomplishment in this fierce deity. As a result, Nupchen Sangyé Yeshé was able to liberate spirits from their samsaric existence, pierce solid rock with his dagger, and extend his life far beyond astrological reckoning.

While he was at Yangdzong, the rule of Dharma began to crumble, as the lineage of Dharma King Trisong Detsen fell to the domain of King Langdarma, who ruled Tibet from 838 to 842. A period of increasing conflict followed, and it was at this time that Nupchen Sangyé Yeshé became inspired to subdue these harmful forces through wrathful, awakened activity. He thus revealed from the Yamantaka tantras the special instructions on fierce spells, incantations, and magic—gathered earlier, while he was in India and Nepal—and was thereby able to quell many of the conflicts tearing Tibet apart at that time.[437]

In the most famous of these episodes, Nupchen, with a mere gesture of his hand, invoked a huge scorpion to appear, terrifying the evil King Langdarma, who thereupon refrained from further persecuting Tibet's white-robed community of yogis.[438] Later, at the prince's invitation, Nupchen Sangyé Yeshé returned to Samye to teach the Dharma, and, in so doing, continued to uphold the lineage of his root teacher, Guru Padmasambhava.[439]

During his lifetime, Sangye Yeshe assisted Khandro Yeshé Tsogyal in compiling and concealing many of Guru Rinpoche's treasures.[440] Furthermore, Nupchen was not only a prolific translator, but he also composed a variety of texts himself. Among those that survive, his commentary on the Anuyoga root tantra the *Gongpa Düpé Do*, entitled *Münpé Gocha* (*Armor Against Darkness*) and his *Samten Migdrön* (*Lamp for the Eye of Contemplation*)—a commentary on meditation according to both the Sutra and Tantra traditions—are especially renowned to this day.[441] Nupchen passed into parinirvana by dissolving into a mass of light at the age of a hundred and eleven—a sign of his accomplishment not only of Yamantaka, but also of the pith instructions of the Great Perfection.[442] Through his combination of scholarship and wrathful activity, Nupchen Sangyé Yeshé thus ensured that the lineage of the Mahaguru would continue authentically, no matter the conditions or obstacles that might arise.

Revelation of the Melong Nyingtik

Like Nupchen Sangyé Yeshé, the renowned early Nyingtik master Melong Dorjé (1243–1303) was born in the Drak Valley.[443] He received the *Vima Nyingtik*—Vimamitra's heart-essence teachings on the Great Perfection—from his root teacher Trulzhik Sengé Gyapa.[444] One of his main retreat places was the Ngarpuk (Cave of Stalks) at Drak Yangdzong, the same remote cave where the Mahaguru and Nupchen had practiced centuries before.

Here at Ngarpuk, Melong Dorjé revealed additional Atiyoga teachings by Vimalamitra, which became renowned as the *Melong Nyingtik* (*The Heart Essence of Melong*)—a treasure later rediscovered by Jamyang Khyentse Wangpo. At Yangdzong, too, Melong Dorjé gave to Rikdzin Kumaraja,[445] Gyalwa Longchenpa's root teacher, the Atiyoga teachings, pointing out the nature of his mind. Melong Dorjé also gave teachings to Rikdzin Kumaraja at Lhodrak Kharchu, the sacred site of the Mahaguru's awakened heart.[446]

Revelation of the Magyü Sangwa Lamkhyer

In the 14th century, Machik Kunga Bum, an emanation of Khandro Yeshé Tsogyal, entered retreat at Drak Yangdzong, in the cave known as Ösal Puk (Clear Light Cave), staying there for seven years and seven days. During this retreat, she revealed the *Magyü Sangwa Lamkhyer* (*The Secret Practices of Mother Tantra*), and opened a 'new' sacred cave, following a prophecy from the female buddha Vajravarahi. This particular practice was widespread in Tibet for a period of time, but later fell into obscurity. In the 19th century, Jamgön Kongtrül retrieved two copies, hidden by Kunga Bum herself, five hundred years earlier, at Drak Yangdzong and Yarlung Sheldrak. When Jamgön Kongtrül showed Chokgyur Lingpa the copies, the Great Tertön recalled receiving the transmission in a former life, when he was Dungtso Repa, the spiritual consort of Kunga Bum. Thereafter, both Jamgön Kongtrül and Chokgyur Lingpa disseminated this precious cycle throughout their lives, with Kongtrül including it in the *Rinchen Terdzö* (*Treasury of Precious Termas*).[447]

Revelation of the Zhijé Lhamo Khordün

> In the thick of the pass of Yortö Dra shall come ༔
> One with the name Ratna and Uddiyana— ༔

A spiritual lord, an emanation of Padma's awakened heart, ⦂
One who will practice supreme Dharma treasures.[448] ⦂

— Revealed by Orgyen Drimé Kunga

On his journey to Lhasa in 1868, the great treasure revealer Chokgyur Dechen Lingpa visited Drak Yangdzong. While practicing Yamantaka there, just as the Mahaguru had done before him, he rediscovered the *Zhijé Lhamo Khordün* (*The Sevenfold Cycle of the Pacifying Goddesses*). This scripture of instructions on The Seven Pacifications had been translated jointly by Guru Rinpoche and Prince Murup Tsenpo, and was later hidden at Lhari Rolpa Drak, to the west of Üshangdo. After the female master Lhatsün Ngönmo had discovered the original in the 12th century, she re-concealed it at Drak Yangdzong, to be re-revealed by Chokgyur Lingpa on this occasion of his visit. Chokgyur Lingpa offered the treasure to Jamyang Khyentsé Wangpo, who transcribed and propagated it widely. The treasure text teaches the pacification of:

1. illness, by means of Buddhalocana
2. epidemics, by means of Shavari
3. enemies, by means of Marici
4. sorcery, by means of Sitatapatra
5. mental distress, by means of Prajñaparamita
6. the eight dangers, by means of Tara
7. untimely death, by means of Mahamayuri[449]

Jamyang Khyentse Wangpo's Vajra Song

On his pilgrimage through central Tibet, Jamyang Khyentse Wangpo also visited the Drak Yangdzong caves. Here, while offering a feast to the mandala of Yamantaka and recalling the many incredible events that had unfolded at this site, the following vajra song arose spontaneously in his mind:

Aho!From within originally pure luminosity
Appears the supreme deity,
The yidam that effortlessly grants the twofold accomplishment,
Complete with face and hands and the excellent marks and signs.
To this mandala of Mañjushri, Vanquisher of Time, I bow.[450]

LHODRAK KARCHU

If, within the total quiescence of dharmadhatu,
Beyond the reach of conceptuality,
One clings to this illusory unity, outer objects will still appear,
Both support and supported. And so, granting relief to all such minds,
We pay constant homage to this Devikota and its host of dakinis![451]

— *Jamyang Khyentsé Wangpo*

Introduction

Long renowned as a potent gathering place of the dakinis, the caves of Lhodrak Karchu were blessed by the Mahaguru as the realm of Yangdak Heruka. This wrathful aspect of Akshobhya-Vajrasattva, embodiment of the awakened heart of the buddhas, thus permeates this magnificent cave complex. Lhodrak Karchu has also been recognized as the sacred mountain of Devikota, renowned in the tantric scriptures as an ideal site for Vajrayana practice. The Mahaguru's heart disciple Namkhé Nyingpo, upon receiving empowerment into the Kagyé mandala, also practiced at Lhodrak Kharchu, attaining full realization of the wrathful deity Yangdak Heruka, and adding further to the blessings of these sacred caves.

Approaching the Sacred Site

Lhodrak (Southern Cliffs), is a region of verdant gorges in South Tibet, with waters that flow down into the lowland jungles of Bhutan.[452] Famed for its beauty and relative seclusion, this area is where the ancient principality of Karchu (Castle River) is located, featuring unimaginable cliffs where caverns, crystalline springs, and self-arisen images of deities have manifested as a practitioner's paradise.[453] The area is renowned for its medicinal plants, its abundant flowers, and for the ancient monastery of Karchu Dudjom Ling, originally established by Melong Dorjé (1243–1303), a Great Perfection lineage holder, developed further by the great Drukpa Kagyü master Pema Karpo (1527–1592), and still later by the Fifth Dalai Lama (1617–1682)—as the seat of Namkhé Nyingpo's reincarnation lineage.

Below this monastic hermitage and the clifftop platform known as the Khandro Drora (Gathering Place of the Dakinis), lies the spiritual center of Karchu, the cave known as Chakpurchen—named after the two iron daggers (*chakpur*) that Guru Chöwang revealed as treasures here. This is the site where

Guru Rinpoche practiced Yangdak Heruka. His disciple, Namkhé Nyingpo, practiced and realized Yangdak Heruka in Palkyi Puk-ring (Vast Cave of Glory), another cave situated downhill from the Chakpurchen. Lhodrak Karchu also features a charnel ground, the Durtrö Lakha (Charnel Pass), which lies on a corner of the cliffside trail near Palkyi Puk-ring. Near to this charnel ground is the temple founded by the great early Atiyoga master Drupchen Melong Dorjé—a site which once housed his physical relics.[454]

Far below the cliffs of Karchu, in a much earlier age, Dharma King Songtsen Gampo built the border-taming temple of Khoting Lhakang, located upon the left elbow of the supine demoness, and home to an especially sacred statue of Buddha Vairocana.[455] And it was from this statue that the 12th century master Nyang Ral Nyima Özer discovered a seminal practice of the wrathful Kaygé deities—*Kagyé Deshek Düpa (The Eight Practices: A Gathering of the Sugatas).*

As highlighted by Jamyang Khyentse Wangpo in his introductory verse above, Lhodrak Karchu has also been recognized by the great Kagyü masters as a Tibetan counterpart of the Indian sacred dakini site of Devikota, one of the twenty-four sacred places associated with the tantric mandala of Chakrasamvara. Specifically, there is a rocky outcrop that resembles a lingam, sacred symbol of divine creativity, on Karchu's southern side. This site, known as Lhamo Karchen, is considered to be the spiritual center of Lhodrak Karchu, and a gathering place for dakinis.[456]

The Mahaguru's Journey

Awakened Heart

> *The blessing of the wisdom mind of Vajra Heruka* ⁞
> *Descended to Garab Dorjé, Manjushrimitra, and Hungchenkara.* ⁞
> *To the masters past, present, and future,* ⁞
> *Of the wisdom heart lineage, we pray!* ⁞
> *To the Lotus-Born Guru of Orgyen, we pray!*[457] ⁞
>
> — *Revealed by Tulku Zangpo Drakpa*

The Lhodrak Karchu are the caves that, through his realization and blessings, came to embody Guru Padmasambhava's awakened heart. Here, Guru Rinpoche entered into retreat to practice Yangdak Heruka.[458] The practice of this wrathful form of Akshobhya-Vajrasattva, the heart-essence of all the buddhas, has the unique capacity to bring one to the profound stage of realization known as *mahamudra vidyadhara*, and it was through practicing Yangdak

Heruka that the vidyadhara Humkara, one of the foremost mahasiddhas in the whole of India, reached his extraordinary level of accomplishment.[459] Guru Padmasambhava was present when Humkara revealed the practice of Yangdak Heruka, his main meditational deity, at the Sitavana charnel ground near Bodh Gaya.[460] Later, Humkara composed several ritual manuals for the Yangdak Heruka practice, mostly living and teaching in Ngatupchen, and in the city of Patan in the Kathmandu valley.[461]

Through this intimate connection, Guru Padmasambhava and the vidyadhara Humkara formed an ever deeper teacher-student relationship. As he attained greater levels of realization, Humkara began to give teachings and transmissions on Yangdak Heruka to the Mahaguru, in both India and Nepal, and it was this sadhana that the Mahaguru later took with him when he returned to Nepal, to the caves of Asura and Yangleshö, where he himself attained the equivalent of buddhahood through the Varjayana path, together with his divine consort Belmo Shakyadevi.[462]

Once the Mahaguru had accomplished this profound deity, he brought the associated teachings to Tibet, and chose the Lhodrak Karchu caves as the sacred site to be established and associated with Yangdak Heruka. Here, by practicing Yangdak Heruka one-pointedly, the Mahaguru not only introduced this powerful practice tradition, but also blessed the site as being identical to his awakened heart. Later, during the *Kagyé* empowerments at Samye Chimpu, Guru Rinpoche entrusted these teachings to Namkhé Nyingpo, whom he instructed to practice at Lhodrak Karchu, so that he too could reap the fruits of Yangdak Heruka. And his own teacher Humkara traveled later to Tibet, where he served as spiritual adviser to King Mutik Tsenpo.[463]

The Mahaguru's Legacy

Master of Yangdak, Namkhé Nyingpo

> Great monk born into the Nup clan, at Lhodrak Karchu
> You accomplished Yangdak Heruka, the awakened heart.
> Hear us, Namkhé Nyingpo, you who ride the rays of the sun:
> Grant us your blessings![464]
>
> —Changdak Tashi Topgyal

Namkhé Nyingpo was born into the Nub family, at a place called Nyang Karda Shambu. Like Nupchen Sangyé Yeshé, he was one of the first Tibetans to be ordained as a monk by Abbot Shantarakshita, and he also became a heart disciple of Guru Padmasambhava. Before long, lotsawa Namkhé Nyingpo was sent to India by King Trisong Detsen to seek out Dharma texts and teachings. Along with four fellow translators, he crossed the border into Nepal and made his way to Ngatupchen (Land of Drummers). These five Tibetan monks were looking for the residence of the master Humkara, a place called Golden Cliff Bird Roost Sanctuary.[465]

When Namkhé Nyingpo and his group reached the residence of the vidyadhara, they offered much gold and requested him to teach the Dharma. There and then, Humkara displayed before them the mandala of wrathful herukas and taught them, step by step, the profound practices of Yangdak Heruka and Secret Mantra. Each of the Tibetan monks gained accomplishment. Namkhé Nyingpo, in particular, thereafter was no longer bound to the earth, for he could fly.

Upon returning to Tibet, Namkhé Nyingpo grew close to King Trisong Detsen. He served as both the royal teacher and healer and transmitted the Yangdak Heruka teachings to the King and other disciples. It was no surprise then, that during the *Kagyé* empowerment at Samye Chimpu, Namkhé Nyingpo's flower fell on the mandala of Yangdak Heruka. Eventually, though, just like Vairocana, Namkhé Nyingpo was cast out of Central Tibet, exiled at the command of scheming ministers. But at Lhodrak Karchu he found refuge in these caves of the awakened heart of the buddhas, and here he entered retreat. Khandro Yeshe Tsogyal visited Namkhé Nyingpo during this time and gave him the necessary instructions and empowerments to progress in his practice.[466] As a result, Namkhé Nyingpo became one of the heart disciples of this wisdom dakini, and he later accompanied her on her journey through Tibet. Eventually, together with Gyalwa Changchup, he recorded Yeshé Tsogyal's biography and hid it as a precious treasure.[467] And just as his teachers Guru Padmasambhava, Humkara, and Khandro Yeshé Tsogyal had done before him, Namkhé Nyingpo accomplished the mahamudra vidyadhara through the practice of Yangdak Heruka. As a sign of his realization, Namkhé Nyingpo was renowned for being able to fly through the sky, riding on the rays of the sun.[468]

The Meeting of the Wisdom Dakinis
Khandro Yeshé Tsogyal and Lhacham Mandarava

> *You journeyed to Karchu, where in meditative equipoise*
> *You actualized the dissolution of experience into its nature.*
> *Sending forth your emanations as guides throughout the six realms,*

You dredged samsara from its depths. To you, we pray![469]

— *Jamgön Kongtrul Lodrö Thayé*

While Namkhé Nyingpo was residing at the Lhodrak caves, Khandro Yeshé Tsogyal also travelled to Lhodrak—on the advice of Guru Rinpoche. There, after granting profound teachings on yogic practices to Namkhé Nyingpo, Khandro Yeshé Tsogyal also entered retreat and remained there for twenty years. Her main focus now was to sustain the experience of the nature of mind that her precious Guru had introduced her to, time and again. Khandro Yeshé Tsogyal described her retreat as follows:

> I abided evenly in the view of the Great Perfection beyond all action, and as the experience dawned on me wherein all phenomena are extinguished in the nature of reality, I was perceived in various forms according to the needs of beings.[470] ⁞

— *Revealed by Samten Lingpa*

Thus, she actualized Great Perfection's highest realization, the dissolution of experience into the nature of reality.

While Khandro Yeshé Tsogyal was still in retreat in Lhodrak, another wisdom dakini arrived in the region. Lhacham Mandarava, the Indian consort of Guru Padmsambahva, had come to meet her spiritual sister. They remained together for thirty-nine days, studying and discussing the Dharma continuously. Mandarava then requested a series of the Mahaguru's pith instructions otherwise unheard of in India, which Yeshé Tsogyal gladly granted. For her part, Yeshé Tsogyal asked Mandarava to give her the instructions on immortality, as well as the practice of Hayagriva, all of which were later hidden as *terma* treasures here. After this profound exchange of teachings, Mandarava vanished like a rainbow into space.[471]

Master of Vajrakilaya, Nyak Jñanakumara

Upon the passing of Prince Muné Tsenpo, heir to Dharma King Trisong Detsen, the great Vimalamitra miraculously travelled back from China to Tibet to preside over the funeral rituals. Delighted at his teacher's return, the lotsawa Nyak Jñanakumara approached him during the ceremonies with an offering of much gold.[472] Vimalamitra asked about Nyak's translation activities and was saddened when Nyak replied that he had been facing all sorts of obstacles, mainly caused by Tibetans still hostile toward Buddhists. He promised to teach his struggling student a method through which he could overcome all obstacles. Thus master and translator went together to Lhodrak Karchu, where the master opened the mandala of Vajrakilaya and granted Nyak the necessary empowerment and oral instructions.

As fruit of their Vajrakilaya practice in Karchu, Nyak was able to summon crows. However, when he pointed his kila-dagger at one of the crows, that crow instantly died. To this, Vimalamitra said: "So you can kill by the power of sorcery, but, I wonder, can you revive by the power of reality? Go ahead and revive it!" This, however, Nyak was unable to do. Vimalamitra, then, with a mere handful of sand cast into the air, breathed life back into the corpse, transforming it into a living crow that soared gracefully into the sky. Turning to Nyak, the master spoke:

> "When you undertake a wrathful rite without first having attained
> the realization with which to 'liberate' the ego of your victim, then,
> even if you succeed in the rite, it is a great crime."[473]

There and then, the master also taught Nyak the practice of *nelung* (guidance of the deceased to the higher realms). Eventually Nyak became an accomplished and renowned Vajrakilaya practitioner, able to circumvent any obstacle he was facing. The body of teachings that he received from Vimalamitra became known as the Nyak Luk Purba (The Vajrakilaya Lineage of Nyak).

The Great Tertön King, Nyangral Nyima Özer

> *A time of unrest will appear throughout the land.*
> *Mantrins will practice magic, which laymen will try to repel.*
> *The killing of a thousand people will be rewarded with statues and scripture.*
> *People will be led from one place to another.*
> *These will be the signs that the time has come to reveal*
> *The termas concealed at Sinmo Barjé and Khoting.*
> *For this, the King's emanation, Nyangral, will appear.*[474]
>
> — *Revealed by Orgyen Lingpa*

Nyangral Nyima Özer (1124–1192), one of the most renowned of the treasure revealers, was born in Lhodrak.[475] He spent much of his youth in retreat in Lhodrak, practicing his family's main yidam, Hayagriva, but also focusing on other important yidam deities. After assimilating the transmissions of his clan during his formative years and honing his skills in his teenage years, the young

Nyangral embarked on a journey away from his birthplace. Throughout his travels, he sought guidance from various masters. Eventually, Nyangral established a sanctuary in the remote location of Mawochok in Lhodrak.

In due course, Nyangral encountered a youthful yogi who bestowed upon him valuable documents pertaining to sacred sites, before vanishing mysteriously. Recognizing the yogi as a manifestation of Guru Padmasambhava, Nyangral interpreted the records to indicate a nearby location called Drak Sinmobarjé—a prominent rock formation situated downstream from his hermitage. Venturing there, he uncovered his first significant cache of *terma* treasures, concealed within a hidden cave which had once served as the grand assembly hall of the Mahaguru. At the heart of the cave, the Mahaguru's throne and sacred objects remained undisturbed, surrounded by several hidden repositories in the ground. It was here that Nyangral discovered numerous vital cycles of teachings, including *The Great Compassionate One*—later known as the *Mani Kumbum*. Additionally, Nyangral unearthed the cycles of *Khandro Sangwa* (*The Secret Dakini*) and, dedicated to Guru Padmasambhava, the *Lama Rikdzin*.

Further, at the border-suppressing temple of Khoting, established by Dharma King Songtsen Gampo just below the sacred caves of Lhodrak Karchu, Nyangral revealed the *Kagyé Deshek Düpa* (*The Eight Instructions: A Gathering of Sugatas*), a foundational Nyingma scripture on the *Kagyé*, which quickly rose to become a revered and major source. Nyangral's biography, the *Salwé Melong* (*Clear Mirror*), tells how Nyangral received the *Kagyé* both as *kama*, an oral lineage going back to Dharma King Trisong Detsen himself, and as a *terma*—the treasure revealed to him at Khoting Lhakang, just below Lhodrak Karchu. Nyangral thereafter merged the *kama* and *terma* traditions to create an extraordinary compendium that gained renown as the *Kagyé Deshek Düpa*.[476] Again, *The Clear Mirror* gives an account of how Nyangral revealed the *Kagyé Deshek Düpa* treasure text from the sacred Vairocana statue at Khoting Lhakang:

> Upon my arrival at the Khoting temple, the centermost of the twenty-one treasure cavities attested in the site manual as being located in the back of the Vairocana statue, did not appear. Later, while walking back up the road from Khoting, I got stuck behind several merchants, one of whom addressed me, saying, "Last night I was circumambulating the temple and happened to find this finger from one of the statues, so I picked it up. Yogin, are you on your way

up or down?" I replied, "I can go wherever." The merchant said, "If you're going back down, please take this to the temple," proffering the statue's forefinger.

With that, I stowed it carefully away and went back down toward Khoting. When I reached the area around Khotöser Lake, a dog ambushed me, and I fell into an irrigation channel. I stripped my sash into bandages and discovered that the statue's finger had crumbled. I found a scroll among the fragments, and the site manual emerged. With that in hand, I returned to the Khoting temple, but the sacristan refused to open the door. I bribed him with a gold coin, entered, and welcomed a great treasure cache from the back of the Vairocana statue. In the treasure repository were two caskets, one dark burgundy and the other grey. From within the burgundy casket emerged six small volumes containing one hundred and thirty distinct works of doctrine—the Mother and Child tantric scriptures of *The Eight Instructions: A Gathering of the Sugatas*, and many abridged liturgies condensed into scrolls.[477]

During his lifetime, Nyangral exclusively unveiled material treasures and relics from various esteemed locations, many of which held imperial significance and were no more than a few days' journey from Mawochok.[478] His most celebrated revelation was the *Zanglingma*, also known as *The Copper Palace*—the first comprehensive biography of the Mahaguru.

Jamyang Khyentse Wangpo's Vajra Song

An extraordinary occurrence took place in the mind of Jamyang Khyentse Wangpo during a pilgrimage to the Lhodrak Kharchu caves. It was there, in the year 1840, that the profound moment unfolded, as he conducted a lavish feast offering to the mandala of Yangdak Heruka within the Palkyi Puk cave. Immersed in the historical significance of the location, his mind brought forth this spontaneous vajra song:

> *Aho! The nature of dharmata,*
> *Pervading all animate and inanimate things,*
> *Dawns visibly as the signs of bliss and emptiness in union,*
> *And movements of temporary confusion dissolve into luminosity.*
> *Bowing to the mandala of the glorious blazing Heruka,*
> *I burst forth and sing of the vajra path of definitive meaning.*[479]

YARLUNG SHELDRAK

The nature of sublime awakening
Dwells not in the extremes of existence or peace.
Its true form is an ocean of freedom and qualities of maturation,
A delight that restores all beings.
On occasion, to be seen as itself, it appears
At the great miraculous vajra site
Amidst virtuous signs of mantra,
As the blazing wish-fulfilling Crystal Cave.[480]

— *Jamyang Khyentsé Wangpo*

Introduction

Yarlung Sheldrak (Yarlung's Crystal Cave) is the life-upholding cave at the Tradruk temple. The Tradruk, built by Dharma King Songtsen Gampo, was Tibet's first and much celebrated temple and was one of many such *tradül*—structures built to suppress the giant ogress lying supine upon Tibet. As such, the Sheldrak cave itself is the vital axis that guards the Tradruk temple and maintains its blessings.[481] The Mahaguru blessed this unique sacred site through his practice of Chemchok Heruka, the wrathful aspect of Buddha Samantabhadra, so that the place itself became identical to his awakened qualities. Following the Mahaguru's advice, his disciple Nyak Jñanakumara later took Yarlung Sheldrak as his own retreat hermitage, an ideal sanctuary for translating, practicing, and accomplishing Chemchok Heruka.

Approaching the Sacred Site

The Yarlung Valley, renowned for its fertility and vibrant greenery, holds within its embrace a rich collection of historical and sacred sites. It is widely recognized as the birthplace of Tibetan civilization, where Tibet first found a unified existence in the 7th century. According to legend, a profound event occurred back in the mists of time in Yarlung, when, in a cave on the slopes of the Gongpo Ri, the Tibetan people came into being through the union of a bodhisattva monkey and an ogress.[482] Also according to legend, the neighboring peak of Lhabab Ri (Divine Descent Mountain), just south of Sheldrak, is the sacred ground where the first kings made their descent from heaven. In the nearby *zorthang* field, which holds the distinction of being Tibet's first cultivated land, the farmers there witnessed the celestial descent, marking the

momentous occasion with their amazement. The Yumbu Lhakang here, the first ever constructed building in Tibet, served as the first king's residence and holds great historical significance. Further up the neighboring Chongyé valley is the final resting place of the Tibetan kings, with special reverence given to the tombs of the foundational Dharma Kings, Songtsen Gampo and Trisong Detsen.[483] Poised above this extraordinary burial site, like a soaring vulture in the sky, lies Sheldrak Puk—the Crystal Cave of the revered Mahaguru. It stands as a testament to the spiritual strength and sanctity of the region.

The pilgrim travelling to Yarlung usually aims to complete the famous *Nesum Tensum* (Three Sanctuaries and Three Stupas) pilgrimage. The *Nesum* or three sanctuaries are: Tradruk, Tibet's first temple, and built by Dharma King Songtsen Gampo, as explained above; Sheldrak, the meditation cave of the Mahaguru; and either Rechung Puk, the meditation cave of Rechungpa (~1083–1161), the renowned disciple of Jestün Milarepa (1040–1123), or Yumbu Lakhang, Tibet's very first building, also described above. The *Tensum* or three stupas are Takchen Bumpa, Göntang Bumpa and Tséchu Bumpa, each of which houses immeasurably precious relics.[484]

The Sheldrak (Crystal Cave) is one of two spiritual centers sacred to the Mahaguru in Yarlung. It is located above the Tséchu Bumpa stupa. The second Guru Rinpoche cave—the Gangki Rawa (Snow Enclosure), perched high on Yarlha Shampo to the south of Yarlung—will be the subject of a later chapter.

Located south of the Tsangpo shore, Yarlung Sheldrak occupies a position beneath a remarkable rocky pinnacle, nestled on the northern side of a steep ravine that descends towards the western rim of the lower Yarlung Valley. The setting is truly awe-inspiring, with panoramic vistas encompassing Yarlung Valley on one side and Tsangpo Valley on the other.[485] It was from the statue of the Dharma protector Rahula, on guard at Sheldrak's entrance, that Orgyen Lingpa brought forth the Mahaguru's profound and sacred autobiography, the *Pema Kathang*, along with other profound treasures.

The central object of devotion in the Sheldrak Cave was the Guru Thong-drolchen statue (The Great Guru that Liberates the Beholder), crafted by the great master Durtrö Rechen, a disciple of Tsangnyön Heruka (1452–1507). The statue, which contained a *kutsap* revealed by Orgyen Lingpa, along with many other precious substances, is considered to be as sacred as the Guru Ngadrama statue at Samye. It was relocated and is now housed at the Tradruk temple.[486] The Sheldrak shrine now houses a newly constructed statue of the Mahaguru flanked by his two consorts Khandro Yeshé Tsogyal and Lhacham Mandarava. To the south lies Tsogyal Sangpuk, the secret meditation cave of Yeshé Tsogyal, where she remained in retreat, made many aspirations, and concealed *terma* treasures.[487] Sheldrak's charnel ground is hailed as equivalent in blessings to the charnel ground of Sitavana. Close to the Sheldrak Cave are two sacred crystalline springs brought forth by Nyak Jñanakumara.

The Mahaguru's Journey

Awakened Qualities

> *The blessing of the wisdom mind of Chemchok Heruka* ⁞
> *Descended into countless emanated dakinis and vidyadharas,* ⁞
> *And all the way down to Mingyur Namkha.* ⁞
> *To all the masters, past, present, and future,* ⁞
> *Of this lineage of noble qualities, we pray!* ⁞
> *To the Lotus-Born Guru of Orgyen, we pray!*[488] ⁞
>
> — *Revealed by Tulku Zangpo Drakpa*

The caves at Yarlung Sheldrak represent Guru Rinpoche's awakened qualities. Here, the Mahaguru focused in retreat on Chemchok Heruka, also known as Mahottara Heruka or Amritakundali.[489] Chemchok Heruka is the wrathful manifestation of Samantabhadra, and the main deity in the mandala of the fifty-eight wrathful deities, which, together with the forty-two peaceful deities, form the mandala of the Hundred Peaceful and Wrathful Deities.[490] Chemchok Heruka is also the central deity in the Mahayoga mandala of the Kagyé and in the mandala of the Anuyoga root tantra the *Gongpa Düpé Do*.[491]

The teachings on Chemchok Heruka were originally revealed by the renowned pandita Vimalamitra—that same legendary vidyadhara, translator and teacher who had greatly supported the establishment of Buddhism in Tibet alongside the Mahaguru. Already back then, the Mahaguru had created the circumstances for Vimalamitra to enter the path of the Dharma,[492] and the two masters had formed an intimate teacher-student relationship. Thus, when meeting the Master again, it was with great joy that Vimalamitra bestowed the teachings of Chemchok Heruka upon Guru Rinpoche. Later, when the two met again at the Sitavana charnel ground, they revealed the Chemchok Heruka teachings together, and the Mahaguru continued to receive teachings on Chemchok Heruka throughout their profound student-teacher relationship. [493]

Seeking to establish in Tibet a sacred site associated with Chemchok Heruka, the Mahaguru chose the Yarlung Sheldrak caves. There, through his own one-pointed practice, he not only introduced the practice tradition but also blessed the site as being identical to his awakened qualities. During the *Kagyé* empowerments at Samye Chimpu, the Mahaguru entrusted the Chemchok Heruka teachings in particular to Dharma King Trisong Detsen and Nyak Jñanakumara. Since the Dharma King could not leave his responsibilities at Samye monastery and go into retreat in a remote mountain cave, he retreated instead into Samye monastery itself, where he practiced and accomplished Chemchok Heruka. Nyak Jñanakumara, however, was not bound by royal duties, and was thus instructed to retreat to Yarlung Sheldrak, so that he too could reap the siddhis of Chemchok Heruka.[494]

The Mahaguru further entrusted Nyak Jñanakumara with the task of translating sacred tantras on Chemchok Heruka at the Crystal Cave of Sheldrak itself, and, once completed, the original translation was concealed within the Pema Tsekpa cave, safeguarding its profound wisdom.[495]

Upon the Mahaguru's advice, Khandro Yeshé Tsogyal and many others went into retreat at Yarlung Sheldrak, and thirty in particular reached great accomplishment, becoming collectively known as "the thirty tantrikas of Sheldrak."[496]

The Covenant

Not long before his departure from Tibet, the Mahaguru returned to the Yarlung Sheldrak cave. As he remained in meditation there, the protector Gyalpo Pehar, whom he had previously bound as the protector of Samye,[497] once again approached the Mahaguru:

> Now the Master Padmasambhava ⁝
> Went to meditate at the wish-fulfilling Crystal Cave. ⁝
> After three days, at dawn, Gyalpo Pehar appeared— ⁝
> Guardian of Samye and of all Tibet's monasteries, ⁝
> Great Upsaka, Gyalpo Shing Chachen, ⁝
> Also known as demon Father Black Lord. ⁝
> Riding in upon a white lioness, accompanied by his retinue, ... ⁝
> He appeared before the master in order to test him. ⁝
> Hailstones as large as sheep fell upon the Master's head. ⁝
> The Master fainted, his effects in disarray. ⁝
> As soon as he came to, through his meditative absorption, ⁝
> He summoned the young upasaka, ⁝
> Who squeezed through the crowd, ⁝
> And came before him, holding a crystal rosary. ⁝

The Master said, "You, who seem to be some kind of yaksha ༓
Yet appear as an upasaka—who is your father?" ༓
The upasaka said, "I am the son of a demon. ༓
Are you able to forge a samaya with the son of a demon?" ༓
And the Master said, "If I am able to forge a samaya, ༓
Are you able to protect the teachings of the Buddha?" ༓
Pehar said, "If, here and now, you entrust to me ༓
All of Tibet's future temples and stupas, ༓
I will protect the teachings. However, if you don't, I will harm them. ༓
I will lash out and trash them, and our samaya will be broken." ༓
Then, the Master Padmasambhava entrusted to Pehar ༓
The temples and stupas that would be built by later generations, ༓
And the supports for Body, Speech, and Mind. ༓
And the upasaka agreed to protect the teachings.[498] ༓

— *Revealed by Orgyen Lingpa*

The Mahaguru had similar encounters with other Dharma protectors during his final days in Tibet. By engaging with them and reminding them of their pledge to protect the Dharma, he ensured that the protectors he had previously entrusted with guarding the Dharma would live up to their promises and continue their role as guardians after his departure.

Empowering a Newly Established Ruler

When the time came for the young Prince Mutik Tsenpo to ascend the throne, the Mahaguru invited the new monarch to his residence at Yarlung Sheldrak. As the new King approached, the Mahaguru came down with his disciples and met him at Tradruk. By performing a *drupchen* of the *Kadü Chökyi Gyatso*, the Mahaguru initiated the new King firmly into the Vajrayana.

Then the Master Padmasambhava, ༓
In the courtyard of Tradruk Monastery, ༓
Opened the Secret Mantra mandala of the *Kadü Chökyi Gyatso* ༓
And conferred twenty-one profound empowerments for this practice ༓
Upon twenty-one disciples, headed by the prince, ༓
On three royal ladies and twenty-one lotsawas, ༓
Headed by their leader, lotsawa Devasambhava, ༓
And on all the patrons, men, and women in the retinue.[499] ༓

— *Revealed by Orgyen Lingpa*

The Mahaguru's Legacy

Master of Chemchok, Nyak Jñanakumara

> At the wish-fulfilling Crystal Cave,
> Through the samadhi of the amrita of appearance and existence
> You made springwater shoot from solid vajra-rock.
> Jñanakumara, please grant your blessings![500]
>
> — Dilgo Khyentsé Rinpoche

Jñanakumara was born into the Nyak clan in Yarlung Chö and later ordained by Abbot Shantarakshita. Showing great interest in the Dharma and a keen and sharp intellect, Jñanakumara quickly became an adept and scholar of both Sutra and Tantra. His four principal teachers were Guru Padmasambhava, the pandita Vimalamitra, and the two lotsawas Vairocana and Yudra Nyingpo. Under their tutelage, he became an excellent translator, fluent in Sanskrit and its vernaculars. In particular, Jñanakumara became an expert in the tantric scriptures of the Mahayoga *Guhyagarbha*, the Anuyoga *Gongpa Düpé Do*, and the Atiyoga teachings. It was also from these four teachers that Jñanakumara received special pith instructions on the Great Perfection, thus becoming one of the esteemed upholders of the early Atiyoga transmission in Tibet.[501]

Nyak is renowned for embodying the "four great rivers of transmitted precepts" imparted by his four primary teachers. These rivers encompassed the realms of textual interpretation, the lineage of oral teachings, blessings and empowerments, and the practical techniques. As such, he is recognized, along with Nubchen Sangyé Yeshé and Zurchen Shakya Jungné, as one of the three masters who established the three lineages of the *kama*, the oral transmission within the Nyingma tradition.[502]

During the *Kagyé* empowerments at Samye Chimpu, Nyak Jñanakumara's flower fell on the mandala of Chemchok Heruka. Consequently, he was instructed to practice Amritakundali at Guru Rinpoche's own meditation cave at Sheldrak. Gaining great accomplishment, Jñanakumara brought forth a sacred spring at Yarlung Sheldrak that still flows today. He was also famous for his Vajrakilaya practice and the transmission received from Vimalamitra at Lhodrak Karchu.[503] The transmission lineage is thus known as Nyak Luk Purba (The Vajrakila Lineage of Nyak). In the end, Jñanakumara achieved the ultimate attainment, and his physical form dissolved into luminosity.[504] Jñanakumara's descendant and emanation Ramo Shelmen Yeshé Zangpo later revealed the Chemchok Heruka teachings at Yarlung Sheldrak, and through them gained accomplishment.[505] Following a prophecy, Yeshé Zangpo then reconcealed the original teachings.

Later, in 1876, Jamyang Khyentse Wangpo rediscovered them on the first day of the first month of the Fire Rat Year. In a vision, Jamyang Khyentsé Wangpo met the mantra protectress Ekajati, who handed him the reconcealed text, written on palm leaves in a mixture of Nagari and symbolic scripts, along with a detailed account of its history. Later, on the tenth day of the fifth month, after supplicating Guru Padmasambhava, Khyentsé Wangpo had a pure vision in which he received the empowerment and complete instructions directly from Guru Rinpoche. Additionally, Khyentsé Wangpo had a vision of Nyak Jñakumara affirming that this instruction was in fact the most essential core teaching on Chemchok Heruka.[506]

The Revelation of the Pema Kathang

As stated in the colophon of the *Pema Kathang*, it was Khandro Yeshé Tsogyal who recorded the words of the Mahaguru when he expounded the *Pema Kathang*:

> Emanation of Sarasvati, Yeshe Tsogyal, ❧
> With her gift of perfect recall, her ability to remember everything, ❧
> Transcribed and concealed, for future generations, ❧
> This precious treasure, *The Chronicles of Padma*, ❧
> Also called *The Extensive Biography of His Lifetime*s ❧
> Or *The Testament of Trisong Detsen*, ❧
> Complete with an index of lotsawas and panditas ❧
> And their Dharma translations. ❧
> May it meet with the fortunate one destined by karma![507] ❧
>
> — *Revealed by Orgyen Lingpa*

The Mahaguru also predicted that the destined treasure revealer Orgyen Lingpa would reveal the *Pema Kathang*:

> A King with ripened conduct will appear in Yarlung; ❧
> A pig will dig in the ground; Mongolia will consume Tibet; ❧
> A hundred and eight fortresses will appear. ❧
> These will be the signs that the time has come for revealing ❧

The *terma* I have concealed in the Crystal Cave. ❈
The *tertön* called Orgyen Lingpa will appear.[508] ❈

— Revealed by Orgyen Lingpa

The final colophon of the *Pema Kathang* then states:

On the eighth day of the fourth month of the Water Dragon Year, a day when the planets, moon, and stars gathered in the thirteenth lunar mansion, at the fortress of Yarlung Sheldrak on the slope of Pema Tsekpa, accompanied by his consort and the Horpa meditator Shakya from Zhukun Rawa, Urgyen Lingpa revealed this treasure from the heart center of Great Rahula, the guardian of Pema Shelphuk. Without a single impure word, this was translated from the Sanskrit letters of the single yellow scroll.[509]

— Orgyen Lingpa

In accordance with the prophecy, during the Water Dragon Year, on the eighth day of the fourth month, guided by the Mahaguru, Orgyen Lingpa ventured to the rear of Yarlung Sheldrak. In that sacred place, where the rocks resemble stacked lotus flowers, stood the extraordinary Crystal Cave. This very cave had witnessed the sublime accomplishments of the great master Uddiyana himself. Within its depths, self-manifested images of peaceful and wrathful deities adorned the walls, while an image of the great Dharma protector Rahula guarded its entrance. It was from this very image that not only the *Pema Kathang*, but also a vast collection of profound *terma* teachings burst forth.

From the upper aspects of the image, Orgyen Lingpa unveiled sadhanas on Guru Padmasambhava and Avalokiteshvara, and instructions on the Great Perfection. From the lower aspects of the image, he revealed the Kagyé cycle, the *Kadü Chökyi Gyatso* (*Ocean of Dharma, Great Gathering of Transmitted Precepts*).[510] From the throat of the image emerged a cycle on the *Hundred Peaceful and Wrathful Deities*, the *Dakini Krodhikali*, and a protector cycle of *Maning*. The heart of the image revealed the profound *Pema Kathang*. And from the serpent-like tail of the image, Orgyen Lingpa unveiled numerous tantras, sadhanas, and applications related to various wisdom protectors, teachings on medicine, and profound instructions on upholding the Dharma. Furthermore, teachings on various arts and crafts were revealed from the arms and the end of the image's tail. [511]

Generations of Blessings

After revealing the treasure teachings from the Sheldrak caves, Orgyen Lingpa publicly taught the *Kadü Chökyi Gyatso* at nearby Tradruk—the very same place where the Mahaguru himself had previously transmitted these to Prince Mutik Tsenpo. Much later, Jamyang Khyentsé Wangpo, the reincarnation of Orgyen Lingpa, visited Tradruk in the Iron Rat Year of 1840, when he was twenty-one. He made one hundred feast offerings there, and composed the following vajra-song:

> *Aho! Deathless wisdom endowed with the most supreme of aspects*
> *Magically appears as the marks and signs of deathless luminosity.*
> *Deathless Lake-Born Vajra Guru,*
> *Who offers this feast of deathless amrita to the fortunate,*
> *I call upon you.*[512]

Eighteen years later, in 1858, Jamyang Khyentsé Wangpo re-revealed the *Kadü Chökyi Gyatso*, following a vision of Orgyen Lingpa. Nearly a century later, in 1956, his reincarnation, Kyapjé Jamyang Khyentsé Chökyi Lodrö then added to the auspiciousness by performing a *drupchö* of the *Kadü Chökyi Gyatso* and giving explanatory teachings:

> On the tenth day of the waning moon of that same month, at the Tradruk temple, he performed the consecration combined with a *drupchö* of the *Ocean of Dharma That Combines All Teachings*, based on a mandala drawn on cloth that was placed on a table in the middle of the assembly hall. He offered an enormous, elegant *tsok*, as well as many other offerings and purification ceremonies, and scattered flowers of consecration throughout all the inner temples large and small, and over the stupas that lined the path outside. He also performed the supreme activities of blessing the amrita, the common long-life practice, the wrathful ritual for averting obstacles, recitations of the fulfillment offering, confession practices, and the accumulation of more than a hundred *tsok* offerings. All these individual practices were performed elaborately in a single day. In an expression of great joy, he declared that the day's ceremonies were even more beneficial than the *drupchen* he had performed earlier at Bentsang. The practice began once the sun had risen, long breaks were taken at various intervals, and it finished early in the evening. To the amazement of everyone present, rainbows appeared in the sky.[513]

Jamyang Khyentse's Vajra Song at Yarlung Sheldrak

In the Iron Rat Year of 1840, on the tenth day of the sixth month, Jamyang Khyentse Wangpo made a pilgrimage to Yarlung Sheldrak. During this visit, he conducted a grand feast offering to the mandala of Chemchok Heruka, all the while reflecting upon the profound historical events that had taken place at this sacred site. It was in this auspicious moment that a vajra song spontaneously emerged within his mind, resonating with divine inspiration:

> *Aho! The natural radiance of luminosity, pure like the unchanging sky,*
> *Dawns as the unceasing activity of the kayas and wisdoms,*
> *And merges with the bindu in which all things are innately present.*
> *Bowing to the mandala of Amrita Qualities,*
> *I sing the song of the yoga of cause, path, and fruition.*[514]

SENGÉ DZONG

The kila of luminous awareness, the perfected nature,
Seals the creation of samsara and nirvana.
From the utterly peaceful dharmadhatu, awakened activity's dance,
The form kayas of Vajrakumara instantly appear,
Peaceful and smiling, granting relief to an ocean of beings,
Within the imputed nature as Ne'u ring Sengé Dzong
(Lion's Fortress in the Vast Meadow).[515]

— *Jamyang Khyentsé Wangpo*

Introduction

Mönkha Nering Sengé Dzong (Lion's Fortress) is the cave complex blessed by the Mahaguru through his practice of Vajrakilaya, the wrathful aspect of Buddha Vajrasattva, establishing it as identical to his awakened activities. Following the Mahaguru's advice, his consort Khandro Yeshé Tsogyal subsequently took Sengé Dzong as her main retreat hermitage. She endured great hardships there, her unwavering commitment to the practice of Vajrakilaya bearing fruit as she unlocked the higher stages of the path of awakening and eventually reaped great siddhis.

Approaching the Sacred Site

The Mahaguru's sacred site of Mönkha Nering Sengé Dzong (Lion's Fortress in the Vast Meadow) lies in northeast Bhutan, close to the Tibetan frontier, nestled among breathtaking cliffs and hidden caverns, pristine mountain springs and the awe-inspiring self-arisen images of deities. Renowned for its enchanting allure and tranquil seclusion, Senge Dzong stands as a testament to natural splendor. Sengé Dzong was originally opened by the great tertön Ratna Lingpa (1403–1478), who received many visions at the site. In more recent times, the treasure revealers Tertön Sogyal, Zilnön Namkhé Dorjé, and Apang Tertön all retrieved treasures from Sengé Dzong. To reach Sengé Dzong these days, one must embark on a challenging three-day journey by foot that starts at Lhuntse Dzong, in the Kuru Chu valley of Bhutan.[516] The cave of Sengé Dzong itself is nestled at the foot of a hill that resembles a leaping lion, hence its name. It rests on a plateau with a distinctive bowl-like shape, surrounded dramatically by the snow-capped peaks of the Himalayan skyline. Adjacent to the cave is a small temple dedicated to the eight forms of Guru Padmasambhava. There are three other sacred caves nearby: Dorjé Dzong to the east, Rinchen Dzong to the west, and Pema Dzong high up on the mountain. Due to this arrangement, the place is commonly referred to as Senge Dzongsum (The Three Lion Fortresses).[517] The great treasure-revealer Lhatsün Namkha Jikmé (1597–1653) composed the best-known guide to Sengé Dzong. Within it he describes the spiritual center of the site:

> At the heart of the sanctuary are the three great Dzongs; in the periphery are the three minor Dzongs, a large plain like the sun and moon conjoined, and its upper and lower parts making another three. In all, there are seven great valleys here, where profound treasures are concealed, and countless minor valleys. In the Sengé Dzong cave itself, having gained accomplishment through her meditation on Vajrakilaya, Jomo Yeshé Tsogyal actually saw the deities face to face, and danced in the sky. She miraculously thrust two crossed kilas of copper and iron into the rock. The Guru's miraculous body-print is there, his incredible hand and footprints, and writing in rock, and at all points of the mandala there are no end of profound treasures, such as the mind series of the Dzokchen teachings. To both east and west, there are many treasure signs, like the Yak's eye sign. At the center of the cave is the Guru's skull-bowl Amritakalasha, with sun and moon decorations. Below, an image of Vajrakilaya with snake design can be seen. On the lintel at the cave entrance are the remains of Mönmo Tashi Khyidren. To the left is the amazing self-arisen natural spring, whose immortal waters grant longevity, and more than a hundred of the Guru's handprints. Above is the concealed 'seed' of the hidden valley of Rolmo Ding, various Guru Rinpoche sacramental substances for ritually blessed medicine, and another wonderful natural spring. To the right is an image of the dark-blue wrathful Guru, a statue of Guru Rinpoche made of minor revealed substances, and a cave inhabited by his karmically ordained followers. The sky above that hill of attainment is in the form of an eight-spoked wheel, and the ground has the form of an eight-petaled lotus. There is the pure perception of a mist of blessings and a cool drizzle of siddhis thoroughly cleansing the stains of the three obscurations.[518]

The Mahaguru's Journey

Awakened Activities

> *The wisdom-heart blessing of awesome Vajrakumara* ⁞
> *Descended to the vidyadharas of spontaneous presence and mahamudra,* ⁞
> *All the way down to Dorjé Tötreng Tsal.* ⁞
> *To the masters, past, present, and future,* ⁞
> *Of the lineage of enlightened activity, we pray!* ⁞
> *To the Lotus-Born Guru of Orgyen, we pray!*[519] ⁞

— *Revealed by Tulku Zangpo Drakpa*

Sengé Dzong are the caves that represent Guru Rinpoche's awakened activities. Here, Guru Rinpoche entered into retreat with a focus on Vajrakilaya.[520] Vajrakilaya is the wrathful form of Vajrasattva, the embodiment of the awakened activity of all the buddhas—manifesting in an intensely wrathful yet compassionate form in order to subjugate the delusion and negativity that arise as obstacles to Dharma practice. In fact, the practice of Vajrakilaya is famous for being the most powerful for removing obstacles, bringing down troublesome spirits and binding them to one's command, and purifying the spiritual pollution so prevalent in this age.[521]

The teachings on Vajrakilaya were in particular taught and spread by the vidyadhara Prabhahasti, one of the foremost mahasiddhas in the whole of India, who later greatly served Nalanda monastery in India. Prabhahasti was also Guru Rinpoche's first guru, meeting him first at Kukkutapada in India, and initiating his training in the outer tantras. This initial meeting created a karmic bond between the two masters that would last long into the future. Guru Rinpoche would continue to learn from and practice with this guru throughout his entire stay in Greater India.[522] Together, later, they revealed the practice of Vajrakilaya in the Sitavana charnel ground near the Vajra Throne in India.[523]

Much later in his journey, deciding it was time to display the supreme siddhi of mahamudra, the Lotus-Born Guru made his way to Nepal, where he met his destined consort, Belmo Shakyadevi. Together they settled in the caves of Asura and Yangleshö.[524] Initially they focused upon the wrathful deity Yangdak Heruka, but were beseiged by powerful demons who plunged the whole country into chaos. Two disciples were dispatched in haste to Nalanda to ask Prabhahasti for help.[525] The disciples hastened back, laden with the teachings on Vajrakilaya. As they drew near, the mere physical presence of these texts had an immediate effect—instantly quelling the demonic tide that was sweeping through the land. Armed with the Vajrakilaya teachings, Guru Rinpoche could get the obstacle-makers under control, meaning that he and his consort Belmo Shakyadevi could gain the realization they were seeking. From then on, Vajrakilaya became the Mahaguru's main yidam deity, and it was mostly through this specific practice that he subdued the hostile forces that he encountered throughout the Himalayas.[526] The Mahaguru discussed and compiled all the Vajrakilaya teachings with his fellow teachers in India, subsequently teaching them in Nepal and bringing them with him to Tibet, where he transmitted them to his students.[527] For establishing a sacred site in Greater Tibet associated particularly with Vajrakilaya, he chose the Sengé Dzong caves. There, by practicing Vajrakilaya one-pointedly, he not only introduced the practice tradition, but also blessed the site as being identical to his awakened activities. During the *Kagyé* empowerments at Samye Chimpu, the Mahaguru entrusted the Vajrakilaya teachings in particular to Khandro Yeshé Tsogyal, subsequently instructing her to practice them at Sengé Dzong.

The Wisdom Dakinis' Journey

Receiving the Vajrakilaya Empowerment

Khandro Yeshé Tsogyal had already received the Vajrakilaya initiation from the Mahaguru at Samye Chimpu and on numerous other occasions. Yet, one momentous day, the wisdom dakini herself—along with her disciples Arya Salé, the Bhutanese girl Dewangmo, and Queen Changchupmen—requested the Mahaguru yet again to grant the Vajrakilaya empowerment. There and then, the Mahaguru manifested the mandala of Vajrakilaya in the sky for everyone to see, and asked:

> "From whom do you wish to receive the empowerment of Vajrakilaya? From the wisdom deities or directly from me?"

To which, the queen replied:

> "Although you are the supreme Guru, since the wisdom deities have come here in actuality, I would like to receive the empowerment from them."

Then, Khandro Yeshé Tsogyal said:

> "Although the wisdom deities have come in actuality, since you embody them and there is no one greater than you, I wish to receive

the empowerment directly from you."

Finally, Arya Salé said:

"May I be united with the wisdom heart of you, the Guru."

Just as he had made the wisdom deities instantly appear, so the Guru made them instantly dissolve into himself, and Khandro Yeshé Tsogyal and Arya Salé were both granted the full empowerment. The queen, however, due to her doubts, only partially received the empowerment. Only later did Khandro Yeshé Tsogyal transmit the full empowerment to her.[528] At Yeshé Tsogyal's request, the Mahaguru then transmitted the entirety of the Vajrakilaya teachings to the queen. In particular the Mahaguru transmitted to her the Vajrakilaya teachings that he himself had compiled, with the pandit Vimalamitra and the Newar King Shilamanju[529] at the Asura and Yangleshö caves in Nepal. Khandro Yeshé Tsogyal noted these teachings all down into a single commentary known as the *Phurdrel Bum Nak* (*The Black Hundred-Thousand Words Commentary on Kilaya*).[530] This masterpiece survives to the present day. Not only is it highly revered, but it also counts among the major Vajrakilaya sources for the Nyingma tradition. Guru Rinpoche gave Yeshé Tsogyal additional teachings and practices, instructing her to hide them as *terma* treasures for future generations, concluding with the words:

"I have entrusted all the Vajrakilaya teachings in their entirety to you, my dear Tsogyal."

Subsequently, Khandro Yeshé Tsogyal transmitted these teachings to Arya Salé and other disciples, and thus the lineage that had begun with the Mahaguru's oral instructions was continued and kept alive throughout the generations, and still persists today.

> *Overcoming great obstacles*
> *In Sengé Dzong I took the sap of healing herbs ¦*
> *And saw the vision of the Medicine deities. ¦*
> *In Nering I subdued and quelled the uproar ¦*
> *Of a host of demons, and attained accomplishment. ¦*
> *I beheld the face of all the deities I practiced, ¦*
> *And I attained accomplishment with ease.[531] ¦*
>
> — *Revealed by Samten Lingpa*

Once Khandro Yeshé Tsogyal had completed her retreat at Zhotö Tidro, she went with her students Arya Salé and Dewangmo to Mönkha Nering Sengé Dzong. Together, the three began practicing at the three Mönka Dzongs, focusing on various methods which gradually refined their meditation practice. Khandro Yeshé, deeply immersed there in the practice of Vajrakilaya, maintained an unwavering vajra posture, refusing to relinquish her steadfast gaze or relax her bodily posture. Malevolent spirits and demons tried to disrupt her focus with seductive and wrathful illusions. Initially, they appeared as various forms of food, clothing, and wealth, tempting the wisdom dakini with worldly pleasures. Yet, with her unwavering concentration, she dispelled these deceptive appearances, recognizing their illusory nature. She developed a profound detachment, causing some illusions to disappear or transform into mundane objects.

As the challenges intensified, Khandro Yeshé Tsogyal's compassion grew. She realized that all beings, even the malevolent spirits, were the product of karma. Determined to remain unafraid, she accepted everything equally, understanding that all experiences arise from the mind's thoughts. Hordes of demons and spirits from different lands and realms unleashed their fury upon the dakini. Thunder, fire, water, and furious storms assailed her, testing her resolve. However, these tribulations only deepened her realization. Her awareness expanded, and her wisdom blossomed.

Undeterred, the demons and spirits continued to obstruct Yeshé Tsogyal. They used all means available, including inciting the local inhabitants against her. Mön, the region where she was staying, was beset by calamities and darkness. A local hunter saw her entering the sacred site of Sengé Dzong and singled out the wisdom dakini as the source of all their troubles. It wasn't long before a group of locals had gathered at the dakini's door, confronting her, demanding that she dispel the evil magic. Unfazed, Tsogyal remained seated, resolute in her vow. They attempted to harm her physically, but her body remained impervious to their attacks. Seeing her unyielding fearlessness, they eventually retreated, acknowledging her indomitable spirit.

Thus is was that the wisdom dakini sat unmovingly in the vajra posture, unperturbed by all obstacles, just as Buddha Shakamuni had done in Bodh Gaya and the Mahaguru at the Asura Cave.[532] Deeply immersed in the practice of Vajrakilaya, the wisdom dakini was able to overcome all obstacles, letting them subside like clouds after a storm, and thus she reaped the crystal-clear sky of accomplishment. The terrors that had plagued the land were instantly transformed into the most delightful situations: timely rains, bountiful harvests, healthy animals, and healthy people. It is said, "When you are able to remove all obstacles, there remains no doubt that all siddhis will come." Indeed, in this place, Khandro Yeshé Tsogyal had attained her highest level of realization to date. The demons and spirits who had tested her came forth and pledged their support, offering their life force and vowing to safeguard her teachings and vanquish her enemies. The locals too approached her in admiration, Seeking forgiveness and requesting that she become their protector and teacher. Khandro Yeshé Tsogyal thus emerged completely transfigured from Sengé Dzong and from her retreat, poised to further her activity for the welfare of all.[533]

Meeting Mönmo Tashi Kyidren

Mönmo Tashi Kyidren, the activity manifestation of Vajravahari, was born in the Mön region of Bhutan. She was the daughter of a local King.[534] Kyidren met Yeshe Tsogyal when the latter was meditating in Senge Dzong in northeastern Bhutan. Having great faith in Khandro Yeshé Tsogyal, Kyidren visited her regularly with offerings of food and drink. Her offerings were accepted with great joy, and it was not long before Kyidren became another of her disciples. Over the span of her stay at Sengé Dzong, Yeshe Tsogyal gave Kyidren many teachings and empowerments. For auspiciousness, she changed her student's name from Kyidren (She who Drives Hounds) to Tashi Kyidren (Propitious Guide of All).[535] Later, when Yeshe Tsogyal concluded her retreat at Senge Dzong in extraordinary fashion, Tashi Kyidren's father realized what an exceptional being she was, and gave his permission for his daughter to go with her and leave. This is how Tashi Kyidren of Mön joined Khandro Yeshe Tsogyal on her enlightened quest.

Mönmo Tashi Kyidren meets the Mahaguru

Not long after this, seeing that Mönmo Tashi Kyidren showed great potential, Yeshe Tsogyal introduced her to Guru Rinpoche at Önpu Taktsang.[536] Seeing that the girl possessed all the marks of a spiritual partner, Guru Rinpoche took her as a consort for the practice of Vajrakilaya. In this way, Tashi Kyidren particularly joined him in the task of subjugating harmful spirits and hiding *terma* treasures. And indeed, as the activity manifestation of Vajravahari, Tashi Kyidren became Guru Rinpoche's 'activity-consort', helping him secure the Dharma for future generations.

The Mahaguru's Legacy

The Blessings of the Site

During his extensive pilgrimage, Jamyang Khyentse Wangpo travelled into Bhutan and made his way to Sengé Dzong, where he entered the sanctuary where Khandro Yeshe Tsogyal had spent years in profound retreat. Accompanied by one of his disciples, Khyentse Wangpo paused in this place, the winter's embrace enfolding them within the snowy landscape. As they sat in the cave, he abruptly instructed his disciple to take refuge behind him and keep still, regardless of what transpired. Draped in his voluminous brown cape, Khyentse Wangpo assumed a poised posture, immersing himself in deep concentration with wide-open eyes fixed on the space before him. Before long, a disturbance echoed from the cave entrance, defying the winter's stillness. Against all odds, a tiger emerged, stepping into the cave. The majestic creature halted in front of the Guru, scrutinizing him with a growl and a menacing sway of its tail. Unperturbed, Khyentse Wangpo maintained his composure, undeterred in his meditative state. After a brief moment, the tiger unleashed a resounding roar, then turned and departed, its purpose fulfilled.

"You can come out now," Khyentse Wangpo calmly declared, his disciple finally given the signal to emerge. "There is no cause for concern anymore." Later, he confided in his disciple that this tiger was no ordinary beast. It was the guardian deity of this sacred place, offering a respectful greeting to the esteemed Guru while simultaneously putting him to the test.

Khyentse Wangpo was known for donning the distinctive patchwork monastic skirt, a traditional garment worn by fully ordained monks. However, this attire was not customary among Bhutanese monks. Thus, when Khyentse Wangpo arrived at Wangdu Podrang, local monks engaged in conversation about the "unusual monk from Tibet, clad in tattered robes," unaware of the spiritual eminence he embodied.

The encounter with the guardian deity and the subsequent discussions among the Bhutanese monks served as testaments to the remarkable presence and spiritual significance of Khyentse Wangpo. His journey to Sengé Dzong and the challenges he faced cemented his revered status as a master of wisdom and perseverance, leaving an indelible mark on those fortunate enough to witness his extraordinary presence.[537]

Jamyang Khyentse Wangpo's Vajra Song

With profound devotion and unwavering faith, Jamyang Khyentse Wangpo made offerings of one thousand feasts to the majestic mandala of Vajrakilaya at Sengé Dzong. A vajra song, filled with blessings and transcendent verses, effortlessly flowed forth from Khyentse Wangpo's being:

> *Aho! The wisdom with sublime attributes*
> *Within the immutable dharmadhatu*
> *And rupakaya's magical display of method and wisdom—*
> *These two, intermingled, show as a symphony of fourfold activity,*
> *Helping in whatever way is needed.*
> *Bowing to the mandala of Bhagavan Vajrakumara,*
> *I burst forth, and sing of the path of the profound secret essence.*[538]

Revelation of the Chimé Soktik

> *Pristine dharmakaya, Padma Amitayus,*
> *Perfect sambhogakaya, All-Holding Padma,*
> *Manifest nirmanakaya, Lake-Born Vajra,*
> *Please bless my mind, I pray!*[539]
>
> — *Düdjom Rinpoche*

Having accomplished the sublime siddhi of the vidyadhara of immortality at the Maratika Caves through the practice of Buddha Amitayus, the Mahaguru brought these most profound pith instructions to Tibet. There, on one occasion, he transmitted them to his disciples Lotsawa Vairocana and Nanam Dorjé Düdjom, who hid them as a *terma* treasure at Sengé Dzong. Both disciples later took rebirth in the single form of the great *tertön* Zilnön Namkhé Dorjé (1868~20th century), the root teacher of Kyapjé Düdjom Rinpoche. In the Water Tiger Year of 1902, Namkhé Dorjé revealed the *Yangsang Trinlé Chüdril (The Extremely Secret Quintessential Vajrakilaya)*, at the Namchak Barwa snow mountain in Pema Kö in Tibet. Subsequently, in the Wood Dragon Year of 1904, the tertön revealed the *Chimé Soktik (Life's Immortal Essence)* as an earth treasure, in public, from one of Khandro Yeshé Tsogyal's meditation caves.[540] The *tertön* kept the actual *Chimé Soktik* practice secret, only transmitting it to the Gyalwang Karmapa, Khakyap Dorjé, in around 1910, and later to Kyapjé Düdjom Rinpoche in 1924. Since Düdjom Rinpoche's receiving and subsequent teaching of the practice, the *Chimé Soktik* has become the main long-life practice of the Düdjom Tersar lineage.

Within his commentary on the *Chimé Soktik*, Kyapjé Düdjom Rinpoche emphasizes the significance of conducting wrathful preliminary rites as a means to overcome obstacles before engaging in the longevity practice itself. Drawing analogies, Rinpoche likens this approach to safeguarding growing crops from potential harm, or a traveling merchant who requires an armed escort for protection. Consequently, Rinpoche proposes that longevity practices often incorporate the presence of wrathful deities like Hayagriva and Vajrakilaya for this very purpose. [541]

YARLHA SHAMPO

The blessing of the wisdom mind of the supreme great heruka ⸵
King of Manifest Perfection ⸵
Descended to the goddess of the Mother Tantras ⸵
Yongkhyu Déma (Blissful Lady of the Total Embrace), ⸵
And all the way down to Dhanasamskrita. ⸵
To the masters of the lineage of the mamos who control existence, ⸵
To these masters past, present, and future, we pray! ⸵
To the Lotus-Born Guru of Orgyen, we pray![542] ⸵

— *Revealed by Tulku Zangpo Drakpa*

Introduction

Yarlha Shampo, with its glistening massif and icy peaks, to the south of the Yarlung Valley, resembles a magnificent snow fortress. Within its central peak resides the mountain protector Yarlha Shampo. When Guru Padmasambhava arrived in Yarlung, he compelled Yarlha Shampo to swear allegiance to the Dharma. Recognizing the spiritual potential of this sacred place, Guru Padmasambhava opened the meditation cave there known as Kangi Rawa (Snow Enclosure), for his followers to have a place where they could engage in transformative practices. Later, the Mahaguru returned to Kangi Rawa and blessed it through the practice of *Mamo Bötong*—where Vajrapani appears as a worldly deity. Following the Mahaguru's guidance, his disciple Drokmi Palkyi Yeshé diligently practiced and successfully accomplished Mamo Bötong at the Yarlha Shampo Kangi Rawa cave.

Approaching the Sacred Site

Journeying to the sixth of the eight great caves brings us back to the majestic Yarlung Valley. Perched high above the Takchen Bumpa stupa, on the western side and at the foot of the icy expanse of the Yarlha Shampo glacier, lies Kangi Rawa (Snow Enclosure). Yarlha Shampo is famous not only for the Mahaguru's meditation cave but also for the presence of the spirit known as Yarlha Shampo that resides on its lofty summit. The presence of Yarlha Shampo, bound under oath by the Mahaguru, played a crucial role in inspiring the establishment of a sanctuary on the slopes of the majestic mountain. In fact, each of the main mountain peaks on the Himalayan plateau is inhabited by a mountain deity, a divine spirit responsible for overseeing the natural world. These spirits were

believed to possess their own domains and could provide assistance to devotees in specific matters. Treating these gods with reverence promised blessings in the form of worldly success and prosperity, while angering them risked triggering natural disasters. Among the most influential of these mountain deities was Yarlha Shampo, who held dominion over all the neighboring rivers, valleys, livestock, crops, and the livelihoods of farmers. Yarlha Shampo would manifest in various guises and forms, often appearing as a majestic white yak. Locals living near his mountain abode would frequently catch glimpses of this divine presence, a testament to his pervasive influence in the region.[543]

The Mahaguru's Journey

Binding Yarlha Shampo

From his elevated dwelling, Yarlha Shampo held sway over the rivers, fertile valleys, crops and livestock that thrived beneath him. Disturbing his divine equilibrium had the potential to unleash devastating natural calamities. Consequently, the Tibetans had long lived in hushed reverence of Yarlha Shampo, doing everything within their means to appease him. However, the local gods and demons, provoked by the initial attempts to construct Samye monastery, were causing widespread destruction not only to the monastery itself but also in the form of various natural disasters. The enraged Yarlha Shampo, feeling threatened in his dominion, descended from his mountain abode in a fit of fury. In an act of retaliation, he caused the Yarlung Tsangpo River to surge and overflow, completely engulfing and obliterating the Pangthang temple. And as Guru Rinpoche traveled through Tibet on his way to Samye Monastery, he was faced with a formidable challenge in the form of the shapeshifting, confrontational Yarlha Shampo:[544]

> Afterward, moving on to the valley of Chephu Shampo, Yarlha Shampo transformed into a white yak the size of a mountain. With his nose steaming like storm clouds, a roar like thunder, and his breath storming a blizzard, he brought down lightning and hail. He then assumed a formidable stance. Master Padma caught the yak by the nose with the hook gesture, bound his middle with the lasso gesture, laid his legs in shackles with the chain gesture, and beat and hacked him with the bell gesture. At this, Yarlha Shampo turned into a young boy with white silken braids. He offered the core of his life and was bound under oath.[545] ፧
>
> — Revealed by Nyangral Nyima Özer

Thus defeated, Yarlha Shampo transformed into a young boy and offered Guru Rinpoche his life-force. This is how Yarlha Shampo became a protector of the Dharma. Since then, Tibetans have been able to call upon the mountain protector as an ally, rather than a foe to be appeased, and invoke him whenever needed, to further their cause.

Bringing the Mamos Under Control

On the tenth day of the Tiger month, ⁏
I went to the charnel ground of Sangchen Rolpé Tsal, ⁏
Where I met the great master Dhanasamskrita ⁏
And requested the empowerment and transmission ⁏
Of the mamos and dakinis. ⁏
Seven days after I had opened the mandala, ⁏
The foremost dakini, Simhamukha, ⁏
Actually appeared and bestowed prophecy, empowerment, and blessings.[546] ⁏

— *Revealed by Dudjom Lingpa*

The Yarlha Shampo Kangi Rawa Cave holds great significance as the site where Guru Padmasambhava compelled the mamos to allegiance. Mamos are indigenous spirit-deities of the natural world, and they respond to human misconduct and environmental abuse by creating obstacles and diseases. The practice of *Mamo Bötong* (*Inciting and Dispatching the Mamos*) affords a unique power for bringing the mamos under control. Rather than being subject to their hindrances, practitioners of *Mamo Bötong* gain the ability to command and direct these spirits, at will.

The *Mamo Bötong* teachings were originally revealed at the Sitavana charnel ground by Guru Padmasambhava and the vidyadhara Dhanasamskrita.[547] Later, when Guru Padmasambhava was continuing his practice in the charnel ground of Sangchen Rolpé Tsal, he once again encountered Dhanasamskrita. On that occasion, Guru Padmasambhava received detailed instructions on *Mamo Bötong*. Remarkably, through just seven days of devoted practice, he attained profound accomplishments.[548]

Upon arriving in Tibet, the Mahaguru chose the Yarlha Shampo Kangi Rawa cave as the sacred site to be associated with *Mamo Bötong*. Here, practicing *Mamo Bötong* with unwavering focus, the Mahaguru not only established the practice tradition but also blessed the site as a place of accomplishment for the *Kagyé* deities and for the binding of spirits. During the *Kagyé* empowerments at Samye Chimpu, the Mahaguru entrusted the *Mamo Bötong* teachings specifically to his disciple Drokmi Palkyi Yeshé, whom he then sent to Yarlha Shampo Kangi Rawa, to put them into practice.

The Wisdom Dakini's Journey

Introducing Seven Bandits to the Nature of Mind

At the Shampo glacier, you introduced seven bandits to the nature of mind
And sent them on their way to Uddiyana.
In Nepal, you took the dakini Kalasiddhi into your care
And gave her the liberating instructions.
Yeshé Tsogyal, to you, we pray![549]

— *Jamgön Kongtrul Lodrö Thayé*

While Khandro Yeshé Tsogyal was meditating at the Shampo glacier, she encountered a group of seven bandits who attacked and robbed her. However, instead of responding with fear or anger, she sang them a song, introducing them to the Four Joys:

Sons, meeting me, your mother, ¦
You have but now received the four empowerments, ¦
Through the strength of merits gathered in the past. ¦
Do not be distracted from the rhythm of the Fourfold Joy![550] ¦

— *Revealed by Samten Lingpa*

As Khandro Yeshé Tsogyal uttered these words, a remarkable transformation took place. The seven thieves, in a mere instant, achieved spiritual maturity and liberation. They acquired profound expertise in manipulating the subtle channels and wind energies within their bodies and became skilled in the harmonious rhythms of the Four Joys.[551] Eventually, these seven robbers became great meditation adepts who dedicated themselves to bringing immeasurable well-being to all sentient beings. Following these extraordinary events, Khandro Yeshé Tsogyal embarked on a journey to Nepal. It was there that she encountered the wisdom dakini Belbang Kalasiddhi.[552]

The Mahaguru's Legacy

Master of Mamo Bötong, Drokmi Palkyi Yeshé

> *In the mountain range of Yarlha Shampo*
> *you accomplished the higher states of cyclic existence.*
> *To you, Drokmi Palyé, who makes mamos his servants,*
> *We pray: Please grant us your blessings![553]*

> — *Changdak Tashi Topgyal*

Palgyi Yeshe was born in Yadrok into the Drokmi (Nomad) clan, and later became a translator at Samye monastery. There he honed his translation skills and worked on numerous sutras and tantras. During the *Kagyé* empowerment ceremony at Samye Chimpu, Drokmi Palgyi Yeshe's flower landed auspiciously on the mandala of *Mamo Bötong*. As a result, he received instructions to practice Mamo Bötong at Yarlha Shampo Gangkyi Rawa. Through dedicated practice, Palgyi Yeshe achieved mastery in *Mamo Bötong*, enabling him to summon the mamos and direct them at will. During his retreat he discovered the life-force stone of Yarlha Shampo itself, which he concealed as a treasure that was later revealed by Kelden Dorjé.[554]

Rikdzin Kumaraja and Gyalwa Longchenpa

> O Longchenpa, in the Kyam Uplands, that wilderness guarded by
> the powerful mountain spirit Yarlha Shampo, your guru Rikdzin
> Kumaraja—Vimalamitra magically in human form—served you
> a feast of the nectar of the Dzokchen teachings. You imbibed the
> quintessence of the three categories and nine expanses, becoming
> drunk on your realization and shattering the contrived philosophies
> of the eight lower approaches.[555]

> — *Rikdzin Jikmé Lingpa*

Rikdzin Kumaraja, accompanied by his student Gyalwa Longchenpa, embarked on a journey to the Shampo Glacier. It was there that Rikdzin Kumaraja imparted numerous empowerments and instructions to Longchenpa, focusing particularly on the teachings of the unparalleled secret wisdom. These teachings encompassed the three cycles of Dzokchen, namely the outer, inner, and secret approaches of utter lucidity. Rikdzin Kumaraja also transmitted the profound pith instructions contained within these four volumes, as well as seventeen tantras, of which the *Dra Talgyur* (*Reverberation of Sound*) stands as the most majestic. Additionally, Rikdzin Kumaraja conveyed one hundred and nineteen pith instructions.

Further, Kumaraja bestowed upon Longchenpa the sadhana cycles, empowerments, and entrustments for the principal guardian deities of the Great Perfection teachings: Ekajati, Za Rahula, and Vajrasadhu. Kumaraja appointed Longchenpa as his primary regent, and the protective deities of the teachings actually manifested and presented their respective sadhanas, pith instructions, and essence mantras to Gyalwa Longchenpa. In particular, Za Rahula made him a promise that none of his lineage holders would be harmed by poison. As a token of this assurance, Rahula offered his own emblem as an amulet, safeguarding him against contamination and poisoning.[556]

PARO TAKTSANG

At Tiger's Lair, in the cave called 'Fulfilment of the Lion's Wishes', ⸙
You subjugated malicious tirthikas, maras and damsi demons. ⸙
In power-places, amid snow and rock, you hid the great termas, ⸙
Gazing all the while in compassion ⸙
On future beings of this degenerate age: ⸙
To Dorjé Drolö Tsal, we pray! ⸙
To the Lotus-Born Guru of Orgyen, we pray![557] ⸙

— *Revealed by Tulku Zangpo Drakpa*

Introduction

Paro Taktsang is central among the thirteen caves blessed by the Mahaguru in his guise as Dorjé Drolö (Wild Vajra Wrath).[558] In this formidable form, the Mahaguru possessed the power to conquer the fiercest demons and shatter even the strongest conceptual thoughts. It was in this unique manifestation that he bestowed his blessings upon Paro Taktsang, revealing hidden *terma* treasures and subduing the local spirits. The Mahaguru further blessed Paro Taktsang through his practice of *Jikten Chötö*, where Vajrapani appears as a worldly deity. Following the Mahaguru's guidance, his disciple Langchen Palkyi Sengé chose Paro Taktsang as his retreat hermitage. There, not only did he engage in translating sacred teachings into Tibetan, but he also diligently practiced and achieved mastery in the profound practice of *Jikten Chötö*.

Approaching the Sacred Site

The Paro valley in western Bhutan holds the distinction of being one of the earliest valleys in the country to enjoy the profound influence of Buddhism. Beginning as a narrow gorge known as Chuzom (Where the Rivers Meet),[559] the valley gradually unfolds into a wider expanse. High above the valley floor, nestled on top of a cliff, stands Taktsang Monastery. When viewed from a distance, this magnificent structure, enfolding the sacred practice cave of Guru Rinpoche, appears seamlessly integrated with the cliff itself. It is renowned by the iconic name of Taktsang (Tiger's Nest, or, more precisely, Tigress Lair). Since the time of Guru Rinpoche, the entire mountain has been filled with hidden treasures. Indeed, Taktsang holds the blessings of the Gawé Tsel (Joyful Grove) charnel ground[560] and encompasses a total of thirteen distinct sacred sites, its spiritual center being the cave of Sengé Samdrub Ké'u Tsang

(Fulfilment of the Lion's Wishes). It was within this cave that the Mahaguru appeared in the form of Guru Dorjé Drolö. The cave is also known as Taksang Pelpuk, and both names pay homage to Langchen Palkyi Sengé, who, following the guidance of the Mahaguru, meditated within this sacred space and attained profound accomplishment. After Palkyi Sengé entered parinirvana, his relics were enshrined in a stupa located at the entrance to the cave.[561]

The Mahaguru's Journey

Manifesting as Guru Dorjé Drolö

As a result of successfully accomplishing Vajrakilaya at Önphu Tatsang (Tigress Lair of the Ön Valley) Guru Rinpoche transformed, along with his disciples.[562] The Guru himself assumed the fiercely wrathful form of Guru Dorjé Drolö, while Mönmo Tashi Kyidren transformed into a tigress, and Khandro Yeshe Tsogyal appeared as Dorjé Drolö's consort, Ekajati. Immersed in the profound meditative absorption of Vajrakilaya, Guru Rinpoche and his consorts emanated countless forms identical to themselves, sending them in all directions.[563] One of these emanations, known as the wrathful Blue-Black Vajrakila, arrived at Paro Taktsang.

There, this emanation of Guru Rinpoche, along with the consorts, proceeded to subdue and bind to oath all the local male and female protectors and spirits of all eight classes that roamed the lands of Mön, Nepal, India, and other such untamed regions to the south. Through this act, they eradicated all malevolence from spirits and prepared the ground for the profound treasures that would be concealed at Paro Taktsang.[564]

Soon after, the Mahaguru, accompanied by Khandro Yeshe Tsogyal, returned to the sacred site of Paro Taktsang. While journeying through the Himalayas, blessing the land and concealing *terma* treasures, the couple had arrived at the hidden valley of Beyul Khenpa Lung (Hidden Valley of Artemisia), near to the sacred site of Sengé Dzong. There, the pair transformed once again into Dorjé Drolö and Ekajati, and miraculously flew to the sacred grounds of Paro Taktsang. During this visit, they spent time in retreat, concealing numerous *terma* treasures and enlisting the local spirits as guardians. Guru Rinpoche declared at that moment:

> This is a place of the Guru's Mind. Whoever practices here will attain the accomplishment of Mahamudra.[565]

Then, Guru Rinpoche blessed the self-arisen images there—Dorjé Drolö, a stupa, and six-syllable mantras—saying:

> When I, the Guru, was in Akanishta, these supports of my Body, Speech, and Mind appeared of themselves.[566] ⅜
>
> — Revealed by Samten Lingpa

It was likely also at this point that the Mahaguru transmitted further profound teachings on Vajrakilaya to Khandro Yeshé Tsogyal, and to the other disciples there.[567]

Bringing the Haughty Spirits under Control

> *The blessing of the wisdom mind of the Bhagavan, Tamer of the Haughty,* ⅜
> *Descended to Rombuguhya Chandra and down to Shakya Sengé.* ⅜
> *To the masters of the lineage of Worldly Offering and Praise,* ⅜
> *To these masters past, present, and future, we pray!* ⅜
> *To the Lotus-Born Guru of Orgyen, we pray!*[568] ⅜
>
> — Revealed by Tulku Zangpo Drakpa

Taktsang Cave also served as the site where the Mahaguru accomplished the practice of *Jikten Chötö* (*Worldly Offering and Praise*). This particular practice brought a unique ability to overpower and bind unruly and arrogant spirits. Alongside the practice of *Vajrakilaya*, the Mahaguru relied extensively throughout his journey on this practice of *Jikten Chötö* to subdue and bind these spirits. By manifesting as Drekpa Kundül (Tamer of the Haughty), the central figure in the *Jikten Chötö* mandala, he cleverly ensured that no spirit could defy his commands. Through this practice, the Mahaguru thwarted the wicked intentions of these spirits and compelled them to swear allegiance.

The teachings on *Jikten Chötö* were originally revealed at the Sitavana charnel ground by the vidyadhara Rombuguhya Chandra and Guru Padmasambhava.[569] Later, as Guru Padmasambhava continued to practice within the charnel grounds, the pair met once again and the Mahaguru received detailed instructions from the vidyadhara on the practice of *Jikten Chötö*.[570]

Upon arriving in Tibet, the Mahaguru chose the Paro Taktsang Cave as the place to establish as a sacred site associated with *Jikten Chötö*. Through his own dedicated practice of *Jikten Chötö* there, he not only introduced the practice tradition but also sanctified the site as a place of accomplishment for the Kagyé deities and in which to subdue arrogant spirits and bind them under oath.

During the *Kagyé* empowerments at Samye Chimpu, the Mahaguru specifically entrusted the teachings of *Jikten Chötö* to Langchen Palkyi Sengé, sending him to Paro Taktsang, where he diligently applied himself in the practice.

The Wisdom Dakinis' Journey

The Siddhi of Immortality

> *At Paro Taktsang, with my three companions,* ⁂
> *I trod the path profound and deep;* ⁂
> *And, as Heruka of Great Bliss,* ⁂
> *I controlled and brought within my power* ⁂
> *The subtle veins, the essence-drops and energies.* ⁂
> *Likewise, the five elements I tamed.* ⁂
> *My body, speech, and mind transfigured as the Triple Kaya,* ⁂
> *And the prophecies of Amitayus came to me.* ⁂
> *From Vajravarahi inseparable,* ⁂
> *I then became the mistress of all mandalas.*[571] ⁂

— *Revealed by Samten Lingpa*

From her retreat place at Sengé Dzong,[572] Khandro Yeshé Tsogyal made her way farther south, accompanied by her disciples Mönmo Tashi Kyidren, Acharya Salé, Monpu Salé and Acharya Pelyang. Their destination was the famous site of Paro Taktsang where, together, they entered retreat. There, through sustaining their bodies with medicinal plants and focusing on the practice of *tsalung*, they underwent great austerities for seven months, focusing one-pointedly on the practice of Buddha Amitayus:

> It was then that she had a vision of the mandala of Amitayus and obtained the immutable diamond body untouched by death and aging, becoming thus a vidyadhara with power over life. It was prophesied that she would remain in this world for two hundred and twenty-five years. Glorious Hayagriva and Vajravarahi banished hindrances. The five dakas and five dakinis accomplished her enlightened activities, following her like her shadow. Bodhisattvas sang their prayers of good augury. As a life-dominating vidyadhara, she received the name Mistress of Eternal Life, Blue Light Blazing.[573] ⁂

— *Revealed by Samten Lingpa*

Thus, they seized the accomplishment of the "vidyadhara with power over life," and Khandro Yeshé Tsogyal received indications that she would live for two hundred and twenty-five years. Khandro Yeshé Tsogyal was able, for the welfare of sentient beings, to remain in her subtle bodies of light without dissolving into the dharmakaya. Having reaped great siddhis, Yeshé Tsogyal and her disciples then continued on to Önphu Taktsang, where they met the Mahaguru and received further teachings.[574]

The Mahaguru's Leagacy

Master of Jikten Chötö, Langchen Palkyi Sengé

> At Patro Taksang in the cave called "Wishes Fulfilled"
> You accomplished Drekpa Dakpo,[575] Tamer of the Haughty.
> To you, Palgyi Sengé, enslaver of gods and demons,
> We pray: Please grant your blessings![576]

— Changdak Tashi Topgyal

Palgyi Senge was born as the eldest son of the Lang clan, to parents named Amé Jangchup Dreköl and Lady Kalden. Even from a young age, he exhibited extraordinary and miraculous abilities. He eventually became a translator at Samye monastery and embarked on a journey to Uddiyana. During the *Kagyé* empowerment ceremony at Samye Chimpu, Palgyi Senge's flower landed on the mandala of Jikten Chötö (Worldly Offering and Praise). The Mahaguru then instructed him to practice *Jikten Chötö* at Paro Taktsang in Bhutan. This he did with dedication, attaining mastery in the practice and gaining control over the eight classes of gods and spirits.[577] When Palgyi Senge eventually entered parinirvana, his relics were enshrined at Paro Taktsang, commemorating his profound spiritual accomplishments. Among the twenty-five disciples of the Mahaguru, Palgyi Senge was the only one who left behind a physical body after passing into parinirvana.[578]

The Mahasiddha Thangtong Gyalpo

On one occasion, the renowned mahasiddha and master of iron bridge-building, Thangtong Gyalpo (1385–1509), arrived at Paro Taktsang to practice Vajrakilaya within the Pelpuk cave. Through his dedicated practice, he experienced a profound vision of the Kagyé deities. During this time, also, a local protector in the form of a nine-headed naga appeared before him and spoke:

Great adept, your Dharma inheritance was bestowed upon you by the Great Teacher of Uddiyana. Therefore, I urge you to extract it from the hidden treasure trove.[579]

Following the naga's guidance, the mahasiddha discovered a treasure trove and retrieved a large paper scroll containing the essential teachings of the sutras and tantras and outlining their key points.

It seemed to the great adept that the mountain range extending from Sengé Puk at Taktsang resembled a venomous black snake, slicing through the heart of the main Paro Valley. Accordingly, he conducted a careful geomantic examination to identify an appropriate location for a stupa. The purpose of this stupa would be to subdue the naga. With precision, he placed an iron spike in each of the four cardinal directions to establish the sacred space. In response to his influence, the local community constructed a Dharma throne on top of a natural rock formation shaped like multiple turtles stacked together on the shoulder of the mountain. This serene spot became Thangtong Gyalpo's preferred evening sitting place, allowing him to engage in meditation and contemplation.[580]

Revelation of the Pudri Rekpung

In the Fire Ox Year of 1937, while Kyapjé Düdjom Rinpoche was in retreat at Paro Taktsang, Khandro Yeshé Tsogyal appeared to him in a dream. Along with Guru Dorjé Drolö's kila dagger, she gave Kyapjé Rinpoche the empowerments, oral transmission, and instructions for the *Pudri Rekpung* (*Razor that Destroys at a Touch*). Khandro Yeshé Tsogyal said, of this teaching:

> The secret teachings and pith instructions of all the tantras, within a single state, this heart essence of the hundred thousand Vajrakilaya teachings is called *Vajrakilaya, Razor That Destroys at a Touch*. It condenses the personal Vajrakilaya practices of the three great masters. Just as Guru Padmasambhava bestowed these teachings, so close to his heart, on the assembly of King and subjects, just so, did they practice them. To secure the Vajrakilaya teachings for future generations, the majority have been transmitted orally, many have been hidden as earth treasures, and some have been hidden in the essence of the wisdom-mind, free of word and fabrication— yet all the core meanings are here. Their extraordinary sharp power and blessings are greater than any other. When later, Guru Padmasambhava was leaving for the southwestern subcontinent to

subdue the cannibals, he inconspicuously handed this profound secret teaching to me, Yeshe Tsogyal, the woman from the Kharchen clan, as a parting gift. So precious is this teaching, I have chosen not to hide it in any common way and instead have sealed it in the heart of the one with pure wisdom-mind and good fortune who is no different from me.[581]

Kyapjé Düdjom Rinpoche recounts the revelation:

In the Fire Ox Year of 1937, on the full moon day in the eight month, I, Jigdral Yeshé Dorjé, was thirty-four years old and practicing Vajrakilaya, making the Dharma nectar medicine according to the sadhana *Sword of Meteorite*, at Paro Taktsang in Bhutan. In a dream, a woman with a beautiful dress and ornaments, whom I knew to be Yeshe Tsogyal, handed me a six-inch clearly detailed phurba of meteorite, and said:

> This is the actual ritual implement that Guru Rinpoche held, when he transformed into Dorjé Drolö here and bound all eight classes of mighty invisible beings, in particular the *gyalpo* and *senmo*, under oath. Later, at Gungtang Mountain Pass, Guru Padmasambhava gave me this *phurba* as a farewell gift. Now I am giving it to you. You must keep it as your heart treasure.

She began to put it in the fold of my *chuba*, and at that moment I was so happy, I grabbed it quickly. Thinking, *I am going to receive an empowerment*, I touched it to my forehead and throat. When I touched it to my heart center, instantly that *phurba* and I became inseparable. The upper part of my body was as it is now, but my lower body had become an iron *phurba* shooting with flames. I was chanting the Vajrakilaya mantra and felt the whole earth tremble and shake. At that moment, the girl said to me:

> That is the real empowerment and blessings. This is the treasure of all tantra teachings and pith instructions, in one single state. Don't neglect this, it has great purpose. Can you remember receiving these teachings, empowerment, and pith instructions from Guru Padmasambhava in ancient times?"

Then she tugged at my hand, extending my arm, and I woke up. In that moment, I remembered many things past, and all the Vajrakilaya teachings I had received came clearly into my mind. If transcribed directly as it was arising within the expanse of rigpa, this Vajrakilaya teaching would have been much larger than those of the two *tertöns* combined. There were many instructions and action practices here that those did not include. Revealing *terma* involves you in a lot of work, with little to show for it, and so I set it aside.[582]

In 1948, eleven years after he had this vision, Dudjom Rinpoche wrote down a condensed version of this Vajrakilaya treasure, calling it *Pudri Rekpung* (*Razor that Destroys at a Touch*). Rinpoche recounts:

> At the age of forty-five, in the Earth-Mouse Year, on the tenth day of the first lunar calendar month, urged by many internal and external circumstances not to neglect my own part in the sharing of the teachings, I transcribed a small portion of these as the heart-drop of the root teachings. Dakinis, and ocean of dharmapalas, you are the owners of these teachings. Please secure them! *I-Thi*. [583]

It was during the same retreat at Paro Taktsang that Kyapjé Dudjom Rinpoche composed his commentary on the *Six Vajra Lines* (the *DüSum Sangyé* prayer), namely *The Ornament of Padmasambhava's Enlightened Vision*.

Transmission of the Wisdom Mind

Kyapjé Dilgo Khyentse Rinpoche was always particularly fond of Orgyen Topgyal, whom he had known since Orgyen Topgyal Rinpoche was a child. Orgyen Topgyal Rinpoche possessed a remarkable ability to elicit answers from Kyapjé Khyentsé Rinpoche that others could not. During his retreat at Paro Taktsang, Kyapjé Khyentse Rinpoche had a vision of Rikdzin Jikmé Lingpa. In this vision, Jikmé Lingpa bestowed upon Khyentse Rinpoche the blessing of his wisdom mind, authorizing him as a lineage holder of the *Nyingtik* teachings in particular.

Meanwhile, Kyapjé Nyoshul Khen Rinpoche was in the process of writing his comprehensive history of the Dzokchen lineage, *A Marvelous Garland of Rare Gems*.[584] When Orgyen Topgyal Rinpoche shared with him the story of Kyapjé Khyentsé's vision, Nyoshul Khen Rinpoche was eager to include it in the chapter dedicated to the life of Kyapjé Dilgo Khyentse Rinpoche. Nyoshul Khen Rinpoche approached Kyapjé Khyentse Rinpoche and inquired about the vision. Initially, Kyapjé Khyentse Rinpoche denied it, suggesting that Orgyen Topgyal Rinpoche's imagination had got the better of him. However,

Orgyen Topgyal Rinpoche insisted that Kyapjé Khyentse Rinpoche himself had shared the vision with him. Consequently, Nyoshul Khen Rinpoche included a sentence in his draft manuscript, stating: "In particular, at Paro Taktsang in Bhutan, Khyentse Rinpoche had a vision of Rikdzin Jikmé Lingpa, who empowered him as a master of the *Nyingtik* teachings."[585]

Nyoshul Khen Rinpoche returned to Khyentse Rinpoche and explained his decision to include the sentence despite the earlier denial. He offered to remove it if it proved inaccurate. Initially hesitant to review the manuscript, Kyapjé Khyentse Rinpoche eventually asked to see the relevant page. After carefully inspecting it, Kyapjé Khyentse Rinpoche quietly informed Nyoshul Khen Rinpoche that there was no need for any changes.[586]

DRAKMAR YAMALUNG

Hrih. In the hermitage of Drakmar Yamalung, ༔
The Great Guru of Uddiyana, Lord of infinite life, ༔
And Queen Yeshé Tsogyal, foremost among dakinis, ༔
Attained supreme vajra-longevity in their inseparable union. ༔
We follow in your footsteps, O sublime ones! ༔
Out of the expanse of your unsurpassed wisdom, have compassion for us! ༔
May the essential vitality of samsara and nirvana ༔
Dissolve in the indestructible bindu! ༔
Shower down your blessings of boundless life and wisdom, and
Grant us the supreme empowerment! ༔
om guru amarani jiwentayé benza ayuke soha[587] ༔

— *Revealed by Jamyang Khyentsé Wangpo*

Introduction

The cave complex known as Drakmar Yamalung received the blessings of the Mahaguru through the practice of *Möpa Drakngak* (*Maledictory Fierce Mantras*), in which Vajrapani manifests as a worldly deity. Acting upon the guidance of the Mahaguru, his devoted disciple and translator Vairocana chose this site of Drakmar Yamalung as his secluded hermitage. Not only did he engage in translation work there, but he also diligently practiced and attained mastery in the *Möpa Drakngak* practice within the cave complex.

At Drakmar Yamalung, Guru Padmasambhava further empowered and consecrated several vases filled with a precious longevity *amrita*. These vases were intended to bestow an extended lifespan upon the King. Unfortunately, the royal ministers, hostile and suspicious, prevented him from partaking of the elixir. In response, the Mahaguru took the decision to conceal the vases as treasure items. His intention was for these hidden treasures to be discovered and utilized by future generations when the time was right.

Approaching the Sacred Site

Drakmar Yamalung (*The Red Rock Cave at Yamalung*) is a revered mountain hermitage located in the hills above the Yamalung meadows, not far to the north of Samye Monastery. Located above the village of Ngamgo, where the valley narrows and steepens, there is a significant confluence of rivers. High above, lies the sacred hermitage of Samye Yamalung. A short walk of less than an hour brings the pilgrim to the base of a tall cliff at the western edge of the valley, and another hour of ascent leads to the hermitage site above. Despite its steep and exposed position, the area boasts abundant growth of juniper and other fragrant shrubs.

In the lower part of the site, nestled amidst a grove of trees, there exists a natural spring known as Water of Longevity. This spring was revealed by Guru Rinpoche himself, who also concealed longevity sadhanas in its proximity. Moving up the slope, one comes upon the Orgyen Puk cave, another cave associated with Guru Rinpoche. It is a spacious, enclosed overhang in the cliff, offering a serene environment for contemplation. Inside this cave are several naturally occurring phenomena, including imprints of the Mahaguru's feet and hands. Taking a central position in the cave, at the rear of the shrine, is a newly crafted statue of Guru Rinpoche. Continuing up the slope, one encounters the humble retreat-cell of the esteemed translator Vairocana, as well as that of the Fifth Dalai Lama. Additionally, there are smaller caves that served as retreat abodes for Khandro Yeshe Tsogyal, Yudra Nyingpo, and Gyalwa Chokyang.[588]

The Mahaguru's Journey

Bringing the Mamos under Control

The awesome blessing of the wisdom-mind of great black Mahabala ॐ
Descended to the master Shantigarbha, ॐ
And thence down to Dorjé Drolö Tsal. ॐ
To the masters of this lineage of maledictory fierce mantras, ॐ
To these masters past, present, and future, we pray! ॐ
To the Lotus-Born Guru of Orgyen, we pray![589] ॐ

— Revealed by Tulku Zangpo Drakpa

Drakmar Yamalung cave holds great significance as the location where the Mahaguru himself engaged in the potent practice of maledictory fierce mantras as a means to subjugate enemies and overcome obstacles. The profound teachings of *Möpa Drakngak* had originally been unveiled at the Sitavana charnel ground by the vidyadhara Shantigarbha in conjunction with Guru Padmasambhava.[590] Later, as Guru Padmasambhava further deepened his esoteric practices in the sacred charnel grounds, he reunited with Shantigarbha and received comprehensive instructions on the practice of *Möpa Drakngak*.[591] Now, upon his arrival in Tibet, the Mahaguru deliberately chose the cave at Drakmar Yamalung to establish a sacred site specifically associated with the practice. By engaging in dedicated practice within this cave himself, he not only introduced the tradition of *Möpa Drakngak* in Tibet, but also bestowed blessings upon the site as a place of accomplishment for the Kagyé deities.

During the auspicious *Kagyé* empowerments held at Samye Chimpu, the Mahaguru entrusted the teachings of *Möpa Drakngak* to the esteemed Lotsawa Vairocana, sending him to Drakmar Yamalung, where he engaged in the practice with utmost devotion and diligence.

The Longevity Empowerment and Ritual

One day, at Drakmar Yamalung, with Khandro Yeshe Tsogyal present, Dharma King Trisong Detsen approached the Mahaguru with a sincere request:

> Due to my excellent merit, all my aspirations have been fulfilled. Especially fortunate it is that the sacred Dharma is being taught and translated, spreading its light like the rising sun. Now I implore you to grant me a teaching to enhance my lifespan and make that most excellent, too. ៖

At this request, and the King's lavishing feast offering, the Mahaguru replied:

> Your Majesty, someone with the most excellent merit cannot also have the longest life. Yet, Your Majesty, since I myself have reached the vidyadhara level of longevity, I shall perform the life-sadhana and confer upon you the empowerment of longevity. ៖

Guru Padmasambhava then one-pointedly practiced the sadhana of longevity, manifesting the mandala for achieving indestructible vajra-life. Visible signs of accomplishment emerged, prompting the Mahaguru to send a message to King Trisong Detsen, inviting him to receive the empowerment of longevity and partake in the nectar of immortality from the long-life vase.

> "Come and I shall give you the empowerment of longevity and pour the nectar of immortality from the vase of life!"[592] ៖

> — *Revealed by Nyangral Nyima Özer*

Predictably, the King's ministers voiced their concerns, warning him against drinking from the vase of longevity. They accused the Master of being an avaricious intruder of ill intent, suggesting that the so-called life-vase might actually contain poison meant to harm the King and seize his kingdom. Undeterred, King Trisong Detsen expressed his unwavering trust in the Mahaguru's omniscience. Despite his confidence, however, the ministers prevailed, blocking the King from receiving the empowerment.

In response, in front of them all, Guru Padmasambhava snapped his fingers, revealing within the vase the entire mandala of Buddha Amitayus, only to dissolve it into space moments later. He drank from the vase himself, and the Mahaguru's entire body became infused with golden vajras, each the size of a rice grain. Filled with remorse, King Trisong Detsen denounced the words of his ministers and pleaded for acceptance from the master.

Responding to the King's plea, Guru Padma once again manifested the mandala of longevity and continued with the practice. As the time for conferring the empowerment arrived, the ministers again spoke up, warning the King that without knowledge of the Master's poison-spells his life would be at risk.[593] Thus the ministers persisted in their objections and once again prevailed. Yet again, the Dharma King was prevented from accepting the empowerment. Guru Padmasambhava countered this by concealing as *terma* treasures various longevity sadhanas and vases of longevity, not only at Yamalung but also at numerous other sacred sites.[594]

King Trisong Detsen, meanwhile, earnestly requested the Mahaguru to provide him with a method to extend his life span, acknowledging that while he personally had no doubt about the longevity empowerment, the opposition of his ministers prevented him from receiving it. In response to his request, the translators and panditas engaged in discussions to determine the most beneficial long-life ceremony for the King. They translated ten sutras, which became known as the *Gyalpö Dochu (The Ten Royal Sutras)*,[595] and the King diligently recited them every day as part of the outer-fulfillment ritual. Additionally, they translated the *Amendment of Breaches of Secret Mantra* and composed four confessions for the inner-fulfillment ritual, addressing various aspects of approach and accomplishment.

With these supportive rituals in place, Guru Padmasambhava successfully extended the Dharma King's life by thirteen years beyond the astrological prediction of fifty-six, which meant he was able to live until the age of sixty-nine. The Mahaguru conveyed to the King that, due to his immense merit, he would now be able to fulfill his entire lifespan without encountering any obstacles, possessing all qualities necessary for such longevity.[596]

Teaching Khandro Yeshé Tsogyal

Wanting to know the profound secret beyond karmic causality,
You received, from the Guru, the samayas beyond transgression.
In Yamalung, to ripen your mind-stream,
He gave you The Ocean of Dharma,
The Great Gathering of Transmitted Precepts. To you, we pray![597]

— *Jamgön Kongtrul Rinpoche*

When Khandro Yeshé Tsogyal became the Mahaguru's disciple and consort, they decided to leave Samye monastery and settle in the nearby Drakmar Yamalung caves. It was here that the Guru commenced Yeshé Tsogyal's training and introduced her to the Dharma, starting with the teachings on the Four Truths of the Noble Ones. Gradually, she received instructions on the complete Buddhist path. When the time came to impart to her the Vajrayana teachings, the Mahaguru unveiled the profound *Kadü Chökyi Gyamtso* (*The Ocean of Dharma, Great Gathering of Transmitted Precepts*). Through this, he introduced the young dakini to the teachings and practices concerning the Kagyé deities.[598]

The Mahaguru's Legacy

Master of Möpa Drakngak, Lotsawa Vairocana

At Yamalung and Liyul Changra
You accomplished Mahabala (The Black Powerful One).
To you, Vairocana, with your wisdom eye,
We pray: Grant us your blessings! [599]

— *Changdak Tashi Topgyal*

Lotsawa Vairocana, an emanation of the Buddha's disciple Ananda, was born at Nyemo Chekhar[600] to the Pakor clan in Tsang. From a young age, he displayed various miraculous abilities and signs. When the time came for the Dharma to be translated into Tibetan, Guru Rinpoche, in his clairvoyance, recognized Vairocana's great potential. Consequently, the boy was brought to Samye monastery to be trained as a translator. There he received extensive teachings on both Sutra and Tantra from Guru Rinpoche and Abbot Shantarakshita. Remarkably, he became fluent in Sanskrit, exceeding the expectations of his teachers. Lotsawa Vairocana pursued his training with great enthusiasm and was one of the first Tibetans to receive ordination from Abbot Shantarakshita. Later, when he was sent to India, he was again in the vanguard as one of the earliest Tibetan translators to visit this sacred land.[601] Despite the hardships and dangers of the journey, his practice in magical emanation allowed him to reach Bodh Gaya safely. In India, he had the good fortune to meet twenty-five great panditas and receive teachings on Atiyoga from the mahasiddha Shri Singha—on the mind (*semdé*) and space (*longdé*) sections of the Great Perfection, in particular. He also managed to bring back the Great Perfection scriptures to Tibet, despite some Indians expressing concern over the potential loss of their priceless Dharma treasure. Upon visiting the Dhumagata charnel ground, Vairocana received the six million four hundred thousand Atiyoga verses directly from Garap Dorjé, the first Dzokchen master, resulting in boundless realization.[602]

For the return journey to Tibet, Vairocana relied on his yogic ability of "swift foot." At Samye, he began transmitting the Dzokchen teachings in secret, at night, to Dharma King Trisong Detsen. He also secretly translated texts on Atiyoga and the highest tantras, with the participation of only the King and several disciples. Before long, however, jealous Indian pandits started spreading rumors about him, that were taken up and adopted by the King's evil-minded officials. As a consequence, Vairocana was banished to Gyalmo Tsawarong, despite the King's best efforts to defend him.[603] Nevertheless, undeterred and in exile, Vairocana continued to teach and transmit the Great Perfection, especially to his heart-disciples Yudra Nyingpo, Pang Mipham Gönpo, and Nyak Jñanakumara.

The banishment of Vairocana, along with several other translators, due to the jealousy of certain evil members of the royal household, had left the kingdom without a complete translation of the Dharma. To solve this problem, the King sent three of his best translators to King Indrabhuti of Kashmir, bearing lavish gifts and requesting the assistance of the King's best pandita, one particularly well-versed in the highest tantras. The request was kindly granted, and the mahapandita Vimalamitra arrived safely at Samye. However, by this time the Tibetan King was once again under the sway of his evil ministers, and their claims that Vimalamitra was a practitioner of black magic meant that initially he refused to receive him. Vimalamitra for his part then performed extraordinary miracles to instill trust in the King. For instance, he emanated a colossal image of Buddha Vairocana, filling all of Samye with the illuminating lights of the five wisdoms. Overwhelmed by such displays, the King finally bowed before Vimalamitra, who proceeded to expound the Dharma, allowing the translation work to continue. Then, on learning of Vairocana's exile from his disciple Yudra Nyingpo, Vimalamitra immediately recognized Vairocana's authenticity and invited him back to the capital, amidst great celebration. Vimalamitra's influence played a significant role in Vairocana's return to Samye, where he resumed his contribution to translating and expounding the Dharma for the King, ministers, and people.

Despite numerous obstacles, therefore Vairocana successfully transmitted the teachings of Dzokchen in Tibet, and translated numerous texts. His contributions benefited the Dharma in Tibet on a vast scale. During the *Kagyé* empowerments at Samye Chimpu, Vairocana's flower fell on the mandala of Möpa Drakngak (Maledictory Fierce Mantras). It was to Drakmar Yamalung that he was sent to do the practice. Through his accomplishment of *Möpa Drakngak*, Vairocana's wisdom expanded to encompass all aspects of knowledge.

The Mahaguru's Legacy

Revelation of the Rikdzin Tuktik

> *This land will be filled with bad dharma,*
> *With outlaws, and samaya breakers.* ⁊
> *The realms of gods and humans will resound with bad news.* ⁊
> *These will be the signs that the time has come to reveal* ⁊
> *The terma I have concealed at Shauk Tago.*[604] ⁊
> *The one called Ugyen Terdak Lingpa will appear.*[605] ⁊
>
> — *Revealed by Orgyen Lingpa*

The esteemed treasure-revealer and founder of Mindrolling Monastery, Rikdzin Terdak Lingpa, also known as Minling Terchen Gyurme Dorie (1646–1714), was a speech emanation of Lotsawa Vairocana. It was at Drak Yamalung, at the age of eighteen, on Guru Rinpoche Day, which fell on Friday, the 15th of June 1663, that Terdak Lingpa revealed the *Rikdzin Tuktik*, (*Heart Essence of the Vidyadhara Guru*), along with the associated samaya substances.[606] Guru Rinpoche had originally given this sadhana to Lotsawa Vairocana, who then transcribed and concealed it at Drakmar Yamalung. As part of the *Rikdzin Tuktik* revelation, Terdak Lingpa also retrieved the longevity sadhana *Tsedrup Yangnying Kundü* (*Union of All Innermost Longevity Practices*), along with two guru *kutsaps* and other sacred substances, from the long-life spring that flowed below the Yamalung caves.[607]

THE THREE VITAL POINTS

Samye Chimpu, Yarlung Sheldrak and Drak Yerpa

Following the establishment of Samye Monastery, there were now three important temples upholding Buddhism in Central Tibet, known collectively as the
Chökhor Sum (The Three Central Dharma Centers):

1. Samye Monastery, established by the Great Abbot Shantarakshita,
   Dharma King Trisong Detsen, and Mahaguru Padmasambhava,
   completed in the Fire Horse Year of 766.
2. The Tradruk (Thundering Falcon) Temple, built by Dharma King
   Songsten Gampo as the first of many *tradül* (structures built with
   the purpose of suppressing the giant demoness dwelling supine in
   Tibet). Specifically, Traduk Temple sits on the left shoulder of this
   demoness. The story goes that a naga was living in a lake at the
   proposed temple site. Songsten Gampo called upon a giant garuda,
   which appeared as a "falcon with thundering cry" (*tradruk*) and
   defeated the naga, clearing the way for the temple's construction.
   [608]
3. The Rasa Trülnang Temple, more commonly known as the
   Jokhang, in Lhasa, and home to the most sacred Jowo Rinpoche
   statue. It was built by Dharma King Songtsen Gampo and his two
   royal consorts, Queen Bhrikuti and Queen Wencheng.

During the *rabné* or consecration ceremony of Samye Monastery, the Mahaguru consecrated all three temples at once:

> Then, in Lhasa, at Tradruk, and later at other temples,
> In one hundred and eight monasteries,
> Guru Padmasambhava threw flowers and carried out the consecration.
> But Samye, without rival under the sun,
> Equaled in splendor the Vajra Throne of India.[609]
>
> — *Revealed by Orgyen Lingpa*

The Mahaguru advised his disciples to continue to uphold the three centers
with utmost care and devotion, since the three are the three vital axes of the
Dharma in Central Tibet. He further stressed that each of these temples had a
vital axis of its own—a particular spiritual life-upholding cave.[610] These, then,
are:

1. The Chimpu Caves, the retreat site for Samye Monastery.
2. Yarlung Sheldrak, the retreat site for the Tradruk Temple.
3. Drak Yerpa, the retreat site for the Rasa Trülnang Temple.

The Mahaguru explained that if spiritual practice at these caves were maintained, this would ensure the wealth and prosperity of the three vital Dharma centers; it would keep their blessings alive and vibrant; and it would protect the temples from any dangers that they might face in the future. Thus, following the advice of the Mahaguru, Dharma King Trisong Detsen commissioned retreat centers at all three.[611] Given their unique importance and blessings, the Mahaguru, when advising his disciples on where to practice, always praised Drak Yerpa, Samye Chimpu and Yarlung Sheldrak as the three most sacred caves in Tibet:

> The three exalted sites are Samye at Chimpu, the Crystal Rock of
>   Yarlung, and the Moon Cave at Yerpa, ᠄
> And each has an associated temple: Samye Monastery, Tradruk,
>   and the Temple of Rasa. ᠄
> There are no pure lands of paradise other than these. ᠄
> Stay and practice in these three places, and the common and
>   supreme siddhis will be attained. ᠄
> Practice here, and anything can be accomplished. ᠄
> Make pilgrimage here, and one enters the ranks of the
>   vidyadharas, ᠄
> And leaving one's mortal body here, one reaches the realm of
>   Khechara.[612] ᠄

> — *Revealed by Orgyen Lingpa*

The Mahaguru thus pointed to these two crucial aspects of the Dharma—the inner and outer. If an active outer center for the Dharma of scripture is to succeed, an inner sacred site that maintains the Dharma of realization is needed. Maintaining the relationship of these two is of vital importance, for without one another they cannot succeed.

Since the sacred sites of Samye Chimpu and Yarlung Sheldrak have been discussed in the previous chapters, the following description will focus on Drak Yerpa alone.

DRAK YERPA

Whoever wears this fresh necklace of amrita
Which wins the deathlessness of awakening's essence,
For them the all-encompassing wisdom of the Lotus-Born Guru will grow.
In this cave which delights the vidyadhara,
Proudly arrayed with these blessings of the jeweled moon,
I offer my praise as a sudden laugh,
With the bright smile of all the hundreds of virtuous signs within
existence and peace![613]

— *Jamyang Khyentsé Wangpo*

Introduction

The Trülnang and Ramoché temples in Lhasa were to house Tibet's most precious Buddha statues, the Jowo Rinpoche and Jowo Mikyö Dorjé, but hindrances were holding up construction. In the midst of this disruption, following
a vision of Avalokiteshvara, Dharma King Songtsen Gampo sought out the
life-upholding caves of Drak Yerpa. By accomplishing a retreat at the caves,
the King cleared the obstacles and the construction of the temples continued
successfully.[614] Later, when the Mahaguru arrived in Tibet, he also practiced
there, entering retreat, hiding *terma* treasures, and further establishing Drak
Yerpa as the vital axis of the Rasa Trülnang temple. Following this retreat, on
many occasions the Mahaguru stressed to his disciples the importance of Drak
Yerpa, greatly praising the blessings of this sacred site as one which could swiftly
unlock the higher stages of realization. Upon the Mahaguru's advice, generations of great masters have entered retreat at Drak Yerpa and likewise reaped
great siddhis. Given Drak Yerpa's immense blessings, many have recognized it
as equal to Drak Yangdzong, a sacred site that truly embodies the Mahaguru's
awakened body.[615]

Approaching the Sacred Site

The narrow Yerpa Valley lies on the north bank of the Kyichu River, east of
Lhasa. As you ascend towards its upper regions, where multiple rivers meet, you
will encounter Drak Yerpa, a majestic cliff studded with caves and wrapped
around by a steep plateau. Giant junipers and clusters of rhododendrons crown
a dense labyrinth of undergrowth, brushwood, and grass, valiantly battling
against the desolation of the rocks. The rock formation in Yerpa resembles the

seated figure of Tara, with her left leg extended and right leg bent inward. Her right breast is Tendrel Puk (Auspicious Cave), and Dawa Puk (Moon Cave) is her left. Additionally, a stream flows out from the hillside below, with unique healing properties for all four-hundred-and-four types of ailments. Below the rock formation, towards the southeast, lies a tapered hill adorned with prayer flags known as Yerpa's Lhari (Divine Hill), which serves as the dwelling place of the local guardian and continues in use as a charnel ground.[616]

Amongst the many caves here, that together make up the sacred number of one hundred and eight, Dharma King Songtsen Gampo stayed in the Chögyal Puk (King's Cave), and the Mahaguru primarily in the Dawa Puk. Several disciples, such as Khandro Yeshe Tsogyal, Vairocana, Namkhé Nyingpo, Khön Lu'i Wangpo, and Gyalwa Chokyang, joined the Mahaguru and displayed great miracles as a result of their practice here. Later, Lhalung Palkyi Dorjé hid at Drak Yerpa after the assassination of King Langdarma. Later still, Drak Yerpa became the celebrated residence of Jowo Atisha—where this great siddha transmitted the teachings of both Sutra and Tantra to his heart disciples.[617]

The Mahaguru's Journey

Auspicious Beginnings

> To you, supremely noble Avalokiteshvara, I pray.
> Watch over me, emanated King, I pray.
> To you, Lord Songtsen Gampo, I pray.
> Inspire me with your blessings, I pray.
> Grant supreme and ordinary attainments, I pray.
> Inspire me, that I may master sublime bodhicitta.
> Inspire me, that I may benefit beings immeasurably.
> Emanated King, may I become your equal![618]

> — Jamyang Khyentsé Chökyi Lodrö

Dharma King Songtsen Gampo divined that Tibet was experiencing a series of enigmatic and detrimental events at the hands of malevolent spirits. In order to suppress these forces, it was crucial to establish a spiritual center somewhere auspicious. In a vision, Songtsen Gampo saw Drak Yerpa as the designated site for this purpose. With his queens, Bhrikuti and Wencheng, the King went to this predestined site and, on close examination, found many self-arisen images and syllables. Also in the vicinity were numerous juniper trees, creating a natural habitat for the local deities. Thus the site's sacredness was confirmed, and building could begin. Songtsen Gampo and his royal consorts dedicated themselves wholeheartedly to the development of this potent site and, once the foundation had been laid, the King spent considerable stretches of time in the Chögyal Puk cave, deepening his spiritual practice and dispelling obstacles that might hinder the construction of the Rasa Trülnang temple.[619]

A Site of Immense Blessings

During the construction of Samye monastery, the Mahaguru visited Drak Yerpa and chose to engage there in retreat, particularly at Dawa Puk, the Moon Cave. Initially, the cave was relatively small. In a miraculous act to enlarge it, Guru Rinpoche thrust his *katvanga* trident into the cave's center, causing three distinct chambers to magically appear. The Mahaguru then entered the cave and spent seven months in retreat, leaving his body imprint on the solid rock as a sign of his presence. He also crafted a small *kutsap*, a likeness of himself, which he blessed so that it could grant liberation upon sight. Upon concluding his retreat, the Mahaguru placed this *kutsap* as his representative and primary sacred object on the shrine.

Following his time at Dawa Puk, the Mahaguru meditated for another month in the Pema Puk (Lotus Cave). It was during this retreat that he encountered a malevolent spirit disguised as a black scorpion. Employing his sandalwood *kila* dagger as a support for his practice, Guru Rinpoche subdued the spirit, putting an end to its harmful activities.[620]

Furthermore, assisted by Khandro Yeshé Tsogyal, Guru Rinpoche concealed numerous treasures at Dawa Puk. In particular, they concealed the relics and begging bowl of the monk Shariputra in the Chörten Tsegu, the nine-pointed stupa located at Drak Yerpa. This magnificent stupa housed a clay pot containing texts written by the Eighty-Four Mahasiddhas. Guru Rinpoche prophesied that these texts would one day circumvent famine and disease among cattle. The stupa was subsequently completed in the 9th century by Lhalung Peldhor and his brothers. Later still, on a full moon day, a government minister discovered the structure and its treasures, and moved them to Samye. From that point onward, the monastery thrived both spiritually and materially.[621]

Following the Mahaguru's advice, Dharma King Trisong Detsen built a meditation center and some stupas at Drak Yerpa with the residual material from Samye. As a result, many more practitioners went into retreat at Drak Yerpa, one hundred and eight of them in particular attaining the rainbow body and becoming collectively known as the 'hundred and eight siddhas of Yerpa'.[622]

The Mahaguru's Legacy

Lhalung Palkyi Dorjé

Lhalung Palkyi Dorjé was born at Dromto Gungmoché in central Tibet. Initially, he served as a guardian of the border between Tibet and China, successfully subduing Chinese invaders. However, deeply moved by the injuries he had inflicted upon his enemies, he renounced his position and ventured to Samye monastery. There he received ordination and teaching from the three presiding masters, Abbot Shantarakshita, Guru Padmasambhava and pandita Vimalamitra.

One day, while Palkyi Dorjé was engaged in meditation in the Dribki Karmo Valley, his shawl was carried away by the wind, eventually landing in Drak Yerpa. Recognizing the geomantic excellence of the site, he decided to practice there and soon reaped great siddhis. While in retreat at the Yerpa caves, he came to hear of the new King Langdarma's ruthless persecution of Buddhists. Determined to protect the Dharma, he vowed to put an end to Langdarma's evil schemes. And so it was that, during a grand royal ceremony, Palkyi Dorjé, disguised in his elaborate costume, skillfully concealed a bow and arrow within the folds of his long robe. Seizing the opportune moment, he successfully assassinated the king and swiftly escaped on a white horse that he had cunningly painted black, using charcoal. To further disguise himself, as he fled, Palkyi Dorjé turned his reversible two-tone robe inside out, with the black side showing. As he crossed a river, the water washed away the charcoal, and the horse reverted to white. He then flipped his robe again, also reverting to white, effectively outwitting the soldiers who were in close pursuit. Following these endeavors, Lhalung Palkyi Dorjé returned and went into hiding in the Pelha Chok Puk cave at Drak Yerpa. In total, he spent twenty-two years at the Drak Yerpa caves. Eventually, towards the end of his life, his body transformed into a mass of light and completely vanished.[623]

A Profound Hayagriva Treasure

The profound treasure, the *Tamdrin Pema Wangchen Yang Sang Kröpa* (*Utterly Secret Wrathful Mighty Lotus Hayagriva*), was brought forth from the Sewalung Rock in Drak Yerpa by three individuals, namely Kyangpo Drakpa Wangchuk, Sumpa Jangchup Tsultrim, and Dre Sherap Lama. They passed it on only once to Nyakton Lhabar of Drutsang. Although the three were initially able to reveal this most profound *terma*, they went on to encounter great obstacles as it had not been theirs to retrieve. Kyangpo got leprosy, Sumpa died tragically, and Dre went mad. The *terma* scrolls eventually came into the possession of a Hayagriva siddha by the name of Shuton, but he struggled to decipher their contents. As a result, for a significant period, there was no continuous or widely recognized lineage for these teachings.

In due course, however, the treasure's destined revealer, the mahasiddha Darcharupa, received the complete empowerments and transmissions of the *terma* directly from Guru Padmasambhava. It happened while the mahasiddha was practicing at Dawa Puk, and Guru Rinpoche advised him to replace the *om* in the mantra with *hrih*, and to engage in the practice.

Darcharupa further sought out Lama Gya of Tanak, the custodian of the *terma*'s previous lineage, and received it from him too. Consequently, Darcharupa became the holder of both treasure lineages and taught the treasure extensively. Eventually, Jamgön Kongtrul Lodrö Thayé included the *Tamdrin Pema Wangchen Yang Sang Kröpa* in his *Treasury of Precious Termas*.[624]

The Blessings of Vajrakilaya

As well as the *Tamdrin Pema Wangchen Yang Sang Kröpa*, the Mahaguru had also concealed the teachings of Vajrakilaya at the Sewalung Rock in Drak Yerpa. While the mahasiddha Darcharupa was practicing in the upper cave of Chomo Nagyel, one day, he had a personal encounter with Guru Padmasambhava. The Mahaguru advised him:

Go and practice in the Dawa Puk (Moon Cave) at Drak Yerpa!

He followed these instructions. And in that place, every morning, Guru Padmasambhava would arrive on horseback on the rays of the rising sun and impart teachings to Darcharupa. Each evening, he would depart in the same way, on the rays of the setting sun, stating that he was off to keep the *rakshasas* under control. It was during this period that Darcharupa discovered a *kila* dagger concealed in Sewalung at Drak Yerpa, and began his practice of Vajrakilaya.

Once, visiting Lhasa on market day, Darcharupa caused chaos in the bazaar with a powerful whirlwind. Going on to Tsang afterwards, he encountered Sakya Pandita there, who happened to be on his way to Kyirong in Mangyul. They stayed together in the same house overnight. Darcharupa had a speech impediment, which meant that he recited the Vajrakilaya mantra as "*om vajra chili chilaya...*"

Sakya Pandita, being a great and learned scholar, earnestly corrected him, saying,

"No, that's not right. You should say, *vajra kili kilaya...!*"

Upon hearing this correction, Darcharupa's pride swelled:

"Even if the mantra is incorrect, I can still accomplish it!"

With great force, he plunged his *kila* dagger into the rock as if it were butter. Recognizing Darcharupa as an accomplished master, Sakya Pandita asked him to accompany him to a debate with heretics in Mangyul. The debate was to be held in Kyirong. Darcharupa agreed, and they set out together.

When they reached Kyirong, it was decided that, following Indian custom, the doctrine of the victorious party would be upheld and their banner raised high. Sakya Pandita engaged in a thirteen-day debate with the heretics' leader Haranandin, ultimately emerging as the winner. However, Haranandin refused to accept the Buddhist teachings and proposed a competition based on displays of spiritual accomplishment. So saying Haranandin deftly tossed his tangled hair aside and, extending his arms like wings, ascended into the sky. Sakya Pandita realized that the only way to subdue him was through the power of mantra. He called out to Darcharupa, saying, "Hey! Vajrachili chilaya! Come here!"

Instantly, the great yoga master plunged his kila dagger into the heart of the heretic's shadow, exclaiming, *"om vajrachili chilaya hung pé!"* Haranandin plummeted to the ground. As a triumphant symbol of his victory in the debate, Sakya Pandita led Haranandin along with him, even though he still refused ordination. This did not conclude matters, however, as Guru Padmasambhava had long since instructed the twelve Tenma Goddesses to protect the Buddhist teachings in Tibet from heretics, and they duly administered their punishment. At the Tibetan border with Mangyul, the heretics began vomiting blood and met their demise. Consequently, there have been no further proponents of non-Buddhist philosophies in Tibet. Although some may have ventured in, none have possessed the intellectual capacity to truly challenge the Buddhadharma.[625]

A Profound Tara Treasure

While Guru Padmasambhava was deeply immersed in longevity practice at the Maratika Caves,[626] an extraordinary event occurred. Noble Tara appeared before him and bestowed a vast array of tantras, transmissions, and pith instructions. The Mahaguru meticulously condensed these teachings into comprehensive, intermediate, and concise manuals, which he later shared with his fortunate disciples in Tibet. To preserve the teachings for future generations, Guru Rinpoche concealed them within three hidden treasures. One of these treasures, the *Drolma Jikpa Kunkyop* (*Tara who Protects against All Dangers*), was hidden in Tramo Drak, a branch of the Uyuk valley in Yakché. It was later revealed by Yakchar Ngönmo but reconcealed at Sewalung Rock in Drak Yerpa.[627] Rongpa Dündül Lingpa subsequently discovered it there, but due to his sudden passing, it was the protectress Mentsün Dorjé Yudrön who retrieved the scrolls. [628] Then, on the eighth day of the first month in the Earth Tiger Year of 1878, the dakini Chandika presented the scrolls to Jamyang Khyentsé Wangpo in a dream, granting her blessings. Upon waking, Khyentsé Wangpo found a greenish-yellow scroll, two fingertips wide and one finger long, covered with symbolic script, right in front of him. He transcribed its contents and began teaching it to fortunate disciples.[629] Jamgön Kongtrul Lodrö Thayé, after receiving this transmission from Khyentsé Wangpo, composed a sadhana liturgy, an empowerment manual, and a war-prevention ritual, incorporating the *Drolma Jikpa Kunkyop* into his *Rinchen Terdzö* (*Treasury of Precious Termas*).

Jamyang Khyentse Wangpo's Vajra Song

While Jamyang Khyentse Wangpo was offering one thousand feasts at the Dawa Puk cave, following a vision of the Mahaguru, he spontaneously composed the following vajra song:

> *Emaho! The play of natural awareness, primordially pure,*
> *Appears as this dance of the illusory net's union;*
> *Immortal Pema Tötreng Tsal, Skull-Garlanded Lotus,*
> *In our inseparability, I pay homage to you!*[630]

TIGRESS LAIR

Paro Taktsang, Önphu Taktsang, and Chimé Karmo Taktsang

On the tenth day of the Ox month, master and disciples conferred,
And in the center and at the borders of the Land of Snows
You concealed millions of terma troves.
With these treasures you safeguarded what remains of the teachings,
All with your constant kindness.
All-powerful Dorjé Drolö, to you we pray:
Grant your blessing, that sudden misfortune never befalls us,
Nor untimely death;
Grant your blessing, so that, as we transfer to the next life,
We are reborn in the pure realm of Great Bliss
And the paradise of Lotus Light,
And in your very presence, Guru,
Thus becoming a source of limitless benefit to living beings![631]

— *Jamgön Kongtrul Lodrö Thayé*

As a buddha and an emanation of the historical Buddha, Guru Padmasambhava re-enacted the twelve deeds (excluding the twelfth, as he did not enter mahaparinirvana). The *Kathang Dé Nga (The Five-Part Chronicles)* provides a detailed account of the different episodes and important individuals in Guru Padmasambhava's life. It portrays the story through a sequence of eleven enlightened deeds, closely echoing those of the Buddha:[632]

1. Forming the enlightened intention to tame beings
2. Descending into the lotus flower
3. Spontaneously taking birth
4. Enjoying princely pleasures
5. Taking ordination
6. Practicing austerities
7. Overcoming the hosts of Mara
8. Attaining complete awakening
9. Turning the Wheel of Dharma
10. Engaging in yogic disciplines
11. Hiding *terma* treasures, so that the Dharma would spread and never wane.

As his final feat and eleventh deed, Guru Padmasambhava hid countless profound *terma* treasures throughout the world—to prevent the destruction of the teachings of Secret Mantra; to avoid corruption of the Vajrayana or its alteration by intellectuals; to preserve the blessings of the lineage; and to benefit future followers. For this activity, the Mahaguru manifested in the extremely wrathful form of Guru Dorjé Drolö (Wild Vajra Wrath).[633] It was in this form, closely linked with his accomplishment of Vajrakilaya, that Guru Rinpoche shattered the conceptual thoughts of disciples, made the gods and demons swear allegiance, dispelled all obstacles that might hinder his lineage in the future, and hid profound and powerful treasures that would uproot ego-clinging in his future disciples.

While the Mahaguru displayed this form in many sites and on multiple occasions, the tradition particularly identifies thirteen sacred sites where he appeared in this profoundly wrathful form.[634] These sacred sites all bear the name Taktsang (Tigress Lair)— after Guru Dorjé Drolö's mount, a tigress. Of these thirteen places, three are highlighted as particularly significant in Khandro Yeshé Tsogyal's biography:[635]

1. Önphu Taktsang, in the Ön Valley, representing the Mahaguru's body
2. Chimé Karmo Taktsang, in Kham, representing the Mahaguru's speech
3. Paro Taktsang, in Bhutan, representing the Mahaguru's heart

Since the sacred site of Paro Taktsang has been discussed in a previous chapter, the following descriptions will focus on Önphu Taktsang and Chimé Karmo Taktsang alone.

ÖNPHU TAKTSANG

For a hundred and eleven years you remained in Tibet,
Concealing the five heart treasures, the twenty-five profound treasures,
The hundred supreme treasures, and countless more besides.
To you, whose kindness toward your followers is extraordinary, I pray!
To the Nirmanakaya of Uddiyana, I pray!
Compassionate Son of the Conquerors, please grant us your blessings![636]

— *Ratna Lingpa*

Introduction

It was at Önphu Taktsang that Khandro Yeshe Tsogyal introduced Mönmo Tashi Kyidren to the Mahaguru. Guru Rinpoche then guided and matured Mönmo Tashi Kyidren and several other close disciples through the mandala of Vajrakilaya. At the culmination of their practice, Guru Rinpoche assumed the extremely wrathful form of Guru Dorjé Drolö (Wild Vajra Wrath). Simultaneously, Mönmo Tashi Kyidren transformed into a tigress, and Khandro Yeshe Tsogyal into the form of the Guru's consort Ekajati. Remaining deeply absorbed in the samadhi of Vajrakilaya, Guru Rinpoche and his consorts emanated countless forms of themselves, which they sent in all directions to subdue all remaining evil spirits. Having accomplished their feat, they hid great *terma* treasures at Önphu Taktsang.

Approaching the Sacred Site

Located at the head of the Ön river, just below the natural divide of a lofty pasture, where mountain passes lead down to Samye monastery, there lies a sanctuary famously known as Önphu Taktsang. To reach this sacred site, one must embark on a day's journey from Dikna, the final village in the upper Ön region. The main cave, Khandro Tsokhang (Assembly Hall of the Dakinis), nestles beneath a group of boulders on the south bank of the river, not far from the Domdom pass. Additionally, there is another cave of significance here, the Zimpuk Gongma (Upper Meditation Cave of the Guru), in which the Mahaguru practiced in retreat. This cave offers breathtaking views of the glacial lake of Taktsang Lhatso (Life-Force Lake of Taktsang).[637]

The Mahaguru and the Journey of the Wisdom Dakinis

Khandro Yeshé Tsogyal's Return to Önphu Taktsang

Before embarking on the path of the Dharma, Khandro Yeshe Tsogyal had sought refuge in the mountains of Önphu Taktsang, motivated by a desire to escape her pursuers, those who sought her hand in marriage. Guided by an intuitive sense of the blessings in that sacred place, she temporarily sought solace there. Her sanctuary was short-lived, unfortunately, as she was soon discovered and brought back against her will, to her previous life.[638] Despite spending only a brief time at Önphu Taktsang, however, a profound karmic connection with the place was nonetheless established—a connection that would later bear fruit, as the site became a catalyst for one of her most significant accomplishments.

And so it was that, much later, having attained great siddhis in Paro Taktsang through her diligent practice of Buddha Amitayus,[639] Khandro Yeshe Tsogyal, accompanied by her devoted disciples, joyfully journeyed to Önphu Taktsang where the Mahaguru was in residence. Upon learning of the progress made by his beloved disciple, the Mahaguru was overjoyed and offered his guidance with these words:

> It is as though the long-life practice is the captain, and Vajrakilaya the protective escort. For this reason, whatever work one does in Secret Mantra, it is important first to practice Vajrakilaya, so as to dispel obstacles. Moreover, *Vajrakilaya* is your yidam deity, and therefore you can do this practice.[640]

> — Revealed by Samten Lingpa

Thus, drawing from his own experience at the Asura and Yangleshö caves,[641] and affirming Khandro Yeshé Tsogyal's prior accomplishment of Vajrakilaya at Sengé Dzong, Guru Rinpoche made it clear to the wisdom dakini that Vajrakilaya is a prerequisite for reaping further siddhis.

Meeting Mönmo Tashi Kyidren

It was at this time that Khandro Yeshé Tsogyal formally introduced Mönmo Tashi Kyidren, one of her most cherished and trusted disciples, to Guru Rinpoche. On this significant occasion, recognizing her remarkable qualities, Guru Rinpoche immediately appointed Tashi Kyidren as his spiritual consort for Vajrakilaya practice. Right there and then, the Mahaguru initiated the assembled group of his closest disciples into the sacred mandala of Vajrakilaya.

This potent ritual aimed to empower disciples both present and future in the means to overcome obstacles and cultivate auspicious circumstances for their spiritual practice and advancement. Once the empowerment was complete, the Mahaguru said:

> It is necessary to disseminate many oral instructions on Vajraku-mara. Otherwise the Secret Mantra will not spread in this foolish land of Tibet, and the yogis who do practice it won't even be able to protect their own lives. As it is, Tibet's multitude of gods and spirits, enemies of the Dharma, will create obstructions, and the spread of Secret Mantra will be halted. And even without these hindrances, it would vanish speedily anyway.[642] ⁛

> — *Revealed by Samten Lingpa*

The Mahaguru then invited his trusted disciples to join him in the practice of Vajrakilaya. The results exceed all expectations, the disciples quickly reaping profound siddhis, and the divine beings of the Vajrakilaya mandala materializing directly before the entire gathering. Guru Rinpoche took on the immensely fierce manifestation of Dorjé Drolö (Guru Vajra Wrath), Mönmo Tashi Kyidren shape-shifted into a tigress, and Khandro Yeshe Tsogyal assumed the form of his sacred companion, Ekajati. Remaining absorbed in the profound meditative state of Vajrakilaya, Guru Rinpoche and his consorts radiated numerous embodiments of themselves, which they dispatched in all directions to subdue any and all present and future obstacles.[643]

As for Mönmo Tashi Kyidren, in becoming Guru Rinpoche's consort for the practice of Vajrakilaya, she joined him in the particular task of subjugating harmful spirits and hiding *terma* treasures. And indeed, as the activity manifestation of Vajravahari, Tashi Kyidren became Guru Rinpoche's 'activity-consort', helping him secure the Dharma for future generations.

Khandro Yeshé Tsogyal attains the Vidyadhara of Immortality

> *At Önphu Taktsang I attained Kila* ⁛
> *And seized the life-force of gods and spirits* ⁛
> *Of a thousand million worlds.* ⁛
> *The deities of Amitayus' mandala I saw* ⁛
> *And reached the level of a deathless vidyadhara,* ⁛
> *Diamond-like, invincible, and indestructible.[644]* ⁛

> — *Revealed by Samten Lingpa*

All those present having successfully and profoundly overcome all obstacles, the Mahaguru generously gave them the initiation and transmission of Buddha Amitayus, along with other associated practices. Then he sent Khandro Yeshe Tsogyal and Lalhung Palkyi Sengé, her destined spiritual consort from Uru, into retreat at Önphu Taktsang. With unwavering focus, their primary objective was to capture the citadel of immortal vajra-life through the practice of Amitayus.

As a result of their dedicated retreat, an extraordinary event unfolded. Buddha Amitayus himself appeared before them in physical form, as he had to the Mahaguru and Lhacham Mandarava at Maratika,[645] bestowing upon them the blessing of eternal life. With remarkable ease, they entered the ranks of the immortal vidyadharas.[646]

Hiding Profound Treasures

Later, the Mahaguru returned to Önphu Taktsang with his devoted disciples, journeying through the majestic Himalayas to get there, bestowing blessings upon the land and concealing sacred *terma* treasures. Once again, they assumed the manifestation of Dorjé Drolö. This time, they devoted themselves to retreat in this sacred place, concealing numerous *terma* treasures and appointing the local spirits as their guardians. It was during this period that Guru Rinpoche declared:

> This is a place of the Guru's Body. Whoever practices here will attain the accomplishment of immortality.[647] §

Then, as he blessed the self-arisen images of the three-syllable mantra, the nine-syllable *rulu* mantra, a stupa, and a vajra, he conveyed the following words:

> When I was born upon the Lake of Dhanakosha, these supports of my Body, Speech, and Mind appeared by themselves.[648] §

> — *Revealed by Samten Lingpa*

The Mahaguru's Legacy

Discovery of the Sacred Site

Initially, the sanctuary of Önphu Taktsang was discovered and unveiled by Orgyen Lingpa (b. 1323). Although he revealed profound treasures inside the cave, it was deemed an unsuitable time for disseminating these teachings, and so he concealed them once again.[649] However, in the 16th century, the sacred site was reopened by the illustrious *changter* master, Rikdzin Lekden Dorjé (1452–1565),[650] recognized as the reincarnation of Rikdzin Gödem.[651] To gain access to the main cave, Lekden Dorjé diligently moved three obstructing boulders that were blocking its entrance.

During his contemplative meditations within the cave, Lekden Dorjé was naturally endowed with insights into the historical significance of the site, as if the wisdom mind of a *tertön*, a revealer of hidden treasures, were unfolding before him. He experienced numerous visions and heard the voices of the dakinis, who proclaimed:

> The Lion-like Pandita of Uddiyana
> Summoned arrogant spirits and outshone them with his brilliance.
> He bound local nagas and land guardians, like Maldro Zican, to oath.
> He left ten-thousand-five-hundred footprints and a hundred self-
> arisen statues. [652]

As the prophecy stated, many naturally arisen syllables and images are indeed found at the sacred site. Subsequently, Lekden Dorjé also revealed profound treasures focused on the Wrathful Guru, Hayagriva, and the dharmapalas. [653]

Revelation of the Taktsang Phurpa

Later still, the renowned *tertön* Samten Lingpa (1655–1708) emerged as a significant figure, unveiling—in his treasure biography dedicated to Khandro Yeshé Tsogyal—the remarkable events that unfolded at Önphu Taktsang. Other esteemed masters of the time, such as Chöjé Lingpa (1682–1720) and his disciple Ratön Topden Dorjé (widely known as Padma Tsewang Tsel), were also frequent visitors to Önphu.[654] It was during their visits that Ratön Topden Dorjé unearthed treasures such as the *Zhiwa Kunzang Tuktik* (*Heart Essence of the Peaceful Samantabhadra*), and various treasures relating to Chemchok Heruka and Black Hayagriva.

One of the treasures unearthed in Önphu by Ratön Topden Dorjé was the Vajrakilaya teachings that the Mahaguru had entrusted to Khandro Yeshé Tsogyal's consort, Langchen Palkyi Sengé.[655] This particular treasure was commonly referred to as the *Taktsang Kila* or *Ratön Kila*.[656] Later, in a visionary encounter at Paro Taktsang, Rikdzin Jikmé Lingpa had the privilege of meeting Ratön Topden Dorjé in a dream, receiving the transmission of these Vajrakilaya teachings from him directly:

At that time, I dreamt I met Padma Tsewang Tsel,
the reincarnation of Langchen Palseng,
and he gave me an initiation into his own Taktsang treasure on
    Vajrakilaya.[657]

Jikmé Lingpa later received the *Taktsang Kila* from Ratön Topden Dorjé in person, which formed the basis for his own writings on Vajrakilaya, namely the *Gyüluk Phurpa* (*Tantra System of Vajrakilaya*). In this unique Vajrakilaya practice, he took the *kama* (oral lineage) of Vajrakilaya from the tantras, merged it with the *terma* or treasure tradition, and thus combined the blessings of both traditions into a single practice.[658]

Jamyang Khyentse's Vajra-Song

Many years later, Jamyang Khyentse Wangpo, reincarnation of both Orgyen Lingpa and Jikmé Lingpa, visited this, his own sacred site, on pilgrimage. He offered a feast, and as a result of his prayers, a vajra song flowed forth:

> *Aho! From the very beginning, all of samsara and nirvana*
> *Has been absolutely perfect, the great mudra of the deity!*
> *So through the power of the truth*
> *Of this inseparability, I pay homage!*[659]

CHIMÉ KARMO TAKTSANG

Among the four valleys, the hidden valley of Meshö
At the foot of Mount Ziltrom is supreme.
Within the palace of the three worldly deities
Lies the Deathless White Tigress Lair of Rongmé.[660]

— *Jamgön Kongtrul Lodrö Thayé*

Introduction

In his wrathful form of Dorjé Drolö, Guru Rinpoche flew far to the east of the Himalayan plateau, to the sacred site that became known as Chimé Karmo Taktsang (Deathless White Tigress Lair). By remaining for one month in the samadhi of vajra wrath, the Mahaguru subjugated evil spirits and sanctified the land. It was at Karmo Taktsang, a true embodiment of the Mahaguru's Speech, that Guru Rinpoche chose to hide a most profound treasure, the *Lamrim Yeshé Nyingpo* (*The Gradual Path of the Wisdom Essence*), a complete and unparalleled presentation of the Vajrayana path.

Approaching the Sacred Site

It is especially due to the blessings of the three great *rimé* masters—Jamyang Khyentsé Wangpo, Jamgön Kongtrul Lodrö Thayé, and Chokgyur Dechen Lingpa—that many of the priceless teachings of the Mahaguru still thrive to this day. Their collaboration was vital for the preservation and continuance of the Mahaguru's teachings, and it was their combined efforts that led to some of the most profound and cherished treasures that are available to us today. The esteemed Dzongsar Monastery, far to the east of Samye, was one of the main centers of their enlightened activity. It was at Dzongsar that the three great masters regularly convened and engaged in profound exchanges, revealing, composing, and refining numerous precious teachings, especially of the Nyingma tradition. Chimé Karmo Taktsang, located in the adjacent Rongmé valley to the north of Dzongsar, stands as a testament to the three great masters' profound legacy, and it was from Dzongsar that they set out when they revealed this unique and sacred site. Since the time of its revelation, Chimé Karmo Taktsang has remained a sanctuary of the Mahaguru's enlightened influence within the realm of Kham. Jokyap Rinpoche (1903–1960), a heart disciple of Jamyang Khyentse Wangpo, describes Karmo Taktsang as follows:

Within the hidden valley in the Zalmo range of Dridza, in the foothills of Ziltrom Dorjé Yungdrung, surrounded by cool snow mountains, to the north of the auspicious, spontaneously self-arisen Shelpuk (Crystal Cave),[661] in the supreme place which is the source of auspiciousness and virtue for the whole domain of Tibet—there, at the head of the White Jewel spring, where Mutak Mizen was tamed by Dorjé Drolö, King of Crazy Wrath; there, on top of the mountain called Poised Haughty Snow Lion, King of the beasts at that time—there, in that place, is the cavern of the Wish-Fulfilling Cave. It is a celestial palace, self-arisen, shaped like a triangle to symbolize the three gates of liberation of emptiness, and so forth, and is adorned all over with numerous forms of the body, speech, and mind of the vast pantheon of peaceful and wrathful deities, and, in particular, with garlands of the vowels and consonants of the Indian and Tibetan scripts, along with the secret symbolic script of the dakinis.[662]

The Mahaguru's Journey

An Initial Blessing

As a result of successfully accomplishing the practice of Vajrakilaya at Önphu Tatsang, Guru Rinpoche, along with his disciples, assumed the fiercely wrathful form of Guru Dorjé Drolö.

Absorbed in this profound meditative state, the Mahaguru and his consorts emanated the wrathful form known as Blood-Red Vajrakilaya, dispatching it to Karmo Taksang. There, this powerful manifestation subdued and vanquished the gods, demons, and spirits that were besieging Kham, Jang, China, Hor, and other more distant lands. By binding them to unbreakable oaths, this wrathful manifestation deprived them of their life force, effectively eliminating all malevolent spirits and creating a fertile ground for the Dharma to spread and be maintained in the far eastern reaches of the Himalayan plateau.[663]

The Gradual Path of the Wisdom Essence

> *To you, Guru Rinpoche, of unmatched kindness,* ⸙
> *We offer our bodies and enjoyments, unreservedly.* ⸙
> *May we never be apart from you until we reach enlightenment;* ⸙
> *May you remember your heart promise and always accept us.* ⸙

May there be peace throughout the realm of Tibet, ༔
And may the teachings of the Buddha remain for a long time. ༔
May we only ever spread the activity of the guru, ༔
Wherever we are reborn—led by our karma or aspirations. ༔
May we thereby bring benefit to whomsoever encounters us, ༔
Whether that be through sight, sound, recollection, or touch, ༔
And may we all, at once, and together, be liberated
Into the expanse of Samantabhadra's mind.[664] ༔

— *Revealed by Chokgyur Dechen Lingpa*

Back at Samye monastery, the Mahaguru was residing in the Shining Turquoise Chamber, Samye's middle storey, when the Dharma King approached, bearing a mandala plate of gold heaped with shining precious turquoise that resembled huge and radiant stars. Following repeated prostrations and the mandala offering, the Dharma King, the prince, the lotsawa Vairocana, and Khandro Yeshé Tsogyal together requested Guru Rinpoche:[665]

There will be no refuge other than you, Guru, ༔
When this ocean of misery drowns Tibet and Kham, ༔
And so we beg you to consider us with kindness, Guru, ༔
Not just for our sake, but for disciples in the future: ༔
Grant us the quintessence of all the profound and vast instructions, ༔
Such as temporarily subjugates the outer and inner maras, ༔
And effortlessly accomplishes the four activities, ༔
And ultimately is the method that attains the bhumi of Unexcelled Wisdom, ༔
The light-body of the fivefold essence.[666] ༔

— *Revealed by Chokgyur Dechen Lingpa*

In response to their request, in an instant the Mahaguru appeared in the wrathful form of Guru Dorjé Drakpo Tsal (Powerful Vajra Wrath), and instantaneously bestowed all the empowerments and oral instructions upon his disciples:

Through the great splendor of blessings, he manifested instantly and everywhere throughout central Tibet and Kham the most magical and miraculous displays of rainbows, lights, rains of flowers, earth tremors, spontaneous sounds, and self-resounding music; and the vajra-wisdom in actuality descended into the fortunate disciples. Once again, the Guru appeared majestically in the form of Padmasambhava, of the nature of light, and uttered, in his vajra voice of dharmata, this teaching, the ultimate vajra speech, the stages of the path condensed to the essence.[667] ༔

— *Revealed by Chokgyur Dechen Lingpa*

Thus it was that the Mahaguru began to teach a most profound treasure, the *Lamrim Yeshé Nyingpo* (*The Gradual Path of the Wisdom Essence*), a complete and unparalleled presentation of the Vajrayana path. Of this, the Second Tsikey Chokling Rinpoche, Könchok Gyurmé, wrote:

This treasure is foremost among hundreds of consequential treasures, including its main text and the four supportive cycles of Guru accomplishment, all of which are potent with scripture, transmission, and pith instruction. Just hearing the name of this profound Dharma that was thus established through commentary and study will rip open the fabric of existence. Studying and contemplating it brings about undefiled wakefulness. Practicing it bestows the fruition of buddhahood. The commentary too is a treasure teaching, sprung from the expanse of wakefulness. No matter how erudite a person might be, no one could compose such a text.

After giving this most profound teaching, the Mahaguru prophesied where the text would be hidden as a *terma* treasure:

After some time, I, the Self-Born Padma, ༔
Will take my leave, amidst a great magical display, ༔
In order to go and subdue my *rakshasa* disciples. ༔
But when one year has passed, ༔
I, Samantabhadra Tötreng, ༔
Will manifest the forms of the eight kinds of wisdom, ༔
The eight supreme aspects of manifestation, ༔
From the natural expression of my eight pure collections. ༔
Among these eight, the Heruka "Wisdom Free from Extremes," ༔
The wild great King of the Wrathful Ones, ༔
Is the great and glorious Dorjé Drolö. ༔
In order to tame the evil ones, perverters of samaya, ༔
He will appear at the place for manifesting delightful magic, ༔

One among thirteen places with the name Taktsang (Tigress Lair). ༈
It lies to the east, in the central land of Dokham, ༈
In the area of the Zalmo range of Dridza, ༈
In the foothills of a hidden valley surrounded by snow mountains, ༈
To the north of the self-appearing Pema Shelpuk (Crystal Cave)— ༈
A place that is the source of auspiciousness for Tibet.[668] ༈

— Revealed by Chokgyur Dechen Lingpa

This was how the Mahaguru foretold his assembled disciples that the *Lamrim Yeshé Nyingpo* would be hidden far to the east at Chimé Karmo Taktsang, a site which he had already blessed when there with Khandro Yeshé Tsogyal and Mönmo Tashi Khyidren.

Concealing Profound Treasures

Not long after that, the Mahaguru went once more to Karmo Taktsang, to further bless and establish this sacred site, accompanied by Khandro Yeshé Tsogyal. Upon reaching Karmo Taktsang, they again assumed the wrathful form of Dorjé Drolö. In the words of the Mahaguru:

At the head of White Jewel spring, ༈
In the place where Mutak Mizen was tamed, ༈
At the top of Poised Haughty Snow Lion mountain, ༈
Lies the cavern of the Wish-Fulfilling Cave. ༈
It is a celestial palace endowed with the three gates of liberation, ༈
Adorned with numerous different forms ༈
Of the peaceful and wrathful deities, ༈
With garlands of the vowels and consonants
Of the Indian and Tibetan syllabaries ༈
And the secret scripts of the dakinis. ༈
At that place, I, the Guru of Uddiyana, did for one month practice ༈
The samadhi of vajra wrath. ༈
Having eliminated obstacles and evil spirits, ༈
I brought forth auspiciousness throughout all Tibet.[669] ༈

— Revealed by Chokgyur Dechen Lingpa

Accordingly, for a month, in the Wish-Fulfilling Cave, the Mahaguru and Khandro Yeshé Tsogyal sustained the samadhi of vajra wrath, binding especially the spirit Mutak Mizen. The couple then entered a further retreat at the summit of this sacred place:

> To the right, for myself, the Guru of Uddiyana, ༔
> And to the left, for the spiritual consort, ༔
> Are the places where we nurtured the secret experiences ༔
> And increased the vajra realization. ༔
> In these places are innumerable profound termas, ༔
> And in particular, as an essence for the future, ༔
> There are symbolic forms of bodily images, ༔
> Profound sign-scripts as representations of speech, ༔
> And—as the vajra of mind— ༔
> The attribute of myself, Draktsal Heruka.[670] ༔
>
> — *Revealed by Chokgyur Dechen Lingpa*

Having dispelled all obstacles, bound all spirits, and blessed the land, the Mahaguru and the wisdom dakini finally hid the most profound of treasures, especially the *Lamrim Yeshé Nyingpo*, at this supreme site. The Mahaguru then stated:

> This is a sacred place of my Speech. Those who practice here will enjoy wide renown and receive great blessings. But those without samaya will meet with much hindrance. Both supreme and worldly accomplishments may be gained here. While I was turning the Wheel of the Doctrine at the Diamond Throne and other places, subjugating demons and those of misguided views, these three images spontaneously appeared here, together with the six-syllable mantra, the three-syllable and twelve-syllable mantras, and so forth, as well as the supports of Mind.[671] ༔
>
> — *Revealed by Samten Lingpa*

The Mahaguru's Legacy

Revelation of the Lamrim Yeshé Nyingpo

The revelation of the *Lamrim Yeshé Nyingpo* was recounted in detail by Chokgyur Dechen Lingpa, who composed a unique first-person account of the *terma* revelations at Karmo Taktsang and the nearby Sengö Yumtso lake. Chokgyur Lingpa was thirty-eight years old when he made the journey to the hermitage cave of Chimé Karmo Taktsang. It was noon on the twenty-fifth day of the ninth month (November 2, 1866) when the Great Tertön arrived, accompanied by Jamyang Khyentsé Wangpo. Chokgyur Lingpa writes:

> As the moon waned during the ninth month of the Fire Tiger Year (1866) and the dakinis gathered on the wholesome twenty-fifth day, we—the descendants of Padma Orgyen Chokgyur Dechen Lingpa and the Gentle Protector Guru, Pema Ösel Dongak Lingpa[672]—were receiving prophecies and having extraordinary visions of the gurus and dakinis while on our way to the Sengé Samdrup Ke'utsang (Cave of Lion's Wishes Fulfilled) at Chimé Karmo Taktsang (Deathless White Tigress Lair).
>
> This extraordinary sacred site is a source of auspiciousness for the Tibetan lands. We arrived there at noon and performed smoke (*sang*) and feast (*tsok*) offerings at the center of the site. Then we entered the cave of Samdrup Ke'utsang and performed further rituals, such as offering another feast.
>
> The next morning, on the twenty-sixth (November 3rd), we climbed to the top of this holy place to get the lay of the land. We performed hundreds of feast and fulfillment offerings, as well as oblation (*torma*) and libation (*serkyem*) to the Three Roots, in order to benefit the Tibetan lands in ways both general and specific.
>
> On the morning of the twenty-seventh day (November 4th), we entered Guru Rinpoche's Secret Cave (Orgyen Sangpuk). There, we looked for signs of a hidden treasure and chipped away at the seal, bit by bit. We used hot coals to melt the rock sealants. Without much difficulty, we revealed a representative statue (*kutsap*) of Guru Rinpoche, a clay casket, and several ritual implements, all within a single afternoon, visible to everyone assembled.[673]
>
> On the previous day, the twenty-sixth (November 3rd), we had waited with anticipation at the door to Yeshé Tsogyal's Secret Cave (Tsogyal Sangpuk), but, due to just a few unfavorable conditions, it had vanished from sight. After sunrise on the twenty-eighth day (November 5th), we cut down a juniper tree and made a ladder.[674] At the place where the cave entrance had previously been spotted, we dug two finger widths into the rock until we saw the outline of the cave's door cut anew. We struggled to excavate the cave using hand tools, but these were too weak, so we left diggers there and came back later in the afternoon.

On the following day, the twenty-ninth (November 6th), we visited the residence of the treasurer Sönam Topgyel and bestowed the treasure empowerment upon the King of Dergé and his ministers. We performed the wrathful enactment, including the obstacle-clearing rituals of *Dorjé Drolö* and *Jampel Parol Goljom*, for the King's wellbeing.[675] On the thirtieth (November 7th), we fulfilled the wishes of the benefactors. On the first day of the tenth month (November 8th), we bestowed the White Tara long-life empowerment upon the King of Dergé and his brother, and performed smoke and mountain cleansing rituals for the benefit of the whole region.

Then, on the second day of the tenth month (November 9th), I[676] returned with a few disciples to Tsogyal Sangpuk. We continued digging into the treasure seal and performed smoke, feast and fulfillment offerings. On the fourth (November 11th), the King of Dergé arrived, and the Gentle Protector Guru also joined us on the sixth (November 12th). From the seventh onwards (November 14th), my disciples and I performed feast, fulfilment, and smoke offerings, as a group.

As we broke through the many treasure seals, one by one, miraculous things emerged, such as plaster of molten gold, and earth of many different colors. On the morning of the ninth (November 16th), I sensed that the treasure was near, and we stopped digging. Later that night, we made a bit of an uproar in order to bring forth the treasure—we sang songs, danced, and melodiously intoned prayers, continuously.

The earth was shaking as we all made our way—myself, my disciples, the King of Dergé, his retinue and ministers—up to the meditation cave. We made a feast offering and sang melodious prayers, loudly and without stopping. Then, as dawn broke on the tenth day of the tenth month (November 17th), we discovered a sign of the treasure near the entrance to the cave. We dug and, without much difficulty, I uncovered the hand-held implement of Rikdzin Dorjé Drakpo Tsel, a meteorite vajra, within the rock. It had pierced through solid rock as if it were mud. To inspire everyone's confidence, I left it only partially exposed, and had everyone come to see it right away. Then, when the sun was up, I revealed the profound treasures concealed both inside and outside the cave, and bestowed the treasure empowerment upon the King of Dergé, his ministers, and a crowd of three hundred people.[677]

Urged on once again by several visions I'd had at different times, I went with my disciples to the shores of Lake Sengö Yumtso on the eleventh (November 18th). The moment we arrived, I had a good feeling. My awareness (*rigpa*) was pristine, and I felt at ease. The sky filled with an effusion of rainbows within the fresh summer clouds.

There was a dilapidated hut, made of slate, which had been home to determined and inspired meditators in the past. There, we arranged offerings and oblations, and prepared a feast. As we performed the feast offering, with fervent prayer, I was suddenly inspired to make my way to the center of the frozen lake. As I struck a large hole in the ice, rainbow light appeared in my eyes and I clearly saw the location of the profound treasure. The Gentle Protector Guru, who had likewise had an extraordinary vision, persuaded the royal nagas guarding the treasure to honor their oaths.

I fastened my sash and lower robe to the top of a stick, and followed Guru Rinpoche's instructions for revealing the profound treasure. As I did this, a rain of flowers fell like snow from a cloudless sky.[678] Bodhisattva naga kings tossed flowers of gold dust on the shore, which flecked with gold. At that moment, the profound treasure was revealed with ease.[679] In return for the treasure, we offered a collection of fine substances, and returned to the center of the sacred site that evening.

The next day (November 19th), we transcribed several of the treasure scrolls retrieved earlier, and then returned home. Thus, without even the slightest obstacle in the form of challenges or problems, we were blessed with auspiciousness from beginning to end.[680]

According to the Great Tertön's account, on the twenty-seventh day, Chokgyur Lingpa revealed an agate scroll containing six different kinds of symbolic script along with a representative statue of Guru Dorjé Drakpo Tsal. The script would later be deciphered and transcribed as the *Damchö Nyingpo Kornga* (*The Essential Sacred Dharma in Five Cycles*).

On the tenth day of the tenth month, the Great Tertön revealed the *Lamrim Yeshé Nyingpo* (*The Gradual Path of the Wisdom Essence*), along with the vajra belonging to Guru Dorjé Drakpo Tsal. Following this revelation, Jamyang

Khyentsé Wangpo gave a spontaneous teaching on the root verses, which Jamgön Kongtrul Rinpoche later wrote down, and which became the famous commentary known as *Yeshé Nangwa* (*Light of Wisdom*).[681] Finally, on the eleventh day of the month, Chokgyur Lingpa drew gold from the Sengé Yumtso lake, and Jamyang Khyentsé revealed the *Tsasum Gyütrul Drawa* (*The Magical Net of the Three Roots*).

Jamgön Mipham Rinpoche's Retreat

Blessed by Mañjushri, Jamgön Mipham Rinpoche (1846–1912) became one of the greatest Tibetan scholars ever to walk this earth. He took Chimé Karmo Taktsang as one of his principal residences from the age of thirty until his parinirvana,[682] spending more than thirteen years here in strict retreat. Mipham Rinpoche's vast and profound writings filled more than thirty volumes, and although he never declared any of his compositions to be treasures, many—due to their profundity—are indeed considered termas. Followers of the Mahaguru especially treasure Jamgön Mipham's profound *White Lotus* commentary on *The Seven-Line Prayer*, which he spontaneously composed in 1870 at the age of twenty-five.[683] In this extraordinary commentary, which many consider a *terma*, Mipham Rinpoche explains the Seven-Line Prayer in the context and application of the main practices of the Nyingma school. Later, in the year 1887, at Karmo Taktsang, Mipham Rinpoche composed a sadhana to accompany his *White Lotus* commentary, namely the *Chinlap Charbep* (*Shower of Blessings*).[684] Of this occasion, Kyapjé Dilgo Khyentsé Rinpoche wrote:

> In this secluded place, a dakini appeared before Mipham Rinpoche and imparted a close lineage transmission. She sang *The Seven-Line Prayer* in an enchanting melody, thus providing the auspicious condition for the composition, the blessings of which are said to be incomparable.[685]

Finally, another story often recounted of Mipham Rinpoche's time in Chimé Karmo Taksang is that of his final words to his attendant, Lama Ösel, shortly before passing into parinirvana there. After entrusting Lama Ösel with a precious teaching on *The Seven-Line Prayer*, Mipham Rinpoche said:

> "Nowadays, if you speak the truth, there is nobody to listen; if you speak lies, everyone thinks it's true.
> What I say now, I have never said before: I am not an ordinary person; I am a bodhisattva who has taken rebirth through aspiration.

The suffering experienced in this body is just the residue of karma; but from now on I will never again have to experience karmic obscuration. ... Now, in this final age, the barbarians beyond the frontier are close to undermining the teachings, so there is no point whatsoever in my taking rebirth here...I have no reason to take birth in impure realms ever again."[686]

WELLSPRINGS OF THE GREAT PERFECTION
Samye Chimpu and Pema Shelpuk

The innate, unblemished state of our primordial nature, which requires no external improvement as it has always been flawless since its very inception, is akin to the boundless sky. It is not something created, yet it effortlessly manifests. The teachings that directly introduce practitioners to this essential nature, transcending the limitations of ordinary mind and embracing awareness itself as the path, are known as Dzokchen—the most profound teachings within the realm of Buddhism. Due to their paramount importance, being the pinnacle of the Buddhadharma, these teachings are cherished and safeguarded with utmost secrecy.

Traditionally, the accomplished masters of Dzokchen transmitted these invaluable teachings directly to devoted disciples, enabling them to attain realization equivalent to that of the buddhas past, present, and future. This convergence of a perfect teacher with perfect students, perfect teachings and in an ideal environment, facilitated the highest level of spiritual attainment.

The profound teachings of Dzokchen initially entered the human realm when Buddha Vajrasattva transmitted them instantaneously to Garap Dorjé during his retreat on Mount Suryaprakasha. With this, Garap Dorjé became the first human Dzokchen master. Following Vajrasattva's instructions, he stayed on Mount Malaya for three years, along with a retinue of dakinis, during which time he codified the six million, four hundred thousand verses of Atiyoga, which were primordially present in his mind.[687]

Garap Dorjé then transmitted the Great Perfection tantras to his disciple Manjushrimita, at Dhanakosha's Isle in Uddiyana and at the Sitavana charnel ground. Manjushrimita subsequently organized these teachings into three sections: mind (*semdé*), space (*longdé*), and pith instructions (*mengak-dé*).[688] The esteemed master Shri Singha then received them from Manjushrimita at the Sosadvipa charnel ground, as well as directly from Garap Dorjé at the Sitavana charnel ground. Shri Singha, in turn, transmitted these Atiyoga teachings to Jñanasutra in the Siljin charnel ground.[689]

The Dzokchen teachings were taken to the Land of Snows by three individuals in particular, who became known as the Wellsprings of the Great Perfection. These three masters all had the mahasiddha Shri Singha as their main Dzokchen teacher:[690]

1. Guru Padmasambhava from Uddiyana, who received the Dzokchen teachings from Garap Dorjé on Dhanakosha's Isle and from Shri Singha in Suvaranadvipa.[691]
2. Pandita Vimalamitra from Kashmir, who received the Dzokchen teachings from Shri Singha in the Siljin charnel ground and from Jñanasutra at the Bashing charnel ground.[692]
3. Lotsawa Vairocana from Tibet, who received the Great Perfection teachings in their entirety from the vidyadharas Garap Dorjé in the Dhumagata charnel ground and Shri Singha in Uddiyana.[693]

Guru Rinpoche entrusted the Dzokchen teachings in their entirety to Princess Pema Sal shortly before she passed away at Samye Chimpu. Similarly, in their entirety, he transmitted them to Khandro Yeshe Tsogyal and numerous dakinis at Zhotö Tidrö. To ensure the preservation and realization of these teachings for future practitioners, the Mahaguru also imparted specific pith instructions to the King and his twenty-five disciples, which later emerged as hidden treasures known as *termas*. Since the principal custodians of these teachings were Khandro Yeshe Tsogyal and Princess Pema Sal, both of whom were dakinis, and since the guardian was the protectress Shaza Khamoché, these teachings were given the name *Khandro Nyingtik* (*Heart Essence of the Dakinis*).[694] Finally, since the Mahaguru's Dzokchen teachings were also hidden as *terma* treasures, the *Khandro Nyingtik* became the *terma* lineage of the Dzokchen teachings.

The vidyadhara Vimalamitra transmitted the Dzokchen teachings to five select students[695] at Samye monastery, appointing Nyang Tingdzin Zangpo as the principal custodian. This particular lineage became known as the *Vima Nyingtik* (*Heart Essence of Vimalamitra*). While parts of the teachings were hidden as treasures, nonetheless, since the core was transmitted orally, this constitutes the *kama* or oral lineage of the Dzokchen teachings.

Lotsawa Vairocana transmitted the Dzokchen teachings to a few select students while he was in exile in Gyalmo Tsawarong. There, he entrusted the Dzokchen teachings especially to Yudra Nyingpo, Pang Mipham Gönpo and Nyak Jñanakumara, who in turn transmitted them orally. Thus began the *kama* lineage of Vairocana's teachings.[696]

After Dharma King Trisong Detsen passed into parinirvana, the Mahaguru, along with Khandro Yeshé Tsogyal, Lotsawa Vairocana, Yudra Nyingpo, and a few other select heart disciples, travelled to Meshö Dzam in Kham where they stayed at Pema Shelpuk (Lotus Crystal Cave). Here, the Mahaguru and

Lotsawa Vairocana discussed the Dzokchen teachings that they had received in India; they put the very heart and core of Vairocana's Dzokchen lineage into writing, and subsequently hid it as a treasure. This became known as the *Vairo Nyingtik* (*Heart Essence of Vairocana*) and constitutes the *terma* lineage of Lotsawa Vairocana's teachings.[697] Since Shri Singha had entrusted especially the mind and space sections to the Lotsawa—unlike the *Khandro Nyingtik* and *Vima Nyingtik* which focus primarily on the pith instructions—the *Vairo Nyingtik* thus contains teachings on all three sections of the Great Perfection: mind, space, and pith instructions[698].

The *Vairo Nyingtik* was revealed in the year 1857 by the three great masters—Chokgyur Dechen Zhikpo Lingpa, Jamyang Khyentsé Wangpo, and Jamgön Kongtrul Lodrö Thayé—as the culmination of their combined treasure revelation activity, and as a treasure teaching entitled the *Dzokchen Desum* (*The Three Sections of the Great Perfection*).

The first two transmissions of the Dzokchen teachings in Tibet by Guru Padmasambhava and pandita Vimalamitra have been detailed in our Samye Chimpu and Zhoto Tidrö chapters. In honor of Lotsawa Vairocana's accomplishments and the legacy of the three great *rimé* masters, we will now present the events at Pema Shelpuk.

PEMA SHELPUK

Kyé! The expression of innate, original purity
Arises as spontaneous clouds of wisdom's play.
From this assembly of lamps arrayed
Come innumerable pure lands of the three kayas,
Among which are the practice places of Dokham.
There are twenty-five great vajra-sites
Of awakened body, speech, heart, qualities, and activities.
The sublime site of the speech aspect of awakened qualities
Has been blessed as indivisible from
the Cool Grove charnel ground of Sitavana
And the great hermitage of glorious Chimpu—
And here it is, the blissful cave of Pema Shelpuk,
Marvelous realm of the five families of wealth deities![699]

— *Dilgo Khyentsé Rinpoche*

Introduction

Of the twenty-five sacred sites of Kham, Pema Shelpuk is the sacred site of the speech aspect of Guru Rinpoche's awakened qualities, and on his third visit to Kham the Mahaguru went there with his heart disciples.[700] Here, for three months, they practiced the *Kagyé Deshek Düpa* (*Assembly of Sugatas*). During this time, Guru Padmasambhava discussed the Dzokchen teachings with his disciple Lotsawa Vairocana. Khandro Yeshé Tsogyal served as their scribe, putting into writing what became renowned as the *Vairo Nyingtik*, the final teachings that resulted from this gathering. Pema Shelpuk, as a true embodiment of the Mahaguru's speech, was his chosen hiding place for the *Vairo Nyingtik*.

Approaching the Sacred Site

Pema Shelpuk lies within a tributary valley to the west of Dzongsar monastery. Surrounded by white mountain cliffs, the Meshö Valley is like an open lotus flower, and the foothills are cloaked in meadows and forests. Flowers grow abundantly in summer, and water flows freely. In the middle, at the heart of the lotus, is a huge white rock with a cave in the center known as Pema Shelpuk (Lotus Crystal Cave). The rock, cave, and surroundings are all white in color. As a result of the Mahaguru's practice, the central cave produced a naturally arisen mandala of the Kagyé deities, into which the deities dissolved in actuality.

Khandro Yeshe Tsogyal practiced in a small cave to the left. The practice caves of Shri Singha and Lotsawa Vairocana, with their self-arisen thrones, are at the top of the rock.[701] The Mahaguru himself described this sacred site as follows:

> This valley, it looks like a blossoming lotus, ៖
> And amidst all its confluences
> There is a white cliff that looks like a crystal dome. ៖
> Here, in the meditation cave of Pema Shelpuk, ៖
> I, Padma of Uddiyana, ៖
> Practiced the *Great Accomplishment of the Assembly of the Sugatas,* ៖
> Such that the spaces of the nine mandalas have naturally arisen
> In all the interior parts of the cave. ៖
> And because the sugatas have dissolved therein, ៖
> Just seeing it closes the gates to the lower realms. ៖
> Outside, on the hillsides to the right of the valley, ៖
> There are boulders that look like garudas in descent, ៖
> And there are stones and earth and wood that have
> Come from the great charnel grounds of India. ៖
> At the valley's center is my wellspring of blessings, ៖
> And natural formations of my awakened body, speech, and heart. ៖
> The white cliff to the left looks like a victory banner,
> And it bears my footprints, the footprints of Uddiyana![702] ៖

> — *Revealed by Jamyang Khyentsé Wangpo*

The Mahaguru and Lotsawa Vairocana's Journey

The Vairo Nyingtik

In Greater India, Lotsawa Vairocana had received three sets of extremely secret Dzokchen teachings from Shri Singha, which he had not yet shared with anyone in Tibet.

At a later point, while meditating at the Black Boulder of Dam, in Kham, Vairocana received the Mahaguru's command to entrust the root verses of these teachings to Khandro Yeshé Tsogyal, Yudra Nyingpo, and a few other select disciples, which he did. Khandro Yeshé Tsogyal gave her promise, as instructed, to write them down within three months and conceal them as a *terma*.

After King Trisong Detsen had passed into parinirvana, the Mahaguru visited Kham for a third and final time, shortly before his departure from Tibet. He entered retreat at the Pema Shelpuk with his disciples Lotsawa Vairocana and Khandro Yeshé Tsogyal. For three months the Mahaguru one-pointedly practiced the *Kagyé Deshek Düpa* (*Assembly of Sugatas*). During this time the Mahaguru and Lotsawa Vairocana were also meeting every day to discuss the Dzokchen teachings that they had received from Shri Singha. The Mahaguru merely focused his mind on his root guru Shri Singha, and the master arrived instantly in his wisdom body. This was when the masters agreed to put in writing the unique set of teachings that Lotsawa Vairocana had received on all three sections of the Great Perfection, and to hide it as a *terma* treasure. As the scene unfolded, Khandro Yeshé Tsogyal joined the masters and received their instructions. The wisdom dakini served as scribe, noting down the final teaching that emerged from this gathering. Subsequently she hid the teaching within Pema Shelpuk itself. Upon the auspicious concealment of the treasure, the Mahaguru stated:

> Blissful Pema Shelpuk, the Lotus Crystal Cave, ౙ
> Is far superior to all others; none can even approach it. ౙ
> For it holds the foremost treasure of all, beneath Tibetan soil. ౙ
> It is the sacred site where resides the sublime teaching, ౙ
> *The Three Classes Of the Great Perfection,* ౙ
> The heart-essence of all learned masters— ౙ
> A treasure chest, a casket of precious gold, ౙ
> That shall remain until the farthest reaches of samsara are emptied![703] ౙ
>
> — *Revealed by Chokgyur Dechen Lingpa*

Just as Samye Chimpu was the primary sacred site for the transmission of the *Khandro Nyingtik* and *Vima Nyingtik*, Pema Shelpuk thus became the sacred site for the transmission of the *Vairo Nyingtik*. Regarding this sublime site, the Mahaguru further said:

> I invoked India's Sitavana charnel ground[704] ౙ
> And dissolved its blessings into the very soil of Chimpu. ౙ
> Likewise, I have transferred these same blessings ౙ
> So that Meshö Dzam in Kham will be identical.[705] ౙ
>
> — *Revealed by Jamyang Khyentsé Wangpo*

Hence, Pema Shelpuk has been praised as a "king of accomplishments" place, and is considered along with Samye Chimpu as one of the two primary residences of the Mahaguru within Tibet.[706]

The Mahaguru's Legacy

Revelation of the Dzogchen Desum

On the third day of the twelfth month, January 28, 1857, Chokgyur Lingpa, Jamyang Khyentsé Wangpo, and Jamgön Kongtrül decided to travel together to Pema Shelpuk—knowing that a *terma* treasure lay hidden within.[707] Up to this point, Pema Shelpuk had been a site feared among locals for its haunting by ghosts. Undeterred by the rumors of one-eyed women and goat-riding spirits, the three masters proceeded nonetheless. Some locals were aghast, fearing for the life of the *tertön*. They soon relaxed, however, as the presence of the three great masters convinced them that something special was unfolding. As the three approached the cave entrance, rainbows filled the sky, and a crowd quickly gathered to witness the event.[708] Before this important revelation, Chokgyur Lingpa had still not been widely recognized as a *tertön*, and many people mockingly referred to him as *Kyater*, or *Kyasu Tertön*. This occasion, however, and the revelation of *The Three Sections of the Great Perfection*, changed all that.[709]

Upon reaching the cave, Kongtrül made an offering to the Dharma protectors, while Khyentsé sang a sacred song to command the local deities. The crowd, for their part, were told to recite the Vajra Guru mantra and pray to Guru Rinpoche. As the three entered the cave, the sound of mantra and prayer resounded. Chokgyur Lingpa's experience suddenly transformed; he flew up from the cave floor, all the way to the ceiling, and from the living rock he pulled out a *terma* box. Within, lay an unprecedented treasure—*The Three Sections of the Great Perfection*, the most complete teaching cycle yet to be uncovered in the Snowy Land of Tibet.[710] This was found, along with nectars blessed by Shri Singha, sacred medicines, Khandro Yeshé Tsogyal's hair, and the hair of Lotsawa Vairocana, all inside this box, all wrapped in Guru Rinpoche's own robes, and drawn out from the depths of the Lotus Crystal Cave. Now there could be no doubt for the onlooking crowd that Chokgyur Lingpa was an authentic *tertön*, blessed to be the revealer of this most amazing of treasures. Those in attendance were promised by Jamyang Khyentsé himself that they would be reborn in the Copper-Colored Mountain, such was the power of that auspicious occasion. From then onward, most of Chokgyur Lingpa's treasures were revealed in public.

As the title suggests, this extraordinary treasure contains teachings on all three sections of the Great Perfection—mind, space, and pith instructions. As such, it is unique among all Great Perfection treasure revelations, which previously had included only one or two of these sections. Never before had all three been discovered together and all at once. While the root text contains the Dzokchen teachings transmitted by Lotsawa Vairocana to his heart disciple Yudra Nyingpo and is therefore also called the *Vairo Nyingtik* (*The Heart Essence of Vairocana*), the *Dzokchen Desum* is a distillation of seven distinct *Nyingtik* teachings revealed by the three masters.[711]

Since Chokgyur Lingpa had retrieved here *The Heart Essence of Vairocana*, he decided to honor the profound teacher-student relationship that safeguarded these most sacred teachings by establishing an auspicious circumstance at the time of its revelation. Chokgyur Lingpa therefore gave the first transmission of these teachings to a reincarnation of Yudra Nyingpo, the original holder of its profound secrets. It so happened that, just six months prior, Yudra Nyingpo had taken rebirth as the Great Tertön's own son, Tsewang Norbu. And so Tersé Tsewang Norbu was brought before the Great Tertön immediately after the treasure was revealed.[712] Auspiciously, Vairocana's emanation was also present, in the form of Jamgön Kongtrül. Thus, with unique interdependent circumstances in place, the Great Tertön bestowed the empowerment upon his infant son, joined by Jamgön Kongtrül and Jamyang Khyentsé Wangpo.

Revelation of the Zabtik Drolchok

A mind treasure emerges when, as Jamyang Khyentsé Wangpo put it, "the treasury of profound secrets that is concealed within the luminous space of the revealer's wisdom-mind bursts open and pours forth, due to the blessings of the Three Roots."[713] While staying at Pema Shelpuk, one morning at dawn, Chokgyur Lingpa beheld Lady Tara in the sky right in front of him. Tara exclaimed "Excellent! (*lekso*)" three times, prompting the *Lekso Sum* (*The Essential Instructions on the Triple Excellence*) to flow forth from the expanse of his realization. With this blessing, the Great Tertön was able to transcribe the mind treasure, *The Profound Essence of Tara*—the root verses for practicing Tara according to the increasingly profound levels of tantra, all the way up to the pinnacle of Atiyoga.[714]

In the wake of this revelation, the Great Tertön traveled to Jamgön Kongtrül Rinpoche's residence at the glorious hermitage of Tsadra Rinchen Drak. There, on the shrine, was a statue of Lady Tara, an embodiment of the wisdom-being who had just bestowed on him *The Essential Instructions on the Triple Excellence*. At his enquiry, Jamgön Kongtrül related that the statue had been given to him by Jamyang Khyentsé Wangpo, who had received it from the treasure guardian of the Tara practice. Indeed, it had once been the personal practice support of the Indian master Arya Nagarjuna.[715] Alongside the *Chimé Phakmé Nyingtik* (*The Heart Essence of the Sublime Lady of Immortality*), discovered by Jamyang Khyentsé Wangpo, *The Profound Essence of Tara* forms part of a larger, yet-to-be revealed *terma* cycle called *Drolma Nyingtik* (*The Heart Essence of Tara*). Since *The Profound Essence of Tara* is easy to practice and its blessings are swift and vast, it has rightly become one of the most famous and widespread Tara sadhanas practiced today.[716]

The Guru Rinpoche Statue at Pema Shelpuk

Both Kyapjé Jamyang Khyentse Chökyi Lodrö and Kyapjé Dilgo Khyentsé Rinpoche spent extended periods of time at Pema Shelpuk. Indeed, it was here that Khyentse Chökyi Lodrö Rinpoche authorized Dilgo Khyentsé Rinpoche as a treasure revealer. In his autobiography, Dilgo Khyentsé Rinpoche recounts the following story, which illustrates the sacredness of Pema Shelpuk, and which he had heard from his own master, there:

> At Crystal Cave there are seven hundred and twenty-five naturally appearing deities, and, when the temple was under construction, Khyentse Wangpo oversaw everything himself, down to the location where the main beams were to be placed. He demanded only the finest materials.
>
> Inside the main statue of Guru Padmasambhava is the root text of Chokgyur Lingpa's *Tukdrup Barché Kunsel* (*The Guru's Heart Practice: Dispeller of All Obstacles*), of which Khyentse Wangpo was the main doctrine holder among ten. For the wisdom-being, he used an inner robe he had inherited from Guru Padmasambhava that bore an image of the Guru in Tsogyal's blood. The statue had to be finished on the tenth day of the Monkey month, but the smith casting the deity had made the head a little crooked. When the consecration was performed, Khyentse Wangpo focused his attention on it, which straightened the head..[717]

Revelation of the Pema Tséyi Nyingtik

In 1935, at Pema Shelpuk, Kyapjé Dilgo Khyentsé Rinpoche revealed one of his most treasured *termas*, the *Pema Tseyi Nyingtik* (*Pema's Heart Essence of Longevity*). His autobiography tells the story:

> Regarding the *Pema Tséyi Nyingtik*, around the Wood-Pig Year

in the 20th century, 1935, I was on pilgrimage and visiting the Pema Shelri (Lotus Crystal Mountain) at Gyamgyal, a pacifying Vajra Family place, and one of the twenty-five sacred places in Dokham. Lotus Crystal Mountain is a permanent glacier in the natural form of the Glorious Heruka, with a white lake in front, in the shape of a long-life vase. Called the Infant Milk Lake, it is known as a place for unchanging long-life practice. I arrived there for that purpose and began by performing the *Dharmakaya Master Amitayus* feast offering from the *Tukdrup Barché Kunsel* (*The Guru's Heart Practice: Dispeller of All Obstacles*). During the feast offering, a square mandala with four gates, and all the higher and lower designs, appeared on the white surface of the lake—the blue-green patterns visible to everyone—while the *Pema Tseyi Nyingtik* clearly dawned in my mind. That night I dreamed that I was reading a commentary on the *Jetari Amitayus Sutra* written by the former Khyentsé, and the next day, when I was reading Lord Taranatha's commentary on the *Amitayus Sutra*, I gained certainty that it mingled as one single stream of blessing with the nine-deity Amitayus of Jetari's tradition.

On my way to Dzongsar, to see my venerable master Chökyi Lodrö Rinpoche at Dzongsar, I stayed one day at Dzamthang, in front of Pema Shelpuk. That night I dreamed that a large juniper tree which had sprouted from Guru Rinpoche's staff was growing above the boulder in front of the sacred place. When I reached this tree, a woman, whom I thought was Tsogyal, gave me a yellow scroll. When I looked at it, the complete cycle of teachings for the *Pema Tseyi Nyingtik* manifested in my awareness.[718]

Following Kyapjé Jamyang Khyentse Chökyi Lodrö's guidance, Kyapjé Dilgo Khyentse Rinpoche put this cycle of teachings in writing, and granted him the complete empowerments and practice instructions.

LEAVING GREATER TIBET

Gungthang Pass

When the Dharma King had reached the age of fifty-nine, a tragic accident led to his passing. However, amid the ensuing turmoil the Mahaguru was able to direct the kingdom and ensure that Prince Mutik Tsenpo was enthroned as the King's heir. With great care, not only did the Mahaguru ensure the worldly transition of power, but also that the young prince was guided on the spiritual path. The prince had, long since, been a devoted disciple of the Mahaguru, but it was only after his father's passing that the Mahaguru gave him the highest teachings of the Great Perfection. Gaining profound realization, Prince Mutik Tsenpo became not only a worldly leader but a spiritual one as well. Having thus ensured the continuation and stability of the kingdom, and its rule of law in accord with the Dharma, the time had come for the Mahaguru to address another pending threat. For a long time, *rakshasa* demons had been gaining strength and building an army, and they were now poised to invade the human realm. In his clairvoyance, the Mahaguru saw that time was running out to stop them. He also knew that he alone had the power to curtail the *rakshasas'* evil schemes, and so he approached the new king and shared his plans for going. The young king listened, initially refusing to let him go, but with deep sadness finally accepting the Mahaguru's decision. Once the news was made public, Tibetans from every corner of the land gathered like a flock of birds around Samye monastery, bringing vast offerings, requesting teachings, and asking for the Mahaguru's parting blessings. With great love and compassion, the Mahaguru taught the Tibetan people and shared his final advice on how to practice the Dharma. Afterwards, many Tibetans joined the farewell party that accompanied the Mahaguru to the Gungthang Pass, his place of departure. There, tents were pitched and the Mahaguru continued to give teachings, especially to his closest disciples, for three more days. Then, on the 10th day of the Monkey month in the Wood Monkey Year, the Mahaguru mounted the supreme steed Balaha and flew off into the sky to deal with the *rakshasa* demons, leaving his disciples sitting in meditation.

GUNGTHANG PASS

King, disciples, abbots, and teachers
All followed you to Mangyul where they bowed in deepest reverence.
When they begged you to stay, you granted prophecies.
To you, loving, compassionate one, I pray!
To the nirmanakaya of Uddiyana, I pray!
Compassionate Son of the Conquerors, please grant your blessings! [719]

— *Ratna Lingpa*

Introduction

After the passing of Dharma King Trisong Detsen, the Mahaguru ensured a smooth transition of power to Prince Mutik Tsenpo. Once the new Dharma King had received comprehensive training in both worldly and spiritual matters, the Mahaguru informed him that it was time for him (the Mahaguru) to leave for the southwest and subdue the *rakshasa* demons. In his great kindness, the Mahaguru made preparations to share his final guidance with the Tibetan people, and as his imminent journey was announced, a sorrowful royal retinue accompanied him to the Gungthang Pass. This high mountain pass not only marked the entry point through which both the Mahaguru and the Abbot had originally arrived in Tibet, but it also became the place of their departure. When all were gathered there, he imparted his final heart advice to his closest disciples. Then, with grace and reverence, he mounted the magnificent horse Balaha and set off towards the isle of the *rakshasas*, his next destination.

Approaching the Sacred Site

The Gungthang Pass serves as a crucial link, connecting central Tibet in the north with Mangyul and Nepal in the south. It serves as a distinct boundary, separating the verdant, foothill valley of Mangyul from the vast, arid grasslands of the Himalayan plateau. Upon reaching the elevated, sandy summit of the pass, visitors are rewarded with awe-inspiring vistas of the snow-capped mountains that envelop the region. A commemorative stupa stands at the spot from whence the Mahaguru departed Tibet, symbolizing the significance of his departure from this sacred land.

The Mahaguru's Journey

The End of an Era

Recognizing the imminent threat posed by the *rakshasa hordes*, the Mahaguru became increasingly aware of the need to leave and avert the impending invasion. With this understanding, he approached Mutik Tsenpo, the newly trained prince, and Tibet's new King to discuss the situation and convey his decision.

> Son, from the time you were small ༔
> You have been my blessing, the core of my heart. ༔
> Now, cleared of the suffering of your father's passing, ༔
> You will bring happiness to this nation ༔
> And spread the teachings of the Buddha. ༔
> I go, not from displeasure, but at a time of increasing excellence. ༔
> I came to Tibet, have done what was needed here, ༔
> And perfected those to be tamed. ༔
> Now the time has come ༔
> To do the same for the demonic *rakshasa* in the south-west. ༔
> Other than me, there is no master with the ability to tame them. ༔
> If I do not do this, they will destroy the Buddhist teachings, ༔
> for they are the very ground of the unhappiness of beings. ༔
> The time has now come. Only son of mine, be well! ༔
> Do not forget me, but forever to me pray! ༔
> When you have yearning faith, you are worthy of blessing. ༔
> We will not be apart. I will never, ever leave you."[720] ༔

— Revealed by Jamgön Kongtrul Lodrö Thayé

Heartbroken, and with tears in his eyes, Mutik Tsenpo replied:

> "I cannot bear the thought of being separated from you. ༔
> Have compassion for us all—please, stay in Tibet! ༔
> My father, our great emperor, is no more, has gone to the skies. ༔
> If you, our Guru, do not stay, but leave for the *rakshasa* lands, ༔
> Won't the valleys of Tibet stand desolate and empty? ༔
> Are beings no longer the focus of your compassion? ༔
> Do not leave—please, stay in Tibet!"[721] ༔

— Revealed by Jamgön Kongtrul Lodrö Thayé

The Mahaguru responded:

> "Mutik Tsenpo, listen! ⸾
> I am the Guru of all beings equally. ⸾
> Are you forcing me to abandon bodhicitta? ⸾
> If I do not tame the south-western land of the *rakshasas*, ⸾
> All beings will sink in the mires of suffering. ⸾
> Then, not a word of the sublime Dharma would be heard by anyone. ⸾
> Would you wish that to happen? ⸾
> I cannot stay, but must be off now, to tame the *rakshasas*. ⸾
> For anyone, man or woman, with faith in me, ⸾
> I, the Lotus Born, have never gone away—I sleep at their door. ⸾
> When the morning light rays shine, and the evening light rays fade, ⸾
> And also at dawn on the tenth lunar day, ⸾
> I will always come, for the welfare of Tibet. ⸾
> For my future disciples who will not meet me directly, ⸾
> They should endeavor in making offerings and paying homage ⸾
> To all supports and places of enlightened body, speech, and mind. ⸾
> For to respect and support the noble Sangha is the same ⸾
> As making offerings in person to Padmasambhava of Uddiyana. ⸾
> My compassion will never fade. ⸾
> I will always benefit and protect the people of Tibet."[722] ⸾

— *Revealed by Jamgön Kongtrul Lodrö Thayé*

Heart Advice for the Tibetan People

Once the news of the Mahaguru's imminent departure became public, the Tibetans were deeply saddened and many quickly came with offerings to receive his blessings and bid farewell.

> None felt joy; many wept in sorrow. ⸾
> The laymen and women of Tibet clustered around, ⸾
> Touching their crowns to the Mahaguru's lotus feet, ⸾
> And offering whatever wealth or possessions they had. ⸾
> Prince Mutik Tsenpo, flanked by his empress and ministers, ⸾
> offered gold and silver, gems of all kinds, ⸾
> silks soft to touch, and all the luxuries of existence.[723] ⸾

— *Revealed by Jamgön Kongtrul Lodrö Thayé*

Moved by the Tibetans' vast display of gratitude and devotion, the Mahaguru addressed them with a final piece of heart advice:

"Listen, people of Tibet! ⚇

Like the udumbara flower, ⚇
The freedoms and advantages are hard to find. ⚇
Like the sun in winter, this human life doesn't last forever. ⚇
There is no end to the sufferings of samsara. ⚇
So, practice virtue, and your beneficial qualities will increase. ⚇
The results of this life's activities, good and bad, ⚇
Will inevitably ripen later. ⚇
Therefore, without distraction, ⚇
Embrace every thought with the Dharma. ⚇
Place your trust in the authentic Guru, and set him above your crown. ⚇
Take refuge, give rise to bodhicitta, and purify your obscurations ⚇
By means of visualization and recitation. ⚇
Accumulate merit by offering mandalas, and practice guru yoga. ⚇
Receive the four empowerments, ⚇
And mingle your mind as one with the Guru's. ⚇
Liberated upon arising, beyond the intellect's reach— ⚇
Maintain this vital point! ⚇
Bring to completion the result— ⚇
The four kayas spontaneously present."[724] ⚇

— Revealed by Jamgön Kongtrul Lodrö Thayé

The Mahaguru continued to give teachings, and in particular the following heart advice to the Dharma practitioners there:

Listen here, Tibetan yogis confident in view and meditation! ⚇
The real yogi is but your unfabricated innate nature. ⚇
"Yogi" means to realize the wisdom of pure awareness. ⚇
That is how you truly obtain the name yogi. ⚇
In the view, be free from ambition; ⚇
Don't indulge in partiality. ⚇
In meditation, be free from reference point; ⚇
Don't indulge in fixating your mind. ⚇
In conduct, be free from accepting and rejecting; ⚇
Don't indulge in self-clinging. ⚇

In the fruition, be free from abandonment and attainment; ፧
Don't indulge in grasping to things as real. ፧
In keeping samaya, be free from limitation; ፧
Don't indulge in fraud and pretense. ፧
Toward the Buddhadharma, be free from bias; ፧
Don't indulge in scholastic sectarianism. ፧
Appearances are delusion; don't indulge in ordinariness. ፧
Food is merely to sustain your life-force; don't grovel for food. ፧
Wealth is illusory; don't indulge in craving. ፧
Clothes are to protect you from cold; don't indulge in opulent fashions. ፧
Equality is nondual; don't indulge in intimate companions. ፧
Be free from preference to country; don't indulge in a homeland. ፧
Make your dwelling an empty cave; don't indulge in monastic life. ፧
Do your practice in solitude; don't indulge in social gatherings. ፧
Be detached and free from clinging; don't indulge in attachment. ፧
Be a self-liberated yogi; don't indulge in charlatanism. ፧
I, Padmakara, am now taking my leave. ፧
Whether you live in the present or will appear in the future, ፧
Tibetan yogis of future generations, keep this in your hearts.[725] ፧

— *Revealed by Nyangral Nyima Özer*

In this way, the Mahaguru continued to give advice.[726]

Final Heart Advice for His Disciples

Once the Mahaguru had finished his final teachings, he left for the Gungthang Pass, accompanied by King Mutik Tsenpo, his closest disciples, and many more.

As the Guru began his journey to the *rakshasa* lands, ፧
The emperor and subjects went along to wave him off. ፧
When they reached Mangyul's upper plain, ፧
The master and his companions rested there for three full days. ፧
To the emperor and every subject, he gave individual advice.[727] ፧

— *Revealed by Jamgön Kongtrul Lodrö Thayé*

Once the party reached the Gungthang Pass, and had pitched their tents, the Mahaguru gave each of his closest disciples specific guidance, heart advice, practice instructions, and prayers. These were then safeguarded like a treasure of gold and subsequently hidden by the disciples as treasures for future generations to discover. Amongst these, the *Le'ü Dün Ma* (*The Prayer in Seven Chapters*) and the *Mahaguru Aspiration Prayer* are some of the best-known and most treasured instructions given by the Mahaguru on this occasion.[728]

Particularly memorable, amongst all the many pieces of heart advice given up there on the Gungthang Pass, are the following final words to his closest disciple Khandro Yeshé Tsogyal, on how to invoke him when he is no longer physically present:

> When you can see me clearly, take empowerments ⸸
> And rest in the View. ⸸
> Until you see me so, persist in meditation. ⸸
> Recite the quintessential Guru Siddhi mantra ⸸
> And, concluding, let your body, speech, and mind ⸸
> Be mingled with the Guru. ⸸
> Call on me with prayers and dedication, ⸸
> And stay within the Great Perfection, ⸸
> The essential sphere beyond all action. ⸸
> Nothing will surpass this, Mistress Tsogyal! ⸸
> Padmasambhava's compassion neither ebbs nor flows; ⸸
> The rays of my compassion for Tibet cannot be severed. ⸸
> There I am, in front of anyone who prays to me— ⸸
> I am never far from those with faith, ⸸
> Nor even from those without it, ⸸
> Though yet they do not see me. ⸸
> My predicted children are forever guarded by my love. ⸸
> In future, henceforth, on the tenth day of the moon, ⸸
> I, the Lotus-Born, will come astride the lordly daystar ⸸
> In forms peaceful, enriching, attractive, and wrathful. ⸸
> At four times I will show myself, ⸸
> And thus will grant attainments to my children.[729] ⸸

> — *Revealed by Samten Lingpa*

The Mahaguru's Departure

In the Wood Monkey Year of 864, on the 10th day of the Monkey month—the same day, month, and year of the astrological cycle which had marked his miraculous birth on a blossoming lotus in the lake of Dhanakosha—the Mahaguru took his leave of Tibet.[730] Once the teachings had concluded, the Mahaguru's disciples sat down and rested in meditation as the Mahaguru prepared for his departure. The *Pema Kathang* relates:

> As they made camp upon the Gungthang Pass, §
> Clouds of white, red, and yellow began swirling in the sky, §
> And from amidst rainbow-colored lights emerged Balaha, §
> King of Steeds, §
> A blue horse of the noblest breed, sporting a jeweled harness. §
> He whinnied loudly, his perfect ears standing erect, §
> As gods and goddesses, old and new, gathered round, §
> All greeting him with the seven royal symbols, §
> The eight auspicious symbols, §
> All kinds of music, and a multitude of dakinis... §
> As Guru Padmasambahva mounted his supreme, bejeweled horse, §
> Dakas of the four classes led the steed and his rider onward, §
> And they took off into the air, into a swirl of rainbow lights. §
> The King and disciples, his closest, were thus left at Gungthang Pass, §
> Like tossing away hot sand, like casting away hunger and thirst. §
> Then the King, his ministers, and the disciples, §
> Rested in meditation until the twenty-fifth day §
> Upon the edge of the Rongthang Sho pond
> In the main town of Mangyul. §
> And as the sun rose, they looked into the space
> Where the Guru had departed, §
> And amidst the sun rays he appeared in the distance like a raven, §
> Flashing in the sky like a flicker of light. §
> Then, as he flew on, like a dove, then a fledgling, §
> Then a bee, then a tiny nit, §
> They gazed after him till their eyes could no longer see him. §
> They stayed in meditation, looking still, §
> But there was nothing more to be seen. §
> Once, when evening fell and they were again in meditation, §
> Then once again they saw him— §
> As a sun ray, far beyond India but not yet reaching Uddiyana, §
> Resting upon the pass of Mount Jambuza. §
> When morning came, they looked out again in their meditation, §
> And saw him pausing near the City of Iron in Sri Lanka, §
> Resting under the cool shade of a magnolia tree. §
> His wise steed was rolling in the golden sand §

And grazing on the *sita* grass, king among medicines. ⸮
Daughters of the *rakshasas* were gathered all around the Guru, ⸮
Beautiful and young, and in the thousands. ⸮
They were all touched by the light of Dharma, their dedication clear. ⸮
Into this iron mansion of the *rakshasas*, which had no doors, ⸮
Strode the Skull-Garlanded One, King of the Rakshasas. ⸮
And they could see the *rakshasas* all bowing in respect.[731] ⸮

— *Revealed by Orgyen Lingpa*

When the Mahaguru was no longer in sight, the disciples bade farewell to the Gungthang Pass and returned to their homes. Although profoundly sad at the departure of their beloved teacher, they also harbored a deep sense of gratitude. They recognized that without the presence and teachings of the Mahaguru, the Buddhadharma would never have taken root in Greater Tibet. Moreover, the disciples found solace in the wealth of parting instructions he had bestowed upon them, providing clarity and guidance for their path and Dharma practice.

While many disciples had expressed a desire to accompany the Mahaguru on his journey, he gently declined their request. Instead, he urged them to remain behind and ensure the continuity of his legacy. The disciples embraced the Mahaguru's words with utmost seriousness, dedicating themselves wholeheartedly to this sacred task. They not only became teachers, passing on the Mahaguru's instructions to future generations of Tibetans, but they also concealed many of his teachings as *terma* treasures for the benefit of future generations. Furthermore, they took vows to reincarnate in future lives in order to carry forward the Mahaguru's legacy and continue his noble work. It is through the unwavering commitment and efforts of these disciples that the Mahaguru's legacy remains unbroken to this day.

The Mahaguru's Legacy

Revelation of the Sampa Lhundrupma

Centuries later, in the Water Dragon Year, 1352, Tulku Zangpo Drakpa revealed the *Le'ü Dün Ma* (*The Prayer in Seven Chapters*), at the Rulak Gyang, and entrusted it to Rikdzin Gödem, who deciphered it from the dakini script.[732] The *Le'ü Dün Ma* is one of the most beloved prayers invoking the Mahaguru, and features seven individual prayers given to his five disciples—Namkhé Nyingpo, Dharma King Trisong Detsen, Khandro Yeshé Tsogyal, Nanam Dorjé Dudjom, and Prince Mutri Tsenpo. The initial six prayers were given in the twelfth month of the Male Fire Horse Year, 766, but the final prayer—the *Sampa Lhundrupma* (*The Prayer to Guru Rinpoche that Spontaneously Fulfills All Wishes*)—was given to Prince Mutri Tsenpo as the Mahaguru's parting testament on the Gungthang pass.[733] The *Sampa Lhundrupma* safeguards the practitioner against conflict, disease, poverty, obstacle-makers, vicious animals, disturbances of the four natural elements, robbers, sudden death, the intermediate state, clinging to reality, and the sufferings of the six classes of beings. Later still, in 1858, Chokgyur Lingpa and Jamyang Khyentse Wangpo revealed the famous practice cycle, the *Lamé Tukdrup Yishin Norbu* (*The Guru's Heart Practice, Wish- Fulfilling Jewel*), along with the guru representative statue known as Guru Kutsap Ngödrup Palbar (Glorious Blaze of Siddhis). The discovery of this priceless teaching transformed the *Sampa Lhündrupma* prayer into a sadhana.[734]

Revelation of the Mahaguru Prayer

The profound *Mahaguru Aspiration Prayer* was discovered in Lhodrak by the renowned treasure revealer Pema Lingpa (1450 – 1521).[735] It contains the last words spoken by Khandro Yeshe Tsogyal to Guru Padmasambhava as he prepared to leave Tibet. This sacred text documents a deeply personal encounter between the Mahaguru and his closest disciple, and thus carries immense blessings. The *Mahaguru Aspiration Prayer* is held in high esteem by numerous revered masters and continues to be recited widely up to the present day. The prayer commences with

Mahaguru, bless me ⁘
That in all my lives to come, ⁘
In your pure land, in the palace, ⁘
Inseparable from you, master, ⁘
I may always be.[736] ⁘

A FINAL PILGRIMAGE

Zangdok Palri, the Glorious Copper-Colored Mountain, is the nirmanakaya pure land manifested by Guru Padmasambhava after his departure from Greater Tibet. It stands as the ultimate destination for Guru Rinpoche and all those who follow in his footsteps. Numerous accomplished masters have recounted their visionary experiences, having traveled to Zangdok Palri in dreams or in visions during their lifetimes. These accounts have been meticulously recorded and preserved.

Furthermore, these masters have identified various sacred sites across the world that bear resemblance to or carry the blessings of Zangdok Palri, including notable places like the island of Sri Lanka.[737] In addition to these visionary experiences and sacred sites, many physical representations of Zangdok Palri have been constructed by devoted practitioners. These visionary accounts, sacred sites, and representations serve not only to inspire disciples but also to bestow blessings, nurture devotion, and act as evidence of pure perception and realization.[738]

Although one might perceive this miraculous realm as beyond our reach, Guru Rinpoche himself, along with countless masters, has demonstrated that the opposite is true. They have shown us that, through sincere practice and devotion, we can establish a profound connection with Zangdok Palri and partake in its blessings and realization.[739]

The key factor that enables us to see, enter, and connect with Zangdok Palri lies within our own perception. Orgyen Topgyal Rinpoche (b. 1951) reminds us that, fundamentally, the world itself has always been a realm of purity. When we come to understand the true nature of reality, we realize that our world has been inherently pure and perfect from the very beginning.[740]

For a highly realized individual who directly experiences this purity, the entire world manifests as Zangdok Palri. As we purify our perception, so our ability expands, and we can perceive Zangdok Palri and other pure lands beyond the constraints of time.[741] Already the sutras have shown us that, upon reaching a certain level of practice, we can visit various buddha realms and receive teachings there.[742]

The appearance of Zangdok Palri within a single body and within a single lifetime is the outcome of pure perception and realization. Consequently, Zangdok Palri is accessible to anyone, at any time, and from any location, through the blessings of pure perception. In response to inquiries about how to reach Zangdok Palri, a dakini revealed the following to Düdjom Lingpa:

Zangdok Palri is a pure land of the manifest body of enlightenment, a celestial realm on earth: When one abandons the ten non-virtuous acts, cultivates stores of merit and wisdom, and makes significant aspirations, one will be born here. In every direction, inside palaces of precious crystal, are golden thrones swathed in silks—seats for all who attain such rebirths.[743]

Affirming that Zangdok Palri depends upon our perception, this dakini explains that practitioners who cultivate merit and wisdom, and make aspiration prayers, will be reborn in Zangdok Palri when their life comes to an end. Therefore, the beautiful *Zangdok Palri Mönlam* (*Aspiration Prayer for rebirth on the Glorious Copper-Colored Mountain*) forms a core part of practice for most followers of Guru Rinpoche. Even though we may not be able to encounter Zangdok Palri in visions and dreams in this lifetime, we can at least ensure that we are reborn there.

ZANGDOK PALRI

South-west of here, in Ngayab Ling, ⁝
On the peak of the Mountain of Glory, ⁝
You rule as sovereign among countless vidyadharas and dakinis, ⁝
And you bind the rakshasa cannibals under oath, ⁝
And, all the while, ceaselessly, you turn your compassionate gaze
On Tibet and all the world. ⁝
To you, the nirmanakaya, and to your kindness, we pray! ⁝
To the Lotus-Born Guru of Orgyen, we pray![744] ⁝

— *Revealed by Tulku Zangpo Drakpa*

Introduction

Guru Rinpoche knew that the demonic *rakshasa* cannibals of Camaradvipa, at the edge of our world-system, posed a grave threat to humanity. Their impending invasion threatened to engulf the Earth and annihilate all human life. Thus, after firmly establishing Buddhism in Tibet, Guru Rinpoche embarked on a mission to avert the looming disaster.

On the tenth day of the Monkey month in the Wood Monkey Year of 864, Guru Rinpoche set out for Camaradvipa. There, he successfully subdued the leader of the *rakshasas*, a demon named Raksha Tötreng (Skull-Garland Rakshasa), and assumed his form. Transforming this perilous and hostile cannibal realm, Guru Rinpoche then manifested the extraordinary Palace of Lotus Light, *Padma Ö*, atop the central mountain known as Zangdok Palri (the Glorious Copper-Colored Mountain). With this, and through Guru Rinpoche's blessings, this once treacherous domain was transformed into a sublime place for spiritual attainment, where the teachings of Tantra flourish and thrive without interruption.

The island of the *rakshasas* thus became Guru Rinpoche's supreme nirmanakaya pure land within our world-system. Residing in the luminous body beyond the confines of birth and death, Guru Rinpoche continues to turn the wheel of the Dharma there, guiding and liberating sentient beings. Emanation after emanation is sent to the human realm, empowered by the blessings of Guru Rinpoche, to ensure the continued guidance and liberation of beings.

Approaching the Sacred Site

Outer Location

Zangdok Palri, known as the Glorious Copper-Colored Mountain, is outwardly situated on the desolate island known as Ngayab Ling in Tibetan and Camaradvipa in Sanskrit. According to ancient Buddhist cosmology, our world-system is centered around the cosmic mountain, the majestic Mount Meru. This Mount Meru is encircled by seven gold mountain rings, with vast oceans filling the spaces in between. Beyond these seven rings are four continents, located in the cardinal directions, each of which consists of two islands. Additionally, there are numerous smaller islands whose specifics are not known.

Our world-system, encompassing all the aforementioned, is further enveloped by a ring of mountains of volcanic iron. According to this ancient cosmology, we inhabit the southern continent known as Jambudvipa, also called the Land of Jambu. This name derives from the presence of a beautiful Jambu tree adorning this continent. The *Le'u Dün Ma* (*The Prayer in Seven Chapters*) points to where Camaradvipa is located:

> *Emaho: O wonder! Yonder, in the south-west,* §
> *To the north-west of the sacred Vajra Seat,* §
> *Lies the continent of Ngayab Ling, land of the rakshasa cannibals,* §
> *Blessed by all the buddhas of past, present and future.* §
> *To this sublime and special realm, we pray!* §
> *To the Lotus-Born Guru of Orgyen, we pray!*[745] §
>
> — Revealed by Tulku Zangpo Drakpa

Camaradvipa is one of the two outlying subcontinents that encircle our terrestrial plane of Jambudvipa, and is positioned to the southwest.[746] This island is inhabited by *rakshasas* (cannibal demons) and, according to Jamgön Kongtrul Lodrö Thayé, it is the only island on Earth to be inhabited by such demons; all other islands are populated by humans.[747]

Although Jambudvipa is sometimes referred to as 'Lanka,' it is important to note that the island-nation we currently know as Sri Lanka, where Sri Pada or Mount Malaya is located, should not be confused with the actual Camaradvipa. However, Chokgyur Dechen Lingpa, in his visionary journey, mentioned that Sri Lanka is one of thirteen islands encountered on the way to the true Camaradvipa. Furthermore, Chokgyur Lingpa revealed that Sri Lanka holds the same sacred essence as Camaradvipa. The dakinis affirmed in Chokgyur

Lingpa's vision that Sri Lanka represents Zangdok Palri, manifesting as an "associated site" within our human realm.[748]

Inner Location

The tantras highlight a profound interconnection between the external and internal realms. They emphasize that the external world is a mirror image of the internal world. In essence, whatever exists in the external environment is also reflected within our own body. Therefore, the tantras not only identify sacred sites in the external world but also describe them as existing within our own being, internally located in our human body. Regarding the 'internal location' of Zangdok Palri, Jamgön Mipham Rinpoche (1846-1912) provided the following, in his insights and writings:

> *Hung Hrih! In the rakshasa city of terror,*
> *On the Glorious Copper-Colored Mountain,*
> *Lies the three-kaya buddha field of Lotus Light,*
> *A wrathful realm, dark red like a raging inferno.*
> *Within our vajra body, this is the city of the heart,*
> *And there—in the palace of vidyadharas, dakas and dakinis—*
> *Dwells the indestructible form of wisdom*
> *That equalizes samsara and nirvana,*
> *The embodiment of all the infinite buddhas—*
> *Padmasambhava, the Lake-born Lord.*[749]

Outwardly Zangdok Palri lies on Camaradvipa, and inwardly, as Mipham Rinpoche states, Zangdok Palri resides in the heart.[750] This external-internal relationship is also emphasized in the *Le'u Dün Ma*, where Zangdok Palri is described as having the shape of the heart:[751]

> *The Glorious Copper-Colored Mountain is shaped as a heart,* §
> *Its base deep down in the domain of the naga king,* §
> *Its slopes, resplendent and majestic,* §
> *Rising into the realm of the dakinis,* §
> *Its soaring peak as high as the world of Brahma.* §
> *To this special king of mountains, we pray!* §
> *To the Lotus-Born Guru of Orgyen, we pray!*[752] §
>
> — *Revealed by Tulku Zangpo Drakpa*

The tantras emphasize the concept of internal pilgrimage by associating sacred sites with vital points in the human body. This means that, through engaging in various tantric practices, practitioners can effectively remove obstructions in the subtle body, such as blockages in the channels, prana (vital energy), and bindu (subtle essence). By doing so, they can evoke a direct experience of Zangdok Palri, even if it may not be possible to reach it physically within the span of this lifetime.[753]

Secret Location

Secretly, Zangdok Palri is the domain of our own enlightened nature. The more we progress on the path and realize our own true nature, the more all phenomena will begin to appear in their true nature as Zangdok Palri. Zangdok Palri will arise as the purity of our own perception.[754] Chokgyur Dechen Lingpa wrote:

> *Lotus-Born, you are inseparable from our original nature.*
> *Your realm, the Glorious Copper-Colored Mountain,*
> *Is our experience in its purity.*
> *May we take birth in this primordially pure realm,*
> *The uncontrived natural state—*
> *Appearance and awareness indivisible![755]*

The Mahaguru's Journey

Liberating the King of the Rakshasas

> *Then you left, and for the Land of Orgyen,* ⚬
> *Where now you subjugate the rakshasa demons;* ⚬
> *Great wonder—surpassing any human being,* ⚬
> *Great marvel—in your phenomenal enlightened actions,* ⚬
> *Great might—with all your miraculous powers:* ⚬
> *With your compassion, inspire us with your blessing!* ⚬
> *With your love, guide us and others along the path!* ⚬
> *With your realization, grant us siddhis!* ⚬
> *With your power, dispel the obstacles facing us all!* ⚬
> *Outer obstacles—dispel them externally,* ⚬
> *Inner obstacles—dispel them internally,* ⚬
> *Secret obstacles—dispel them into space!* ⚬

In devotion, I pay homage and take refuge in you! ⁝
om ah hung benza guru pema siddhi hung[756] ⁝

— Revealed by Chokgyur Dechen Lingpa

Raksha Tötreng, a formidable ogre characterized by nine heads and eighteen arms, held dominion over Camaradvipa from his imposing fortress. The fortress, standing nine stories tall, was constructed using a macabre arrangement of human skulls, some bloodied, some bleached.. Accompanying Raksha Tötreng was his demon consort, a fearsome red-colored entity whose presence was said to be too intimidating to behold directly. Surrounding the cannibal king and queen was an entourage of a thousand ogres, engaging in ghastly acts of blood-drinking, innocent lives taken, and relentless terror inflicted upon the surrounding islands.

Recognizing that Raksha Tötreng was impervious to conventional methods of subjugation, Guru Rinpoche employed a transformative approach. Through cutting his life-force and liberating his consciousness, Guru Rinpoche successfully subdued Raksha Tötreng, bringing an end to his reign of terror.[757]

Attaining the Spontaneously Accomplished Vidyadhara

Endowed with wisdom body, speech, and mind, ⁝
You are our glorious guide; ⁝
You have freed yourself of obscurations ⁝
And know the three realms with vivid clarity; ⁝
You have attained the supreme siddhi ⁝
And possess the supreme body of great bliss. ⁝
All the obstacles to our enlightenment—eliminate them for good![758] ⁝

— Revealed by Chokgyur Dechen Lingpa

Simultaneously, as he liberated the *rakshasa* king, Guru Rinpoche displayed the fourth vidyadhara level, the "spontaneously accomplished vidyadhara." The Mahaguru thus attained the immortal *vajra-kaya*. In this form beyond birth and death, he has assumed sovereign rule over all Camaradvipa, maintaining control over the *rakshasas* into perpetuity. From there, Guru Rinpoche tirelessly emanates countless manifestations, each with the purpose of liberating sentient beings, and he will continue to do this for as long as the cycle of samsara persists. Kyapjé Dudjom Rinpoche has written about this matter:

There he presides as King, with an emanation in each of the eight rakshasa continents, giving teachings such as *The Eight Great Methods of Attainment* of the Kagyé, and protecting the people of this world of Jambudvipa from fears for their life. Even to this day, he reigns as the vajradhara supreme, the 'vidyadhara with spontaneous accomplishment of the ultimate path'; and thus he will remain, without ever moving, until the end of the universe.[759]

Padma Ö: The Inconceivable Palace of Lotus Light

Then, the Mahaguru manifested the inconceivable Palace of Lotus Light, (Padma Ö), which has been beautifully described in Rikdzin Jikmé Lingpa's *terma* treasure, *Secret Path to the Glorious Mountain*, revealed at Samye Chimpu:[760]

Nirmanakaya

om ah hung benza guru pema siddhi hung. ॰
Its nature is utterly pure, beyond conceptual mind, ॰
A primordial expanse where a ceaseless radiance shines, ॰
bliss and emptiness indivisible, ॰
Sambhogakaya's display appearing as a pure land, ॰
A nirmanakaya aspect of Endurance, this world of ours— ॰
May we be born on this Glorious Copper-Colored Mountain! ॰

The Vajra seat, very center of our world ॰
Is that sacred place where buddhas, ॰
Past, present, and future, turn the Wheel of Dharma. ॰
North-west of there, lies the land of Ngayab Langka Ling— ॰
May we be born on this Glorious Copper-Colored Mountain! ॰

A spontaneous array, a mountain rising in the shape of a heart, ॰
Its base resting on the crown of the hooded King of the Nagas, ॰
Its slopes thronging with formless dakas and dakinis ॰
Celebrating the ganachakra feast, its peak reaching to the heights ॰
Of the form realms' states of meditative absorption— ॰
May we be born on this Glorious Copper-Colored Mountain! ॰

On the summit of this king of mountains, ॰
Rises a palace beyond all measure, ॰
The eastern side of crystal, the south of lapis lazuli, ॰
The west of ruby, and the north of emerald, ॰

And all translucent like a rainbow, no outside, inside or in-between— ⁞
May we be born on this Glorious Copper-Colored Mountain! ⁞

Corridors, corners, and parapets pulsate in rainbow outlines, ⁞
With terraces, friezes, and hanging garlands with jewels and tassels, ⁞
And water-spouts, roofs, door ornaments, and porches, ⁞
And the Wheel of Dharma, the parasol and finial, ⁞
All perfect in symbols, in meaning, and signs— ⁞
May we be born on this Glorious Copper-Colored Mountain ⁞

There are wish-fulfilling trees here and fountains of nectar, ⁞
Green groves sweet with the fragrance of healing plants, ⁞
And rishis, vidyadharas, flocks of birds and swarms of bees, ⁞
All quivering with the sounds of mystic song ⁞
And vibrant with the three vehicles, the Dharma— ⁞
May we be born on this Glorious Copper-Colored Mountain![761] ⁞

— Revealed by Rikdzin Jikmé Lingpa

On Camaradvipa there is a heart-shaped mountain, with blue base, white flanks, and a red summit, and around it, a vast plain and cliffs resembling arrows, spears, tridents, and swords.[762] On the top of the mountain stands a magnificent and resplendent fortress of awakened perfection. This is the renowned Palace of Lotus Light, (Padma Ö), the sacred dwelling of the great Mahaguru Padmasambhava.

With its structure of five types of gemstones and minerals, the celestial Palace of Lotus Light radiates with unparalleled brilliance. The ground floor of the palace represents the nirmanakaya field of Guru Rinpoche, while the middle floor embodies the sambhogakaya field of Avalokiteshvara, and the top floor the dharmakaya field of Amitabha. Adorned with melodious bells and delicate silk canopies, the three-tiered palace is ablaze with grandeur and beauty. The eastern side is crafted from crystal, the south from lapis lazuli, the west from ruby, and the north from emerald.

The entire palace exudes a translucent quality akin to rainbow light, devoid of distinctions between exterior and interior. Within each level, in every direction nook, and cranny, throughout the galleries and doorways, the expressions of awakened body, speech, and mind manifest as dakas, dakinis, gods, and goddesses of light. They dance, sing, and emanate boundless clouds of outer, inner, and secret offerings. Outside the palace, rainbows and light-spheres illuminate the surroundings, while the ground appears adorned with intricate embroidery, like the finest silk brocade. Gentle breezes carry enchanting scents from meadows of beautiful flowers and medicinal plants. Merely touching the earth, inhaling the air, beholding the environment, and hearing the celestial song, one's whole being fills with boundless exaltation.

A palace vast and limitless, and, at its heart, §
Upon an eight-cornered jewel, a seat of lotus, sun and moon, §
Padmakara spontaneously appears, as all the sugatas in one, §
Embodying the three kayas, resplendent in an aura of rainbow light— §
May we be born on this Glorious Copper-Colored Mountain! §

Through your wisdom of great bliss, profound and luminous, §
Emptiness manifests as compassion, and, as its magical display, §
In every direction of space, and especially the land of Tibet, §
Your emanations stream out, on and on, §
In their thousands and millions— §
May we be born on this Glorious Copper-Colored Mountain! §

On your right, the stretching rows of vidyadharas from India and Tibet, §
Their minds suffused in the boundless Dzokchen view, §
'The vajra play of luminosity;' §
On your left, the rows of scholars and sages of India and Tibet, §
Their voices sounding the Dharma, revealing their experience §
And realization, from teaching and practice— §
May we be born on this Glorious Copper-Colored Mountain! §

Around them the King and subjects, the twenty-five disciples, §
And nirmanakaya tertöns and sovereigns among the siddhas, §
All practicing the cycles of the nine graded vehicles, §
And, one-pointed, keeping the yogic discipline §
Of unwavering realization— §
May we be born on this Glorious Copper-Colored Mountain! §

The four cardinal and eight intermediate directions, §
And the corners and internal galleries, §
Are all filled with dakas, dakinis, gods and goddesses, §
With their vajra hymns and dance, moving like mirages, §
Sending out clouds of offerings, outer, inner and secret— §
May we be born on this Glorious Copper-Colored Mountain![763] §

— Revealed by Rikdzin Jikmé Lingpa

The ground floor of the Palace of Lotus Light encompasses the entire realm of emanation, known as the nirmanakaya. Within this sacred space, Guru Rinpoche, who embodies all the qualities of guru, yidam, and dakini, sits upon a majestic throne adorned with precious jewels. From this exalted position, he imparts teachings of Secret Mantra to an inconceivably vast assembly. This ocean-like gathering includes the twenty-five main disciples, the hundred treasure revealers, the hundred great scholars, the hundred great translators, as well as countless vidyadharas, dakas, dakinis, and realized adepts. Khandro Yeshé Tsogyal holds a foremost position in the assembly, as the primary dakini of Zangdok Palri. Having lived for two-hundred years, fulfilling aspirations and working to benefit sentient beings, she ultimately dissolved into luminosity and made the journey to Zangdok Palri without abandoning her physical form. There she remains as the heart consort of the Guru, eternally united in their sacred bond.[764]

Sambhogakaya

Above, lies the palace of the sambhogakaya, §
Limitless, an array of utter beauty, §
Where Padmapani, Lord of the World, presides, §
Encircled by an entourage that surpasses the imagination, §
Utterly destroying discursive thought §
And habit patterns, subtle enemies and negativity— §
May we be born on this Glorious Copper-Colored Mountain![765] §

— Revealed by Rikdzin Jikmé Lingpa

The magnificent celestial assembly hall on the middle floor of the Palace of Lotus Light represents the sambhogakaya, the realm of unimaginable and expansive expressions of bliss. The presiding deity in this celestial hall is the Great Compassionate One, Avalokiteshvara, also known as Padmapani.

Dharmakaya

Above, in the joyful pure land of the dharmakaya, §
Samantabhadra, the ground, the essence of primordial wisdom, §
Appearing as Amitabha (Limitless Light), symbolically grants teachings
to an entourage no different from his own awareness, §
Where teacher and disciples possess equal realization §
And enlightened activity— §

May we be born on this Glorious Copper-Colored Mountain![766] ❊

— *Revealed by Rikdzin Jikmé Lingpa*

The boundless celestial palace on the top floor of the Palace of Lotus Light manifests as an unbounded mansion of lapis lazuli, representing the indescribable nature of the dharmakaya. Within this sacred abode resides the Protector Amitabha, accompanied by an expansive retinue that seamlessly embodies the luminous awareness of his enlightened state.

Conclusion

At the four gates the Four Great Kings keep their vows. ❊
The eight classes of gods and demons, outer, inner, and secret, ❊
Dispatched as envoys, subjugate heretics and transgressors. ❊
An ocean of oath-bound protectors beat the victory drum ❊
To show their might— ❊
May we be born on this Glorious Copper-Colored Mountain! ❊

Now, through the power of visualizing vividly the details of the pure land, ❊
And through aspiring with our inner awareness ❊
Toward this external Copper-Colored Mountain of Glory, ❊
So, inside this very body of ours, here in this world of 'Endurance', ❊
May our entire experience actually arise, ❊
Here and now, as the Glorious Copper-Colored Mountain! ❊

When, through the profound and unique interaction ❊
Of generation and completion, ❊
The knots of the three channels and five centers are freed, ❊
Then, in the great palace of the Glorious Copper-Colored Mountain ❊
In the center of our hearts, ❊
May we perfect the powerful play of innate primordial wisdom ❊
And so meet the Lord Padmakara, our own awareness, face to face! ❊

The five paths of Accumulation, Preparation, Seeing, Meditation, ❊
And No-More-Learning, ❊
The bhumis from 'Perfect Joy' up to 'Universal Radiance', ❊
The two supreme stages of the Vajrayana, ❊
In particular the extraordinary stage of Clear Light Dzokpachenpo, ❊
The 'unexcelled wisdom', the yeshé lama— ❊
Effortless, unaltered, and at ease, may we complete them all, ❊

And so be liberated in the space of the ground, the Lotus Light! ※

Yet, if we cannot perfect the full strength of realization, ※
Nonetheless, through the power of our fervent prayer and aspiration, ※
When death arrives with all its overpowering force, ※
Let the messengers of Padma, the dakinis, gracefully dancing, ※
Actually take us by the hand, ※
Just as they did Kharchen Za and Guna Natha,[767] ※
And lead us to the paradise of Lotus Light! ※

By the truth of the utterly pure dharmadhatu, ※
And through the compassion of the ocean
Of Three Jewels and Three Roots, ※
May we accomplish all our aspirations, just as we wish, ※
And so become a guide, each and every one of us, ※
To lead all beings to the pure land of Lotus Light![768] ※

— *Revealed by Rikdzin Jikmé Lingpa*

The Mahaguru's Legacy

Among the many visionary journeys to Zangdok Palri—both recorded and unrecorded—we would like to share now three accounts by the great *rime* masters—Chokgyur Dechen Zhikpo Lingpa, Jamyang Khyentsé Wangpo, and Jamgön Kongtrul Lodrö Thayé—who have deeply inspired and influenced this series of pilgrimage books.

Chokgyur Dechen Lingpa's Visionary Journey

During Chokgyur Lingpa's visionary journey to Zangdok Palri, the dakinis instructed him to remember every detail and describe it with precision upon his return. They emphasized the importance of having the imagery depicted in paintings, so that the disciples of the Mahaguru could visualize Zangdok Palri and hold that image in their minds at the time of their own death, aspiring to be reborn in that sacred realm. Following the guidance of the dakinis, the Great Tertön shared his visionary experience with his students, who diligently recorded it and commissioned a thangka, a traditional Tibetan scroll painting, to depict Chokgyur Lingpa's account.

The following excerpts are taken from the extensive visionary narrative of the Great Tertön as later recorded in his biography by Könchok Tenpé Gyaltsen (1871–1939), himself the recognized reincarnation of Chokgyur Lingpa:[769]

The great awareness holder Chokgyur Lingpa and five dakinis boarded the great ship and miraculously arrived at the other shore in a single instant... The dakinis led the way and together they reached the eastern side of the mountain. They continued on their journey... Looking in the four directions, he saw the bathing pools of the four activities, gardens of different kinds of flowers, many types of birds, and deer with melodious and modulating voices. These animals spoke in human language and were discussing the Dharma in accordance with their individual characters and abilities. The trees, water, and wind were also emitting the sound of Dharma. So pleasant was it, that he felt even staying for eons would not be long enough...

Nirmanakaya, The First Storey of the Central Palace

In the large central Palace of Lotus Light, the great Guru Padmasambhava was surrounded by a retinue of a hundred great panditas, a hundred great translators, a hundred awareness holders, and a hundred treasure revealers. There, he opened the mandala of *The Ocean of Dharma, the Gathering of Transmitted Precepts*. For the section on the inner showering of resplendent blessings, dakinis of the four classes performed a dance in front of the mandala, with the Dharma King Trisong Detsen and his sons seated before them as the event's benefactors.

Upon witnessing this, Chokgyur Lingpa felt boundless faith and devotion, and blissful elation, as if he had attained the first *bhumi*, 'Truly Joyful'. He felt not even the slightest puff of pride at having arrived in this place without first having to discard his body—these aggregates that perpetuate defilement...

Sambhogakaya, The Second Storey of the Central Palace

As they reached the middle level, they saw the Lotus-Born Guru with a hundred thousand vidyadharas, including the eight great vidyadharas of India. He was turning the great Dharma Wheel of the mind, space, and pith-instruction sections of the Great

Perfection. Chokgyur Lingpa paid homage and made mandala offerings. During these deeply felt supplications, Guru Rinpoche proclaimed, "The Great Perfection is primordial purity, free from all action and effort!" Then, directing his gaze into midair, he uttered, *Ah ah ah, phat*! and remained in a sky-like state that defies expression.

Dharmakaya, The Third Storey of the Central Palace

There on the upper level, he beheld Guru Rinpoche in the five aspects of Tötreng Tsal. Clustered all around him were the five sambhogakaya families in inconceivable array, emanating and reabsorbing throughout the whole of space. He was teaching by means of the dharmakaya speech that is the nature of nonarising, the sambhogakaya speech of symbolic intent, and the nirmanakaya speech of verbal expression. Robed in the attire of the supreme nirmanakaya buddhas of the ten directions, he was seated in the midst of an inconceivable retinue and accompanied by countless offering goddesses who were there to make offerings and receive teachings. The scene was completely beyond description...

Jamyang Khyentsé Wangpo's Visionary Journey

Jamyang Khyentsé Wangpo recounts his own visionary journey to Zangdok Palri in his autobiography, written in verse and requested by his disciple Dodrupchen Jikmé Tenpé Nyima (1865–1926). He recounts how he received the sutras and tantras in their entirety directly from Guru Rinpoche and was established as a holder of the seven transmissions:

> On the tenth day of the fourth month of my sixteenth year
> I was transported at dawn to
> Guru Padmasambhava's 'Lotus Light' palace.
> There, in a cave on a magically formed rock mountain,
> Quite incommensurate with ordinary landscapes,
> Amidst white clouds most beautiful,
> I beheld Tsokyé Dorjé surrounded by the dakini assembly.
> He conferred his mental blessing and symbolic empowerment
> And granted me authorization for the seven transmissions.
> After that, fixing his eyes in a gaze, he declared:

"Maintaining naked presence in the union of awareness and emptiness,
Untainted by objects falsely perceived as external,
Unaffected by the false viewpoint of the perceiver,
This is the mind of all the buddhas."
He then dissolved into me, whereupon,
In the state of his mind mingling indistinguishably with my own,
I just about gained recognition of the way things really are.
Inspired thereby with joy
and supplicating him one-pointedly in faith, I received all
the transmitted teachings of the old translation tradition (1),
Physical Revelations (2), Revelations of reconcealed treasures (3),
Mental revelations (4), Visionary revelations (5),
Oral transmissions (6),
and Revelations through recollection of past lives (7).[770]

Jamgön Kongtrul Lodrö Thayé's Visionary Journey

Jamgön Kongtrul Lodrö Thayé shared this visionary journey to Zangdok Palri in his autobiography. He was in his late twenties when he gave an elaborate account of his vision to his devoted disciple Nesar Karma Tashi Chöpel, but only mentioned it briefly in his autobiography:[771]

> One night, in my dreams, I felt I was about to die and, turning to face the southwest, I flew in that direction, thinking to go to Zangdok Palri. When it seemed that I had gone about halfway, I saw both Orgyen and his consort, together with a third figure, Vimalamitra, all on the slopes of a verdant col on a very high mountain. Descending to earth, I circumambulated them and made prostrations. Bowing my head, I requested some indication of their intent toward me, that there might yet be some things for me to accomplish which would make it unnecessary to go to the continent of Chamara. Although they spoke many words of advice, I could not keep these in mind. At a certain point, I came back to my room. I received a summons stating that I had to return with all haste, whereupon I flew back until I could see my spiritual master's monastic seat in vivid brilliance. With that thought, I awoke from sleep.[772]

EPILOGUE

Mahaguru Padmasambhava's thousand-year presence in this world fulfilled his enlightened activity here. Throughout his journey across the vast subcontinent of Greater India and the majestic Himalayan plateau, the Mahaguru served as an enlightened beacon, spreading the teachings of the Dharma far and wide. With his blessings, he sanctified the land, established sacred sites, concealed treasures, and transformed Greater Tibet into a sanctuary where the pure teachings of scripture and realization would thrive for over a millennium, awaiting the time when they would radiate throughout the entire world.

While the Mahaguru's physical pilgrimage has been meticulously recorded and shared in this series of books, his true impact and blessings surpass all imagination. The external sacred sites, brimming with profound blessings, serve as skillful means to guide us toward the hidden realms of our direct experience—our own mind's true nature. In this context, the Mahaguru embodies the essence of our innate nature, manifesting as the ultimate guru who leads and directly points us toward this deepest realization. In truth, we have never been separate from the Guru, this active aspect of our buddha-nature, working tirelessly on our behalf, guiding us back to this profound awakening, assuming infinite external forms and, most importantly, appearing as our own root teacher.

PART THREE

Invoking the Lotus-Born Guru

ESSENTIAL PRAYERS
TO THE LOTUS-BORN GURU

The following pages offer but a single droplet from the ocean of devotional prayers to the Lotus-Born Guru. Here we find the very the essence of his blessed speech, and the sacred words that past masters have evoked to call upon the Mahaguru. We hope that wherever you are, they may be a source of inspiration, strength, and blessings. For those who are interested, many more prayers and accounts have been translated as supplements to this book and are now readily accessible on the Nekhor website.

THE PATH OF AN AUTHENTIC PILGRIM

— *Phakchok Rinpoche*

While on pilgrimage to the sacred sites of Guru Padmsambhava in Bhutan, Phakchok Rinpoche gave the following teaching.[773] *Seated in the ancient temple of Kyichu Lhakang, built by Dharma King Songtsen Gompo in the seventh century, Rinpoche gave a full lesson in how to make the experience of visiting holy places more transformative. In his direct way, he shows us how to truly bring pilgrimage onto the spiritual path.*

Pilgrimage is an important act of devotion and faith. It enables us to accumulate merit and purify our defilements and obscurations of body, speech, and mind, all through the power of the blessings of sacred sites. In the *Mahaparinirvana Sutra*, Buddha Shakyamuni says, "Monks, after my passing away, all sons and daughters of good family and all the faithful, so long as they live, should go to the four holy places and remember: here in Lumbini, the Enlightened One was born; here in Bodh Gaya, he attained enlightenment; here in Sarnath, he turned the Wheel of Dharma; and here in Kushinagar, he entered parinirvana. Monks, after my passing away there will be those who circumambulate and prostrate to these places . . . a pilgrimage to these four holy places will help to purify their previously accumulated negative karmas, even the five heinous actions."

Now we are in a sacred place where buddhas, bodhisattvas, Mahaguru Padmasambhava, and countless realized beings have all been before us and therefore blessed the place. The intensity of blessings received from such a site depends entirely on the student; they fall into three categories. Those with greater faith, devotion, and pure perception will have greater results. The medium ones, with medium devotion, faith, and pure perception, will reap medium results. And finally, as in today's day and age, people who have difficulty supplicating and generating faith, devotion, and pure perception will similarly find it difficult to receive the blessings of such a sacred site.

Sometimes, students have difficulty with the term *supplication*. This English translation may confuse us a bit, but we should take the time to investigate what we are requesting when we make a supplication. If we are correctly supplicating, we are asking to come to see, to realize the nature of our own mind. We supplicate our root guru, who is the person who introduces us to this precious gem. Thus, we are not requesting a gift from outside ourselves. Instead, we are asking the kind guru to bring us to understand our own nature. Similarly, when we supplicate all the buddhas and bodhisattvas, we are making the firm wish that we gain and then stabilize this awareness of the natural state. When you go to visit a pilgrimage site, the first and most important thing to know is how to do *prostrations*. First, you go to the shrine. Right away, you think of and invoke all the enlightened buddhas and teachers, right there in front of you. Feel them in the presence of Guru Rinpoche's shrine. It is amazing that we can actually come so close to one of the places where the Mahaguru practiced. Not only that, many great masters have come to these places and blessed them as well. So, whenever you go on pilgrimage, the first thing you need to remember is to perform three prostrations.

After doing prostrations, the second thing to do is bring up your *motivation*. Quietly, sit down and think, "I'm here on pilgrimage not only for myself, and I would like to dedicate this pilgrimage to all sentient beings that are going through difficulties. I wish that all beings be freed from these difficulties, and that's why I'm now doing this pilgrimage and practice." You should always generate good intentions and remember these good intentions, because when you come to spiritually enhancing places like this, you might become selfish and think, "Oh, now I'm getting blessings, now I'm accumulating merit. I'm so blessed, I'm so happy!" Becoming selfish is easy, and that is why it is very important to recall your motivation. Bodhicitta is very important!

Thirdly, *receive the blessings*. How do you receive the blessings? You think, "Oh, Guru Rinpoche, you are the embodiment of all the sugatas, all your blessings, all your kindness, wisdom, siddhis, realizations—all your everything—is laid open like a wish-fulfilling jewel before me, yet due to my karmic obscurations and lack of merit, I cannot see that my nature is enlightened. Oh! How dreadful and how blinded I am with my habitual tendencies; they always take me astray from the true path!" With a yearning so deep, pray and supplicate to Guru Rinpoche to grant you blessings so that your defilements are cleared and you see the true path.

Then, visualize the Mahaguru radiating light and that you are receiving his empowerments. White light comes from his forehead and dissolves into yours. Red light comes from his throat and blue light from his heart, and both enter your throat and heart. If you cannot visualize these kinds of details, then just think that you receive the radiance, compassion, wisdom, dignity, and blessings of the Guru. This is very important. Whenever you go on pilgrimage, you need to know how to empower yourself in this way: this is how to receive blessings. Guru Rinpoche says that while you are receiving the blessings, you need to be firm and realize that now your defilements are purified, the two merits are accumulated, that you have received the four empowerments and received all the siddhis and blessings. This is key.

Fourth, make some *offerings*. No shortcuts! If you spend so much energy travelling to the pilgrimage site and just do a shortcut prayer and make a feeble offering, it's not worthwhile.

The word for "feast offering" in Sanskrit is *ganachakra*, which if translated into Tibetan is *tsok kyi khorlo*, or, literally, "circle of accumulation". Gathering the two accumulations of merit and wisdom is the supreme and indispensable method for clearing away the cloud of obscurations that prevent us from realizing our buddha nature. The practice of feast offerings is one of the most skillful ways to swiftly gather the accumulations and also purify our obscurations and mend our broken samayas. In many of Guru Rinpoche's treasure teachings, it says that performing feast offerings generates tremendous merit. There even have been many instances when Guru Rinpoche himself has appeared in person during feast offerings and blessed the practitioners who were calling upon him with unwavering devotion.

Although we all may be doing different sadhana practices, all of which have their own, individual feast offering texts, they all have the same benefits and the same purpose: gathering the accumulations of merit and wisdom and purifying our obscurations. For those of you performing feast offerings at sacred sites, and especially if it falls on Guru Rinpoche day (the tenth day of the lunar month) and Dakini day (the twenty-fifth day of the lunar month), I would like to make one simple suggestion: in order to create auspicious coincidences (*tendrel*) for yourself and others, it's very important to begin your practice by supplicating Guru Rinpoche with the Seven-Line Prayer. For those of you who are not yet familiar with the practice of feast offerings, simply reciting this prayer at least three times on those days will be extremely beneficial for your practice.

One of the treasure teaching revelations of Guru Chöwang, one of the five Tertön Kings, contains directions for supplicating Guru Rinpoche with the Seven-Line Prayer:

> Pray in this way over and over again. Create a feeling of yearning and longing so intense that tears spring from your eyes. If the rapture of devotion overwhelms you, breathe out strongly, and then leave everything as it is. Clear and awake, focused and undistracted, look within.[774]

When we talk about *the guru*, there are actually different levels of meaning: the outer, inner, and secret levels. The Seven-Line Prayer addresses the outer guru, who is symbolized or represented by the manifestation of Guru Rinpoche in a physical form. On the inner and the secret levels, though, the Seven-Line Prayer addresses, respectively, emptiness and co-emergent wisdom. Finally, no matter the practice you follow, be sure to seal your feast offering with the aspiration of bodhichitta: "May all sentient beings benefit tremendously from this feast offering, may the cloud of obscurations be cleared away, and may the blazing sun of wisdom shine through!"

After the offerings are finished, always make *aspirations*. What is your aspiration in doing this pilgrimage? What is your aspiration in sitting in front of Guru Rinpoche? You aspire to benefit all beings, to uphold the Dharma, and to reach enlightenment. So, we start by taking refuge, performing prostrations. Second, we generate our motivation. Third, we receive the siddhis, the blessings. Fourth, we pray and make offerings. Finally, of course, we dedicate the merit and make aspirations. We should continually remind ourselves to make aspirations that everything we do may not lead us astray from enlightenment, but rather lead us toward enlightenment. One sutra tells of how Buddha Shakyamuni counseled a King, saying, "O King, whether you are walking, sitting, talking, whatever you may do, never forget the aspiration for enlightenment. When you have this in mind, you will never go astray from the path."

There is a famous saying about the power of aspiration: "Guru Rinpoche resides upon the crown of all who have faith in him." Keep this in mind as you supplicate with devotion and make aspirations for rebirth in Zangdok Palri, the Glorious Copper-Colored Mountain. For a devoted practitioner, Zangdok Palri is truly present, here and now. There are many accounts of visionary journeys to the Glorious Copper-Colored Mountain by the great treasure revealers and by devoted students. Our bodies may be subject to time, but our minds are not. Therefore, if one truly has devotion, one can reach the Copper-Colored Mountain in a finger snap. Devotion is the key word here. Without devotion, one can neither receive blessings nor perceive the signs of blessings. Clear faith and devotion will dispel any doubts that arise during meditation practice, as these precious qualities endow our minds with trust and confidence.

My beloved root Gurus Kyabjé Tulku Urgyen Rinpoche, Kyabjé Nyoshul Khen Rinpoche and Kyabjé Soktse Rinpoche were both incredibly knowledgeable and scholarly. However, when they taught, the first thing they would say was, "If you do not have faith, devotion, or compassion, you're done. It's no use trying anything else." This was always the very first thing they taught. Therefore, please relax your critical mind and generate the mind of devotion and pure perception; then let the blessings of the sacred site seep down into the core of your being.

༄༅། །ཁྲ་མ་གསང་འདུས་ལས་གསུངས་པའི་ཚིག་བདུན་གསོལ་འདེབས་བཞུགས་སོ། །ཁྱད་པར་བླ་སྒྲུབ་ཚིག་

ACCOMPLISHING THE LAMA THROUGH THE SEVEN-LINE PRAYER: A SPECIAL TEACHING FROM THE LAMA SANGDÜ

Revealed by Guru Chöwang

The Seven-Line Prayer is the most famous and widely chanted of all prayers to Guru Padmasambhava. This, the original revelation, includes further instructions on how to invoke Guru Rinpoche through these seven lines.

ཕྱགས་འཚལ་བླ་མ་ཡི་དམ་ལྷ་ལ་ཕྱག་འཚལ་ལོ༔

Homage to the yidam deity! ༔

ཕྱི་རབས་སྐལ་ལྡན་རིགས་ཀྱི་བུ༔ ཨོ་རྒྱན་བདག་ལ་སྐྱབས་འཚོལ་ན༔ དབེན་པའི་གནས་སུ་རང་
འདུག་ནས༔ མི་རྟག་སྐྱོ་སྣང་བ་དང་༔ འཁོར་བས་སུན་པ་རབ་ཏུ་གཅེས༔

Fortunate men and women of the future, sons and daughters of enlightened family, when you turn to me, the Guru of Orgyen, for refuge, take yourself to an isolated place and arouse deep feelings of melancholy at impermanence and disgust with samsara. This is vital. ༔

བློ་སྙིང་བྲང་གསུམ་ང་ལ་གཏོད༔ གཞན་ཡང་སྐྱབས་གྱུར་རེ་ས་རྣམས༔
ཨོ་རྒྱན་བདག་ལ་རྟོགས་པར་སོམས༔ སྐྱིད་སྡུག་རེ་ལྟོས་ཁྱེད་ཤེས་ཀྱིས༔

Then, rely on me completely, heart and soul. Reflect how every kind of refuge and all your hopes are all fulfilled and complete within me, the Guru of Orgyen. Whether in happiness or in sorrow, have total trust and confidence in me. ༔

མཆོད་བསྟོད་མི་འཚལ་རྒྱ་གསོག་སྤོངས༔ ཕྱས་དག་ཡིད་གསུམ་གུས་པ་ཡིས༔ ཚིག་བདུན་འདི༔
ཡིས་གསོལ་བ་ཐོབ༔

There is no need to make offerings or praise. Set aside all accumulations. Simply let devotion flood your body, speech, and mind, and pray. Pray with these seven lines: ༔

ཧཱུྃ༔   ཨོ་རྒྱན་ཡུལ་གྱི་ནུབ་བྱང་མཚམས༔

hung ༔   orgyen yul gyi nupjang tsam ༔

Hung! ༔   In the northwest of the land of Uddiyana ༔

པདྨ་གེ་སར་སྡོང་པོ་ལ༔

pema gesar dongpo la ༔

In the heart of a lotus flower, ༔

ཡ་མཚན་མཆོག་གི་དངོས་གྲུབ་བརྙེས༔

yamtsen chok gi ngödrup nyé ༔

Endowed with the most marvellous attainments, ༔

པདྨ་འབྱུང་གནས་ཞེས་སུ་གྲགས༔

pema jungné zhé su drak ༔

You are renowned as the Lotus-Born, ༔

འཁོར་དུ་མཁའ་འགྲོ་མང་པོས་བསྐོར༔

khor du khandro mangpö kor ༔

Surrounded by many hosts of dakinis. ༔

ཁྱེད་ཀྱི་རྗེས་སུ་བདག་བསྒྲུབ་ཀྱི༔

khyé kyi jesu dak drup kyi ༔

Following in your footsteps, ༔

བྱིན་གྱིས་བརླབ་ཕྱིར་གཤེགས་སུ་གསོལ༔

jingyi lap chir shek su sol ༔

I pray to you, come, inspire me with your blessing! ༔

གུ་རུ་པདྨ་སིདྡྷི་ཧཱུྃ༔

guru pema siddhi hung ༔

guru pema siddhi hung ༔

ཞེས་པས་ཡང་ཡང་གསོལ་བ་ཐོབ༔

Pray in this way, over and over again. ༔

གདུང་བ་དྲག་བསྐྱེད་མཆི་མ་ཕྱུང་༔ དད་པས་ཁམས་འདུས་འབྱུང་ཤིད་ན༔

ཏུག་གིས་ཐོབ་ལ་ས་ལེར་ཞོག༔ སང་རེ་ཡེ་རེ་མ་ཡེངས་ལྟ༔

Create a feeling of yearning and longing so intense that tears spring from your eyes. If the rapture of devotion overwhelms you, breathe out strongly, and then leave everything as it is. Clear and awake, focused and undistracted, look within. ༔

འདི་ལྟར་གསོལ་བ་འདེབས་པའི་བུར༔ ང་ཡིས་སྐྱོབ་པ་སྨོས་ཅི་དགོས༔ དུས་གསུམ་རྒྱལ་བའི་སྲས༔ སུ་འགྱུར༔ དབང་ཆེན་རང་རིག་སེམས་ལ་ཐོབ༔ ཏིང་འཛིན་མཐུ་བཏུན་ཡེ་ཤེས་རྒྱས༔

For children of mine who pray like this, it goes without saying that they will have my protection, for they will be the sons and daughters of the buddhas of past, present, and future. They will receive complete empowerment into the awareness of their own enlightened mind. Their samadhi will be so powerful and stable that wisdom will naturally blossom and expand. ༔

བྱིན་རླབས་རང་བྱུང་ཆེན་པོ་ཡིས༔ རང་སྨིན་གཞན་སྨྱོད་སྡུག་བསྔལ་སེལ༔ རང་ཉིད་འགྱུར་ཚེ་གཞན༔ སྣང་རྣམས༔ དུས་མཉམ་འགྱུར་ཞིང་ཕྲིན་ལས་འགྲུབ༔ ཡོན་ཏན་ཐམས་ཅད་རང་ལ་རྫོགས༔

This great blessing, which arises of its own accord, will dispel all suffering that will ripen on you or be experienced by others. When your mind is transformed, others' perceptions will simultaneously change. You will accomplish enlightened activity, and all noble qualities will be complete within you. ༔

བདག་ཉིད་ཆེན་པོ་ཆོས་ཀྱི་སྐུར༔ སྨིན་ཅིང་གྲོལ་བའི་ཐབས་ཆེན་འདི༔ ཕྲགས་ཀྱི་སྲས་དང་འཕྲད་པར་ཤོག༔

May the sons and daughters of my heart meet with this extraordinary skillful means, one which ripens and liberates into the dharmakaya realization of my enlightened being. ༔

ཁྱད་པར་བྱིན་རླབས་ཀྱི་སྐྱབས་པ་ཆིག་བདུན་མའི་གསོལ་འདེབས་ཤིན་ཏུ་ཟབ་ཕྱིར་ཕྲགས་ཀྱི་ཡང་གཏེར་གསང་བར་གདམས་པ༔ ཤེས་རབ་བློ་ལྡན་སྙིང་རྗེ་ཆེ༔ ཆོས་ཀྱི་དབང་ཕྱུག་དེ་དང་འཕྲད་པར་ཤོག༔ ཅེས་སོ།། །།

A practice with a uniquely powerful blessing, the Seven Line Prayer is exceptionally profound; so let this instruction be an extremely secret treasure of my enlightened mind. May it meet with one who possesses a mind of wisdom, and is endowed with great compassion, called Chökyi Wangchuk.[775] ༔

༄༅། །བླ་མའི་རྣལ་འབྱོར་མདོར་བསྡུས་བཞུགས་སོ། །

A CONCISE GURU YOGA

— *Chokgyur Dechen Lingpa*

Beginning with a brief visualization, this concise guru yoga centers around the famous Prayer in Six Vajra Lines. After accumulating this prayer, the practitioner may wish to add any other prayers or mantras invoking Guru Padmasambhava, such as his vajra guru mantra. The guru yoga concludes with receiving the empowerments, dissolving the visualization, and reciting the brief Zangdok Palri Mönlam, an aspiration prayer to be reborn in Guru Rinpoche's pure land of the Copper-Colored Mountain. Since the Prayer in Six Vajra Lines and the Zangdok Palri Mönlam can be recited independently from this Guru Yoga, they are also presented individually in the pages that follow.

སྤྱི་གཙུག་པདྨ་ཉི་ཟླའི་སྟེང་། །

chitsuk pema nyidé teng

Above my head on a blossoming lotus and seat of sun and moon disc,

གུ་རུ་པདྨ་འབྱུང་གནས་ནི། །

guru pema jungné ni

Appears Guru Padmasambhava, the Lotus-Born,

རྒྱལ་ཀུན་འདུས་པའི་ངོ་བོར་བསམ། །

gyal kün düpé ngowor sam

Embodiment of all the Victorious Ones.

དུས་གསུམ་སངས་རྒྱས་གུ་རུ་རིན་པོ་ཆེ༔

düsum sangyé guru rinpoché ༔

Embodiment of buddhas of past, present, and future, Guru Rinpoche; ༔

དངོས་གྲུབ་ཀུན་བདག་བདེ་བ་ཆེན་པོའི་ཞབས༔

ngödrup kün dak dewa chenpö zhab ༔

Master of all siddhis, Guru of Great Bliss; ༔

བར་ཆད་ཀུན་སེལ་བདུད་འདུལ་དྲག་པོ་རྩལ༔

barché kün sel düdul drakpo tsal ༔

Dispeller of all obstacles, Wrathful Subjugator of Maras— ༔

གསོལ་བ་འདེབས་སོ་བྱིན་གྱིས་བརླབ་ཏུ་གསོལ༔

solwa dep so jingyi lap tu sol ༔

To you I pray: inspire me with your blessing ༔

ཕྱི་ནང་གསང་བའི་བར་ཆད་ཞི་བ་དང་༔

chi nang sangwé barché zhiwa dang ༔

So that outer, inner, and secret obstacles are dispelled ༔

བསམ་པ་ལྷུན་གྱིས་འགྲུབ་པར་བྱིན་གྱིས་རློབས༔

sampa lhün gyi drupar jingyi lob ༔

And all my aspirations are spontaneously fulfilled. ༔

གུ་རུའི་སྐུ་ཡི་གནས་བཞི་ནས། །

gurü ku yi ne zhi né

From the four centers on the Guru's body,

འོད་འཕྲོས་བདག་གི་གནས་བཞིར་ཐིམ། །

ö trö dak gi ne zhir tim

Light radiates out and dissolves into my four centers.

སྒྲིབ་བཞི་དག་ནས་དབང་བཞི་ཐོབ། །

drip zhi dak né wang zhi top

Through this, the four obscurations are purified, and I obtain the four empowerments.

འོད་ཞུ་རང་དང་གཉིས་མེད་འདྲེས། །

ö zhu rang dang nyimé dré

Guru Padmasambhava dissolves into light and becomes one with me,

བླ་མ་རང་སེམས་དབྱེར་མེད་བསྒོམ། །

lama rangsem yermé gom

And I meditate on the inseparable unity of the Guru and my own mind.

ཞེས་དགེ་སློང་ཚེ་དབང་བདེ་ཆེན་ངོར། མཆོག་གྱུར་གླིང་པས་བྲིས།།

This was written by Chokgyur Lingpa at the request of the monk Tsewang Dechen.

གདོད་མའི་གཤིས་དང་དབྱེར་མེད་པདྨ་འབྱུང་། །

dömé shi dang yermé pema jung

Padmasambhava, you are inseparable from the primordial nature.

རང་སྣང་དག་པའི་ཟངས་མདོག་དཔལ་རིའི་ཞིང་། །

rangnang dakpé zangdok palri zhing

Your realm, the Glorious Copper-Colored Mountain, is the purity of our own perception.

སྣང་རིག་དབྱེར་མེད་མ་བཅོས་གཉུག་མའི་ངང་། །

nang rik yermé machö nyukmé ngang

May we be born in this primordial pure realm,

གདོད་ནས་རྣམ་དག་ཞིང་དུ་སྐྱེ་བར་ཤོག །

döné namdak zhing du kyewar shok

The unfabricated natural state, the indivisibility of appearance and awareness!

ཅེས་རིམ་གཉིས་ཟབ་མོའི་རྣལ་འབྱོར་བླ་མ་བྱང་ཆུབ་བསྐུལ་ངོར། མཆོག་གྱུར་གླིང་པས་གང་ཤར་དོན་དམ་པར་སྒྱུར་ནས་བྲིས།།

To fulfill the request of Lama Changchup, a practitioner of the profound development and completion stages, I, Chokgyur Lingpa, wrote down whatever came to mind, while maintaining recognition of the absolute.[776]

ༀ། །ཀུ་རུའི་གསོལ་འདེབས་བསམ་པ་མྱུར་འགྲུབ་མ་བཞུགས་སོ། །

SAMPA NYUR DRUPMA—THE PRAYER THAT SWIFTLY FULFILLS ALL WISHES

— Omniscient Longchenpa and Rikdzin Jikmé Lingpa

This prayer to Guru Padmasambhava for the swift fulfillment of all wishes begins with a verse from Longchenpa's Khandro Yangtik, the Heart Essence of the Dakinis, and concludes with several verses written by Jikmé Lingpa. It is renowned for its power to pacify illness, prevent famine and invasions, and contribute to the welfare of the teachings and beings.

ཨེ་མ་ཧོ། མཚོ་དབུས་གེ་སར་པདྨའི་སྡོང་པོ་ལ། །

emaho, tso ü gesar pemé dongpo la

Emaho! In the heart of a blossoming lotus, upon the waters of a lake,

སྐུ་ལྔ་ཡེ་ཤེས་ལྷུན་གྱིས་གྲུབ་པའི་ལྷ། །

ku nga yeshé lhün gyi drupé lha

You are the deity who is the spontaneous presence of the five kayas and wisdoms.

རང་བྱུང་ཆེན་པོ་པདྨ་ཡབ་ཡུམ་ནི། །

rangjung chenpo pema yapyum ni

O great, naturally arisen Padma Yabyum,

མཁའ་འགྲོའི་སྤྲིན་ཕུང་འཁྲིགས་ལ་གསོལ་བ་འདེབས། །

khandrö trinpung trik la solwa dep

Surrounded by clouds of dakinis—to you we pray.

བསམ་པ་མྱུར་དུ་འགྲུབ་པར་བྱིན་གྱིས་རློབས། །

sampa nyurdu drupar jingyi lop

Grant your blessing so that all our wishes be quickly fulfilled!

ལས་ངན་སྤྱད་པའི་རྣམ་སྨིན་མ་ཐུས་བསྐྱེད་པའི། །

lé ngen chepé nammin tü kyepé

As a result of our negative karma, whenever we suffer

ནད་གདོན་བར་གཅོད་དམག་འཁྲུགས་མུ་གེ་སོགས། །

né dön barchö mak truk mugé sok

From illness, malevolent spirits, döns and obstacles, warfare and violence,
famine and starvation,

ཁྱོད་ཞལ་དྲན་པའི་མོད་ལ་ཟད་བྱེད་པའི། །

khyö zhal drenpé möla zé jepé

Then remember your promise that even simply to think of you will
immediately dissolve all such suffering.

ཞལ་བཞེས་སྙིང་ནས་བསྐུལ་ལོ་ཨོ་རྒྱན་རྗེ། །

zhalzhé nying né kul lo orgyen jé

O Lord of Orgyen, we implore you from the depths of our hearts,

བསམ་པ་མྱུར་དུ་འགྲུབ་པར་བྱིན་གྱིས་རློབས། །

sampa nyurdu drupar jingyi lop

Grant your blessing so that all our wishes be quickly fulfilled!

དད་དང་ཚུལ་ཁྲིམས་གཏོང་ལ་གོམས་པ་དང་། །

dé dang tsultrim tong la gompa dang

To practice devotion, discipline, and generosity,

ཐོས་པས་རྒྱུད་གྲོལ་ཁྲེལ་ཡོད་དོ་ཚ་ཤེས། །

töpé gyü drol trelyö ngotsa shé

To free the mind through hearing the Dharma, and to have dignity,
self-control,

ཤེས་རབ་ཕུན་སུམ་ཚོགས་པའི་ནོར་བདུན་པོ། །

sherap pünsum tsokpé nor dünpo

And discriminating awareness—make these seven, noble human qualities

སེམས་ཅན་ཀུན་གྱི་རྒྱུད་ལ་རང་ཞུགས་ནས། །

semchen kün gyi gyü la rang zhuk né

Fill the hearts and minds of all sentient beings

འཇིག་རྟེན་བདེ་སྐྱིད་ལྡན་པར་དབུགས་འབྱིན་མཛོད། །

jikten dekyi denpar ukjin dzö

And so bring peace and happiness to the world.

བསམ་པ་མྱུར་དུ་འགྲུབ་པར་བྱིན་གྱིས་རློབས། །

sampa nyurdu drupar jingyi lob

Grant your blessing so that all our wishes be quickly fulfilled!

གང་ལ་ནད་དང་སྡུག་བསྔལ་མི་འདོད་རྐྱེན། །

gangla né dang dukngal mindö kyen

When oppressed by illness, suffering, and unwanted circumstances,

འབྱུང་པོའི་གདོན་དང་རྒྱལ་པོས་ཆད་པ་དང་། །

jungpö dön dang gyalpö chepa dang

Falling prey to harm from negative forces and punishment from Kings and leaders,

མེ་ཆུ་གཅན་གཟན་ལམ་འཕྲང་འཇིགས་པ་ཆེས། །

mé chu chenzen lamtrang jikpa ché

Threatened by fire, water, vicious animals, and journeys of great danger,

ཚེ་ཡི་ཕ་མཐར་གཏུགས་པའི་གནས་སྐབས་ཀུན། །

tsé yi patar tukpé nekap kün

When this life is spent and death arrives—at these times

སྐྱབས་དང་རེ་ས་གཞན་དུ་མ་མཆིས་པས། །

kyap dang resa zhendu machipé

We have nowhere to turn except to you!

ཐུགས་རྗེས་ཟུངས་ཤིག་གུ་རུ་ཨོ་རྒྱན་རྗེ། །

tukjé zung shik guru orgyen jé

Care for us with your great compassion, O Great Orgyen Guru!

བསམ་པ་མྱུར་དུ་འགྲུབ་པར་བྱིན་གྱིས་རློབས། །

sampa nyurdu drupar jingyi lop

Grant your blessing so that all our wishes be quickly fulfilled!

ཞེས་བོད་ཁམས་ནད་མུག་མཐའ་དམག་ཞི་ཞིང་བསྟན་འགྲོའི་བདེ་སྐྱིད་གསོ་བར་ཕན་ན་སྐྱམ་པ་དད་ལྡན་རྣམས་ཀྱིས་ཐུགས་ལ་གཞུག

This prayer should be kept in the hearts of all those with faith, who wish to benefit the land of Tibet, pacify illness, prevent famine and border invasions, and contribute to the welfare of the teachings and beings.

ཅེས་པ་འདིའི་ཚིག་ག་དང་པོ་ཀུན་མཁྱེན་ཀློང་ཆེན་པའི་མཁའ་འགྲོ་ཡང་ཏིག་གི་རྒྱབ་ཆོས་ཟབ་དོན་རྒྱ་མཚོའི་སྤྲིན་ཕུང་གི་མཆོད་བརྗོད་ལས་བྱུང་ཞིང་། དེ་ཕྱིན་ཀུན་མཁྱེན་གཉིས་པ་རིག་འཛིན་འཇིགས་མེད་གླིང་པའི་རྡོ་རྗེའི་གསུང་བྱིན་རླབས་ཅན་ནོ། །

The first stanza is taken from the verses of praise in the *Infinite Cloud Banks of Profound Meaning* (*Zabdön Gyatsö Trinpung*), the background teachings to the omniscient Longchenpa's *Khandro Yangtik*; and the later verses are the blessed vajra words of the second omniscient one, Rikdzin Jikmé Lingpa.[777]

༄༅། །བསམ་ལྷུན་བསྒྲུབས་པ་ཕྱགས་རྗེའི་གློག་ཞགས་བཞུགས་སོ། །

THE LIGHTNING BOLT OF COMPASSION— A PRAYER THAT SPONTANEOUSLY FULFILLS ALL WISHES

— Do Khyentsé Yeshé Dorjé

This is a condensed version of the famous Barché Lamsel, a prayer for the elimination of all obstacles on the spiritual path.

ཨེ་མ་ཧོཿ   དཀོན་མཆོག་རྩ་གསུམ་བདེ་གཤེགས་ཀུན་འདུས་དཔལ།   །
emaho könchok tsa sum deshek kündü pal
Emaho: O wonder! O Guru Rinpoche, in your glory you embody Buddha, Dharma, and Sangha; lama, yidam and khandro; and all the sugatas.

སྙིགས་དུས་འགྲོ་བ་མགོན་མེད་སྐྱབས་གཅིག་པུ།   །
nyikdü drowa gönmé kyap chikpu
You are the sole refuge of beings, without protection in this dark age.

ཐུགས་རྗེ་གློག་ལྟར་མྱུར་བའི་ཐོད་ཕྲེང་རྩལ།   །
tukjé lok tar nyurwé tötreng tsal
Your compassion is as swift as lightning, Tötreng Tsal.

མ་ཧཱ་གུ་རུ་པདྨ་ཧེ་རུ་ཀར།   །
maha guru pema herukar
Mahaguru, wrathful Padma Heruka,

མོས་གུས་གདུང་ཤུགས་དྲག་པོས་གསོལ་བ་འདེབས།   །
mögü dungshuk drakpö solwa dep
With fervent longing and devotion, we pray to you.

དགྲ་གདོན་བགེགས་དང་བར་ཆད་བྱུད་ཕྱུར་བྲློགས།   །
dra dön gek dang barché jepur dok
Avert enemies, döns, obstructing forces, obstacle makers, curses and spells.

མ་རུངས་རྒྱལ་བསེན་འབྱུང་པོ་དམ་ལ་ཐོག །

marung gyal sen jungpo dam la tok

Bring all negative forces, gyalpo, senmo, and jungpo demons under your subjugation.

བསམ་པ་ལྷུན་གྱིས་འགྲུབ་པར་བྱིན་གྱིས་རློབས། །

sampa lhün gyi druppar jingyi lob

Grant your blessings so that all our wishes be spontaneously fulfilled.

ཞེས་པ་འདི་ཡང་དུས་རྟགས་མཚོན་གྱུར་གྱི་སྐབས་སུ་འཕགས་ཡུམ་སྲས་ཀྱི་ཐུགས་བཞེད་ལྟར་ཕུགས་ གཏེར་འཛིན་ལུས་རྡོ་རྗེས་སྨྲས་སོ། །

When the signs of the times became apparent, at the request of the noble consort and son, Jalü Dorjé uttered this, as a treasure from his wisdom mind.[778]

༄༅། །བར་ཆད་ལམ་སེལ་ཤིན་ཏུ་བསྡུས་པ་བཞུགས་སོ། །

A VERY BRIEF BARCHÉ LAMSEL—
THE PRAYER FOR CLEARING OBSTACLES
FROM THE PATH

— Do Khyentsé Yeshé Dorjé

This is a condensed version of the famous Barché Lamsel, a prayer for the elimination of all obstacles on the spiritual path.

ཨོཾ་ཨཱཿ་ཧཱུྃཿ   ཆོས་སྐུ་སྣང་མཐའ་ལོངས་སྐུ་སྤྱན་རས་གཟིགས། །
om ah hung, chöku nangta longku chenrezik
Om ah hung! Dharmakaya Amitabha, sambhogakaya Avalokiteshvara,

སྤྲུལ་སྐུ་པདྨ་འབྱུང་གནས་དྲག་པོ་རྩལ། །
tulku pema jungné drakpo tsal
Nirmanakaya Padmasambhava, wrathful Drakpo Tsal,

གསོལ་བ་འདེབས་སོ་ཐུགས་རྗེའི་ཤུགས་ཆུང་ལ། །
solwa dep so tukjé shuk chung la
We pray to you. With the force of your compassion,

ཕྱི་ནང་གསང་བའི་བར་ཆད་དབྱིངས་སུ་སོལ། །
chi nang sangwé barché ying su sol
Dissolve all obstacles, outer, inner, and secret, into space!

དུས་ངན་སྙིགས་མའི་འགྲོ་བ་སྡུག་བསྔལ་ཚེ། །
dü ngen nyikmé drowa dukngal tsé
When beings suffer in this decadent dark age,

ཁྱེད་ལས་རེ་ས་མེད་དོ་སྙིང་ཁོང་ནས། །
khyé lé resa mé do nying khong né
We have no other hope but you. From the depth of our hearts,

མོས་གུས་གདུང་བས་ལྷང་ལྷང་གསོལ་བ་འདེབས། །

mögü dungwé lhang lhang solwa dep

With fervent devotion and longing, urgently we pray.

འགལ་རྐྱེན་ཕྱི་ནང་གསང་བའི་བར་ཆད་བཟློག །

galkyen chi nang sangwé barché dok

Avert bad circumstances, outer, inner, and secret obstacles.

ཚེ་བསོད་དཔལ་ལ་རླུང་རྟ་དར་རྒྱས་ཤོག །

tsé sö pel la lungta dargyé shok

Let our life span and merit increase, and our vitality strengthen and grow!

ཅེས་པའང་གཏེར་མིང་འཛིན་པ་འཇའ་ལུས་རྡོ་རྗེས་སོ། །

By the one who holds the name of a treasure revealer, Jalü Dorjé.[779]

༁ཿ །གསོལ་འདེབས་དངོས་གྲུབ་ཀུན་འབྱུང་བཞུགས་སོ། །

THE SOURCE OF ALL TRUE REALIZATION

— Jamgön Mipham Rinpoche

This is a short prayer to the eight manifestations of Guru Padmasambhava, the eight vidyadharas, the eight Bodhisattvas, and the eight Kagyé deities.

སྤྲུལ་པའི་གུ་རུ་མཚན་བརྒྱད་དང་། །
trulpé guru tsen gyé dang
To the eight manifestations of Guru Rinpoche,

གྲུབ་པའི་རིག་འཛིན་ཆེན་པོ་བརྒྱད། །
drupé rikdzin chenpo gyé
The eight great accomplished vidyadharas,

བྱང་སེམས་ཉེ་བའི་སྲས་བརྒྱད་དང་། །
changsem nyewé sé gyé dang
The eight great bodhisattvas,

སྒྲུབ་ཆེན་བཀའ་བརྒྱད་ལྷ་ཚོགས་ལ། །
drupchen kagyé lhatsok la
And the eight mandalas of Kagyé with all their deities,

གསོལ་བ་འདེབས་སོ་བྱིན་གྱིས་རློབས། །
solwa dep so jingyi lop
To all of you we pray—inspire us with your blessings!

ཕྱི་ནང་གསང་བའི་བར་ཆད་སོལ། །
chi nang sangwé barché sol
Dispel all obstacles outer, inner, and secret!

བསམ་པ་ཡིད་བཞིན་འགྲུབ་པ་དང་། །

sampa yizhin drupa dang

Fulfill all our aspirations!

མཆོག་དང་ཐུན་མོང་དངོས་གྲུབ་སྩོལ། །

chok dang tünmong ngödrup tsol

Grant us attainments ordinary and supreme!

གསེར་འཕྱུང་མེ་བྱ་སྨིན་ཟླའི་དམར་ཕྱོགས་དགའ་བ་དང་པོའི་ཉིནར་ལ་འཇམ་དཔལ་རྡོ་རྗེའི་ཡིད་མཚོ་ལས་བརྡོལ་བའོ། །

This arose from the lake of the mind of Jampal Dorjé at dawn on the first day of the waning moon of the month of Pleiades in the Fire Bird Year (1897).[780]

༄༅། །རྡོ་རྗེ་ཚིག་རྐང་དྲུག་གི་གསོལ་འདེབས་བཞུགས་སོ། །

THE PRAYER IN SIX VAJRA LINES

—Revealed by Chokgyur Dechen Lingpa

Popularly known also as the Düsum Sangyé, this prayer is a key supplication to Guru Padmasambhava. It is seen as the distillation of all the most important of the Guru's Tukdrup, or Heart Practices, revealed by Chokgyur Lingpa. It carries immense blessings and is an incredibly swift supplication intended specifically for our time. Chanting these six lines alone is equivalent to reciting the entirety of Chokgyur Lingpa's Heart Practice cycles. As we recite them, we request Guru Padmasambhava to bless us, to remove all outer, inner, and secret obstacles, and to fulfill all of our prayers and wishes.

དུས་གསུམ་སངས་རྒྱས་གུ་རུ་རིན་པོ་ཆེ༔

düsum sangyé guru rinpoché ༔

Embodiment of buddhas of past, present, and future, Guru Rinpoche; ༔

དངོས་གྲུབ་ཀུན་བདག་བདེ་བ་ཆེན་པོའི་ཞབས༔

ngödrup kün dak dewa chenpö zhab ༔

Master of all siddhis, Guru of Great Bliss; ༔

བར་ཆད་ཀུན་སེལ་བདུད་འདུལ་དྲག་པོ་རྩལ༔

barché kün sel düdul drakpo tsal ༔

Dispeller of all obstacles, Wrathful Subjugator of Maras— ༔

གསོལ་བ་འདེབས་སོ་བྱིན་གྱིས་བརླབ་ཏུ་གསོལ༔

solwa dep so jingyi lap tu sol ༔

To you I pray: inspire me with your blessing ༔

ཕྱི་ནང་གསང་བའི་བར་ཆད་ཞི་བ་དང་༔

chi nang sangwé barché zhiwa dang ༔

So that outer, inner, and secret obstacles are dispelled ༔

བསམ་པ་ལྷུན་གྱིས་འགྲུབ་པར་བྱིན་གྱིས་རློབས༔

sampa lhün gyi drupar jingyi lob ༔

And all my aspirations are spontaneously fulfilled. ༔

ཞེས་གཏེར་ཆེན་མཆོག་གྱུར་བདེ་ཆེན་གླིང་པས་སེང་ཆེན་གནམ་བྲག་གི་གཡས་ཟུར་བྲག་རི་རིན་ཆེན་བརྩེགས་པ་ནས་སྤྱན་དྲངས་པའི་དུས་བབས་ཀྱི་གསོལ་འདེབས་འདི་ཉིད་བྱིན་རླབས་ཤིན་ཏུ་ཆེ་བས་ཀུན་གྱིས་ཁ་ཏོན་དུ་གཅེས་པར་ཟུངས་ཤིག །

Discovered by the great treasure revealer Chokgyur Dechen Lingpa, from the right-hand side of the Sengchen Namdrak rock on Mount Rinchen Tsekpa, 'The Pile of Jewels.' Because the blessing of this prayer, one intended for this present time, is so immense, it should be treasured by all as their daily practice.[781]

༄༅། །ཨོ་རྒྱན་རིན་པོ་ཆེར་གསོལ་འདེབས་བཞུགས་སོ། །

THE PRAYER TO GURU RINPOCHE
FOR ATTAINMENTS

— The First Dodrupchen Rinpoche

This four-line prayer is among the most popular to Guru Padmasambhava, and it is usually added to the end of the Prayer in Six Vajra Lines, featured above. In the colophon, the First Dodrupchen, Jigmé Trinlé Özer, declares that it was spoken by the Mahaguru himself during a visionary encounter.

ཨོ་རྒྱན་རིན་པོ་ཆེ་ལ་གསོལ་བ་འདེབས། །

orgyen rinpoché la solwa dep

To Orgyen Rinpoche we pray!

འགལ་རྐྱེན་བར་ཆད་མི་འབྱུང་ཞིང་། །

galkyen barché minjung zhing

Grant us, without impediment or obstacles arising,

མཐུན་རྐྱེན་བསམ་པ་འགྲུབ་པ་དང་། །

tünkyen sampa drupa dang

Favorable circumstances, the fulfillment of our aspirations,

མཆོག་དང་ཐུན་མོང་དངོས་གྲུབ་སྩོལ། །

chok dang tünmong ngödrup tsol

And attainments, ordinary and supreme.

ཅེས་པ་འདི་ནི་གྲུབ་ཆེན་རིན་པོ་ཆེ་འཇིགས་མེད་ཕྲིན་ལས་འོད་ཟེར་མཁའ་སྤྱོད་དཔལ་གྱི་ཙ་རི་ཏྲ་ཕེབས་ སྐབས་སྤྲུལ་དཔོན་རིན་པོ་ཆེ་ཞལ་གཟིགས་པའི་དུས་ཕོལ་བྱུང་དུ་གསུངས་པའི་གསོལ་འདེབས་བྱིན་རླབས་ ཅན་ནོ། མངྒ་ལོ། །

The precious master, Guru Padmasambhava, appeared in a vision to Dodrupchen Rinpoche, Jikmé Trinlé Özer, while he was visiting Khachö Palgyi Tsaridra. Immediately, he spoke the words of this prayer; such is its blessing. Mangalam![782]

THE ASPIRATION OF THE VAJRADHATU MANDALA

—*Revealed by Chokgyur Dechen Lingpa*

Guru Padmasambhava recited this dedication and aspiration prayer in the turquoise chamber on the second floor of Samyé on the occasion of opening the Vajradhatu mandala. The text was later discovered as a treasure by Chokgyur Dechen Lingpa and transcribed by Jamgön Kongtrul.

ན་མོ་གུ་རུ༔

Namo Guru! ༔

སྐྱེལ་ལོ་སྐྱིལ་སྟར་བའི་ཆོས་བཅུ་ལ༔   བསམ་ཡས་བར་ཁང་གཡུ་ཞལ་ཅན་དུ་ཇོ༔ དྲུ་ཙེ་རྡོ་རྗེ་དབྱིངས་ཀྱི་དཀྱིལ་
འཁོར་ནས་ཕྱེས་ཚེ་ཨོ་རྒྱན་གྱིས་སྨོན་ལམ་འདི་གསུངས་པས་རྗེ་འབངས་ཐམས་ཅད་ཀྱིས་ཐུགས་དམ་ནར་
མར་མཛད༔   ཕྱི་རབས་རྣམས་ཀྱིས་འདི་ལ་ཕུགས་དམ་རྩེ་གཅིག་ཏུ་མཛོད༔

On the tenth day of the Monkey month of the Monkey Year, the Guru of Uddiyana said this aspiration prayer in the Turquoise-Covered Shrine on the second floor of Samyé, at the time of opening the Vajradhatu mandala. The King and his subjects made it their constant heart practice. Future generations should also maintain it one-pointedly. ༔

ཕྱོགས་བཅུ་དུས་བཞིའི་རྒྱལ་བ་སྲས་དང་བཅས༔

chok chu dü zhi gyalwa sé dang ché ༔

Buddhas and bodhisattva, heirs of the ten directions and the four times, ༔

བླ་མ་ཡི་དམ་མཁའ་འགྲོ་ཆོས་སྐྱོང་ཚོགས༔

lama yidam khandro chö kyong tsok ༔

Lama, yidam, khandro, and the hosts of dharmapalas who guard the teachings, ༔

མ་ལུས་ཞིང་གི་རྡུལ་སྙེད་གཤེགས་སུ་གསོལ༔

malü zhing gi dul nyé zhek su sol ༔

All of you without exception, as numerous as the atoms in the universe, please come here ༔

མདུན་གྱི་ནམ་མཁར་པད་ཟླའི་གདན་ལ་བཞུགས༔

dün gyi namkhar pe dé den la zhuk ༔

In the space in front of me and take your seats on these cushions of lotus and moon. ༔

ལུས་ངག་ཡིད་གསུམ་གུས་པས་ཕྱག་འཚལ་ལོ༔

lü ngak yi sum güpé chaktsal lo ༔

I pay homage with devotion in body, speech, and mind. ༔

ཕྱི་ནང་གསང་བ་དེ་བཞིན་ཉིད་ཀྱིས་མཆོད༔

chi nang sangwa dézhin nyi kyi chö ༔

I make outer, inner, and secret offerings and the offering of suchness. ༔

རྟེན་མཆོག་བདེ་གཤེགས་རྣམས་ཀྱི་སྤྱན་སྔ་རུ༔

ten chok dezhek nam kyi chen nga ru ༔

In the presence of the supreme support, the sugatas, ༔

སྔོན་གྱི་སྡིག་པའི་ཚོགས་ལ་བདག་གནོང་ཞིང་༔

ngön gyi dikpé tsok la dak nong zhing ༔

I feel remorse for all my accumulated negative actions of the past; ༔

ད་ལྟའི་མི་དགེ་འགྱོད་པས་རབ་ཏུ་བཤགས༔

daté migé gyöpé rap tu zhak ༔

And with regret, I confess my present nonvirtues. ༔

ཕྱིན་ཆད་དེ་ལས་ལྡོག་ཕྱིར་བདག་གིས་དམ༔

chinché dé lé dok chir dak gi dam ༔

From now on, I vow to turn away from them all. ༔

བསོད་ནམས་དགེ་ཚོགས་ཀུན་ལ་ཡི་རང་ངོ༔

sönam gé tsok kun la yirang ngo ༔

I rejoice in all accumulations of virtue and merit. ༔

རྒྱལ་བའི་ཚོགས་རྣམས་མྱ་ངན་མི་འདའ་བར༔

gyalwé tsok nam nyangen midawar ༔

I beseech all the Victorious Ones not to pass beyond sorrow, ༔

སྡེ་སྣོད་གསུམ་དང་བླ་མེད་ཆོས་འཁོར་བསྐོར༔

dénö sum dang lamé chö khor kor ༔

But to turn the Wheel of the three pitakas and of the unsurpassed Dharma. ༔

དགེ་ཚོགས་མ་ལུས་འགྲོ་བའི་རྒྱུད་ལ་བསྔོ༔

gé tsok malü drowé gyü la ngo ༔

I dedicate all accumulations of virtue, without exception, to the minds of beings. ༔

འགྲོ་རྣམས་བླ་མེད་ཐར་པའི་སར་ཕྱིན་ཤོག༔

dro nam lamé tarpé sar chin zhok ༔

May they all reach the ground of unsurpassable liberation! ༔

སངས་རྒྱས་སྲས་བཅས་བདག་ལ་དགོངས་སུ་གསོལ༔

sangyé sé ché dak la gong su sol ༔

Buddhas and their bodhisattva heirs, turn your attention toward me! ༔

བདག་གིས་བཙམ་པའི་སྨོན་ལམ་རབ་བཟང་འདི༔

dak gi tsampé mönlam rapzang di ༔

May this excellent aspiration that I am now making ༔

རྒྱལ་བ་ཀུན་ཏུ་བཟང་དང་དེ་སྲས་དང་༔

gyalwa kuntuzang dang dé sé dang ༔

Emulate the prayers ༔

འཕགས་པ་འཇམ་དཔལ་དབྱངས་ཀྱིས་མཁྱེན་པ་ལྟར༔

pakpa jampalyang kyi khyenpa tar ༔

Of the victorious Samantabhadra with his bodhisattva heirs, ༔

དེ་དག་ཀུན་གྱི་རྗེས་སུ་བདག་སློབ་ཤོག༔

dédak kun gyi jésu dak lop zhok ༔

And noble Manjughosha's omniscient wisdom. ༔

བསྟན་པའི་དཔལ་གྱུར་བླ་མ་རིན་ཆེན་རྣམས༔

tenpé palgyur lama rinchen nam ༔

May the precious lamas, the glory of the teachings,༔

ནམ་མཁའ་བཞིན་དུ་ཀུན་ལ་ཁྱབ་པར་ཤོག། ༔

namkha zhintu kun la khyapar zhok ༔

Pervade everywhere like space itself ༔

ཉི་ཟླ་བཞིན་དུ་ཀུན་ལ་གསལ་བར་ཤོག། ༔

nyi da zhintu kun la selwar zhok ༔

And illuminate everything like the sun and moon. ༔

རི་བོ་བཞིན་དུ་རྟག་དུ་བརྟན་པར་ཤོག། ༔

riwo zhintu taktu tenpar zhok ༔

May they always be with us, steadfast like mountains. ༔

བསྟན་པའི་གཞི་མ་དགེ་འདུན་རིན་པོ་ཆེ༔

tenpé zhima gendun rinpoché ༔

May the precious Sangha, the bedrock of the teachings, ༔

ཐུགས་མཐུན་ཁྲིམས་གཙང་བསླབ་གསུམ་གྱིས་ཕྱུག་ཤོག། ༔

tuk tün trim tsang lap sum gyi chuk zhok ༔

Remain in harmony, maintain pure discipline, and be rich in the three higher trainings. ༔

བསྟན་པའི་སྙིང་པོ་གསང་སྔགས་སྒྲུབ་པའི་སྡེ༔

tenpé nyingpo sang ngak drubpé dé ༔

May the practitioners of the secret mantrayana, the heart of the teachings, ༔

དམ་ཚིག་ལྡན་ཞིང་བསྐྱེད་རྫོགས་མཐར་ཕྱིན་ཤོག། ༔

damtsik den zhing kyé dzok tarchin zhok ༔

Keep their samaya commitments and perfect the generation and completion stages. ༔

བསྟན་པའི་སྦྱིན་བདག་ཆོས་སྐྱོང་རྒྱལ་པོ་ཡང་༔

tenpé jindak chökyong gyalpo yang ༔

For the King who protects the Dharma, the benefactor of the teachings, ༔

ཆབ་སྲིད་རྒྱས་ཤིང་བསྟན་ལ་སྨན་པར་ཤོག། ༔

chapsi gyé zhing ten la menpar zhok ༔

May his kingdom flourish and may he be of benefit to the Dharma. ༔

བསྟན་པའི་ཞབས་འདེགས་རྒྱལ་རིགས་བློན་པོ་ཡང་ །

tenpé zhap dek gyal rik lönpo yang ༔

May those who serve the teachings, warriors and ministers, ༔

བློ་གྲོས་རབ་འཕེལ་རྩལ་དང་ལྡན་པར་ཤོག ༔

lodrö rap pel tsal dang denpar zhok ༔

Possess increasing skills and supreme intelligence. ༔

བསྟན་པའི་གསོས་བྱེད་ཁྱིམ་བདག་འབྱོར་ལྡན་རྣམས ༔

tenpé söjé khyimdak jorden nam ༔

May the wealthy householders who sustain the teachings ༔

ལོངས་སྤྱོད་ལྡན་ཞིང་ཉེར་འཚེ་མེད་པར་ཤོག ༔

longchö den zhing nyertsé mépar zhok ༔

Be prosperous and always free from harm. ༔

བསྟན་ལ་དད་པའི་ཡངས་པའི་རྒྱལ་ཁམས་ཀུན ༔

tenpa dépé yangpé gyalkham kun ༔

May all Buddhist nations, where there is faith in the teachings, ༔

བདེ་སྐྱིད་ལྡན་ཞིང་བར་ཆད་ཞི་བར་ཤོག ༔

dékyi den zhing barché zhiwar zhok ༔

Enjoy happiness and well-being, with all obstacles pacified. ༔

ལམ་ལ་གནས་པའི་རྣལ་འབྱོར་བདག་ཉིད་ཀྱང་ ༔

lam la népé naljor daknyi kyang ༔

And for me, this yogi on the path, ༔

དམ་ཚིག་མི་ཉམས་བསམ་པ་འགྲུབ་པར་ཤོག ༔

damtsik minyam sampa drupar zhok ༔

May my samaya never decline, and may my wishes be fulfilled. ༔

བདག་ལ་བཟང་ངན་ལས་ཀྱིས་འབྲེལ་གྱུར་གང་ ༔

dak la zang ngen lé kyi drel gyur gang ༔

May whoever makes a connection with me, through positive or negative karma, ༔

གནས་སྐབས་མཐར་ཐུག་རྒྱལ་བས་རྗེས་འཛིན་ཤོག །

nékap tartuk gyalwé jédzin zhok

Always be blessed by the buddhas' care,

འགྲོ་རྣམས་བླ་མེད་ཐེག་པའི་སྒོར་ཞུགས་ནས། །

dronam lamé tekpé gor zhuk né

And may all beings cross the gate of the supreme vehicle

ཀུན་བཟང་རྒྱལ་སྲིད་ཆེན་པོ་ཐོབ་པར་ཤོག །

kunzang gyalsi chenpo topar zhok

And reach Samantabhadra's great kingdom.

དེ་ལྟར་གྱི་སྨོན་ལམ་དུས་དྲུག་ཏུ་བརྗོན་པར་བྱ༔   ས་མ་ཡ༔

You should practice this aspiration diligently at the six times of the day. Samaya. Gya.

སྤྲུལ་སྐུ་རུ་དྲག་རྣམས་འཕུལ་གཏེར་ཆེན་མཆོག་གྱུར་བདེ་ཆེན་གླིང་པས་གནས་མཆོག་སེང་ཆེན་གནམ་བྲག་
གཡས་ཟུར་བྲག་རི་རིན་ཆེན་བརྩེགས་པའི་གོང་མོ་འོག་མ་ནས་ཁྲོམ་གཏེར་དུ་སྤྱན་དྲངས་པའི་ཡི་གེའི་སྲ་
ཆོས་དར་ཤོག་ངོས་མཆོག་རྒྱལ་ཕྲུག་ཡེ་ཤེས་འཕྱུར་མ་ལས། དེ་འཕྲལ་ཉིད་དུ་པདྨ་གར་དབང་བློ་
གྲོས་མཐའ་ཡས་ཀྱིས་དག་པར་བཀུས་པ་དགེ་ལེགས་འཕེལ།། ‖

The great *tertön* Chokgyur Dechen Lingpa, who was an emanation of Prince Murub Tsenpo, revealed this treasure publicly, below the peak of Drakri Rinchen Tsekpa, Precious Rocky Mountain, on the right-hand edge of the most sublime place, Sengchen Namdrak, Great Lion Sky Rock. The *terma* was originally written down by Yeshé Tsogyal in formal Tibetan handwriting upon silk paper made from the Dharma robe of Vairotsana, and was immediately and perfectly transcribed by Pema Garwang Lodrö Thayé upon discovery. May virtue and well-being increase and spread! [783]

༄༅། །ཨ་རྟུ་གུ་རུ་གསོལ་འདེབས་བཞུགས་སོ། །

THE MAHAGURU ASPIRATION

Revealed by Pema Lingpa

This aspiration prayer made by Khandro Yeshé Tsogyal, the Mahaguru's closest disciple, holds great blessings. It is highly treasured by many great masters and widely recited amongst the followers of the Mahaguru to this present day.

ན་མོ་གུ་རུ༔

Namo Guru: homage to the Guru! ༔

སློབ་དཔོན་ཆེན་པོ་པདྨ་འབྱུང་གནས་ལྷོ་ནུབ་སྲིན་པོའི་ཡུལ་དུ་གཤེགས་པའི་དུས༔ མང་ཡུལ་གུང་ཐང་ལ་ཐོག་ཏུ་ཡེ་ཤེས་མཚོ་རྒྱལ་གྱིས་ཕྱག་དང་བསྐོར་བ་བྱས༔ གུ་རུའི་ཞབས་ལ་སྤྱི་བོར་བླངས་ནས་སྨོན་ལམ་འདི་ལྟར་བཏབ་པ༔

The great master Padmasambhava was on the verge of leaving Tibet for the south-west and the land of the rakhasas, when, high on the Gungthang Pass in Mangyul, Yeshé Tsogyal prostrated and circumambulated him. Then she touched the crown of her head to his feet, and made this prayer of aspiration:

མ་ཧཱ་གུ་རུའི་བྱིན་རླབས་ཀྱིས༔

maha gurü jinlap kyi ༔

Mahaguru, bless me ༔

བདག་ཀྱང་ཚེ་རབས་ཐམས་ཅད་དུ༔

dak kyang tserap tamché du ༔

So that in all my lives to come, ༔

ཞིང་ཁམས་དག་པའི་ཕོ་བྲང་དུ༔

zhingkham dakpé podrang du ༔

In the palace in your pure land, ༔

བླ་མ་འབྲལ་མེད་བསྟེན་པར་ཤོག༔

lama dralmé tenpar zhok ༔

I may be always at your side, master, never apart from you. ༔

མོས་གུས་བརྟེམས་རྐྱང་མེད་པ་ཡིས༔

mögü tem kyang mepa yi ༔

With unswerving devotion, ༔

མཉེས་པའི་ཞབས་ཏོག་འགྲུབ་པ་དང་༔

nyepé zhaptok drupa dang ༔

I will serve you and please you ༔

དགོངས་པ་ཟབ་མོ་ཐུགས་ཀྱི་བཅུད༔

gongpa zapmo tuk kyi chü ༔

And receive, as nectar, the transmission of your blessing, ༔

བྱིན་རླབས་བདུད་རྩིའི་ལུང་ཐོབ་ཤོག༔

jinlap dütsi lung top zhok ༔

Your profound realization, the very essence of your wisdom mind. ༔

སྐུ་གསུང་ཐུགས་ཀྱི་བྱིན་རླབས་ཀྱིས༔

ku sung tuk kyi jinlap kyi ༔

Let the blessings of your enlightened body, speech, and mind ༔

ལུས་ངག་ཡིད་གསུམ་སྨིན་པ་དང་༔

lü ngak yi sum minpa dang ༔

Ripen my own body, speech, and mind ༔

ཟབ་མོའི་བསྐྱེད་རྫོགས་རྣམ་གཉིས་ལ༔

zapmö kyedzok nam nyi la ༔

So that I gain mastery over the profound ༔

དབང་ཐོབ་སྒྲུབ་པ་བྱེད་པར་ཤོག༔

wang top drupa jepar zhok ༔

Stages of generation and completion. ༔

ལོག་ཏོག་བདུད་ཀྱི་ཚོགས་རྣམས་དང་༔

loktok dü kyi tsok nam dang ༔

May all the demons of wrong views be eliminated ༔

ནད་གདོན་བར་ཆད་ཞི་བ་དང་༑

nedön barché zhiwa dang ༔

And, with them, illness, harmful influence, and obstacles; ༔

འཁོར་དང་ལོངས་སྤྱོད་རྒྱས་པ་ཡིས་༔

khor dang longchö gyepa yi ༔

And may good companions and resources multiply ༔

བསམ་པ་ཡིད་བཞིན་འགྲུབ་པར་ཤོག་༔

sampa yizhin drupar zhok ༔

So that all my wishes are fulfilled, just as I desire. ༔

དུར་ཁྲོད་རི་ཁྲོད་གངས་ཁྲོད་སོགས་༔

durtrö ritrö gang trö sok ༔

In charnel grounds, hermitages, retreats amid the snows, ༔

ཕུན་སུམ་ཚོགས་པའི་གནས་ཉིད་དུ་༔

pünsum tsokpé né nyi du ༔

And in other secluded places with all the perfect qualities, ༔

ཏིང་འཛིན་ཟབ་མོའི་དགོངས་བཅུད་ལ་༔

tingdzin zabmö gong chü la ༔

Let the quintessence of deep samadhi meditation ༔

རྟག་ཏུ་སྒྲུབ་པ་བྱེད་པར་ཤོག་༔

taktu drupa jepar zhok ༔

Be my constant practice. ༔

སྒྲུབ་པ་བྱས་པའི་འབྲས་བུ་ཡིས་༔

drupa jepé drebu yi ༔

And, as the result of this practice of mine ༔

ཕྲིན་ལས་རྣམ་བཞི་འགྲུབ་པ་དང་༔

trinlé nam zhi drupa dang ༔

May I accomplish the four kinds of activity, ༔

ལྷ་སྲིན་བྲན་དུ་ཁོལ་ནས་ཀྱང་༔

lhasin dren du khol né kyang ༔

Turn even gods and rakshasas into my servants, ༔

སངས་རྒྱས་བསྟན་པ་བསྲུང་བར་ཤོག༔

sangyé tenpa sungwar zhok ༔

And so be able to protect the Buddha's teachings. ༔

སྟོན་པས་གསུངས་པའི་དམ་ཆོས་རྣམས༔

tönpé sungpé damchö nam ༔

May all the sublime teachings taught by Buddha༔

རྩོལ་མེད་རྒྱུད་ལ་འཆར་བར་ཤོག༔

tsolmé gyü la charwar zhok ༔

Appear, with no effort, before my mind; ༔

མཁྱེན་པ་མཆོག་ལ་མངའ་བརྙེས་ནས༔

khyenpa chok la nga nyé né ༔

And by mastering this supreme knowledge, ༔

རྟོགས་པ་མཆོག་དང་ལྡན་པར་ཤོག༔

tokpa chok dang denpar zhok ༔

May I then attain supreme realization. ༔

བྱང་ཆུབ་སེམས་ཀྱི་རྟེན་འབྲེལ་གྱིས༔

changchup sem kyi tendrel gyi ༔

Through the interdependence of my genuine bodhicitta wish, ༔

སྐྱེ་འགྲོ་མ་ལུས་དབང་བསྡུས་ནས༔

kyendro malü wang dü né ༔

Let me magnetize and influence every single being, ༔

ཐོགས་མེད་ཡིད་བཞིན་ནོར་བུའི་མཐུས༔

tokmé yizhin norbü tü ༔

And let the power of this wish-fulfilling jewel, utterly unobstructed, ༔

འབྲེལ་ཚད་དོན་དང་ལྡན་པར་ཤོག༔

dreltsé dön dang denpar zhok ༔

Make any connection we have into one of deepest benefit and meaning. ༔

སངས་རྒྱས་བསྟན་པ་དར་བའི་མཐུས༔

sangyé tenpa darwé tü ༔

May I be the cause for the Buddha's teachings to spread ༔

བརྒྱུད་འཛིན་ཆོས་སྟོན་རྒྱས་པ་དང་༔

gyü dzin chö tön gyepa dang ༔

So that lineage holders and teachers of Dharma increase, ༔

འགྲོ་ཀུན་བདེ་ལ་འཁོད་ནས་ཀྱང་༔

dro kün dé la khö né kyang ༔

So that all beings may be ushered into bliss, ༔

ཞིང་ཁམས་ཐམས་ཅད་དག་པར་ཤོག༔

zhingkham tamché dakpar zhok ༔

And so that all realms be purified into buddhafields. ༔

བདག་གི་ལུས་ངག་ཡིད་གསུམ་གྱིས༔

dak gi lü ngak yi sum gyi ༔

From my body, speech, and mind, ༔

གདུལ་བྱ་སོ་སོའི་བློ་ཡུལ་དུ༔

dulja sosö lo yul du ༔

To benefit each of those to be trained, ༔

གང་ལ་གང་འདུལ་སྤྲུལ་པའི་སྐུ༔

gang la gang dul trulpé ku ༔

Everyone according to their need, ༔

དཔག་ཏུ་མེད་པར་འབྱུང་བར་ཤོག༔

pak tu mepar jungwar zhok ༔

Let my emanations appear in infinite profusion. ༔

མདོར་ན་འཁོར་འདས་མ་ལུས་ཀུན༔

dorna khordé malü kün ༔

May I realize samsara and nirvana. ༔

གུ་རུ་ཉིད་དང་དབྱེར་མེད་ཅིང༔

guru nyi dang yermé ching ༔

All are your manifestation, Guru, indivisible from your very nature, ༔

སྐུ་གསུམ་འདུ་འབྲལ་མེད་པ་ཡི ༔

ku sum dudral mepa yi ༔

And so may I understand the three kayas to be inseparably one, ༔

རྣམ་མཁྱེན་སངས་རྒྱས་མྱུར་ཐོབ་ཤོག༔

namkhyen sangyé nyur tob zhok ༔

And may I swiftly attain the omniscience of buddhahood. ༔

སེམས་ཅན་གསོལ་བ་འདེབས་པར་ཤོག༔

semchen solwa debpar zhok ༔

May sentient beings make prayers, ༔

བླ་མས་བྱིན་གྱིས་རློབས་པར་ཤོག༔

lamé jingyi lop par zhok ༔

May masters grant their blessings, ༔

ཡི་དམ་དངོས་གྲུབ་སྟེར་བར་ཤོག༔

yidam ngödrup terwar zhok ༔

May yidam deities grant attainments, ༔

མཁའ་འགྲོས་ལུང་བསྟན་བྱེད་པར་ཤོག༔

khandrö lungten jepar zhok ༔

May dakinis grant predictions! ༔

ཆོས་སྐྱོང་བར་ཆད་བསལ་བར་ཤོག༔

chökyong barché salwar zhok ༔

May Dharma protectors dispel obstacles, ༔

སངས་རྒྱས་བསྟན་པ་དར་ཞིང་རྒྱས་པར་ཤོག༔

sangyé tenpa dar zhing gyepar zhok ༔

May the Buddha's teachings spread and grow, ༔

སེམས་ཅན་ཐམས་ཅད་བདེ་ཞིང་སྐྱིད་པར་ཤོག༔

semchen tamché dé zhing kyipar zhok ༔

May all beings enjoy happiness and well-being, ༔

ཉིན་དང་མཚན་དུ་ཆོས་ལ་སྤྱོད་པར་ཤོག༔

nyin dang tsen du chö la chöpar zhok ༔

May they live out the Dharma day and night! ༔

རང་གཞན་དོན་གཉིས་ལྷུན་གྱིས་གྲུབ་པར་ཤོག༔

rangzhen dön nyi lhün gyi drupar zhok ༔

May our own and others' aims be spontaneously accomplished! ༔

རང་བཞིན་དག་པའི་དགེ་བ་འདིས༔

rangzhin dakpé gewa di ༔

Through this merit, stainless by its very nature, ༔

འཁོར་བ་ངན་སོང་དོང་སྤྲུག་ནས༔

khorwa ngensong dong truk né ༔

Let samsara's depths, the lower realms, be emptied ༔

སྲིད་མཚོར་སླར་ཡང་མི་གནས་ཞིང་༔

si tsor lar yang mi né zhing ༔

So that we remain no more in this ocean of existence, ༔

ཕྱམ་གཅིག་སྐུ་གསུམ་མངོན་གྱུར་ཤོག༔

chamchik ku sum ngön gyur zhok ༔

But actualize the three kayas together, all as one! ༔

རྒྱལ་བ་ཀུན་གྱི་གསང་ཆེན་མཛོད༔

gyalwa kün gyi sang chen dzö ༔

Great, secret treasure of all the buddhas, ༔

བླ་མེད་མཆོག་གི་བསྟན་པ་འདི༔

lamé chok gi tenpa di ༔

Supreme and unsurpassable teaching, ༔

ཇི་ལྟར་མཁའ་ལ་ཉི་ཤར་བཞིན༔

jitar kha la nyizhar zhin ༔

Like a sun rising in the sky, ༔

རྒྱལ་ཁམས་ཡོངས་ལ་དར་རྒྱས་ཤོག༔

gyalkham yong la dargyé zhok ༔

Shine forth and spread through the entire world! ༔

བདག་གི་དགེ་བའི་རྩ་བ་འདི་དང་དགེ་བའི་རྩ་བ་གཞན་དག་ཀྱང་བསྐྱེད་ནས༔

dak gi gewé tsawa di dang gewé tsawa zhendak kyang kyé né ༔

May this merit grow, along with my other roots of virtue, ༔

དཔལ་ལྡན་བླ་མའི་ཐུགས་དགོངས་ཡོངས་སུ་རྫོགས་པའི་ཡོན་ཏན་དང་ལྡན་པར་གྱུར་ཅིག༔

palden lamé tukgong yongsu dzokpé yönten dang denpar gyur chik ༔

So that I possess all qualities that please and fulfill the glorious master's wishes; ༔

སངས་རྒྱས་ཀྱི་བསྟན་པ་རིན་པོ་ཆེ་དར་ཞིང་རྒྱས་པར་བྱེད་པའི་སྐྱེས་བུ་སྟོབས་ལྡན་དུ་གྱུར་ཅིག༔

sangyé kyi tenpa rinpoché dar zhing gyepar jepé kyebu tobden du gyur chik ༔

That I am fired with the power to spread and increase the Buddha's precious teachings; ༔

མཁྱེན་པ་དང་བརྩེ་བ་ནུས་པ་གསུམ་མཐར་ཕྱིན་ནས་རྫོགས་པའི་སངས་རྒྱས་སུ་གྱུར་ཅིག༔

khyenpa dang tsewa nüpa sum tarchin né dzokpé sangyé su gyur chik ༔

That I attain ultimate wisdom, love, and capacity and become a perfect buddha; ༔

འགྲོ་བ་རིགས་དྲུག་ན་གནས་པའི་སེམས་ཅན་ཐམས་ཅད་འཁོར་བ་སྡུག་བསྔལ་གྱི་རྒྱ་
མཚོ་ལས་བསྒྲལ་ཏེ་མྱུར་དུ་མངོན་པར་རྫོགས་པར་སངས་རྒྱས་པར་གྱུར་ཅིག །

drowa rik druk na nepé semchen tamché khorwa dukngal gyi gyatso lé
dral té nyurdu ngönpar dzokpar sangyé par gyur chik §

And so that all sentient beings throughout the six realms are freed from
samsara's great ocean of suffering, quickly realizing complete and perfect
buddhahood. §

བདག་འདྲ་པདྨ་གླིང་པས་ལྷོ་བྲག་སྨན་མདོའི་བྲག་སེང་གེའི་གདོང་པ་ཅན་ནས་གདན་དྲངས་པའོ། །

This was revealed by Pema Lingpa from the rock shaped like a lion's head in the medicinal valley of Lhodrak.[784]

༄༅། །མར་མེའི་སྨོན་ལམ་བཞུགས་སོ། །

LIGHT OFFERING PRAYER

— Jamgön Mipham Rinpoche

This is a profound four-line prayer for offering butter lamps.

རིག་པ་ཀ་དག་སྣང་གསལ་མར་མེ་འདི། །

rigpa kadak nangsal marmé di

This brightly shining lamp of primordial pure awareness,

རིག་འཛིན་དཀྱིལ་འཁོར་པད་འབྱུང་ལྷ་ལ་འབུལ། །

rikdzin kyilkhor pejung lha la pul

We offer to Padmasambhava and the deities of the mandala of vidyadharas.

རིག་པས་གར་ཁྱབ་མ་གྱུར་འགྲོ་བ་རྣམས། །

rigpé gar khyap magyur drowa nam

Wherever awareness pervades, may all mother sentient beings

རིག་སྟོང་ཆོས་སྐུའི་གོ་འཕང་ཐོབ་པར་ཤོག །

riktong chökü gopang topar shok

Realize the dharmakaya, unity of awareness and emptiness.

མི་ཕམ་པས་སོ།།

Written by Mipham.[785]

༄༄། །ཞིངས་མཆོག་དཔལ་རིའི་སྨོན་ལམ་བཞུགས་སོ། །

ASPIRATION TO BE REBORN ON THE GLORIOUS COPPER-COLORED MOUNTAIN

— Chokgyur Dechen Lingpa

This is a four-line prayer to be reborn in the Glorious Copper-Colored Mountain, or Zangdok Palri, the pure land where Guru Padmasambhava and his retinue reside.

གདོད་མའི་གཤིས་དང་དབྱེར་མེད་པདྨ་འབྱུང་། །

dömé zhi dang yermé pema jung

Padmasambhava, you are inseparable from the primordial nature.

རང་སྣང་དག་པའི་ཟངས་མདོག་དཔལ་རིའི་ཞིང་། །

rangnang dakpé zangdok palri zhing

Your realm, the Glorious Copper-Colored Mountain, is the purity of our own perception.

སྣང་རིག་དབྱེར་མེད་མ་བཅོས་གཉུག་མའི་ངང་། །

nang rik yermé machö nyukmé ngang

May we be born in this primordial pure realm,

གདོད་ནས་རྣམ་དག་ཞིང་དུ་སྐྱེ་བར་ཤོག །

döné namdak zhing du kyewar shok

The unfabricated natural state, the indivisibility of appearance and awareness!

མཚོག་གྱུར་གླིང་པས་སོ།།

Written by Chokgyur Lingpa.[786]

ENDNOTES

1.   Zangpo Drakpa 2010a. Please note that our translation differs slightly from the quoted source.

2.   Traditionally, in Tibetan the biography or life-story of a great master is called a *namthar*. Namthar translates literally as complete freedom or complete liberation. It is the recounting of the story of the attainment of complete freedom. A namthar is thus the telling of the most sublime story—that of the attainment of complete freedom from suffering and its causes, and also of subsequent deeds which liberate others from their limitations (Ngawang Zangpo 2002, 115).

3.   Jamgön Kongtrul 2018a.

4.   The western Himalayan kingdom of Ladakh was included in our India volume, for although it has traditionally held to Tibetan cultural and linguistic practices, it also falls within the scope of the India's Eight Great Charnel Grounds.

5.   For an English translation of Jamyang Khyentse Wangpo's Guide to Central Tibet, see: Akester 2016.

6.

7.   For the most recent publication, see: Gustave-Charles Toussaint 2000.

8.   For this translation and publication, see: Yeshé Tsogyal 1978.

9.   For an English translation of the *Zanglingma*, see: Yeshé Tsogyal 1999.

10.   Khyentsé Wangpo 2016.

11.   These texts are available online for free, at *Lotsawa House*.

12.   For Yeshe Tsogyal's biography, see: Gyalwa Changchub 2002. For Mandarava's biography, see: Padmasambhava 1998.

13.   So far, no individual treasure biographies of Shakyadevi, Kalasiddhi and Tashi Kyidren have been revealed. Brief information about their lives is found in the various biographies of Guru Rinpoche, Yeshé Tsogyal and Mandarava. For very short biographies of Shakyadevi, Kalasiddhi and Tashi Kyidren, see: Jamgön Kongtrul 2011, 62–65. For a life summary prayer to Yeshé Tsogyal by Jamgön Kongtrul (1813–1899) based on Samten Lingpa's revelation, see: Jamgön Kongtrul 2017.

14.   For a translation, see: Jamgön Kongtrul 2011.

15.   Dudjom Rinpoche 1991.

16.   For an English translation of Jamyang Khyentse Wangpo's *Guide to Central Tibet*, see: Akester 2016. And, for a German translation of Katok Situ Chökyi Gyatso's *Pilgrimage Guide to Central Tibet*, see: Everding 2019.

17.   Samye Translations 2023a, 75.

18. Samye Translations 2023a, 117.

19. Samye Translations 2023a, 29.

20. Also known as the Kaliyuga.

21. Avalokiteshvara.

22. The five fields of knowledge are: craftsmanship, logic, grammar, medicine, and the "inner science" of Dharma.

23. This is a reference to the three outer tantras of kriya-, carya-, and yoga-tantra.

24. Prahevajra is the Sanskrit name for Garap Dorjé.

25. *The Net of Illusion, the Secret Essence Tantra* or *Mayajala Guhyagarbha Tantra* is one of the eighteen main Mahayoga scriptures of the Nyingma School.

26. This biography lists Shri Singha instead of Rambuguhyacandra as one of the eight vidyadharas.

27. Mahottara Heruka or Chemchok Heruka is the central figure of the Eight Sadhana Teachings.

28. Mañjushri Yamantaka or Jampel Shinjé is the central figure of the *Mañjushri Cycle on Awakened Form* from the *Eight Sadhana Teachings*.

29. Lotus Speech refers to the *Lotus Tantras on Awakened Speech* from the *Eight Sadhana Teachings*, and has Hayagriva of Tamdrin as the central figure.

30. Mind of Perfect Purity refers to the *Tantras on the Perfectly Pure Awakened Mind* from the *Eight Sadhana Teachings*, and has Yangdak Heruka as the main deity.

31. Amrita Qualities refers to the Amrita Tantras on Awakened Qualities from the *Eight Sadhana Teachings*, and has Amritakundalin as the main deity.

32. Kila Activity refers to the *Kila Cycle* on *Awakened Activity* from the *Eight Sadhana Teachings*, and has Vajrakilaya or Dorjé Phurba as the main deity.

33. *Sublime Knowledge of Kila* or *Vidyottama Tantra* is one of the main Vajrakilaya tantras.

34. Jikten Chötö or Lokastotrapuja (*Worldly Offering and Praise*) is a reference to the *Offerings and Praises to Protect the Teachings*, one of the three worldly practices from the Eight Sadhana Teachings.

35. Mantrabhiru or Möpa Drak-ngak or Mantrabhiru, "Fierce Mantras," is a reference to the Cycle on Fierce Mantras, one of the three worldly practices from the *Eight Sadhana Teachings*.

36. The Tripitaka is Sanskrit for the Three Collections of Scriptures and comprises the common teachings of Buddha Shakyamuni: Sutra, Abhidharma, and Vinaya.

37.   Namely, the Asura Cave.

38.   'Great Seal' is a direct translation of Mahamudra.

39.   The "eight great masters" mentioned here are the eight vidyadharas of India.

40.   Sitavana or Silwé Tsel, in the vicinity of the Vajra Throne at Bodh Gaya.

41.   The Shankarakuta Stupa or Chöten Deché Tsekpa.

42.   Dakini Karmendrani, also known as Khandroma Lékyi Wangmo, is the dakini to whom Vajradharma entrusted the Kagyé teachings, sealed in caskets and placed within the Shankarakuta Stupa in the Cool Grove charnel ground in India.

43.   *The Eight Sadhana Teachings, Assembly of Sugatas* or the *Kagyé Deshek Düpa* was later revealed as a terma by Nyangral Nyima Özer (1124/1136–1192/1204).

44.   Nanam Dorjé Düdjom, Palgyi Sengé, and Shakyaprabha.

45.   The Tenma Sisters, or Twelve Guardian Sisters, are a group of twelve goddesses connected to twelve different mountains and lakes in Tibet.

46.   Gangkar Shamé (Fleshless Lady of the White Glacier) is a "female deity of Lhabu Gangkar mountain in Shang." Guru Rinpoche subdued her and gave her the secret name Shamé Dorjé Yü Drönma (Turquoise Lamp, Fleshless Vajra Lady) (Rikey 2011, 125 and 129).

47.   Tinglomen is "the goddess of Lake Mendong in the west of Rutok in northern Tibet" (Rikey 2011, 125). The northern region of Tibet is known as 'Jang', which literally means 'the North'.

48.   Local guardians are local spirits protecting various parts of the Tibetan land.

49.   Dorjé Lekpa, or Vajrasaddhu, is an important protector deity.

50.   Osham and Tanglha seem to refer to Yarlha Shampo and Nyenchen Thangla, two mountain deities (Rikey 2011, 125).

51.   Constellation gods are the deities ruling the twenty-eight lunar mansions.

52.   Planetary demons are spirits ruling the planets of our solar system.

53.   Medicine ladies are aboriginal Tibetan goddesses.

54.   Naga goddess is a type of female naga spirit, a cross between the menmo goddesses and the nagas.

55.   This is a reference to the deity of Mount Magyel.

56.   Plague mothers are a particular type of mamo goddess.

57.   *Gongpo* demons are a type of malevolent spirit hostile to the Tibetan

rulers.

58.   *Genyen* is also the name for householders holding the lay vows. The spirits of that name seem to be of different sorts and often in the retinue of other deities.

59.   Warrior deities seem to be a type of warrior spirit, which are sky-travelling, war-like demons.

60.   Warrior nagas are a cross between nagas and warrior spirits.

61.   Body guardians are a type of spirit that specifically protects the human body.

62.   The *gya* deities might be a reference to the gods of the *Gya* heaven.

63.   Sovereign spirits are higher ranking spirits who ruled the land before the advent of Buddhism.

64.   Earth lords are local spirits who dwell in the earth.

65.   Hammer-wielders are a type of sky-travelling spirit who possess children and cause disunity and quarrel. As patrons of blacksmiths, they sometimes hold hammers and ride goats.

66.   Demon nagas are a cross between maras and nagas.

67.   'Spirits of meadows and crags' is a literal translation of the Tibetan *yapang*.

68.   Divine nyen or *lhanyen* are in fact spirits of an evil nature, said to make people lame. They usually dwell between earth and sky.

69.   Literally 'deputy ministers,' these are spirits attending on other, higher-ranking spirits. Indeed, many protectors have their own "court," including ministers, to attend them.

70.   Great *nyen* or *nyenchen* are a type of *nyen*. There also exist minor *nyen*.

71.   *Dümen* possibly refers here to a cross between a naga and a *menmo* goddess.

72.   Warrior demons are a cross between maras and warrior spirits.

73.   A demon king is a king of maras.

74.   May be a reference to Buchu Lhakang of Kongpo, one of twelve geomantic temples built during the reign of Songtsen Gampo to tame a supine ogress stretched out across Tibet, and thus to guard the country.

75.   Hunting gods are a set of thirteen deities who are ancestral spirits of the kings (Rikey 2011, 121.

76.   *Mudü* are a type of mara, possibly related to the Mu clan, one of the six principal clans of Tibet.

77.   Valley demons are a type of mara.

78.   The four *semo* sisters number among the twelve tenma goddesses.

79.   Mother goddesses are a type of ferocious goddess.

80.   The Four Great Kings are also known as the Four Guardian Kings of the cardinal directions, namely Dhritarashtra (East), Virudhaka (South), Virupaksha (West) and Vaishravana (North).

81.   This description of Samye corresponds to the Indian cosmological order, as presented in mandalas. Indeed, Mount Meru is believed to be at the center of the universe, flanked by the sun and moon. Around these, in the four cardinal directions and eight intermediary directions, are the four great continents and eight minor islands, respectively. The whole is within an ocean surrounded by a rim of iron mountains.

82.   *Vairocana's Awakening* or the *Vairocanabhisambodhi tantra* is a major Charya Tantra scripture.

83.   The Vajra Space mandala or the Vajradhatu mandala consists of thirty-seven deities. Its central figure is Vairocana, who is surrounded by the four Buddhas: Akshobhya, Ratnasambhava, Lokeshvararaja (Amitabha) and Amoghasiddhi. The Vajradhatu mandala appears in several tantras of both the Nyingma and Sarma Schools. For example, it is the primary mandala of the *Sarvatathagatatattvasamgraha.*

84.   The Great Awakened One, or Mahabodhi, is an epithet of Buddha Shakyamuni.

85.   The Latin botanical name for Arura is *Terminalia chebula.* In Tibetan medicine, *arura* is considered a panacea. Due to its great healing power, the Medicine Buddha is depicted carrying an *arura* branch in his right hand.

86.   The Abbot and Master are Shantarakshita and Padmasambhava, respectively.

87.   Lotsawa is the Indian word for 'translator,' which is also used in Tibetan.

88.   The three—Ka, Chok and Zhang—are Kawa Paltsek, Chokro Luyi Gyaltsen and Zhang Yeshé Dé, respectively.

89.   *Paramita* is short here for *Prajñaparamita,* the sutras of the *Perfection of Wisdom.*

90.   The *Mahaparinirvana sutra* is an important Mahayana scripture on *tathagatagarbha* (Buddha-nature), belonging to the third or final turning of the Wheel of the Dharma.

91.   The *Vajra Summit tantra,* or *Vajrashekhara Mahaguhya Yogatantra,* is one of the four major sections of Yoga Tantra.

92.   The famous middle storey of Samye.

93.   Dzo is a type of cattle, a cross between a yak and a cow.

94. Mahottara is short for Mahottara Heruka.

95. These eight correspond respectively to the principal deities of each of the *Eight Sadhana Teachings*.

96. *The Ocean of Dharma, the Great Gathering of Transmitted Precepts* is a teaching cycle that focuses on the Kagyé deities. It was discovered as a *terma* treasure by Orgyen Lingpa and was subsequently rediscovered as a *yangter* by Jamyang Khyentsé Wangpo.

97. The Border Taming and Further Taming Temples were two sets of four temples, built by King Songtsen Gampo, Trisong Detsen's ancestor and the first Dharma King of Tibet, and set in geomantic locations, in order to subdue the negative forces of the land.

98. The two supreme tertöns are Guru Chökyi Wangchuk and Nyang Nyima Özer.

99. Lingpa is a characteristic tertön name.

100. Here referring to Prince Mutri Tsenpo, who received the *Sampa Lhundrupma* prayer and associated practice cycle from Guru Rinpoche.

101. i.e. the *Sampa Lhundrupma*, the *Prayer that Spontaneously Fulfils All Wishes*.

102. This refers to the famous *Sampa Lhündrup* practice cycle.

103. For the initial introduction of Buddhism to Tibet, we are following the account given by Sakyapa Sonam Gyaltsen (1312–1375) in *The Clear Mirror: A Royal Genealogy*. This work presents Tibetan history in terms of the origins of the Tibetans and how the Dharma arrived in Tibet. For a translation and discussion, see e.g.: Sørensen 1994.

104. Sørensen 1994, 111–132.

105. Sørensen 1994, 138. The Yarlung Valley is an important historical and sacred place that is home to several sacred sites—one of them the Yarlung Sheldrak cave, which Guru Rinpoche blessed extensively. For a discussion of Yarlung Sheldrak, see our chapter on Yarlung Sheldrak. For a further discussion of the Yarlung Valley and its sacred sites, see: Akester 2016, 404–429; Gyurme Dorjé 2009, 190–196; Dowman 1996, 171–195; Everding 2019 Vol. II, 3–49; Chan 1994, 515–543; and Sørensen and Hazod 2005.

106. The farmers are said to have first encountered Nyatri Tsenpo as he was descending a mountain that was subsequently named Lhabab Ri (*Descent from the Heavens Mountain*). For a further discussion of Lhabab Ri, see the references mentioned in the previous footnote.

107. Yumbu Lhakhang stands on a hill, perched like a castle, on the eastern bank of the Yarlung River in the Yarlung Valley. While the original palace,

believed to be one of Tibet's oldest buildings, was damaged in the cultural revolution, it was reconstructed in 1983. For a further discussion of Yumbu Lhakhang, see the references mentioned in the footnote above.

108. For an English translation of this particular sutra, see Buddha Shakyamuni 2013.

109. For a complete list of the relics, see e.g.: Sørensen 1994, 150.

110. The Trülnang Temple, more commonly also known as the Jokhang, is the most sacred shrine in the whole of Tibet. Situated in Lhasa, it is home to the sacred Jowo Rinpoche statue. It was completed in the year 647 and faces west towards Nepal in recognition of the key role played in its construction by Queen Bhrikuti. The Ramoche Temple in Lhasa was founded by Queen Wencheng at the same time as the Jokhang. It originally housed the famous Jowo Rinpoche statue. Later, in response to the threat of an invasion, the Jowo Rinpoche was moved to the Jokhang, where it was initially hidden in a secret chamber. As a replacement, the Jowo Mikyö Dorjé, which had been brought to Tibet from Nepal by Queen Bhrikuti, was removed from the Jokhang and installed as the central image in Ramoche. For a full discussion of these events, see: Sørensen 1994, 197–298. For a further discussion of Lhasa's sacred sites, see: Akester 2016, 63–130; Gyurme Dorjé 2009, 68–130; Dowman 1996, 171–195; Everding 2019 Vol. I, 239–296; Chan 1994, 62–139.

111. Namely the Arya Lokeshvara statue which was later placed in the Potala Palace in Lhasa. For more on King Songtsen Gampo's quest to bring a sacred image of his tutelary deity Avalokiteshvara to Tibet and thus bless the land, see the later chapter on Mangyul. See also: Sørensen 1994, 189–195.

112. Dudjom Rinpoche 1991, 510–511; and Tenzin 1982, 84.

113. Sørensen 1994, 167–173. For a list of the texts that Thönmi translated into Tibetan, see e.g.: Sørensen 1994, 173.

114. The aspirations of the three brothers were made during the time of the previous Buddha, Kashyapa, according to *Liberation Upon Hearing: The History of the Jarung Kashor Stupa*. For a full translation of the story, see: Shakya Zangpo 2017. For a summary of the history and the further events unfolding at the Boudha Stupa, see the chapter entitled *The Great Jarung Kashor Stupa* in our Nepal Volume: Padmasambhava 2019, 81–94. We also refer to this story again in the prologue and the Drakmar Drinzang chapter of this book.

115. For the encounters of the Tibetan envoys with the Mahaguru, see the chapter on Mangyul.

116. See, e.g.: Jamgön Kontrul 2018a.

117. The aspirations of the four brothers were made during the time of the

previous Buddha, Kashyapa, according to *Liberation Upon Hearing: The History of the Jarung Kashor Stupa*. For a full translation of this text, see: Shakya Zangpo 2017. For a summary of the history and further events unfolding at the Boudha Stupa, see the chapter entitled *The Great Jarung Kashor Stupa* in our Nepal Volume: Padmasambhava 2019, 81–94. We also reference this story again in the Drakmar Drinzang chapter of this book.

118. Tsumagari 2012, 195.

119. For a further discussion of Drakmar Drinzang, see: Akester 2016, 303–304; Gyurme Dorjé 2009, 181; Dowman 1996, 233; Everding 2019 Vol. I, 417.

120. Khyentsé Wangpo 2016.

121. Translated from: nyang ral nyi ma 'od zer. 2007. For an alternative English translation, see also: Yeshe Tsogyal 1999, 55.

122. Jinchen (b. 698) was a daughter of Li Shouli, a prince of Tang China. Jinchen was married to King Tridé Tsuktsen to form an alliance between China and Tibet. During her time in Tibet she helped to promote Chinese culture and Buddhism. Modern scholars doubt that Jinchen was actually King Trisong Detsen's mother, since she is believed to have passed away in 739, three years prior to Trisong Detsen's birth. These scholars argue that one of Tridé Tsuktsen's other queens, namely Queen Mangmo Jé Shiteng from the Nanam clan, was likely Trisong Detsen's birth mother (see eg. Kapstein 2000, 26–30 for a discussion). In any case, we are following, here, the *Pema Kathang* and the majority of Tibetan sources, all of which state that Trisong Detsen's mother was Jinchen.

123. There are some speculations as to the exact birthdate of the King. Here, we are following his most commonly accepted birthdate. See also: Doney 2011, 7 fn. 3.

124. Translated from: o rgyan gling pa 1987, 341.

125. Doney 2011, 7.

126. Yeshe Tsogyal 1999, 55–56.

127. Translated from: o rgyan gling pa 1987, 344.

128. Khyentsé Wangpo 2016.

129. Akester 2016, 305.

130. See the corresponding chapter on inviting the Bodhisattva Abbot, in our India Volume: Padmasambhava 2021, 241–243.

131. Other biographies of Guru Padmasambhava suggest that the abbot Shantarakshita was in fact Lhacham Mandarava's brother and, thus, the son of King Vihardhara.

132. While the *Pema Kathang* does not specify where the Tibetan emissaries met Shantarakshita, various biographies of Guru Padmasambhava suggest that this meeting took place at Nalanda (Yeshé Tsogyal 1999, 57). Other sources suggest that Shantarakshita had already left his homeland in Zahor and was traveling to Nepal. When King Trisong Detsen got wind of the news that Shantarakshita was in the neighboring country of Nepal, he immediately seized the opportunity and extended an invitation (Akester 2016, 305; Diemberger 2000, 43, 47 and 51).

133. Translated from: o rgyan gling pa 1987, 348–349.

134. The Vajradhatu mandala consists of thirty-seven deities. Its central figure is Vairocana, who is surrounded by the four Buddhas—Akshobhya, Ratnasambhava, Lokeshvararaja (Amitabha) and Amoghasiddhi. The Vajradhatu mandala appears in several tantras of both the Nyingma and Sarma Schools.

135. Akester 2016, 306. Diemberger 2000, 64.

136. The monastic center of Uddandapura, also known as Odantapuri and Pulahari, is located within walking distance of Nalanda, about 10 km away. It was established in the 7th century by King Gopala (660–705 CE), who also served as its main patron. Like Nalanda, it was one of Ancient India's most prestigious mahaviharas (great monasteries). It is said to have been the model for Samyé Monastery in Tibet (Buswell and Lopez 2014, 601; Butön Rinchen Drup 1931b, 189; Dutt 1988, 354–358). According to Gendun Chöpel, this was the place known as Pulahari, the residence of Naropa, where Marpa is believed to have met his root teacher Naropa (Gendün Chöpel 2000, 51–53). For an interesting summary of the mythical origins of Uddandapura, see Akester 2016, p. 308 fn. 21.

137. Translated from: o rgyan gling pa 1987, 351–352.

138. Taranatha 2019.

139. Khyentsé Wangpo 2016.

140. Translated from: o rgyan gling pa 1987, 351–352.

141. According to Taranatha (Taranatha 2019; see also: Diemberger 46–47), the obstacles opposing the establishment of the Dharma were created not only by demons, but also by ministers in opposition, and were so fierce that even Shantarakshita's life was in danger. Fearing for the abbot's life, King Trisong Detsen pleaded with him to leave for Nepal to avoid the threat. The Great Abbot acquiesced to the King's plea and waited in Nepal for the arrival of Guru Padmasambhava, only returning to Samye once the spirits were pacified.

142. Translated from: o rgyan gling pa 1987, 352.

143. Guru Padmasambhava's full account was hidden and later revealed as a

treasure by Ngakchang Shakya Zangpo (b. 15th century) while on pilgrimage to Samyé Monastery. This treasure, entitled *Liberation upon Hearing: The History of the Great Jarung Kashor Stupa*, became one of the most beloved accounts of the history of the Boudha Stupa. For a full translation of the story, see: Shakya Zangpo 2017. For the story of the *Liberation upon Hearing*'s discovery, see our later chapter on Samye monastery. For a summary of the history and the further events unfolding at the Boudha Stupa, see the chapter entitled *The Great Jarung Kashor Stupa* in our Nepal Volume: Padmasambhava 2019, 81–94.

144. Translated from: o rgyan gling pa 1987, 352.

145. Depending on the biography consulted, King Trisong Detsen's envoys met Guru Rinpoche at different locations. Here, following the *Pema Kathang*, they first met in Bodh Gaya. We have also told this story within our India volume: Padmasambhava 2019, 251–266).

146. Translated from: o rgyan gling pa 1987, 356–357.

147. Jamgön Kongtrul 2012, 42.

148. Jamgön Kongtrul 2012, 313–314.

149. These were the *Tukjé Chenpo Semnyi Ngelso (The Great Compassionate One Resting in Comfort and Ease)*, and the bone relics of the twenty-one brahmins (Akester 2016, 304 fn. 10).

150. Akester 2016, 303–304. Jamgön Kongtrul 2012, 195–196 and 312.

151. There have been many accounts of Khandro Yeshé Tsogyal's life story. For one of the most famous and beloved of them, see: Gyalwa Changchub 2002.

152. These are variations on the name Tsogyal Sangpuk, or Tsogyal's Secret Cave.

153. Orgyen Tobgyal Rinpoche 2002.

154. Chökyi Lodrö 2004.

155. For more details, see the later chapter on Drak Yangdzong..

156. Chan 1994, 320.

157. For further information on Tsogyal Lhatso, see: Akester 2016, 344; Gyurme Dorjé 2009, 164; Dowman 1996, 214–215; Chan 1994, 319–320; and Everding 2019 Vol. I, 417–419.

158. Jamgön Kongtrul 2017.

159. Gyalwa Changchub 2002, 6–8. As also noted by Jamgön Kongtrul (2011, 44), the names of Khandro Yeshé Tsogyal's parents vary depending upon the source consulted. Here we are following Taksham Nüden Dorjé's treasure biography of Yeshé Tsogyal.

160. Gyalwa Changchub 2002, 9.

161. Nyoshul Khenpo 2005, 61.

162. Gyalwa Changchub 2002, 8–11.

163. Gyalwa Changchub 2002, 11.

164. Jamgön Kongtrul 2017.

165. Gyalwa Changchub 2002, 17. For a further description, see the later chapter on Önphu Taktsang.

166. Gyalwa Changchub 2002, 12–22.

167. Khyentse Wangpo 2020.

168. Jikmé Lingpa 2019a. For a translation of the *Yumka Dechen Gyalmo* Sadhana, see: Jikmé Lingpa 2019b.

169. Translated from: mkhyen brtse'i dbang po 1980, 372.

170. Chokgyur Dechen Lingpa 2017a.

171. These include e.g. the great Indian and Tibetan siddhas and pilgrims Marpa Lotsawa (1012–1097), Arya Atisha (982–1054), Ngatso Lotsawa (b. 1011), Ngok Loden Sherap (1059–1109), Mahapandita Gayadhara (d. 1103), Padampa Sangyé (d.1117), Milarepa (1040–1123), Sakya Pandita (1182–1251), Orgyen Rinchen Pal (1230–1309), Rigdzin Gödem (1337–1408), Chokyi Dronma (1422–1455) and Kathog Rigdzin Tsewang Norbu (1698–1755), to name just a few (Ehrhard 2004, 290; Ehrhard 2014, 24; and: Gö Lotsawa 1949, 130, 207, 767, 916, 1034)..

172. Translated from: ngag dbang blo bzang rgya mtsho 2009, 26.

173. For a further description and hiker's guide to Mangyul, see: Chan 1994, 924–939.

174. Davidson 2008, 132.

175. For example, the famous dharani, *Vanquishing Constraints of Body, Speech and Mind*, which was translated by the Indian pandita Gayadhara and the Tibetan lotsawa Shakya Yeshé at the Arya Vati Zangpo temple in Mangyul. For a translation of this dharani, see: Buddha Shakyamuni 2023. For further information on translation activities here, see: Ehrhard 2004, 290 and fn. 249.

176. For instance, during a time of demon-fueled turmoil in Lhasa, Mangyul temporarily served as a refuge for the statue of Shakyamuni Buddha known as Jowo Rinpoche (Precious Lord) which was brought to Tibet by the Chinese princess Wencheng during the reign of Dharma King Songtsen Gampo (Go Lotsawa 1949, 44).

177. Mills 2007, 2.

178. Ehrhard 2004, 283; and Mills 2007, 34.

179. Ehrhard 2014, 15–16. As well as revealing several hymns of praise composed in the presence of Arya Vati Zangpo (see e.g. in English: Ehrhard 2014, 33–39; and in Tibetan: Ehrhard 2004, 523–534), and various treasure

revelations (see e.g.: Jamgön Kontrul 2012, 36, 213 and 267), the treasure revealer Zhikpo Lingpa (1524–1583)—whose awakened activity had been predicted by the Mahaguru in the *Pema Kathang*—discovered a sadhana featuring four of the Avalokiteshvara Brothers. The fifth Brother, in this case, is the practitioner's own physical body. The sadhana arose in Zhikpo Lingpa's pure vision, dictated to him by an emanation of Guru Padmasambhava, and it provided the means to bring the Brothers' blessings directly into the practitioner's own experience. The Brothers thus remain as extraordinary supports for connecting to the energy of enlightened compassion, inseparable from Guru Rinpoche himself. For a translation of this sadhana, see: Shikpo Lingpa 2017.

180. The full list of the five and their locations is as follows: 1. Arya Vati Zangpo at Kyirong in Mangyul, 2. and 3. Arya Akham and Arya Bukham in Patan, 4. Arya Jamali in Kathmandu, and 5, Arya Lokeshvara in the Potala Palace in Lhasa. For further details on how to visit the three Avalokiteshvara Brothers in Nepal, see our Nekhor app and our Nepal volume (Padmasambhava 2019, 185-193).

181. Following Decleer 2006, 77. For a German translation of *The Emerald Horse* and a discussion of all three histories, see: Ehrhard 2004.

182. Translated from: O rgyan gling pa 1987, 357.

183. For the Mahaguru's activity at Asura and Yangleshö caves, see our Nepal volume: Padmasambhava 2019, 139–154.

184. For a full account of the events unfolding at *E Vihara*, see, within our Nepal volume, the chapter entitled E Vihara: Padmasambhava 2019, 171–184.

185. There are two sacred lakes of particular significance in the Kathmandu Valley: Lake Taudaha, on the way to Pharping, and Lake Nagdaha, near Patan. These are the two sacred lakes which are said to have remained when Manjushri drained the great lake that once filled the whole valley. They are said to be the home of the naga King Karkotaka and are visited annually by migrating water birds, due to the purity of the water compared to that of the many other (polluted) lakes in the valley.

186. It appears that there are at least four sacred sites associated with the Mahaguru that are referred to as Slate Mountain. The *Pema Kathang*'s Chapter 45 and the *Sertrengwa* both speak of a Slate Mountain Cave within the bounds of Kosala. Both seem to indicate that the first site lies somewhat near Bodh Gaya, though it remains unidentified to date (see our India volume for more details: Padmasambhava 2021, 217–222). According to the histories of the Vajrakilaya teachings, Guru Rinpoche retreated to a Slate Mountain Cave on the borders of Nepal and India (also referred to as Yari Nak, see our Nepal

volume: Padmasambhava 2019, 155–160). Several biographies recount how Guru Padmasambhava practiced in a Slate Mountain Cave at Mangyul upon entering Tibet (Ehrhard 2004, 284 and fn. 177. Please note that fn. 177 also identifies two of the three locations referred to as Slate Mountain.) Finally, the *Pema Kathang's* Chapter 60 also speaks of Yari Gong in Tolung (see the next chapter on Shongpa Lhachu).

187. Newar Buddhists hold that this site is actually present-day Godawari, a sacred, forested area in the southeast of the Kathmandu Valley. A *hari* sandalwood tree is a particular kind of sandalwood tree.

188. There are several stories recounting the origin of the statues. One of their main differences lies in the number of "Brothers." For a short discussion, see: Decleer 2006, 78–80.

189. For a full account of the history of the five Self-Arisen Avalokiteshvara Brothers, see, within our Nepal volume, the chapter entitled *The Avalokiteshvara Brothers*: Padmasambhava 2019, 185–193. For further details on how to visit the three Avalokiteshvara Brothers in Nepal, see our **Nekhor** app. (The story is further also summarized, examined, and discussed by Decleer 2006; Sørensen 1994, 189–194; Sonam Gyaltsen 2006, 111–117; and Ehrhard 2004.)

190. Ehrhard 2014, 22.

191. For a full list of sacred sites in Mangyul, including those of Guru Padmasambhava, see: Ehrhard 2004, 280–292.

192. Yeshe Tsogyal 1999, 59–61.

193. Diemberger 2007, 35.

194. Ehrhard 2004, 284 and fn. 176. Please note that the number and names of disciples who were present in Mangyul varies depending upon the source consulted. Here we are following the *Pema Kathang*, which states that the three envoys who met Guru Rinpoche in Mangyul were Kawa Paltsek, Nanam Dorjé Düdjom (who also led the first search party), and Chokro Lu'i Gyaltsen.

195. Gö Lotsawa 1949, 44.

196. Yeshe Tsogyal 1999, 62.

197. For this dialogue between Guru Padmasambhava and the King, see: Taranatha 2019 or Ngawang Zangpo 2002, 169. For a brief discussion of this three-part subjugation of spirits, see Mayer 2008, 296–297 fn. 13. Please note that authors often differ as to details of time and place when describing the subjugation of certain spirits. Given the need for certain spirits to be tamed more than once, it seems that some narratives present a summary of their taming, an event that, when explained in detail, took place at several locations and

over a longer period of time. For example, some accounts relate that Lang Palgyi Sengé assisted Guru Padmasambhava in the taming of the Tenma goddesses (Mayer 2008, 299) when King Trisong Detsen's delegates met the Mahaguru at Yangleshö (Yeshe Tsogyal 1999, 59–61). For the Mahaguru's first encounter with the Tenma Goddesses at Asura and Yangleshö caves, see the section *Binding the Tenma Goddesses*, in our Nepal volume: Padmasambhava 2019, 147–148. And for a detailed discussion of the taming of the Tenma goddesses, see: Mayer 2008, 296–308.

198. Rikey 2011, 125 and 129.

199. Jamgön Kongtrül 2011, 65.

200. Gyalwa Changchub 2002, 129.

201. Gyalwa Changchub 2002, 146.

202. For a full account of Belbang Kalasiddhi's life-story, see the chapter on Ngatupchen in our Nepal volume: Padmasambhava 2019, 120–128. The current paragraph is based on: Gyalwa Changchub 2002, 129–132 and 197–198. Jamgön Kongtrul 2011, 66–67.

203. Sardar-Afkhami 2001, 63–64.

204. Rikdzin Gödem's *Beyul Chi'i Themjang* (*The Outer Pass-key to the Hidden-Lands*), recounts how the Mahaguru first introduced the Tibetans to the *beyuls*. Accordingly, while Guru Rinpoche was residing at Samye Chimpu, Dharma King Trisong Detsen invited him to Samye. Having offered the Guru a feast, the King inquired about the future of the Dharma. In particular, King Trisong Detsen was eager to find out where in the future the Mahaguru's followers could practice the Dharma undisturbed. It is at that point that the Mahaguru explained the *beyuls* to the King (Sardar-Afkhami 2001, 40).

205. As mentioned in our introduction, a full discussion of the *beyuls* goes beyond the scope of the present book series. Rather than discussing them here, we feature our ever-expanding research into the *beyuls* on our Nekhor website and app.

206. These four are: 1. Pema Ling (Lotus Sanctuary); 2. Dremo Jong (Valley of Rice); 3. Khenpa Jong (Valley of Artemisia); 4. Lungsum Jong (Valley of the Three Regions). (See in Tibetan: O rgyan gling pa 1987, 589–590).

207. For more information on Nanam Dorjé Düdjom, see our chapter on Mount Hepori.

208. According to the *Gurü Ga'u Dünma* (*The Guru's Seven Amulets*), the seven are: 1. Kyimolung (Valley of Happiness) in Nubri and Kutang, Nepal; 2. Pema Tsal/Ling (Lotus Grove) in Yolmo, Nepal; 3. Rolpa Khandro Ling in Khumbu, Nepal; 4. Khenpalung (Valley of Artemisia) in Khumbu, Nepal and

Bhutan. (There are two beyuls named Khenpalung, one discovered by Rikdzin Gödem in Nepal, and a second one by Pema Lingpa in Bhutan. For a discussion, see e.g.: Diemberger 1997); 5. Lha'i Phodrang Ding (Lofty Palace of the Gods), the precise location of which, as with several of the *beyuls*, is yet to be identified: see: Samuel 2020, 63); 6. Dremo Jong (Valley of Rice) in Sikkim; and 7. Dromo Khü (Cleft of Wheat Fields) in Chumbi Valley, Nepal (Samuel 2020, 63–64).

209. In addition to Kyimolung, Ridzin Gödem is particularly remembered for opening the *beyul* Dremo Jong (Valley of Rice) in Sikkim, in 1373. Rikdzin Gödem opened Dremo Jong by performing several miracles at its spiritual center Tashi Ding, where he blessed the Drakar Phuk (White Rock Cave) and established a monastery. In 1408, at the age of seventy-one, Rikdzin Gödem entered *mahaparinirvana* at Zilnön in Sikkim (Boord 2013). Later, Lhatsün Namkha Jikmé (1597–1653) blessed Tashi Ding and re-opened the *beyul*.

210. Boord 2013; and Samuel 2020, 66.

211. Jamgön Kongtrul 2011, 148; and Solmsdorf 2013, 123–124.

212. Burroughs 2013; and Solmsdorf 2013, 129, fn. 31.

213. Khyentsé Wangpo 2016.

214. Translated from: O rgyan gling pa 1986, 55.

215. It appears that there are at least four sacred sites associated with the Mahaguru that are referred to as Yari Gong (Slate Mountain). For more information, see "The Mahaguru's Journey to Tibet" in our previous chapter on Mangyul.

216. For further information on Shongpa Lhachu, see: Akester 2016, 192–193; Gyurme Dorjé 2008, Dowman 1996, 134; and Everding 2019 Vol. I, 239.

217. Yeshe Tsogyal 1999, 64.

218. Translated from: o rgyan gling pa 1987, 366–367.

219. Translated from: o rgyan gling pa 1987, 367.

220. Translated from: o rgyan gling pa 1987, 368.

221. Translated from: mkhyen brtse'i dbang po 1980a, 386–387.

222. Khyentsé Wangpo 2016.

223. The five negative emotions are ignorance, anger, pride, attachment, and jealousy, and the five associated Wisdom Families are represented by Vairocana, Akshobhya, Ratnasambhava, Amitabha, and Amoghasiddhi, respectively.

224. For a further description of Zurkhar, see: Akester 2016, 342; Gyurme Dorjé 2009, 172; Dowman 1996, 219–221; and Leschly 2007a.

225. Some of the shorter biographies of Guru Padamsambhava state that

the King received the Mahaguru either directly at his palace (Chokgyur Lingpa 2020) or on Mount Hepori (Yeshé Tsogyal 1999, 65). Here we are following the story as detailed in the *Pema Kathang*, where the King received the Mahaguru at Zurkhar Do, then invited him to his palace, and finally led him to Mount Hepori, where he (the Guru) subdued the spirits of Tibet.

226. Translated from: o rgyan gling pa 1987, 368.

227. Translated from: o rgyan gling pa 1987, 375.

228. Translated from: o rgyan gling pa 1987, 376.

229. Akester shares an alternative story, where the stupas symbolize the five aspects of the ideal guru-patron relationship. Here, the stupas were miraculously built by five Newar master-craftsmen who were miraculously summoned by the Mahaguru (Akester 2016, 342).

230. Tsumagari 2012, 195; Dudjom Rinpoche 1991, 513–514; Akester 2016, 303.

231. Translated from: o rgyan gling pa 1987, 569–570.

232. For a biography of Longchenpa, see eg.: Nyoshul Kheno 2005, 98–161; Tulku Thondup 1999, 109–117.

233. For a brief survey, see e.g.: Dezhung Rinpoche and Dilgo Khyentse Rinpoche 2023.

234. For more details, see our later chapter on Samye Chimpu.

235. Dudjom Rinpoche 199, 585; and Ford 2021. For more details, see the chapter on Samye Chimpu.

236. Jamgön Kongtrul 2011, 123–124; and Leschly 2007a.

237. These are the opening lines of the song. Translated from: mkhyen brtse'i dbang po 1980a, 429.

238. Chokgyur Dechen Lingpa 2017a.

239. For a further description of Mount Hepori, see: Akester 2016, 328 and Gyurme Dorjé 2009, 179.

240. For the events unfolding at Samye Chimpu, see the chapter on Samye Chimpu.

241. Translated from: o rgyan gling pa 1987, 376–377.

242. While this initially pacified the nagas, their final subjugation, including that of King Manasvi, took place at Samye Chimpu. For this episode, see the chapter on Samye Chimpu.

243. Translated from: o rgyan gling pa 1987, 378.

244. A *drupchen* (*Great Accomplishment*) is a form of intensive group practice that lasts at least nine days, and is said to be equivalent to spending many years in solitary retreat.

245. This explanation is based on a teaching on *sangchö* (Smoke Offering), given by Orgyen Topgyal Rinpoche in July 2002 at Rangjung Yeshe Gomde, California.

246. Drimé Ösel Lingpa 1999.

247. Khenpo Namdrol 1999, 25.

248. Namkha Tsewang Chokdrup 2019.

249. This likely refers to the site on Mount Hepori where Dharma King Trisong Detsen discovered the Buddha images. For more information, see the section *Furnishing Samye with Statues and Relics* within the chapter on Samye Monastery.

250. *Zikhyim* (*zi khyim*) is a word imported from Chinese; it is also called *li* in Tibetan. *Zikhyim* mostly refers to a special alloy that consists of seven or more metals used for casting statues, bells and other precious ritual objects. Depending on the percentage of each metal, the colour changes. It can also refer to native copper extracted from the earth. Both the alloy and the native copper are regarded as very precious, and thus ritual objects made from *Zikhyim* are not usually gilded.

251. Jikmé Lingpa 2022a.

252. Jikmé Lingpa 2022b.

253. Jamgön Kongtrul 2013.

254. Chokgyur Lingpa 2017a.

255. Apparently referring to traditional sources, Akester claims that "inconceivable" describes the monastery's cosmic scale; "unchanging" describes Samye's blessing; and "spontaneously accomplished" describes the fact that it was built by non-humans (Akester 2016, 304 fn. 12).

256. For more on Uddandapura, see the section entitled *Inviting the Bodhisattva Abbot* in the chapter on Drakmar Drinsang. Jamgön Kongtrul suggests that Samye was modeled after Vikramashila, the former monastic home of Abbot Shantarakshita (Padmasambhava 2004, 50).

257. Yeshe Tsogyal 1999, 73.

258. For a detailed description of the entire monastic complex, see especially: Akester 2016, 318–328; Gyurme Dorjé 2009, 172–179; Dowman 1996, 216–225; and Everding 2019 Vol. I, 373–407. Also: O rgyan gling pa 1987, 382–383.

259. Jamgön Kongtrul 2011, 123–124; and Leschly 2007a.

260. Zangpo Drakpa 2010d.

261. Translated from: o rgyan gling pa 1987, 379–380. For a detailed

description of the layout of Samye and its individual temples and stupas, see: Ibid., 307–314.

262. Translated from: O rgyan gling pa 1987, 381.

263. The precise occasion when Khandro Yeshe Tsogyal becomes the spiritual consort of the Guru varies, as also noted by Jamgön Kongtrul (2011, 44). In consideration of the main sequence of events, we are following Khandro Yeshé Tsogyal's life story, according to which she becomes the Mahaguru's consort shortly after she met him (Gyalwa Changchub 2002, 21–22). According to the *Zanglingma*, it appears that Khandro Yeshé Tsogyal becomes the Guru's consort at a later point, after the translation of the Dharma into Tibetan had been completed (Yeshe Tsogyal 1999, 122). The *Pema Kathang* does not mention any particular point at which Khandro Yeshé Tsogyal met the Mahaguru.

264. Drakpa Gyaltsen 2021. Given the auspicious circumstances at the time these lines were first recited—the King requesting the Guru to teach the Dharma—they have since become the most popular mandala offering for requesting Dharma teachings. The precise origin of this famous four-line mandala offering is unclear, however. Here we are following Kyapjé Nyoshul Khen Rinpoche, who states that the verse was composed by King Trisong Detsen himself (Nyoshul Khenpo 2005, 56).

265. Gyalwa Changchub 2002, 19–22.

266. Diemberger 2000, 64–65; and Akester 2016, 307–308..

267. The story is recounted in various ways. Here we are following it as told in Shakabpa (2010, 140) and Akester (2016, 312 fn. 27).

268. Translated from: o rgyan gling pa 1987, 384.

269. This may refer to the Uighur people who inhabited the Gansu corridor of modern-day China.

270. For a brief discussion of this story, see: Akester 2016, 311 fn. 26. Just before the Mahaguru left Tibet, Gyalpo Pehar visited the Mahaguru at Yarlung Shelrak. For this encounter, see the chapter on Yarlung Sheldrak.

271. Khyentsé Wangpo 2016.

272. Akester 2016, 304 fn. 13.

273. Translated from: o rgyan gling pa 1987, 386.

274. Chokgyur Lingpa 2020.

275. Translated from: o rgyan gling pa 1987, 390.

276. Khyentsé Wangpo 2016.

277. Chokgyur Lingpa 2020.

278. Chokgyur Lingpa 2020.

279. Khyentsé Wangpo 2016.

280. The other two extant lineages of ordination according to the Vinaya are the Theravadin and the Dharmaguptika.

281. For more information on Nalanda and Vikramashila, see the chapters on Zahor and Nalanda in our India volume: Padmasambhava 2021, 201–202 and 234–246. The monasteries were some of the prime locations for the activity of translation.

282. For example, the two Indian panditas Vibhuticandra and Danashila not only translated a vast number of scriptures into Tibetan, but even composed treatises directly in Tibetan. It appears that Tibetan translators were held in great esteem, as possibly shown by the fact that one such Tibetan scholar even became guardian of one of Vikramashila's gates (Dutt 1988, 351). Furthermore, one of the temples at the monastery currently identified as Vikramashila was built by Tibetans.

283. Lotsawa is the title used for native Tibetan translators who worked with Indian scholars or panditas to translate major Buddhist texts into Tibetan from Sanskrit and other Asian languages; it is said to derive from *lokacakshu*, literally "eyes of the world".

284. For the enlightened activity of both the Guru and Vimalamitra at the Sitavana charnel ground, see: Padmasambhava 2021, 152–154. The 50th chapter of the *Pema Kathang* recounts how Guru Rinpoche, as part of his enlightened activity, creates the auspicious circumstances for Vimalamitra to take birth in Kashmir. Since the precise location of this event is unknown, we did not include this story in our India Volume. According to the *Pema Kathang*, as part of his thousand-year stay on the Indian subcontinent, the Mahaguru skillfully created the circumstances for some of the greatest upholders of the Buddhadharma to appear, including Nagarjuna (Padmasambhava 2021, 229–233), Aryadeva (Ibid., 233), Vasubandhu, Lavapa (Ibid., 100–102), and Humkara (Padmasambhava 2019, 122–128).

285. Nagasawa 2017.

286. In chapters 68 to 82, the *Pema Kathang*, in illustrating the effort involved in translating the Dharma into Tibetan, goes into great detail about the training of each of the Tibetan translators and their individual journeys. We have refrained from sharing these stories for fear of presenting too much detail. Instead, in the chapters that follow, on the sacred caves, we will share some of the stories of how these translators attained accomplishment. Similarly, for this summary of events from the *Pema Kathang*, under the heading *Establishing the Support of Enlightened Speech* we have chosen to cite *The Wish-Fulfilling Tree*, Guru Padmasambhava's own account of his life story, revealed by Chokgyur

Dechen Lingpa, a treasure text which provides a concise and beautiful synopsis of the events told in more detail in the *Pema Kathang*.

287. Khyentsé Wangpo 2016.

288. Chokgyur Lingpa 2020.

289. Khyentsé Wangpo 2016.

290. Gyalwa Changchub 2002, 104–125. Diemberger 2000, 60–62.

291. Tashi Topgyal 2016.

292. For a discussion of the events unfolding at Samye Chimpu, see the chapter on Samye Chimpu.

293. For a short biography of King Trisong Detsen, see: Tulku Thondup 1996, 96–99.

294. Yeshe Tsogyal 1999, 126.

295. For this account, see the earlier chapter on Mount Hepori.

296. Translated from: o rgyan gling pa 1987, 602–603.

297. Translated from: o rgyan gling pa 1987, 604.

298. Yeshe Tsogyal 1999, 143.

299. For a short biography of Rigdzin Kumaraja, see: Nyoshul Khenpo 2005, 93–97; and Garry 2007c.

300. Nyoshul Kheno 2005, 130

301. For a full translation of the story, see: Shakya Zangpo 2017.

302. Ibid

303. Ibid

304. Ibid

305. Jamgön Kongtrul 2023.

306. For a translation of the *Tsokyé Nyingtik* sadhana, see: Khyentsé Wangpo 2022.

307. The 'Zahor-style' of depicting Guru Padmasambhava.

308. Jamgön Kongtrul 2012, 241.

309. Translated from: mkhyen brtse'i dbang po 1980a, 360.

310. Gyalwa Changchub 2002, 23–29. For more details, see the chapters on Samye Chimpu and Drakmar Yamalung.

311. For more on Drakmar Yamalung, see the chapter on Drakmar Yamalung.

312. Gyalwa Changchub 2002, 30–34.

313. See the chapter on Samye Chimpu.

314. Nyangral Nyima Özer 2017.

315. Gyalwa Changchub 2002, 34–59.

316. For a further description of Zhotö Tidro, see: Akester 2016, 182–186;

Gyurme Dorjé 2009, 152; Dowman 1996, 117–121; Chan 1994, 344–346; Everding 2019 Vol. I, 113–114; and Loseries 1994.

317. While this may be a reference to Khandro Yeshé Tsogyal, this emanation was later associated with the protectress of the Drikung Kagyü tradition, Achi Chökyi Drolma.

318. A cycle that combines Dzokchen and Mahamudra, practiced in the Drikung tradition. According to the Drikung masters, it is a separate Nyingtik cycle (and not a sub-cycle or part of either the *Vima or Khandro Nyingtik*). Loseries 1994 48–50.

319. Jamgön Kongtrul 2017.

320. The last two paragraphs were adapted from Taranatha 2019. Taranatha follows the *Bashé (Testament of Ba)*, which describes the Guru's seeming departure before Samye was even consecrated (see eg. Diemberger 2000, 58–59). According to Khandro Yeshe Tsogyal's life story, the couple take their leave, miraculously visible to all in a palanquin of light (Gyalwa Changchub 2002, 35).

321. Chökyi Lodrö 2022.

322. These quotes, included in Nyoshul Khen Rinpoche's history of Dzokchen in Tibet, are drawn from the introduction to the *Khandro Yangtik*, Longchenpa's transmission history of the *Khandro Nyingtik*. See: Nyoshul Khenpo 2005, 69–70.

323. While the Mahaguru had already been in Tibet for some time, he had not yet shared the highest teachings of Dzokchen, the Great Perfection, with anyone. The Tibetan population did not even know that such teachings existed. The Dharma King, however, who paid close attention to the Mahaguru's teachings, had found some clues, and in his curiosity asked the Mahaguru to share these highest of teachings with his heart disciples. The Mahaguru eventually gave in and granted his disciples the empowerment and initial transmission into the Great Perfection teachings at Samye and Samye Chimpu (see the following chapter on Samye Chimpu). Earlier, while Dharma King Trisong Detsen's beloved daughter, Princess Pema Sal, was passing away, the Mahaguru had entrusted the Dzokchen teachings to her as a *terma* treasure. However, nobody was allowed to be present when he transmitted these teachings to the princess. Thus, the Mahaguru had not yet transmitted the Great Perfection teachings to any of his living disciples, until now.

324. This is drawn from the *Sertrengwa, The Golden Rosary*, which consists of a series of questions asked by Khandro Yeshé Tsogyal regarding meditation practice, and the answers given by Guru Padmasambhava. This dialogue forms

part of the *Khandro Nyingtik*, revealed by Pema Ledrel Tsel. For an English translation of *The Golden Rosary* text, see: Padmasambhava 1994, 44–60.

325. For the events unfolding at Chimpu, see the later chapter on Samye Chimpu.

326. Jamgön Kongtrul 2017.

327. For Khandro Yeshe Tsogyal's journey, see our Nepal volume: Padmasambhava 2019, 91–92; 124–125; 151–152; 183–184 and 198–201. Otherwise, the stories can be found in Khandro Yeshe Tsogyal's biography (Gyalwa Changchub 2002, 45–57).

328. Gyalwa Changchub 2002, 34–44.

329. Gyalwa Changchub 2002, 57–59.

330. Gyalwa Changchub 2002, 59–61.

331. Gyalwa Changchub 2002, 57–61.

332. Gyalwa Changchub 2002, 61–63.

333. Jamgön Kongtrul 2017.

334. Gyalwa Changchub 2002, 135–136 and 147. This story is also told in our Nepal volume, see: Padmasambhava 2019, 198–201;

335. Gyalwa Changchub 2002, 150–151.

336. Gyalwa Changchub 2002, 100, 147, 152.

337. Nyoshul Khenpo 2005, 114–115.

338. Translated from: o rgyan gling pa 1987, 570–571.

339. The cave where this was revealed is at Dorjé Kyé Rock in Yeru Shang (Jamgön Kongtrul 2011, 140–143).

340. According to Kathok Rikdzin Tsewang Norbu (1698–1755), the *Dorsem Nyingtik* forms the fourth branch of *The Fourfold Heart Essence* teachings, initially synthesized by Gyalwa Longchenpa (Dezhung Rinpoche and Dilgo Khyentse Rinpoche 2023).

341. Pema Kunsang 2006, 340. On pp. 341–345, Erik Pema Kunsang offers two short translations of texts from the *Dorsem Nyingtik*.

342. Jamgön Kongtrul 2011, 143.

343. For a brief overview of the *Gongpa Yangzab* and a detailed account of Je Rinchen Phuntsok's revelation, see Burghart 2017, 176–193.

344. Jamgön Kongtrul 2012, 182.

345. Translated from: mkhyen brtse'i dbang po 1980a, 401.

346. While this is a commonly accepted list of the eight caves, it is important to remember that many sites exhibit similar spiritual qualities. Also, depending upon the source consulted, exactly which caves are included may differ. The current arrangement is not intended to discredit or devalue other

sacred sites. On the contrary, it is intended to highlight a mere droplet in the vast ocean of sacred spaces blessed by the Mahaguru. The present list of eight caves is given, for example, by: Orgyen Lingpa 2008, Tashi Topgyal 2016; and Jamgön Kongtrul 2011, 31–50. For lists of the eight caves that exchange one or several caves with others, see e.g.: Orgyen Lingpa 2016; Gyalwang Changchub 2002, 63–64; Padmasambhava 2004, 240 fn. 139; and Dilgo Khyentse 2022.

347. For a detailed discussion of the eight great charnel grounds, see: Padmasambhava 2021, 124 ff.

348. Translated from: mkhyen brtse'i dbang po 2008, 2–3.

349. Akester (2016, 329), for example, states that the caves of Samye Chimpu served as an important pre-Buddhist charnel ground. Similarly, Longchenpa famously likened Samye Chimpu to the Sitavana charnel ground of India (Nyoshul Khenpo 2005, 120).

350. Together with the eight vidyadharas of India, the Mahaguru revealed the profound instructions and practices collectively known as the *Kagyé* (*The Eight Instructions*), in the Sitavana charnel ground in India. For more information on the revelation of the *Kagyé*, see: Padmasambhava 2021, 152-154. For a list of the *Kagyé* that the Mahaguru practiced in the eight great charnel grounds, see: Ibid., 143.

351. Both Dharma King Trisong Detsen and Nyak Jñanakumara received the practice of Chemchok Heruka. The Dharma King entered retreat in Samye monastery itself, where he accomplished Chemchok Heruka and is accordingly counted as one of the eight vidyadharas of Tibet. Nyak Jñanakumara was sent to the cave of Yarlung Sheldrak where he also accomplished Chemchok Heruka. Although Nyak Jñanakumara is not counted as one of the eight vidyadharas of Tibet, his realization was equally great.

352. The *Barché Lamsel* prayer here invokes Guru Rinpoche in the form of Kalden Drenze, the Mahaguru indivisible from all eight Kagyé deities. Chokgyur Lingpa 2017a.

353. For more information on the connection between the Chimpu caves and Samye Monastery, see the chapter entitled The Three Vital Points.

354. Jamyang Khyentse Wangpo praised Chimpu as identical to the Sosadvipa or Kula Dzokpa charnel ground (Akester 2016, 330 fn. 82) and Gyalwa Longchenpa praised the site as identical to Sitavana (see the quotation below).

355. Jikmé Lingpa 2017. Jikmé Lingpa takes his first line from the *Pema Kathang* itself. The five lines that follow are Jikmé Lingpa's explanation.

356. For a further detailed explanation of the Samye Chimpu caves and their sacred features, see: Akester 2016, 329–334; Gyurme Dorjé 2009,

180–181; Jikmé Lingpa 2017; Dowman 1996, 226–232; and Everding 2019 Vol. I, 409–415.

357. Tashi Topgyal 2016.

358. Akester 2016, 334 and Jikmé Lingpa 2017. The biography of Khandro Yeshé Tsogyal tells the story of the Mahaguru defeating several evil ministers by means of the syllable *hung*, when they attempted to ambush him at the Chimpu caves (Gyalwa Changchub 2002, 16).

359. Khyentsé Wangpo 2016a.

360. For the initial truce between the humans and the nagas, and especially their King Manasvi, see the previous chapter on Mount Hepori.

361. This is a summary of the story as told by the *Pema Kathang*. For slightly different versions of this story, see especially: Yeshe Tsogyal 1999, 128–130; Khyentsé Wangpo 2016b, 307–309; and Taranatha 2019.

362. Taranatha 2019.

363. Zangpo Drakpa 2010d.

364. According to Yeshe Tsogyal 1999, 144.

365. As a result of the Mahaguru and Lhacham Mandarava's long-life practice at the Maratika caves, Amitayus appeared in front of them and blessed them—the Mahaguru as Hayagriva, and Mandarava as Vajravarahi (Yeshe Tsogyal 1999, 45). For a full account of the events unfolding at the Maratika caves, see our Nepal Volume: Padmasambhava 2019, 105–116. The "vidyadhara with power over life" is the third of the four vidyadhara levels. According to the Nyingma school of Tibetan Buddhism, the four stages of the tantric path to awakening, or four vidyadhara levels, are increasingly refined stages of realization and spiritual accomplishment. For a more detailed discussion of these, see for example: Tulku Thondup 2001, 218–221.

366. For a full account of Madram Rudra's liberation and Guru Rinpoche's involvement therein, see our India Volume: Padmasambhava 2021, 152–154.

367. For the two masters' joint revelation of the *Prajñaparamita* as well as their student-teacher relationship, see our India Volume: Padmasambhava 2021, 229–233. For a short biography of Nagarjuna in relation to the *Kagyé* teachings, see: Dudjom Rinpoche 1991, 479–480. Nagarjuna's life story varies, depending upon the source consulted. For a brief discussion of the various versions of Nagarjuna's life story, see: Shaoyong 2019, 336–340. And, for a Tibetan version, see eg.: Abhayadatta 1979, 112–117.

368. For the story surrounding the revelation of the practice of Yamantaka at the Sitavana charnel ground, see our India Volume: Padmasambhava 2021, 124–135.

369. Zangpo Drakpa 2010d.

370. For more information on the revelation of the *Kagyé*, see: Padmasambhava 2021, 152–154. For a list of the eight Kagyé deities that the Mahaguru practiced in the eight great charnel grounds, see: Ibid., 143.

371. The stories of these eight disciples will be shared in this and the following chapters. Please note that beyond the particular yidam deity practice that each received during the *Kagyé* transmission, each of the eight also received and practiced a wide variety of other teachings and sadhanas, many of which they hid as *terma* treasures, often discovered by their own later reincarnations.

372. Yeshe Tsogyal 1999, 122–126 and Gyalwa Changchub 2002, 62–64.

373. Nyang Ral Nyima Özer revealed the *Kagyé Deshek Düpa*, Guru Chöwang revealed the *Kagyé Sangwa Yongdzok*, and Rigdzin Gödem revealed the *Kagyé Rangshar*. These three *terma* are collectively known as the *Kagyé Nam Sum* (*The Three Kagyé Collections*). Furthermore, the author of the *Pema Kathang*, Orgyen Lingpa, also revealed another major *Kagyé* cycle in a treasure known as the *Kadü Chökyi Gyatso* (*The Ocean of Dharma, the Great Gathering of Transmitted Precepts*), at the Yarlung Sheldrak caves (see the following chapter). The *Kadü Chökyi Gyatso* was later rediscovered as a *yangter* by Jamyang Khyentsé Wangpo. As mentioned in the *Pema Kathang*, Guru Rinpoche had previously practiced the *Kadü Chökyi Gyatso* during his time in Greater India (see Padmasambhava 2021, 102–103 and 219–220).

374. For the story told in this section we are following primarily Orgyen Topgyal Rinpoche's oral account (2014b).

375. Orgyen Topgyal Rinpoche 2014b; Erik Pema Kunsang 2014. For more on Buddhaguhya and the exchange between the Dharma King and Buddhaguhya, see e.g.: Nagasawa 2017. For a partial translation of the actual letter that Buddhaguhya sent to Dharma King Trisong Detsen, see: Snellgrove 2002, 446–450.

376. Orgyen Topgyal Rinpoche 2014b.

377. Orgyen Topgyal Rinpoche 2014b.

378. For the meeting of Shri Singha and Guru Padmasambhava in Greater India, see: Padmasambhava 2021, 194–195.

379. Following Orgyen Tobgyal Rinpoche 2014b and Pema Kunsang 2014.

380. Pema Kunsang 2006, 165.

381. For a full discussion of the events unfolding at the Boudha Stupa in Nepal, see: Ibid., 81–94. For the former lives of the princess, see Padmasambhava 2019, 91 and Shakya Zangpo 2017.

382. This revelation would later occur at Tramo Drak in the Dang Valley.

For a short biography of Pema Ledreltsel, see: Nyoshul Khenpo 2005, 70–73; and Garry 2007a. For a short biography of Gyalsé Lekden, see: Nyoshul Khenpo 2005, 70–75.

383. Nyoshul Khenpo 2005, 70; Dudjom Rinpoche 1991, 554–555 and Akester 2016, 332–333. For the story of how Vimalamitra established the Great Perfection teachings in Tibet, see the following section.

384. Gyalwa Changchub 2002, 129, 150–152 and 156–160.

385. Tashi Topgyal 2016.

386. For short biographies of Gyalwa Chokyang, see eg.: Jamgön Kongtrul 2000, 38–39; Tulku Thondup 1996, 101; and Mandelbaum 2007a.

387. Akester 2016, 330 fn. 84.

388. Nyoshul Khenpo 2005, 98.

389. Jamgön Kongtrul 2011, 39.

390. Khyentsé Wangpo 2016.

391. The 50ᵗʰ chapter of the *Pema Kathang* recounts how Guru Rinpoche, as part of his enlightened activity, created the auspicious circumstances for Vimalamitra to take birth in Kashmir. Since the precise location of this event is unknown, we did not include this story in our India Volume. According to the *Pema Kathang*, as part of his thousand-year stay on the Indian subcontinent, the Mahaguru skillfully created the circumstances for some of the greatest upholders of the Buddhadharma to appear––including Nagarjuna (Padmasambhava 2021, 229–233), Aryadeva (Ibid., 233), Vasubandhu, Lavapa (Ibid., 100–102), and Humkara (Padmasambhava 2019, 122–128).

392. Almogi suggests that Vimalamitra's birthplace might have been the city of Hatinapur in Uttar Pradesh (Almogi 2016, 7).

393. For the Guru's and Vimalamitra's enlightened activity at the Sitavana charnel ground, see: Padmasambhava 2021, 152–154.

394. Nyoshul Khenpo 2005, 75–83; Dudjom Rinpoche 1991, 555–556 and Gruber 2012.

395. Akester 2016, 331.

396. Nyoshul Khenpo 2005, 84–85. Dudjom Rinpoche 1991, 555–550.

397. Accounts differ as to the order, time and location of Longchenpa's reception and transmission of the *Nyingtik* teachings. Compare e.g.: Nyoshul Khenpo 2005, 106–107; Dudjom Rinpoche 1991; Tulku Thondup 1996, 111–112; Dahl 2010, 228; and Ford 2021.

398. Tulku Thondup 1996, 112.

399. These earth *termas* were included in Pema Lingpa's *Kunzang Gongdü* (*Wisdom Assembly of Samantabhadra*). Longchenpa did not discover many

earth termas. Due to his profound realization, the majority of Longchenpa's termas are mind termas (Jamgön Kongtrul 2011, 131).

400. Dudjom Rinpoche 1991, 593 andOr Nyoshul Kheno 2005, 130. Also quoted in Jikmé Lingpa, 2017.

401. For a biography of Rikdzin Jikmé Lingpa, see eg.: Nyoshul Kheno 2005, 198–215; Tulku Thondup 1996, 118–135; and Gardener 2010.

402. For more information on Jikme Lingpa's visionary journey to the Jarung Kashor stupa, see our Nepal Volume: Padmasambhava 2019, 92–93.

403. Tulku Thondup 1996, 43.

404. Tulku Thondup 1996, 124.

405. Tulku Thondup 1996, 43.

406. Dudjom Rinpoche 1991, 837. Tulku Thondup 1996, 128.

407. In fact, Jikmé Lingpa composed two *Zangdok Palri* prayers while residing at Samye Chimpu. The second prayer, *Secret Path to the Mountain of Glory*, forms the basis of this volume's final chapter, Zangdok Palri (see also Jikmé Lingpa 1999).

408. These are the opening lines of the prayer. Jikmé Lingpa 2010.

409. Jikmé Lingpa 2010.

410. Akester 2016, 330 fn. 82.

411. Translated from: mkhyen brtse'i dbang po 2020, 54.

412. Translated from: mkhyen brtse'i dbang po 1980, 356–357.

413. These are the opening lines of the song. Translated from: mkhyen brtse'i dbang po 1980, 433.

414. These are the opening lines. Translated from: mkhyen brtse'i dbang po 1980, 357.

415. Jamgön Kongtrul 2012, 127–128.

416. Translated from: mkhyen brtse'i dbang po 2020, 52.

417. There are a few variations in the Tibetan spelling of this name, such that it is sometimes pronounced *Drak Yongdzong*.

418. For a further detailed explanation of the Drak Yangzong and Dzong Kumbum caves and their sacred features, see: Akester 2016, 345–352; Gyurme Dorjé 2009, 164; Dowman 1996, 210–214; Chan 1994, 317–326; and Everding 2019 Vol. I, 419–421.

419. For a description of Tsogyal Lhatso, see our previous chapter of that title.

420. Akester 2016, 349. Gyurme Dorjé (2009, 164) suggests that the hilltop is identical to the Sitavana charnel ground. (For a discussion of the Kula Dzokpa charnel ground, see: Padmasambhava 2021, 157–160.)

421. Akester 2016, 347.

422. Zangpo Drakpa 2010d.

423. According to Yeshé Tsogyal 1999, 144.

424. Dudjom Rinpoche 1991, 478.

425. Yeshé Tsogyal 1999, 42–43. For the story unfolding at Mount Malaya, see our India Volume: Padmasambhava 2021, 126–138. For the story of Manjushri becoming a disciple of Garap Dorjé, see our India Volume: Padmasambhava 2021, 83–85. For a short biography of Manjushrimitra in relation to the *Kagyé* teachings, see: Dudjom Rinpoche 1991, 477–479. For Manjushrimitra's role of transmitting the Great Perfection teachings, see eg.: Ibid., 490–494.

426. For the story surrounding the revelation of the practice of Yamantaka at the Sitavana charnel ground, see our India Volume: Padmasambhava 2021, 152–154.

427. King Vasudhara of Nepal became an important lineage holder of the Yamantaka teachings. For more on the teacher-student relationship between Guru Rinpoche and Vasudhara, see our Nepal volume: Padmasambhava 2019, 177, 184 and 209.

428. Yeshé Tsogyal 1999, 118.

429. Gyalwa Changchub 2002, 121.

430. Tashi Topgyal 2016.

431. The Drongmoché village is nowadays simply called Dramda. For a discussion of this particular sacred site, see: Akester 2016, 343.

432. Esler 2014, 8.

433. Esler 2014, 8.

434. Esler 2014, 10. Lotsawa Ché Tsenkyé is believed to have translated the *Gongpa Düpa Do*, the Anuyoga root tantra, from the Burushaki language, a dialect spoken around Gilgit, under the guidance of the panditas Dharmabodhi and Dhanarakshita (Dalton 2002, 266–268).

435. Esler 2014, 8–11.

436. Esler 2014, 8–11.

437. Dudjom Rinpoche 1991, 609-610.

438. Esler 2014, 14.

439. Esler 2014, 16.

440. Tarthang Tulku 1975, 47.

441. For a discussion of Sangye Yeshé's compositions, see: Esler 2014, 15–16. For a translation of *Lamp for the Eye of Contemplation*, see: Esler, 2022.

442. Dudjom Rinpoche 1991, 614.

443. For a short biography of Melong Dorjé, see: Nyoshul Khenpo 2005,

91–93; and Garry 2007b.

444. For a short biography of Trulzhik Sengé Gyapa, see: Nyoshul Khenpo 2005, 90–92.

445. For a short biography of Rigdzin Kumaraja, see: Nyoshul Khenpo 2005, 93–97; and Garry 2007c.

446. For more details, see the later site description of Lhodrak Kharchu.

447. For Machik Kunga Bum, see: Gardner 2016; Jamgön Kongtrul 2011, 202–203; Jamgön Kongtrul 2003, 124; and Akester 2006, 347. For Dungtso Repa, see: Leschly 2007; and Jamgön Kongtrul 2011, 203–204.

448. Jamgön Kongtrul 2011, 300.

449. Jamgön Kongtrul 2012, 225: and Akester 2016, 347.

450. Translated from: mkhyen brtse'i dbang po 1980a, 430.

451. Translated from: mkhyen brtse'i dbang po 2020, 56.

452. Akester 2016, 445.

453. For a further detailed explanation of the Lhodrak Karchu caves and their sacred features, see: Akester 2016, 460–463; Gyurme Dorjé 2009, 208–211; Chan 1994, 693–696; and Everding 2019 Vol. II, 77–89.

454. For more on Drupchen Melong Dorjé, see our previous chapter on Drak Yangdzong.

455. For a detailed explanation of Khoting Lhakhang and its sacred features, see: Akester 2016, 458–459; Gyurme Dorjé 2009, 208; Chan 1994, 692. and Everding 2019 Vol. II, 89.

456. For more information on Lhamo Karchen, see: Akester 2016, 462 and Chan 1994, 694.

457. Zangpo Drakpa 2010d.

458. According to Yeshe Tsogyal 1999, 145.

459. According to Jikmé Lingpa, when the practitioner reaches the stage of mahamudra vidyadhara, his or her body transforms completely into the deity, and all enlightened activities are effortlessly mastered (Jikmé Lingpa, Patrul Rinpoche and Getse Mahapandita 2006, 61). The mahamudra vidyadhara is the third of the four vidyadhara levels. According to the Nyingma school of Tibetan Buddhism, the four stages of the tantric path to awakening, or four vidyadhara levels, are increasingly refined stages of realization and spiritual accomplishment. For a more detailed discussion of these, see for example: Tulku Thondup 2001, 218–221.

460. For the story surrounding the revelation of the practice of Yangdak Heruka at the Sitavana charnel ground, see our India Volume: Padmasambhava 2021, 152–154.

461. Macdonald 1987, 104. For more information on Humkara and the events unfolding at Ngatupchen, see our chapter on Ngatupchen in the Nepal volume: Padmasambhava 2019, 117–128. For a short biography of Humkara in relation to the Kagyé teachings, see: Dudjom Rinpoche 1991, 475–477.

462. For the events unfolding at the Asura and Yangleshö caves, see our Nepal Volume: Padmasambhava 2019, 139–154.

463. Taranatha 1983, 63. While it is certain that Humkara continued to transmit and teach the practices and instructions related to Yangdak Heruka that greatly influenced the Nyingma tradition, it is uncertain what else he did in Tibet.

464. Tashi Topgyal 2016.

465. This story about Namkhé Nyingpo has been adapted from our Nepal Volume. For more on the events unfolding at Ngatupchen, see our chapter on Ngatupchen in the Nepal volume: Padmasambhava 2019, 117–128.

466. Gyalwa Changchub 2002, 160.

467. Gyalwa Changchub 2002, 165 and 208.

468. Yeshé Tsogyal 1999, 83–89.

469. Jamgön Kongtrul 2017.

470. Gyalwa Changchub 2002, 160–161.

471. Gyalwa Changchub 2002, 162–165.

472. Nyak Jñanakumara was one of the twenty-five disciples of Guru Rinpoche. For more information on Nyak Jñanakumara, see the following chapter on Yarlung Sheldrak.

473. Dudjom Rinpoche 1991, 603.

474. Translated from: o rgyan gling pa 1987, 563.

475. For a biography of Nyangral Nyima Özer, see e.g.: Hirshberg 2013 and 2016; Dudjom Rinpoche 1991.

476. Trautz 2019, 41–42.

477. Hirshberg 2016, 128–129.

478. Hirshberg 2013.

479. Translated from: mkhyen brtse'i dbang po 1980, 435.

480. Translated from: mkhyen brtse'i dbang po 2020, 57.

481. For more information on the connection between Yarlung Sheldrak and the Tradruk Temple, see the chapter entitled The Three Vital Points.

482. For more on Gongpo Ri, see e.g.: Akester 2016, 409.

483. For more information on the graves of these two Dharma Kings, see: Akester 2016, 436–437; and Dowman 1996, 196–204. For a detailed

examination of the burial mounds, see: Romain 2022.

484. For further explanations of each of these sacred sites, see Akester 2016, 404–429; Dowman 1996, 171–204; and Chan 1994, 515–543.

485. For a detailed explanation of the Yarlung Sheldrak caves and their sacred features, see: Akester 2016, 425–428; Gyurme Dorjé 2009, 190–191; Dowman 1996, 191–193; Everding 2019 Vol. II, 23–27; Chan 1994, 522–524; and Sørensen and Hazod 2005, 107–109.

486. For more information on the two sacred Guru Rinpoche statues, namely the Guru Thongdrolchen and Guru Ngadrama, see e.g.: Akester 2016, 308 and 427. For more information on the Guru Ngadrama statue, see also the final story in our earlier chapter on Samye.

487. Gyalwa Changchub 2002, 152.

488. Zangpo Drakpa 2010d.

489. According to Yeshe Tsogyal 1999, 145.

490. The Hundred Peaceful and Wrathful Deities feature in several practices and cycles of teachings, most notably the *Bardo Tödrol Chenmo* (*The Tibetan Book of the Dead*) and the *Guhyagarbha Tantra*, which is the primary source describing this mandala.

491. Notably, Nupchen Sangyé Yeshé composed an important commentary on the *Gongpa Düpé Do*, entitled *Münpé Gocha* (*Armor Against Darkness*). For more information, see the section on Nupchen Sangyé Yeshé in the chapter on Drak Yangdzong.

492. For more on Vimalamitra and his student-teacher relationship with Guru Rinpoche, see the section on Vimalamitra in the chapter on Samye Chimpu.

493. For the story surrounding the revelation of the practice of Chemchok Heruka at the Sitavana charnel ground, see our India Volume: Padmasambhava 2021, 124–135.

494. For more information on the King's retreat, see the section entitled "The King's Retreat" in the chapter on Samye monastery.

495. Jamgön Kongtrul 2012, 217–218.

496. Gyalwa Changchub 2002, 121 and 152.

497. See the chapter on Samye for the story on how the Mahaguru bound the protector Gyalpo Pehar.

498. Translated from: o rgyan gling pa 1987, 648–649.

499. Translated from: o rgyan gling pa 1987, 616.

500. Translated from: dil mgo mkhyen brtse 2008, 183–184.

501. Jñanakumara received the *rigpé tselwang* from Guru Padmasambhava, the *Nyingtik* teachings from Vimalamitra, and the Atiyoga transmissions from Lotsawa Vairocana and his disciple Yudra Nyingpo (Erik Pema Kunsang 2014; Nyoshul Khenpo 2005, 50–51 and 57).

502. Garry 2007d.

503. For the events that took place at Lhodrak Karchu, see the chapter on Lhodrak Karchu.

504. Dudjom Rinpoche 1991, 601–605.

505. Jamgön Kongtrul 2012, 217–219.

506. Jamgön Kongtrul 2012, 218–219.

507. Translated from: o rgyan gling pa 1987, 711.

508. Jamgön Kongtrul 2012, 122–123. Translated from: o rgyan gling pa 1987, 711–712.

509. Translated from: o rgyan gling pa 1987, 711–712.

510. For the story of how Guru Padmasambhava transmitted the *Kagyé* teachings in Tibet, see the chapter on Samye Chimpu. As mentioned in the *Pema Kathang*, Guru Rinpoche had previously practiced the *Kadü Chökyi Gyatso* in Greater India (See Padmasambhava 2021, 102–103 and 219–220). The *Kadü Chökyi Gyatso* was later rediscovered as a *yangter* by Jamyang Khyentsé Wangpo.

511. Jamgön Kongtrul 2011, 123–124.

512. Translated from: mkhyen brtse'i dbang po 1980, 427

513. Dilgo Khyentse and Orgyen Tobgyal 2017, 370.

514. Translated from: mkhyen brtse'i dbang po 1980, 439.

515. Translated from: mkhyen brtse'i dbang po 2020, 61.

516. Although Sengé Dzong is located just a day's travel to the east of Lhakhang Dzong in Tibet, it is presently only accessible from the Bhutanese side due to restrictions on crossing the border. Sengé Dzong lies in a restricted area of Bhutan and a special permit from the Bhutanese government is needed in order to access the site.

517. Following Matthew Akester, who provides a detailed explanation of the Sengé Dzong caves and their sacred features (Akester 2016, 455–458).

518. Akester 2016, 457.

519. Zangpo Drakpa 2010d.

520. According to Yeshe Tsogyal 1999, 144.

521. Khenchen Namdrol 1999, 7.

522. For this initial meeting and the events unfolding at Kukkutapada, see our India Volume: Padmasambhava 2021, 117–123.

523. For the story surrounding the revelation of the practice of Vajrakilaya at the Sitavana charnel ground, see our India Volume: Padmasambhava 2021, 152–154.

524. For the events unfolding at the Asura and Yangleshö caves, see our Nepal Volume: Padmasambhava 2019, 139–154.

525. For a more detailed account of this story, see our India Volume: Padmasambhava 2021, 240–241.

526. For the Mahaguru's subjugation of hostile forces by means of Vajrakilaya, at the sacred sites of Asura and Yangleshö, Yarinak and Chumik Changchup in Nepal, see: Padmasambhava 2019, 155–170. And, for the subjugation of hostile forces through Vajrakilaya at Bodh Gaya in India, see: Padmasambhava 2021, 259–260.

527. For the story of how the Mahaguru compiled and subsequently transmitted the Vajrakilaya teachings, see our Nepal Volume: Padmasambhava 2019, 149–152.

528. The story which originates from the Vajrakilaya commentary entitled *Phurdrel Bum Nak* (see below) is frequently told by Vajrakilaya practitioners of the Nyingma tradition. The current version follows the account of the *Phurdrel Bum Nak* as translated by Martin Boord (Boord 2002, 124–126).

529. For the story of how the Mahaguru compiled and subsequently transmitted the Vajrakilaya teachings, see our Nepal Volume: Padmasambhava 2019, 149–152.

530. Boord 2002, xxvii–xxviii and 109.

531. Gyalwa Changchub 2002, 101.

532. For the Mahaguru's subjugation of hostile forces by means of Vajrakilaya at the sacred sites of Asura and Yangleshö in Nepal, see: Padmasambhava 2019, 144–147.

533. Gyalwa Changchub 2002, 78–89. Although Khandro Yeshé Tsogyal's biography offers a detailed narrative of the wisdom dakini's retreat, it does not explicitly establish a direct correlation between her meditation practice and the yidam Vajrakilaya. However, recognizing that Sengé Dzong is the site where the dakini attained mastery over Vajrakilaya, we have highlighted this profound connection.

534. The name of this King varies depending on the source consulted. Some suggest that she was the daughter of the legendary King of the Iron Palace, Sindhu Raja, who invited the Guru to Bhutan to cure him of his disease.

535. Gyalwa Changchub 2002, 83 and 88–89. Gyalwa Changchub 2002, 90.

536. Gyalwa Changchub 2002, 90.

537. Jamgön Kongtrul 2012, vi–vii.

538. Translated from: mkhyen brtse'i dbang po 1980, 441–442.

539. Dudjom Rinpoche 2020.

540. Cantwell and Mayer 2010, 66.

541. Cantwell and Mayer 2010, 67.

542. Zangpo Drakpa 2010d.

543. For a brief explanation of the Yarlha Shampo Kangi Rawa cave and its sacred features, see: Akester 2016, 419–420; and Dowman 1996, 184–185. For more details on the mountain protector Yarlha Shampo, see: Jisheng 2001, 344–346.

544. Taranatha 2019 and Akester 2016, 306–307.

545. Yeshe Tsogyal 1999, 63. For another account of how the Mahaguru tamed Yarlha Shampo, see: Taranatha 2019.

546. Dudjom Lingpa 2017.

547. Dudjom Lingpa 2017.

548. Dudjom Lingpa 2017.

549. Jamgön Kongtrul 2017.

550. Gyalwa Changchub 2002, 127.

551. Gyalwa Changchub 2002, 127.

552. For the events that unfolded in Nepal meeting of the two dakinis, see Padmasambhava 2019, 124–125.

553. Tashi Topgyal 2016.

554. Jamgön Kongtrul 2011, 46..

555. Nyoshul Khenpo 2005, 207–208.

556. Nyoshul Khenpo 2005, 104–105.

557. Zangpo Drakpa 2010e.

558. See our later chapter entitled Tigress Lair.

559. That is the point where the Paro River meets the Thimpu River.

560. Lopen Thinley Kunzang 2008, 121.

561. For a further discussion of Paro Taktsang and its sacred features, see: Lopen Thinley Kunzang 2008, 116–129 and Gyurme Dorjé 2009, 846–849.

562. For a further description of Önphu Taktsang, see the chapter on Önphu Taktsang.

563. Gyalwa Changchub 2002, 96.

564. Gyalwa Changchub 2002, 96.

565. Gyalwa Changchub 2002, 134.

566. Gyalwa Changchub 2002, 134.

567. Li 2018, 55.

568. Zangpo Drakpa 2010d.

569. For the story surrounding the revelation of the practice of Chemchok Heruka at the Sitavana charnel ground, see our India Volume: Padmasambhava 2021, 124–135.

570. Dudjom Lingpa 2017.

571. Gyalwa Changchub 2002, 100.

572. For this story, see our chapter on Sengé Dzong.

573. Gyalwa Changchub 2002, 90.

574. For a continuation of the story, see the chapter on Önphu Taktsang.

575. Drekpa Kundül, chief figure in the mandala of Jikten Chötö.

576. Tashi Topgyal 2016.

577. Yeshe Tsogyal 1999, 127.

578. Tulku Urgyen Rinpoche 2004, 182.

579. Stearns 2007, 252.

580. Stearns 2007, 254.

581. Khenpo Tsewang Dongyal 2008, 184.

582. Khenpo Tsewang Dongyal 2008, 184–187.

583. Khenpo Tsewang Dongyal 2008, 184–187.

584. Nyoshul Khenpo 2005.

585. Nyoshul Khenpo 2005, 314.

586. Dilgo Khyentse 2010, xxx–xxxi.

587. Translated from: mkhyen brtse'i dbang po 2013b, 68.

588. For a further explanation of the Drakmar Yamalung caves and sacred spring, and their sacred features, see: Akester 2016, 301–302; Dowman 1996, 233–234; and Everding 2019 vol. I, 415–417.

589. Zangpo Drakpa 2010d.

590. For the story surrounding the revelation of the practice of Chemchok Heruka at the Sitavana charnel ground, see our India Volume: Padmasambhava 2021, 124–135.

591. Dudjom Lingpa 2017.

592. Yeshé Tsogyal 1999, 117.

593. Yeshé Tsogyal 1999, 117–118.

594. According to the *Zanglingma* (Yeshé Tsogyal 1999, 118), Guru Padmasambhava hid two such vases at Yarlung Sheldrak and Drak Yangdzong. Rikdzin Terdak Lingpa subsequently discovered the longevity sadhana *Tsedrup Yangnying Kundü* (*Union of All Innermost Longevity Practices*), at Yamalung itself (Akester 2016, 301 and 302 fn. 4). The Third Gyalwa Karmapa discovered

two longevity treasures at Yamalung and Chimpu (Dudjom Rinpoche 1991, 573 and Akester 2016, 301). Another longevity vase was borne by dakinis to Pel Chuwori and dissolved into the rock at the head of the Tsechu Köpa Labrang spring (Akester 2016, 246 and 247 fn. 78).

595. For a translation of *The Ten Royal Sutras*, see: Buddha Shakyamuni 2021.

596. Yeshé Tsogyal 1999, 119–120.

597. Jamgön Kongtrul 2017.

598. Gyalwa Changchub 2002, 23–28.

599. Tashi Topgyal 2016.

600. As also noted by Jamgön Kongtrul (2011, 48), his birthplace differs depending upon the source consulted. Here we are following the *Pema Kathang*.

601. We include here a brief summary of the story as told in the *Pema Kathang*. Lotsawa Vairocana's life story has been translated and published in English. Thus, for a full account of these events, see: Yudra Nyingpo 2004.

602. Nyoshul Khenpo 2005, 50.

603. Gyalmo Tsawarong was a district between eastern Tibet and China. Not to be confused with the valley of Tsawa Rong in Nuwakot in Nepal, a discussion of which you will find in our Nepal Volume.

604. At Shauk Tago, a sacred site in Bhutan, on Friday, the 23rd of August 1680, Terdak Lingpa revealed in public the *Tukjé Chenpo Deshek Kundü* (*The Great Compassionate One; the Universal Gathering of the Sugatas*) (Dudjom Rinpoche 1992, 828).

605. Jamgön Kongtrul.

606. Dudjom Rinpoche 1992, 828.

607. Akester 2016, 302 fn. 4.

608. Sørensen 2005, 56–58.

609. Translated from: O rgyan gling pa 1987, 390.

610. Akester provides a quotation from the *Lhodrak Chöjung*, highlighting this relationship (2016, 133).

611. Gyalwa Changchub 2002, 124.

612. Translated from: O rgyan gling pa 1987, 590.

613. Translated from: mkhyen brtse'i dbang po 2020, 64.

614. Akester 2016, 133.

615. Depending upon the source consulted, Drak Yerpa may replace Drak Yangdzong as the sacred site of the Mahaguru's awakened body. See e.g.: Dilgo Khyentse 2022.

616. Akester 2016, 137.

617. For a further explanation of the Drak Yerpa caves and their sacred features, see: Akester 2016, 133–139; Gyurme Dorjé 2009, 141–142; Dowman 1996, 73–79; Chan 1994 338–343; and Everding 2019 Vol. I, 279–287.

618. Chökyi Lodrö 2020.

619. Chan 1994, 339.

620. Akester 2016, 136–137.

621. Chan 1994, 340.

622. Gyalwa Changchub 2002, 121–123. Depending upon the source consulted, the number of siddhas may vary. Jamgön Kontrul (2018a) states: "eighty of the Guru's students attained rainbow body at Yerpa."

623. Mandelbaum 2007b.

624. There are varying accounts as to the revelation of this particular Hayagriva practice. According to Jamgön Kongtrul Rinpoche, it was revealed by the combined efforts of three tertöns (Jamgön Kongtrul 2011, 191–192 and Akester 2016, 136 fn. 8).

625. Following the story as told by Dudjom Rinpoche (1991, 714–716).

626. For more information on Maratika, see our Nepal Volume: Padmasambhava 2019, 105–116.

627. For a brief biography of Yakchar Ngönmo, see: Jamgön Kongtrul 2011, 112–113.

628. For a brief biography of Düdul Lingpa, see: Jamgön Kongtrul 2011, 113 and 249–250.

629. Jamgön Kongtrul 2012, 227–228.

630. Translated from: mkhyen brtse'i dbang po 1980, 394.

631. Jamgön Kontrul 2013.

632. For a further description of the Mahaguru's eleven deeds, see our India Volume: Padmasambhava 2021, 57–59.

633. For Chögyam Trungpa Rinpoche's explanation of the deeper psychological meaning of this aspect, see: Chögyam Trungpa 2001, 167–182. For a further explanation of Guru Dorjé Drolö, see also: Khenchen Palden Sherab Rinpoche and Khenpo Tsewang 2012, 97–102.

634. However, according to Kyapjé Tulku Urgyen Rinpoche only five of them are known (Padmasambhava 2004, 209 fn. 13). For a list, see e.g.: Padmasambhava 2013, 225 fn. 46.

635. Gyalwa Changchub 2002, 94–96 and 134–135.

636. Ratna Lingpa 2019.

637. Following Matthew Akester's description (2016, 370). For more

information on Önphu Taktsang, see also: McCue 2010, 97–99.

638. Gyalwa Changchub 2002, 17. For more on this story, see our chapter on Tsogyal Lhatso.

639. For this story, see our chapter on Paro Taktsang.

640. Gyalwa Changchub 2002, 95.

641. For the Mahaguru's accomplishment of Vajrakilaya at the Asura and Yangleshö caves, see our Nepal Volume: Padmasambhava 2019, 139–154.

642. Gyalwa Changchub 2002, 94.

643. Gyalwa Changchub 2002, 96.

644. Gyalwa Changchub 2002, 101.

645. For the Mahaguru's accomplishment of Buddha Amitayus at the Maratika caves, see our Nepal Volume: Padmasambhava 2019, 105–116.

646. For the Mahaguru's accomplishment of Buddha Amitayus at the Maratika caves, see our Nepal Volume: Padmasambhava 2019, 105–116.

647. Gyalwa Changchub 2002, 134.

648. Gyalwa Changchub 2002, 134.

649. Jamgön Kongtrul 2011, 124; Akester 2016, 370 fn. 87.

650. For a biography of Rikdzin Lekden Dorjé, see e.g.: Samten Chhosphel 2013; and Jamgön Kongtrul 2011, 238–239.

651. For more on Rikdzin Gödem, see the earlier chapter on Mangyul.

652. Akester 2016, 370 fn. 87.

653. Akester 2016, 370 fn. 87; Samten Chhosphel 2013; Jamgön Kongtrul 2011, 239.

654. For a short biography of Ratön Topden Dorjé, see: Jamgön Kongtrul 2011, 273–275.

655. For more on Langchen Palkyi Sengé, see the earlier chapter on Paro Taktsang.

656. Li 2018, 114.

657. Gyatso 1998, 46–47.

658. Li 2018, 92–93.

659. Translated from: mkhyen brtse'i dbang po 1980, 418.

660. Translated from the Tibetan: blo gros mtha' yas 2005b, 128.

661. Pema Shelpuk (The Lotus Crystal Cave), at Meshö Dzam in Kham. For a description of this sacred site, see the chapters that follow.

662. Padmasambhava 2013, 225 fn. 46.

663. Gyalwa Changchub 2002, 96.

664. Padmasambhava 2013, 117.

665. Padmasambhava 2004, 6.

666. Padmasambhava 2004, 7.

667. Padmasambhava 2004, 7-8.

668. Padmasambhava 2013, 110.

669. Padmasambhava 2013, 111.

670. Padmasambhava 2013, 111–112.

671. Gyalwa Changchub 2002, 134-135.

672. Jamyang Khyentse Wangpo.

673. According to Jamyang Khyentse Wangpo, Chokgyur Lingpa primarily revealed the *Damchö Nyingpo Kor-nga* (*The Essential Sacred Dharma in Five Cycles*), featured in Volume 31 of the Chokling Tersar.

674. The ladder was needed in order to reach the cave.

675. Jampal Parol Goljom (Destroyer of External Hindrances), is a wrathful form of Mañjushri.

676. Chokgyur Dechen Lingpa.

677. Along with a representative statue (*kutsap*) of Guru Dorjé Draktsal, Chokgyur Lingpa revealed the *Lamrim Yeshé Nyingpo* (*The Gradual Path of the Wisdom Essence*) at this site of Chimé Karmo Taktsang. He revealed an associated sadhana, *The Secret Practice of Dorjé Draktsal*, from Yegyal Namkha Dzö.

678. Chokgyur Lingpa removed his yogic skirt and tied it with his belt to a stick. Using it as a net, he caught and retrieved the treasure (Orgyen Tobgyal 1990, 15).

679. This refers to the gold which Chokgyur Lingpa drew forth from the lake. For a detailed account of this revelation, see also Orgyen Tobgyal Rinpoche 1990, 14–16. Additionally, as described, Jamyang Khyentsé Wangpo retrieved a *terma* treasure entitled the *Tsasum Gyütrul Drawa* (*Magical Net of the Three Roots*) from the lake, the text of which is found in Volume 3 of his Collected Writings.

680. Chokgyur Dechen Lingpa 2013.

681. For a translation of *The Light of Wisdom*, see: Padamsambhava 2003.

682. For more information on Mipham Rinpoche's stay at Karmo Taktsang, see e.g.: Dilgo Khyentse 2020, 62–65.

683. For a translation of Mipham Rinpoche's *White Lotus* commentary, see: Mipham Rinpoche 2015a.

684. For a translation of the sadhana, see: Mipham Rinpoche 2015b. And, for a commentary on this sadhana, see: Dilgo Khyentse 2021.

685. Dilgo Khyentse 2021.

686. Rigpa Translations. For an alternative translation and the full story

surrounding Mipham Rinpoche's passing, see: Dilgo Khyentse 2020, 112.

687. Tulku Thondrup 1996, 56–57; and Padmasambhava 2021, 135–136.

688. For these stories, see: Padmasambhava 2021, 83–85 and 149; and Tulku Thondrup 1996, 56–57.

689. Nyoshul Khenpo 2005, 50.

690. Nyoshul Khenpo 2005, xliv.

691. For the meeting of Garap Dorjé and Guru Padmasambhava, see: Padmasambhava 2021, 83–85. For the meeting of Shri Singha and Guru Padmasambhava, see: Padmasambhava 2021, 194–195.

692. Nyoshul Khenpo 2005, 50; and Tulku Thondrup 1996, 66–67.

693. Orgyen Topgyal Rinpoche 2014; and Nyoshul Khenpo 2005, 49–50.

694. Orgyen Topgyal Rinpoche 2014.

695. These five were Dharma King Trisong Detsen, Nyang Tingdzin Zangpo, Prince Muné Tsepo, Kawa Paltsek and Chokro Lu'i Gyaltsen.

696. Nyoshul Khenpo 2005, 50–51.

697. Orgyen Topgyal Rinpoche 2014.

698. Nyoshul Khenpo 2005, xliv–xlv and 50.

699. Translated from the Tibetan: dil mgo mkhyen brtse 1994, 134.

700. Samye Translations 2023a, 132.

701. Orgyen Tobgyal Rinpoche 1990, 8. For more information on how to reach Pema Shelpuk, see e.g.: Gyurme Dorjé 2009, 464–465; and McCue 2010, 301–303. For a visual journey to Pema Shelpuk, see: Samye Translations 2023a, 224–233.

702. Translated from: mkhyen brtse'i dbang po 2008, 3–4.

703. Translated from: mchog 'gyur gling pa 2013, 10–11.

704. The original text states Sosadvipa (Sosa ling) instead of Sitavana charnel ground. However, in this chapter's initial quotation Kyapjé Dilgo Khyentsé Rinpoche clarifies that Sosadvipa is to be understood here as referring to the Sitavana charnel ground.

705. Translated from: mkhyen brtse'i dbang po 2008, 3.

706. Dilgo Khyentse and Orgyen Tobgyal 2017, 518.

707. Khyentse Wangpo 2023. Please note that we've also shared the story of the *Dzokchen Desum* revelation in our previous publication, *Terchen Chokgyur Dechen Zhikpo Lingpa*, featuring the treasure sites of Chokgyur Lingpa. See: Samye Translations 2023b, 132–133.

708. Orgyen Tobgyal Rinpoche 1990, 8–9.

709. Samye Translations 2023a, 81.

710. Orgyen Tobgyal Rinpoche 1990, 9.

711. Following the revelation of the *Vairo Nyingtik*, Chokgyur Lingpa and Jamyang Khyentse Wangpo revealed: the *Garap Nyingtik* from Meshö Dzamnang Drakar Yangtsé; the *Jampel Nyingtik* from Drinyen Dong; the *Tsogyel Nyingtik* from Sengé Namdrak; and the *Pema Garwang Nyingtik*, *Sangdak Nyingtik* and *Riksum Nyingtik*, from Yegyel Namkha Dzö (Khyentsé Wangpo 2023; and Jamgön Kongtrul 2012, 210).

712. Tulku Urgyen Rinpoche 2005, 70.

713. Khyentse Wangpo 2023. Please note that we've also shared the story of the *Zabtik Drolchok* revelation in our previous publication, *Terchen Chokgyur Dechen Zhikpo Lingpa*, which features the treasure sites of Chokgyur Lingpa. See: Samye Translations 2023b, 263.

714. Tulku Urgyen Rinpoche and Trulshik Adeu Rinpoche 2007, 66.

715. Jamgön Kongtrul 2012, 208.

716. Tulku Urgyen Rinpoche and Trulshik Adeu Rinpoche 2007, 66.

717. Dilgo Khyentse 2010, 105.

718. Dilgo Khyentse 2010, 145.

719. Ratna Lingpa 2016.

720. Here, and for the quotations below, instead of the *Pema Kathang*, we are following *A Garland of Vajra Gems* revealed by Jamgön Kongtrul (2018b), which presents a succinct account of the exchanges between the Mahaguru and Prince Mutik Tsenpo.

721. Jamgön Kongtrul 2018b.

722. Jamgön Kongtrul 2018b.

723. Jamgön Kongtrul 2018b.

724. Jamgön Kongtrul 2018b.

725. Yeshe Tsogyal 1999, 170–171.

726. For further pieces of the Mahaguru's heart advice, see especially: Yeshe Tsogyal 1999, 155–197. See also our chapters on Samye and Yarlung Sheldrak for the heart advice that the Mahaguru granted to the queen and the two dakinis.

727. Jamgön Kongtrul 2018b.

728. For translations of these prayers, see: Zangpo Drakpa 2010 and Pema Lingpa 2014. A translation of the *Mahaguru Aspiration Prayer* is included in the prayer section at the back of this book.

729. Gyalwa Changchub 2002, 141.

730. While the treasure biographies generally agree that the Mahaguru left Tibet in a Wood Monkey Year and on the 10th day of the Monkey month, the total duration of the Mahaguru's time in Tibet varies. For a brief discussion of

this, see e.g.: Yeshé Tsogyal 1999, 9–11 and Taranatha 2019.

731. Translated from: o rgyan gling pa 1987, 697–703.

732. For a short biography of Tulku Zangpo Drakpa, see Valentine 2016. For more on Rikdzin Gödem, see our earlier chapter on Mangyul.

733. For a full translation of the *Le'ü Dün Ma*, see: Zangpo Drakpa 2010.

734. For a translation of the extensive *Tukdrup Yishin Norbu Sadhana*, see: Jamyang Khyentse Wangpo and Chokgyur Dechen Lingpa 2023.

735. For a biography of Pema Lingpa, see: Harding 2003; or Maki 2011.

736. For a translation of this prayer, see the final prayer section of this book. For a teaching by Phakchok Rinpoche on the significance of the prayer, see our Nepal Volume: Padmasambhava 2019, 37–47.

737. See the following chapter on Zangdok Palri for the connection between Zangdok Palri and Sri Lanka in particular.

738. For the visionary journeys to Zangdok Palri, see e.g.: Samye Translations 2023b; Dudjom Lingpa 2011; Jatsön Nyingpo 2017; Jikme Lingpa 2022c. For a breathtaking visual journey featuring thangka depictions and constructed representations of Zangdok Palri, see especially: Pui Lamsam 2013.

739. See e.g.: Samye Translations 2023b, 37–38.

740. Orgyen Topgyal Rinpoche at Gomde Denmark, September 1st, 2012.

741. Orgyen Topgyal Rinpoche at Asura Cave, May 9th, 2014.

742. Samye Translations 2023b, 176.

743. Dudjom Lingpa 2011.

744. Zangpo Drakpa 2010e.

745. Zangpo Drakpa 2010c.

746. Jamgön Kongtrul 1995, 109–113.

747. Jamgön Kongtrul 1995, 113.

748. For more on Sri Lanka as a sacred Vajrayana site, see the Mount Malaya chapter in our India Volume: Padmasambhava 2021, 126–138. For Chokgyur Lingpa's visionary journey, see: Samye Translations 2023b, 181–223. For more on the relationship between Sri Lanka and Camaradvipa, see: Dudjom Rinpoche 1991, 455 and Bogin 2014, 11.

749. Mipham Rinpoche 1999.

750. See also Phakchok Rinpoche's explanation: Samye Translations 2023b, 38.

751. See also Bogin (2004, 9), who also outlines this connection.

752. Zangpo Drakpa 2010c.

753. For a detailed discussion of 'internal pilgrimage', see: Ngawang Zangpo 2001 and Huber 2008, 86–93.

754. For a teaching by Phakchok Rinpoche on this prayer, see: Samye Translations 2023b, 224–230.

755. Chokgyur Dechen Lingpa 2018.

756. Chokgyur Lingpa 2017a.

757. Parallels can be drawn between this event and the final subjugation of Rudra at the hands of Hayagriva or Vajrapani. Guru Rinpoche's subjugation of the rakshasa King can thus be seen as a re-enactment of the Rudra subjugation myth. See: Bogin 2014, 9.

758. Chokgyur Lingpa 2017a.

759. Dudjom Rinpoche 1991, 520–521.

760. For more on Samye Chimpu, see our chapter on Samye Chimpu. For a further detailed examination and explanation of this prayer, see especially: Jikme Lingpa 2022c.

761. Jikmé Lingpa 1999.

762. With reference to the description by Dudjom Lingpa (Dudjom Lingpa 2011, 65).

763. Jikmé Lingpa 1999.

764. Ngawang Zangpo 2002, 303.

765. Jikmé Lingpa 1999.

766. Jikmé Lingpa 1999.

767. Khandro Yeshe Tsogyal and Yuthok Yönten Gönpo.

768. Jikmé Lingpa 1999.

769. For Chokgyur Lingpa's full visionary account, see: Samye Translations 2023b, 181–223. Please note that, in Chokgyur Lingpa's own visionary account, the descriptions of the middle storey of the palace (the sambhogakaya) and the upper (the dharmakaya) differ from those found in Rigdzin Jikmé Lingpa's aspiration prayer, cited above. This of course does not imply that one is right and the other wrong. Rather, it reflects that Zangdok Palri can arise differently according to the perception of beings.

770. Jamgön Kongtrul 2012, 9–10. For a further explanation of this by Jamgön Kontrul, see: Ibid., 22 and 190–191.

771. Jamgön Kongtrul 2003, 374.

772. Jamgön Kongtrul 2003, 65.

773. This teaching took place on September 19, 2015.

774. Guru Chöwang 2004.

775. Guru Chöwang 2004.

776. Chokgyur Dechen Lingpa 2017b.

777. Longchenpa and Jikmé Lingpa 2005.

778. Do Khyentsé Yeshé Dorjé 2016.
779. Do Khyentsé Yeshé Dorjé 2015.
780. Mipham Rinpoche 2004.
781. Chokgyur Dechen Lingpa 2015.
782. Trinlé Özer 2011.
783. Chokgyur Dechen Lingpa 2019.
784. Pema Lingpa 2011.
785. Mipham Rinpoche 2018
786. Chokgyur Dechen Lingpa 2018.

BIBLIOGRAPHY

Tibetan

We have translated excerpts from the following Tibetan source texts for our book. Most of the original texts can be easily accessed via BDRC (https://www.tbrc.org).

Bdud 'joms ye shes rdo rje. 1996. *Bdud 'joms chos 'byung.* Khreng tu'u: Si khron mi rigs dpe skrun khang.

O rgyan gling pa. 1986. *Bka' thang sde lnga.* Pe cin: mi rigs dpe skrun khang.

———. 1987. *Pad+ma bka' thang.* Khreng tu'u: Si khron mi rigs dpe skrun khang.

O rgyan 'jigs med chos kyi dbang po. 2013. *kun bzang bla ma'i zhal lung.* Delhi: Chosspyod Publication.

Sangs rgyas gling pa. 2007. *Bka' thang gser phreng.* Lha sa: Bod ljongs mi dmangs dpe skrun khang.

Slob dpon sems dpa' rdo rje. 2017. *rgya gar nang pa'i gnas chen khag dang rgyud sde las byung ba'i yul nyer bzhi dang dur khrod brgyad kyi byung ba mdor bsdu.* Kalimpong: Shri Diwakar Publications.

Toh. 2092. Vimalamitra. *mtshan don gsal bar byed pa'i sgron ma.* rgyud, tshi 1b1-38b2.

Printed Publications and Online Resources

For our research we have relied on the following books, academic journals, and translations kindly made available online by *Lotsawa House* (http://lotsawa-house.org) and *Lhasey Lotsawa* (http://lhaseylotsawa.org).

Abhayadatta. 1979. *Buddha's Lions: Lives of the Eighty-four Siddhas.* Emeryville: Dharma Publishing.

Alak Zenkar. 2005. "A Brief Presentation of the Nine Vehicles." On *Lotsawa House.* Trans. Adam Pearcey. https://www.lotsawahouse.org/tibetan-masters/alak-zenkar/nine-yanas.

———. 2006. "Brief Biography of Jamyang Khyentse Wangpo the Great." On *Lotsawa House.* Trans. Adam Pearcey. https://www.lotsawahouse.org/tibetan-masters/alak-zenkar/brief-biography-of-jamyang-khyentse-wangpo.

Almogi, Orna. 2016. "Tantric Scriptures in the rNying Ma Rgyud 'bum Believed to Be Transmitted into Tibet by Kāśmirian Panditas: A Preliminary

Survey." In *Around Abhinavagupta*, ed. Eli Franco and Isabelle Ratié. Münster: LIT Verlag.

Antonini, C. S. "Preliminary Notes on the Excavation of the Necropolises Found in Western Pakistan." *East and West 14* (1963): 13-26.

Aryashura. 2009. *Garland of the Buddha's Past Lives, Vol. I*. Translated by Justin Meiland. New York University Press.

Ashvaghosha. 2008. *Life of the Buddha*. Translated by Patrick Olivelle. New York: Clay Sanskrit Library.

Beal, Samuel. 1884a. *Si-yu-ki. Buddhist Records of the Western World Vol. I*. Translated from the Chinese of Hiuen Tsiang, AD 629. London: Trübner & Co., Ludgate Hill, 1884.

———. 1884b. *Si-yu-ki. Buddhist Records of the Western World Vol. II*. Translated from the Chinese of Hiuen Tsiang, AD 629. London: Trübner & Co., Ludgate Hill, 1884.

———. 1914. The Life of Hiuen-Tsiang: By the Shaman Hwui Li with an Introduction Containing an Account of the Works of I-Tsing. London: Trübner & Co., 1914.

Beer, Robert. 1999. The Encyclopedia of Tibetan Symbols and Motifs. Boston: Shambala.

Bischoff, F.A., and C. Hartman. 1971. "Padmasambhava's Invention of the Phur-bu: Ms. Pelliot Tibétain 44." In A. Macdonald (ed.) *Études tibétaines dédiées à la mémoire de Marcelle Lalou*. Paris, Adrien Maisonneuve: 11–27.

Bogin, Benjamin. 2014. "Locating the Copper-Colored Mountain: Buddhist Cosmology, Himalayan Geography, and Maps of Imagined Worlds." In *Himalaya, the Journal of the Association for Nepal and Himalayan Studies* 34, no. 2.

Boord, Martin. 1993. *The Cult of the Deity Vajrakilaya*. Tring: The Institute of Buddhist Studies.

———. 2002. *A Bolt of Lightning from the Blue*. Berlin: Khordong.

Buddha Shakyamuni. 2012. "The Glorious King of Tantras That Resolves All Secrets." On *84000*. Trans. Dharmachakra Translation Committee, 2012. https://read.84000.co/translation/toh384.html.

———. 2013. "The Play in Full." On *84000*. Trans. Dharmachakra Translation Committee, 2013. https://read.84000.co/translation/toh95.html.

Buswell, Robert E. and Donald S. Lopez Jr. 2014. "Otantapurī." In *The Princeton Dictionary of Buddhism*. Princeton, NJ: Princeton University Press, 601.

Butön Rinchen Drup. 1931a. *History of Buddhism (Chos 'Byung) Vol. I.* Trans. Eugéne Obermiller. Heidelberg: In Kommission bei O. Harrassowitz.

———. 1931b. *History of Buddhism (Chos 'Byung) Vol. II.* Trans. Eugéne Obermiller. Heidelberg: In Kommission bei O. Harrassowitz.

Cantwell, Cathy. 1989. "An Ethnographic Account of the Religious Practice in a Tibetan Buddhist Refugee Monastery in Northern India." *PhD dissertation.* University of Kent.

———. 2014. "Jacob P. Dalton The Taming of the Demons: Violence and Liberation in Tibetan Buddhism." In *History of Religions, Vol. 54, No. 1* (August 2014): 106–112.

Chatral Rinpoche. 2016. "A Guide to Uddiyana (Ujjain)." On *Lotsawa House.* Trans. Lhasey Lotsawa. https://www.lotsawa./house.org/tibetan-masters/chatral-rinpoche/guide-to-uddiyana.

Chittadhar Hridaya. 2010. *Sugata Saurabha.* Translation by Todd T. Lewis and Subarna Man Tuladhar. Oxford: Oxford University Press.

Chögyam Trungpa. 2001. *Crazy Wisdom.* Ed. Sherab Chödzin. Boston: Shambala.

Chokgyur Dechen Lingpa. 2015. "The Prayer in Six Vajra Lines." On *Lotsawa House.* Trans. Patrick Gaffney. http://www.lotsawahouse.org/tibetan-masters/chokgyur-dechen-lingpa/prayer-in-six-vajra-lines

———. 2017a. "Barche Lamsel—The Prayer that Removes All Obstacles from the Path." On *Lotsawa House.* Trans. Rigpa Translations. http://www.lotsawahouse.org/tibetan-masters/chokgyur-dechen-lingpa/barche-lamsel.

———. 2017b. "A Concise Guru Yoga." On *Lotsawa House.* Trans. Lhasey Lotsawa. http://www.lotsawahouse.org/tibetan-masters/chokgyur-dechen-lingpa/concise-guru-yoga.

———. 2018. "A Prayer of Aspiration for the Copper-Coloured Mountain of Glory." On *Lotsawa House.* Trans. Lhasey Lotsawa. http://www.lotsawahouse.org/tibetan-masters/chokgyur-dechen-lingpa/zangdokpalri-monlam.

———. 2020. "*The Wish-Fulfilling Tree*: The Life-Story of the Master of Uddiyana as found in Padmasambhava's Sevenfold Cycle of Profundity." On *Lhasey Lotsawa.* Trans. Lhasey Lotsawa. https://lhaseylotsawa.org/library/the-wishfulfilling-tree.

Chökyi Lodrö. 2018a. "A Song of Perfect Joy." On *Lotsawa House.* Trans. Adam Pearcey. https://www.lotsawahouse.org/tibetan-masters/jamyang-khyentse-chokyi-lodro/rajgir-vulture-peak-nalanda-praise.

———. 2018b. "In Praise of Tso Pema." On *Lotsawa House.* Trans.

Adam Pearcey. https://www.lotsawahouse.org/tibetan-masters/jamyang-khyentse-chokyi-lodro/tso-pema-praise.

———. 2018c. "Gathering Auspiciousness." On *Lotsawa House*. Trans. Adam Pearcey. https://www.lotsawahouse.org/tibetan-masters/jamyang-khyentse-chokyi-lodro/gathering-auspiciousness-mahabodhi-prayer.

———. 2020. "Vajra Seat Aspiration." On *Lotsawa House*. Trans. Adam Pearcey. https://www.lotsawahouse.org/tibetan-masters/jamyang-khyentse-chokyi-lodro/vajra-seat-aspiration.

———. 2021. "A Guru Yoga of Śavari." On *Lotsawa House*. Trans. Lhasey Lotsawa. https://www.lotsawahouse.org/tibetan-masters/jamyang-khyentse-chokyi-lodro/shavari-guru-yoga.

Cunningham, Alexander. 1892. *Mahabodhi or the Great Buddhist Temple under the Bodhi Tree at Buddha-Gaya*. London: W.H. Allen.

Dalai Lama. 1985. *The Kalachakra Tantra*. Trans. Jeffrey Hopkins. London: Wisdom Publications.

———. 2005. "A Prayer to Kindle the Three Kinds of Faith Addressed to the Seventeen Great Panditas of Glorious Nalanda." On *Lotsawa House*. Trans. Adam Pearcey. http://www.lotsawahouse.org/tibetan-masters/fourteenth-dalai-lama/seventeen-great-panditas-nalanda.

Dalton, Catherine. 2019. "Enacting Perfection: Buddhajñānāpāda's Vision of a Tantric Buddhist World." *PhD dissertation*. UC Berkeley.

Dalton, Jacob. 2002. *The uses of the dgongs pa 'dus pa'i mdo in the development of the rnyinng-ma school of Tibetan Buddhism*. Asian Language and Cultures: Buddhist Studies. The University of Michigan, 2002.

———. 2011. *The Taming of the Demons*. London: Yale University.

———. 2016. *The Gathering of Intentions: A History of a Tibetan Tantra*. New York: Columbia University Press.

Davidson, Ronald M. 2008. *Tibetan Renaissance: Tantric Buddhism in the Rebirth of Tibetan Culture*. Motilal Banarsidass Publisher.

Decaroli, Robert. 2004. *Haunting the Buddha: Indian Popular Religions and the Formation of Buddhism*. Oxford: Oxford University Press.

Devers, Quentin. "Buddhism before the First Diffusion? The case of Tangol, Dras, Phikhar and Sani-Tarungtse in Purig and Zanskar (Ladakh)." In *Études mongoles et sibériennes, centrasiatiques et tibétaines, 51* (2020).

Dilgo Khyentse and Orgyen Tobgyal. 2017. *The Life and Times of Jamyang Khyentse Chökyi Lodrö: The Great Biography by Dilgo Khyentse Rinpoche and Other Stories*. Boston: Shambhala Publications.

Do Khyentsé. 2015. "A Very Brief Barché Lamsel." On *Lotsawa House*.

Trans. Rigpa Translations. https://www.lotsawahouse.org/tibetan-masters/do-khyentse/very-brief-barche-lamsel.

―――. 2016. "The Lightning Bolt of Compassion—a Short Sampa Lhundrupma." Trans. Rigpa Translations. On *Lotsawa House*. https://www.lotsawahouse.org/tibetan-masters/do-khyentse/lightning-bolt-of-compassion.

Dudjom Lingpa. 2017. "The Biography of the Great Orgyen that Naturally Liberates on Sight." On *Lotsawa House*. Trans. Nick Schmidt. https://www.lotsawahouse.org/tibetan-masters/dudjom-lingpa/biography-of-great-orgyen.

Dudjom Rinpoche. 1987. "A Brief Analysis of Some Important Chronological Events in the History of Buddhism and Tibet," The Tibet Journal Vol. 12, No. 3 (Autumn 1987), 5–16.

―――. 1991. *The Nyingma School of Tibetan Buddhism: Its Fundamentals and History*. Trans. and edited by Gyurme Dorje and Matthew Kapstein. Somerville, MA: Wisdom Publications.

―――. 2013. "The Concise Benefits of the Festival of the Tenth Day." On *Lotsawa House*. Trans. Rigpa Translations. https://www.lotsawahouse.org/tibetan-masters/dudjom-rinpoche/concise-benefits-of-festival-of-the-tenth-day.

Dutt, Sukumar. 1988. *Buddhist Monks and Monasteries of India*. Delhi: Motilal Banarsidass.

Eck, Diana L. 1982. *Banares: City of Light*. New York: Alfred A. Knopf, Inc.

―――. 2012. *India: A Sacred Geography*. New York: Harmony Books.

English Elizabeth. 2002. *Vajrayogini: Her Visualization, Rituals, and Forms*. Boston: Wisdom Publications.

Filigenzi, Anna. 2001. "A Vajrayanic Theme in the Rock Sculpture of Swat (NWFP, Pakistan)". In G. Verardi and S. Vita (eds.) *Buddhist Asia 1*, Papers from the First Conference of Buddhist Studies Held in Naples in May 2001: 37-55.

―――. 2011. "Post-Gandharan Swat. From the Late Buddhist rock-sculptures to the Turki Śāhis dynastic centers", in Ghani-ur-Rahman and Luca M. Olivieri (eds.) *Italian Archaeology and Anthropology in Northern Pakistan (1955-2011) of Journal of Asian Civilizations*, 2011: 193-210.

―――. 2015. *Art and Landscape: Buddhist Rock Sculptures of Late Antique Swat/Uddiyana*. Wien: Austrian Academy of Sciences Press.

Garab Dorjé. 2008. "The Three Statements that Strike the Vital Point." On *Lotsawa House*. Trans. Rigpa Translations. https://www.lotsawahouse.org/indian-masters/garab-dorje/three-statements-that-strike-vital-point.

Geiger, Wilhelm. *The Mahavamsa or The Great Chronicle of Ceylon*. London: Pali Text Society 1912.

Gendün Chöpel. 1985. *Dhammapada: Translation of Dharma Verses with the Tibetan Text*. Trans. into Tibetan by Gendün Chöpel and trans. into English by Dharma Publishing Staff. Berkeley: Dharma Publishing.

———. 2000. *A Guide to India: A Tibetan Account by Amdo Gendun Chöpel*. Translated by Toni Huber. Delhi: Library of Tibetan Works and Archives, 2000.

———. 2014. *Grains of Gold: Tales of a Cosmopolitan Traveler*. Trans. Thupten Jinpa and Donald S. Lopez Jr. Chicago: University of Chicago Press.

Gö Lotsawa. 1949. *The Blue Annals*. Trans. George Roerich. Calcutta: Royal Asiatic Society of Bengal.

Gönpo Tseten. 2018. "A Bouquet of Udumbara Flowers: An Explanation of the Tenth Day." On *Lotsawa House*. Trans. Lhasey Lotsawa. https://www.lotsawahouse.org/tibetan-masters/gonpo-tseten-rinpoche/bouquet-of-udumbara-flowers.

Guru Chöwang. 2004. "Accomplishing the Lama through the Seven Line Prayer." On *Lotsawa House*. Trans. Rigpa Translations. https://www.lotsawahouse.org/tibetan-masters/guru-chowang/seven-line-prayer.

Gustave-Charles Toussaint. 2000. *Padmasambhava: Le Dict de Padma*. Paris: Editions Les Deux Océans.

Gyalwa Changchub and Namkhai Nyingpo. 2002. *Lady of the Lotus-Born: The Life and Enlightenment of Yeshe Tsogyal*. Trans. by the Padmakara Translation Group. Boston: Shambala.

Herdman, Hilary. 2017. "Encircling the Sacred." *Unpublished Dissertation*. University of Bristol.

Hikosaka, Shu. 1998. "The Potiyil Mountain in Tamil Nadu and the Origin of the Avalokiteśvara Cult." Buddhism in Tamil Nadu: Collected Papers. Chennai, India: Institute of Asian Studies. 119–141.

Holt, Sree Padma and A. W. Barber. 2009. *Buddhism in the Krishna River Valley of Andhra*. Albany: State University of New York Press.

Huber, Toni. 2008. *The Holy Land Reborn: Pilgrimage and the Tibetan Reinvention of Buddhist India*. University of Chicago Press.

Jamgön Kongtrul. 2001. Sacred Ground: Jamgon Kongtrul on "Pilgrimage and Sacred Geography". Trans. By Ngawang Zangpo. Ithaca: Snow Lion Publications.

———. 2003. *Timeless Rapture: Inspired Verses of the Shangpa Masters*. Transl. by Ngawang Zangpo. Ithaca: Snow Lion Publications.

———. 2010. *The Treasury of Knowledge: Buddhism's Journey to Tibet*. Trans. Ngawang Zangpo. Ithaca: Snow Lion.

———. 2011. *The Hundred Tertöns*. Trans. Yeshe Gyamtso. Woodstock: KTD Publications.

———. 2013. "The Prayer of the Tenth Days in Guru Rinpoche's Life Story entitled 'The Nucleus of Blessings'." On *Lotsawa House*. Trans. Rigpa Translations. https://www.lotsawahouse.org/tibetan-masters/jamgon-kongtrul/nucleus-of-blessings.

———. 2018. "The Life and Liberation of Padmakara, the Second Buddha." On *Lotsawa House*. Trans. Lhasey Lotsawa. https://www.lotsawahouse.org/tibetan-masters/jamgon-kongtrul/life-and-liberation-of-padmakara.

Jikmé Lingpa. 2019. "Yumka Dechen Gyalmo." On *Lotsawa House*. Trans. Han Kop. https://www.lotsawahouse.org/tibetan-masters/jigme-lingpa/yumka-dechen-gyalmo-sadhana

———. 2020. "Palchen Düpa." On *Lotsawa House*. Trans. Han Kop. https://www.lotsawahouse.org/tibetan-masters/jigme-lingpa/palchen-dupa.

Jikmé Phuntsok. 2019. "Lament Recalling the Guru of Oddiyāna." On *Lotsawa House*. Trans. Adam Pearcey. https://www.lotsawahouse.org/tibetan-masters/khenpo-jigme-phuntsok/spontaneous-lament-recalling-great-guru.

Khenchen Palden Sherab Rinpoche and Khenpo Tsewang. 2012. *Liberating Duality with Wisdom Display: Eight Emanations of Guru Padmasambhava*. Sidney: Dharma Samudra.

Khyentsé Wangpo. 2016. "A Beautiful and Wondrous Udumbara Garland." On *Lotsawa House*. Trans. Lhasey Lotsawa. https://www.lotsawahouse.org/tibetan-masters/jamyang-khyentse-wangpo/beautiful-wondrous-udumbara-garland.

———. 2018. "The History of the Hearing Lineage of the Profound and Secret Practice of Simhamukhā." On *Lotsawa House*. Trans. Lhasey Lotsawa. https://www.lotsawahouse.org/tibetan-masters/jamyang-khyentse-wangpo/history-of-simhamukha.

Kinnard, Jacob N. 2014. *Places in Motion: The Fluid Identities of Temples, Images, and Pilgrims*. Oxford: Oxford University Press.

Kunzang Pelden. 2007. *The Nectar of Manjushri's Speech*. Trans. Padmakara Translation Group. Boston: Shambala.

Kragh, Ulrich Timme. 2018. "Chronotopic Narratives of Seven Gurus and Eleven Texts." *Cracow Indological Studies, 20(2)*: 1–26.

Lerap Dewa Tsal. 2017. "Lives and Liberation of Mandāravā." On *Lotsawa House*. Trans. Lhasey Lotsawa. https://www.lotsawahouse.org/tibetan-masters/samten-lingpa/prayer-lives-and-liberation-of-mandarava.

Lhasey Lotsawa. 2016. *The Great Tertön*. Kathmandu: Lhasey Lotsawa.

Lamotte, Etienne. 1988. History of Indian Buddhism: From the Origins to the Saka Era. Translated from the French by Sara Webb-Boin under the supervision of Jean Dantinne. Louvain Paris: Peters Press.

La Vaissière, Etienne de. 2018. "Inherited Landscapes in Muslim Bactra." In *Eurasian Studies 16.1-2* (2018): 124–141.

Li, Rongxi. 1996. *The Great Tang Dynasty Record of the Western Regions*. Berkeley: Numata Center for Buddhist Translation and Research, 1996.

Li, Brenda WL. 2011. "A Critical Study of the Life of the 13th-Century Tibetan Monk U rgyan pa Rin chen dpal based on his Biographies." *PhD dissertation*. Oxford: Oxford University.

Lokesh Chandra. "Oddiyāna: A New Interpretation." In M. Aris & Aung San Suu Kyi, *Tibetan Studies in Honour of Hugh Richardson*, Warminster, 1980: 73–78.

Longchenpa and Jikmé Lingpa. 2005. "Sampa Nyur Drupma." On *Lotsawa House*. Trans. Rigpa Translations. https://www.lotsawahouse.org/tibetan-masters/longchen-rabjam/sampa-nyur-drupma.

Lopez, Donald. 2019. *Seeing the Sacred in Samsara: An Illustrated Guide to the Eighty-Four Mahāsiddha*. Boston: Shambala.

Mani, Vettam. 1975. *Puranic Encyclopaedia: A Comprehensive Dictionary with Special Reference to the Epic and Puranic Literature*. Delhi: Motilal Banarsidass.

Mayer, Robert. 2012. "Padmasambhava in Early Tibetan Myth and Ritual, Part 3: 'Miraculous births' and 'Womb births.'" On *kīli kīlaya*. http://blogs.orient.ox.ac.uk/kila/2012/09/05/padmasambhava-in-early-tibetan-myth-and-ritual-part-3-miraculous-births-and-womb-births/.

———. 2020. "Uddiyāna, the North West, and Treasure: another piece in the jigsaw?" On *kīli kīlaya*. https://blogs.orient.ox.ac.uk/kila/2020/07/15/uddiyana-the-north-west-and-treasure-another-piece-in-the-jigsaw/

Mendis, Garrett Champness. 1996. *The Early History of Ceylon and its Relations with India and Other Foreign Countries*. Delhi: Asian Educational Services.

Mipham Rinpoche. 2004. "The Prayer which is the Source of All True Realization." On *Lotsawa House*. Trans. Rigpa Translations. https://www.lotsawahouse.org/tibetan-masters/mipham/source-of-all-true-realization.

———. 2015. *White Lotus: An Explanation of the Seven-line Prayer to Guru Padmasambhava*. Trans. by The Padmakara Translation Group. Boston: Shambala.

———. 2018. "Light Offering Prayer." On *Lotsawa House*. Trans. Lhasey Lotsawa. https://www.lotsawahouse.org/tibetan-masters/mipham/light-offering-prayer.

Nagarjuna. 2015. *The Root Stanzas on the Middle Way*. Transl. Padmakara Translation Group. Boulder: Shambhala.

———. 2016. "Great Praise of the Twelve Acts of the Buddha." On *Lotsawa House*. Trans. Rigpa Translations. https://www.lotsawahouse.org/indian-masters/nagarjuna/great-praise-twelve-acts-buddha.

Ngawang Zangpo. 2002. *Guru Rinpoche: His Life and Times*. Ithaca: Snow Lion Publications.

Namkhai Norbu. 2011. "Oddiyana and Shambala." In *The Mirror: Newspaper of the International Dzogchen Community 113* (Nov. – Dec. 2011), 2–4.

Nyang-ral Nyima Özer. 2017. On *Lotsawa House*. Trans. Lhasey Lotsawa. "A Prayer Recalling the Life and Liberation of the Precious Master Padmasambhava." https://www.lotsawahouse.org/tibetan-masters/nyang-ral-nyima-ozer/prayer-recalling-life-and-liberation.

———. 2018. "The Abbreviated 'Prayer in Seven Chapters.'" On *Lotsawa House*. Trans. Rigpa Translations. https://www.lotsawahouse.org/tibetan-masters/nyang-ral-nyima-ozer/short-leu-dunma.

Nyoshul Khenpo. 2005. A Marvelous Garland of Rare Gems. Junction City: Padma Publishing.its,snowy landrotsana renturned

Olivieri, Luca Maria. 2016. "Guru Padmasambhava in Context: Archaeological and Historical Evidence from Swat/Uddiyana (c. 8th century CE)." *Journal of Bhutan Studies 34* (2016), 20–42.

———. 2017. "The itinerary of O rgyan pa in Swat/Uddiyana (second half of 13th Century)." *Journal of Asian Civilizations 40, no. 1* (2017): 87–101.

Orgyen Lingpa. 2016. "A Concise History of Orgyen Padma's Enlightened Deeds." On *Lotsawa House*. Trans. Lhasey Lotsawa. https://www.lotsawahouse.org/tibetan-masters/orgyen-lingpa/concise-history-of-orgyen-padmas-enlightened-deeds.

Padmasambhava. 1998. *The Lives and Liberation of Princess Mandarava*. Trans. Lama Chonam and Sangye Khandro. Boston: Wisdom Publications.

———. 2004. *Light of Wisdom*. Vol. 1. Translated by Erik Pema Kunsang. Kathmandu: Rangjung Yeshe.

———. 2019. *Following in Your Footsteps: The Lotus-Born Guru in Nepal*. Compiled and narrated by Lhasey Lotsawa. Kathmandu: Rangjung Yeshe.

Paranavitana, S. 1958. "The God of Adam's Peak." *Artibus Asiae*. Supplementum, vol. 18, 1958, 5–78.

Patrul Rinpoche. 1998. *The Words of My Perfect Teacher*. Translated by Padmakara Translation Group. Boston: Shambala.

———. 2012. "Clarifying the Two Truths." On *Lotsawa House*. Trans. Adam Pearcey. https://www.lotsawahouse.org/tibetan-masters/ patrul-rinpoche/two-truths-view-mahayana.

Quagliotti, Anna Maria. 2008. "New Considerations on some Gandhāran Fasting Buddhas." In *Miscellanies about the Buddha Image*, edited by Claudine Bautze-Picron, 65–76. Oxford: Archaeopress.

Radich, Michael. 2015. *The Mahaparinirvana-Mahasutra and the Emergence of Tathagatagarbha Doctrine*, ed. Michael Zimmmermann. Hamburg: Hamburg University Press.

Ratna Lingpa. 2019. "The Invocation of Uddiyana on the Tenth Day. On *Lotsawa House*. Trans. Lhasey Lotsawa. https://www.lotsawahouse.org/ tibetan-masters/ratna-lingpa/tenth-day-invocation.

Revire, Nicolas. 2011. "Facts and Fiction: The Myth of Suvannabhūmi through the Thai and Burmese Looking Glass." *Mahachulalongkorn Journal of Buddhist Studies, 4* (2011): 79–80.

Rich, Bruce. 2010. *To Uphold the World: A Call for a New Global Ethic from Ancient India*. Boston: Beacon Press.

Rigpa Translations. 2004. *A Great Treasure of Blessings*. Lodeve: The *Tertön* Sogyal Trust.

Rizvi, Janet. 1998. *Ladakh, Crossroads of High Asia*. Oxford: Oxford University Press.

———. *Trans-Himalayan Caravans – Merchant Princes and Peasant Traders in Ladakh*. Oxford: India Paperbacks, 2001.

Sahoo, Akhil Kumar. "Tāmralipta: The Ancient Port in Odisha." In Odisha Review June 2013. Bhubaneswar: Department of Information & Public Relations, 2013): 48–51.

Salvini, Mattia. 2018. "Recollecting the Pilgrimage to Mount Potalaka." On *Levekunst*. http://levekunst.com/recollecting-the-pilgrimage-to-potalaka/.

Sanderson, Alexis. 2007. "The Śaiva Exegesis of Kashmiri" in *Mélanges tantriques à la mémoire d'Hélène Brunner / Tantric Studies in Memory of Hélène Brunner*, edited by Dominic Goodall and André Padoux, Collection Indologie

106, Pondicherry: Institut français d'Indologie / École française d'Extrême-Orient, 2007: 231–442.

———. 2009. "The Śaiva Age: The Rise and Dominance of Śaivism during the Early Medieval Period." In *Genesis and Development of Tantrism*, edited by Shingo Einoo, Institute of Oriental Culture Special Series, 23. Tokyo: Institute of Oriental Culture, University of Tokyo, 2009: 41–350.

Schopen, Gregory. 1996. "Immigrant Monks and the Proto-Historical Dead: The Buddhist Occupation of Early Burial Sites in India." In *Festschrift fü Dieter Schlingloff*, edited by F. Wilhelm, 215–238. Munich: Reinbek.

———. 2004. *Buddhist Monks and Business Matters: Still More Papers on Monastic Buddhism in India*. Honolulu: University of Hawai Press.

Shaoyong, Ye. 2019. "Nagarjuna." In Jonathan A. Silk (ed.) *Brill's Encyclopedia of Buddhism, Vol. II: Lives*, 335–347. Leiden: Brill.

Sherab Drime. 2021. "Buddhagupta-nātha." On *Treasury of Lives*. http://treasuryoflives.org/biographies/view/Buddhagupta-natha/6412.

Spagnesi, Piero. 2006. "Aspects of the Architecture of the Buddhist Sacred Areas in Swat". In: Luca M. Olivieri (ed[s]): *Special Issue for the 50th Anniversary of the IsIAO Italian Archaeological Mission in Pakistan* of *East and West*, 2006: 151–175.

Sogyal Rinpoche. 2002. *The Tibetan Book of Living and Dying*. Edited by Patrick Gaffney, and Andrew Harvey. New York: Harper Collins.

Sonam Gyaltsen. 2006. *The Clear Mirror: A Traditional Account of Tibetan's Golden Age*. Translated by McComas Taylor. Ithaca: Snow Lion Press.

Sørensen, Per K. 1994. *Tibetan Buddhist Historiography: The Mirror Illuminating the Royal Genealogies: An Annotated Translation of the XIVth Century Chronicle rGyal-rabs gsal-ba'i me-long*. Asiatische Forschungen Band 128. Wiesbaden: Harrassowitz Verlag.

Stein, M. Aurel. *Ancient Khotan: Detailed Report of Archaeological Explorations in Eastern Turkestan*. Oxford: Clarendon Press, 1907.

Strong, John S. 1992. *The Legend and Cult of Upagupta: Sanskrit Buddhism in North India and Southeast Asia*. Princeton: Princeton University Press.

———. 2014. *The Legend of King Aśoka: A Study and Translation of the Asokavadana*. Princeton: Princeton University Press.

Sugiki, Tsunehiko. 2009. "The Structure and Traditions of the Systems of Holy Sites in Buddhist Samvara Cycle and its Related Scriptural Cycles in Early Medieval South Asia." In: S. Einoo (ed.) *Genesis and Development of Tantrism*, Institute of Oriental Culture, University of Tokyo, 515–558.

Suzuki, D.T. 1932. *The Lankavatara Sutra: A Mahayana Text*. London: Routledge Kegan Paul.

Tarthang Tulku. 1991. *Lineage of Diamond Light: Crystal Mirror Series, Volume V*. Berkeley: Dharma Publishing.

Taranatha. 1983. *The Seven Instruction Lineages (Bka' babs bdun ldan)*. Trans. David Templeman. Library of Tibetan Works and Archives: Dharamsala.

———. 1990. *History of Buddhism in India*. Trans. Lama Chimpa and Alaka Chattopadhyaya. Delhi: Motilal Banarsidass.

———. 2019. "Three Reasons for Confidence: A Work Telling the Life and Liberation Story of the Great Master Padmakara." On *Lotsawa House*. Trans. Lhasey Lotsawa. https://www.lotsawahouse.org/tibetan-masters/taranatha/three-reasons-for-confidence.

Tenzin, Acharya Kirti Tulku Lobsang, and K. Dhondup. 1982. "Early Relations between Tibet and Nepal (7th to 8th Centuries)." In *The Tibet Journal* 7, no. 1/2.

Tertön Sogyal. 2019. "A Synopsis of the Vajra-Guru Mantra." On *Lotsawa House*. Trans. Lhasey Lotsawa. https://www.lotsawahouse.org/tibetan-masters/terton-sogyal/vajra-guru-mantra.

Tenpé Nyima. 2019. "Garland of Night-Blooming Water Lilies." On *Lotsawa House*. Trans. Lhasey Lotsawa. https://www.lotsawahouse.org/tibetan-masters/dodrupchen-III/garland-of-night-blooming-water-lilies.

Thich Nhat Hanh. 1987. *Old Path White Clouds: Walking in the Footsteps of the Buddha*. Berkeley: Parallax Press.

Thomas F. W. 1935. *Tibetan Literary Texts and Documents Concerning Chinese Turkestan*. London: The Royal Asiatic Society.

Thuken Losang Chokyi Nyima. 2017. *The Crystal Mirror of Philosophical Systems: A Tibetan Study of Asian Religious Thought*. Trans. Geshe Lhundub Sopa, and ed. Roger R. Jackson. Boston: Wisdom Publications.

Trinlé Özer. 2010. "A Constant Stream of Blessings." On Lotsawa House. Trans. Rigpa Translations. https://www.lotsawahouse.org/tibetan-masters/dodrupchen-I/constant-stream-of-blessings.

———. 2011. "The Prayer to Guru Rinpoche for Attainments." On *Lotsawa House*. Trans. Rigpa Translations. https://www.lotsawahouse.org/tibetan-masters/dodrupchen-I/prayer-for-attainments.

Tsogdruk Shabkar Rangdrol. 1994. *The Life of Shabkar: The Autobiography of a Tibetan Yogin*. Trans. Matthieu Ricard. Albany: State University of New York Press.

Tucci, Guiseppe. 1940. *Travels of Tibetan Pilgrims in the Swat Valley*. Calcutta: Greater India Society.

Tucci, Guiseppe. 1999. *Tibetan Painted Scrolls, Two Volumes*. Bangkok: SDI Publications.

Tulku Thondup. 1996. *Masters of Meditation and Miracles*, edited by Harold Talbott. Boston: Shambhala.

———. 2001. *Enlightened Journey*. Ed. Harold Talbott. Boston: Shambhala.

Van der Kuijp, Leonard W.J. 2010. "Za hor and its Contribution to Tibetan Medicine, Part One: Some Names, Places, and Texts." In *Bod Rig Pa'i Dus Deb, Journal of Tibetology* 6: 21–50.

———. 2013. *On the Edge of Myth and History: Za hor, its Place in the History of Early Indian Buddhist Tantra, and Dalai Lama V and the Genealogy of its Royal Family*. Shanghai: Zhongxi Book Company.

Vidyarthi, L.P. 1961. *Sacred Complex in Hindu Gaya*. New Delhi: Asia Publishing.

Vostrikov, Andrei Ivanovich. 1994. Tibetan Historical Literature. Trans. Harish Chandra Gupta. London and New York: Routledge Curzon.

Walser, Joseph. 2005. *Nagarjuna in Context: Mahayana Buddhism and Early Indian Culture*. New York: Columbia University Press.

———. 2002. "Nāgārjuna and the Ratnāvalī. New Ways to Date an Old Philosopher." *Journal of the International Association of Buddhist Studies* (2002): 209–262.

Weinberger, Steven. 2003. *The Significance of Yoga Tantra and the Compendium of Principles (Tattvasagraha Tantra) within Tantric Buddhism in India and Tibet*. University of Virginia.

Whitfield, Roderick. 2012. *Korean Buddhist Culture: Accounts of a Pilgrimage, Monuments, and Eminent Monks*. Seoul: Jogye Order of Korean Buddhism.

Yeshé Tsogyal. 1978. *The Life and Liberation of Padmasambhava, Vol. I & II*. Padma bKa'i Thang. Rediscovered by Terchen Urgyan Lingpa, translated into French by GC Toussaint, and into English by K. Douglas and G. Bays. Emeryville: Dharma Publishing.

———. 1999. *The Lotus-born: The Life Story of Padmasambhava*. Trans. Erik Padma Kunsang, ed. Marcia Binder Schmidt. Boston: Shambhala.

Zangpo Drakpa. 2010a. "Le'u Dünma— The Prayer in Seven Chapters to Padmakara, the Second Buddha, Chapter One, The Prayer to the Three Kaya Guru." On *Lotsawa House*. Trans. Rigpa Translations. https://www.lotsawa-house.org/tibetan-masters/tulku-zangpo-drakpa/leu-dunma-chapter-1.

———. 2010b. "Le'u Dünma— The Prayer in Seven Chapters to Padma-kara, the Second Buddha, Chapter Two, The Prayer Requested by King Trisong Detsen." On *Lotsawa House*. Trans. Rigpa Translations. https://www.lotsawa-house.org/tibetan-masters/tulku-zangpo-drakpa/leu-dunma-chapter-2.

———. 2010c. "Le'u Dünma—The Prayer in Seven Chapters to Padma-kara, the Second Buddha, Chapter Three: The Prayer Requested by Khandro Yeshé Tsogyal." On *Lotsawa House*. Trans. Rigpa Translations. https://www.lotsawahouse.org/tibetan-masters/tulku-zangpo-drakpa/leu-dunma-chapter-3.

———. 2010d. "Le'u Dünma—The Prayer in Seven Chapters to Padma-kara, the Second Buddha, Chapter Five: The Prayer Requested by Nanam Dorjé Dudjom." On *Lotsawa House*. Trans. Rigpa Translations. https://www.lot-sawahouse.org/tibetan-masters/tulku-zangpo-drakpa/leu-dunma-chapter-5.

———. 2010e. "Le'u Dünma—The Prayer in Seven Chapters to Padma-kara, the Second Buddha, Chapter Six: The Prayer Requested by Prince Mutri Tsenpo." On *Lotsawa House*. Trans. Rigpa Translations. https://www.lotsawa-house.org/tibetan-masters/tulku-zangpo-drakpa/leu-dunma-chapter-6.

Teachings

For our research we have relied on the following teachings and instructions:

Orgyen Topgyal Rinpoche. 2012. *Teaching at Gomde Denmark*. Denmark, Knebel, Gomde Denmark, September 1, 2012.

———. 2014. *Teaching at Asura Cave*. Nepal, Pharping, Asura Cave, May 9, 2014.

———. 2015a. *Teaching at Nalanda*. India, Bihar, Nalanda, March 7, 2015.

———. 2015b. *Teaching at Mount Malaya*. Sri Lanka, Sri Pada, December 15, 2015.

Phakchok Rinpoche. *The Path of an Authentic Pilgrim*. Bhutan, Kyichu Lhakang, September 19, 2015.

———. *Sacred Sites and Pilgrimage*. Nepal, Asura Cave, March, 2021.

RANGJUNG YESHE PUBLICATIONS

www.rangjung.com

PADMASAMBHAVA • *Treasures from Juniper Ridge* • *Advice from the Lotus-Born, Dakini Teachings* • *Following in Your Footsteps*

PADMASAMBHAVA AND JAMGÖN KONGTRÜL • *The Light of Wisdom, Vol. 1, & Vol. 2, Vol. 3, Secret, Vol. 4 & Vol. 5*

PADMASAMBHAVA, CHOKGYUR LINGPA, JAMYANG KHYENTSE WANGPO, TULKU URGYEN RINPOCHE, ORGYEN TOBGYAL RINPOCHE, & OTHERS • *Dispeller of Obstacles* • *The Tara Compendium* • *Powerful Transformation* • *Dakini Activity*

YESHE TSOGYAL • *The Lotus-Born*

DAKPO TASHI NAMGYAL • *Clarifying the Natural State*

TSELE NATSOK RANGDRÖL • *Mirror of Mindfulness* • *Heart Lamp*

CHOKGYUR LINGPA • *Ocean of Amrita* • *The Great Gate* • *Skillful Grace* • *Great Accomplishment* • *Guru Heart Practices*

TRAKTUNG DUDJOM LINGPA • *A Clear Mirror*

JAMGÖN MIPHAM RINPOCHE • *Gateway to Knowledge, Vol. 1, Vol. 2, Vol. 3, & Vol. 4*

TULKU URGYEN RINPOCHE • *Blazing Splendor* • *Rainbow Painting* • *As It Is, Vol. 1 & Vol. 2* • *Vajra Speech* • *Repeating the Words of the Buddha* • *Dzogchen Deity Practice* • *Vajra Heart Revisited*

ADEU RINPOCHE • *Freedom in Bondage*

KHENCHEN THRANGU RINPOCHE • *King of Samadhi* • *Crystal Clear*

CHÖKYI NYIMA RINPOCHE • *Present Fresh Wakefulness* • *Bardo Guidebook*

TULKU THONDUP • *Enlightened Living*

ORGYEN TOBGYAL RINPOCHE • *Life & Teachings of Chokgyur Lingpa* • *Straight*

TALKDZIGAR KONGTRÜL RINPOCHE • *Uncommon Happiness*

TSOKNYI RINPOCHE • *Fearless Simplicity* • *Carefree Dignity*

MARCIA BINDER SCHMIDT • *Dzogchen Primer* • *Dzogchen Essentials*
• *Quintessential Dzogchen* • *Confessions of a Gypsy Yogini*
• *Precious Songs of Awakening Compilation*

ERIK PEMA KUNSANG • *Wellsprings of the Great Perfection*
• *A Tibetan Buddhist Companion* • *The Rangjung Yeshe Tibetan-English Dictionary of Buddhist Culture* • *Perfect Clarity*

SAMYE TRANSLATIONS

samyetranslations.org

Terchen Chokgyur Dechen Zhikpo Lingpa
by Guru Padmasambhava,
Chokgyur Lingpa, Jamyang Khyentsé Wangpo, Jamgön Kongtrül,
Orgyen Tobgyal Rinpoche, and Phakchok Rinpoche

The Great Tertön Revised Edition
by Guru Padmasambhava,
Chokgyur Lingpa, Jamyang Khyentsé Wangpo, Jamgön Kongtrül,
Orgyen Tobgyal Rinpoche, and Phakchok Rinpoche

Following in Your Footsteps: The Lotus-Born Guru in Nepal
by Guru Padmasambhava

Following in Your Footsteps: The Lotus-Born Guru in India
by Guru Padmasambhava

A Glimpse of Buddhadharma
by Phakchok Rinpoche

A Glimpse of Mind Training
by Phakchok Rinpoche

A Lamp Illuminating the Path to Liberation
by Khenpo Gyaltsen

Keys to Happiness & a Meaningful Life
by Phakchok Rinpoche

The Eightfold Supreme Path of Mind Training
Compiled by Phakchok Rinpoche

The Noble Wisdom of the Time of Death
Sutra and Commentaries by Prajnasamudra and Shantideva